D0895473

CALGARY PUBLIC LIBRARY

FEB   2015

Belief without Borders

ALSO BY LINDA A. MERCADANTE

Bloomfield Avenue
A Jewish-Catholic Jersey Girl's Spiritual Journey

Victims & Sinners
Spiritual Roots of Addiction and Recovery

Gender, Doctrine, and God
The Shakers and Contemporary Theology

From Hierarchy to Equality
A Comparison of Past and Present Interpretations of 1Cor11:2–16 in
Relation to the Changing Status of Women in Society

Belief without Borders

Inside the Minds of the Spiritual but not Religious

LINDA A. MERCADANTE

OXFORD
UNIVERSITY PRESS

OXFORD
UNIVERSITY PRESS

Oxford University Press is a department of the University of Oxford.
It furthers the University's objective of excellence in research, scholarship,
and education by publishing worldwide.

Oxford   New York
Auckland   Cape Town   Dar es Salaam   Hong Kong   Karachi
Kuala Lumpur   Madrid   Melbourne   Mexico City   Nairobi
New Delhi   Shanghai   Taipei   Toronto

With offices in
Argentina   Austria   Brazil   Chile   Czech Republic   France   Greece
Guatemala   Hungary   Italy   Japan   Poland   Portugal   Singapore
South Korea   Switzerland   Thailand   Turkey   Ukraine   Vietnam

Oxford is a registered trademark of Oxford University Press
in the UK and certain other countries.

Published in the United States of America by
Oxford University Press
198 Madison Avenue, New York, NY 10016

© Linda A. Mercadante 2014

All rights reserved. No part of this publication may be reproduced, stored in
a retrieval system, or transmitted, in any form or by any means, without the prior
permission in writing of Oxford University Press, or as expressly permitted by law,
by license, or under terms agreed with the appropriate reproduction rights organization.
Inquiries concerning reproduction outside the scope of the above should be sent to the
Rights Department, Oxford University Press, at the address above.

You must not circulate this work in any other form
and you must impose this same condition on any acquirer.

Library of Congress Cataloging-in-Publication Data
Mercadante, Linda A.
Belief without borders : inside the minds of the spiritual but not religious /
Linda A. Mercadante.
pages cm
Includes bibliographical references and index.
ISBN 978–0-19–993100–2 (cloth : alk. paper)   1. Spirituality—History—20th century.
I. Title.
BL624.M45 2014
200.973′090512—dc23
2013033364

1 3 5 7 9 8 6 4 2
Printed in the United States of America
on acid-free paper

*To my wonderful, kind, and thoughtful husband, José Luis Mas,
who, for some reason, has never once thought of himself as
"spiritual but not religious"*

Contents

A *Personal Prelude*

CONFESSIONS OF A FORMER SBNR

WHEN I WAS little, I was nothing. At least that is what everyone told me. I was not Jewish like my Russian-Austrian mother. I was not Catholic like my Italian immigrant father. I was not Protestant like the Presbyterians who gathered at the big brick church blocks away in Forest Hill. Nor was I like the black Baptist families in the urban church near our apartment. I especially envied these mothers and fathers and children on Sunday mornings when I saw them happily greeting each other as they gathered on the sidewalk before services. Their church was less than a block from our family business, an Italian pastry shop on busy Bloomfield Avenue in Newark, NJ. I lived in a Will Herberg kind of world where, as he wrote in 1955—if you wanted to be part of mainstream America—you were either Protestant, Catholic, or Jewish.[1] When I was growing up, it was not popular to answer "nothing" when asked what religion you were. Certainly no one ever said they were "spiritual but not religious."

My two grandmothers had not wanted my parents to marry. In those days a "mixed" marriage was considered a shameful thing. Therefore, although my parents never denied their heritages, once married they completely stopped all external religious practices. I cannot be sure about their inner lives, but I know that neither of them ever mentioned prayer and our home contained no sacred scriptures of any kind. While it was clear that my other relatives practiced their respective faiths, our home was a "no religion" zone. My parents treated religion like an unwanted gift they kept on a back shelf in the closet. While they gladly passed on their respective food ways and proud cultural histories, they never spoke to me about God, took me to services, or told me what they believed. With the events of the Second World War fresh in their memories, what they did agree on and teach me was that religious prejudice is wrong. Beyond that, I knew I could not probe.

I was not happy to be nothing. I sensed—as many children do—that there was something spiritual beyond my mundane reality and I wanted to connect with it. So at about age 8, I chose to be baptized as a Roman Catholic. The choice seemed obvious. There were no Jews near where we lived. And the few Protestants, regardless of race, were regarded as almost another species—one, I was warned, which did not like Jews, Catholics, or immigrants. In my North Ward neighborhood with its rich Italian immigrant heritage and the magnificent Sacred Heart Cathedral just a few blocks away, Catholicism seemed the only game in town. But it was a powerful and evocative one, with more answers—and questions—than I had ever dared broach at home. Not just the beliefs, but also the music, rituals, and architecture all called to me in ways I could not fully explain.

I was exultant once I had a religious identity and a way to satisfy my spiritual needs and theological questions. But neither of my parents was happy about this. My father, concerned that my mother already felt like an outsider among her Italian Catholic in-laws and neighbors, did not want me to offend her, so he never encouraged me in my choice. My mother had Hitler's decimation of the Jewish people still fresh in her mind. It was clear she saw my choosing Christianity as a rejection of her and one more loss to Judaism.

Although my parents did not actively prevent me, they largely ignored my religious practices. Those times when it was difficult to ignore—like when I wanted a Christmas tree, a white dress for First Communion, or to wear a crucifix—the tension broke through the surface. So I kept a low profile when it came to religion. It had to be my own decision and effort that got me to Mass and catechism classes. Left without much guidance, I was able to treat Roman Catholicism like many people treat Alcoholics Anonymous, that is, "take what you like and leave the rest." I heard the message of God's peace, joy, and abundant life and I imbibed moral precepts. But no religion-related prohibitions or shame were evident in my home.

No doubt my neighborhood also played a part in allowing me this latitude. The Catholicism practiced among the Italian immigrants there had many elements of folk religion "from the old country." While many wore a small crucifix around their neck, even more hedged their bets by also wearing a "cornicello," a tiny horn amulet, as protection from evil. They would go to Mass, take communion, and make novenas. But they also buried statues for good luck, deserted any patron saint that did not deliver on their requests, and gave each other the "evil eye" when angry. Most important, and unlike Irish and German American Catholics, the Italians took everything the church said "with a grain of salt." Even if their beliefs and practices were looked down upon by the Irish clergy that ran our local churches, that did not seem to bother the people I knew.

In this milieu, I did not feel much overt compulsion about literal biblical interpretation or rigid "orthodoxy," as I might have had I been brought up evangelical Protestant. At the same time, I also imbibed much from my Jewish background through frequent contact with my mother's side of the family. Therefore, my spiritual formation was mixed from the beginning. But this was not an era where overt religious hybridity was welcome. Different from today, when people actively mix various religious practices and alternative spiritualities, I could not exult in my mixed-faith background.

Reinforcing this was the religious prejudice I felt all around me. Both my parents' religions seemed to believe in a loving God. But outside my family I heard Christians call Jews "Christ killers," witnessed anti-Semitism, and was deeply troubled by the Nazi Holocaust. And even the Baltimore Catechism, which I appreciated for its many answers, told me that the Jewish faith had been superseded by the Christian religion.[2] Nor was it optimum for me as a girl in religious America. In church I was not allowed behind the altar, but instead made to feel inferior and told what I could and could not do with my life. I observed that my Jewish background, too, circumscribed female lives. Things got worse when my parents—concerned about drugs at nearby Barringer High School—had me commute daily to the public, but very Protestant, suburban Glen Ridge High School. There I found it was a liability to be Roman Catholic, Jewish, Italian, and from Newark.[3]

Even away at college, I could not escape the influence of religion. I wanted an active social life, but was appalled to learn that there were separate sororities and fraternities for Jewish and Christian students. Given all this background, it should come as no surprise that I gladly left religion behind when the cultural revolution of the late 1960s and early 1970s emerged, with its liberation movements and burgeoning spiritual alternatives. In this exhilarating atmosphere, I chose to become a newspaper reporter. It gave me a perfect excuse to ask endless questions, interview persons on the cutting edge, and get an overview of the ferment going on in American society. Although I was no longer a practicing Catholic, my first job was with a Catholic diocesan paper. I met numbers of dedicated, even saintly, people, but I also saw confusion, hypocrisy, power grabbing, and the mundane realities of a religious institution filled with human beings. Seeing religion from the inside pushed me from non-religious to atheist. I moved on to a secular daily newspaper job and got involved in social action groups.

Eventually, however, I could not deny the emptiness at my spiritual center and the many unanswered questions I still had, so I resumed the seeker road. I avoided religion, but did try many things on the burgeoning menu of alternative spiritualities. Although few people said this in the 1970s, I had become "spiritual but not religious." Like many seekers today, I tried one thing after another: yoga, meditation, vegetarianism, jogging, alternative health practices, Unity, social action groups, and spirituality retreats. I even joined an ashram. But I found nothing that could answer my theological questions or satisfy my spiritual needs. Desperate for something I could not fully articulate, I quit my job and left for a year-long hitchhiking trip to Europe. Along the way, I encountered a brand of evangelical Christianity that impressed me. I met fervent, loving, accepting believers living like hippies in the Swiss Alps. They introduced me to both the Hebrew Bible and New Testament, respected my Jewish roots, and helped me appreciate my mixed religious background. They entertained my endless questions, did not flinch from my challenges, and put up with my barely concealed suspicion of religion. They demonstrated that intellect must be married to heart, and heart needed to be nurtured in community. They helped me see that Christ promoted reconciliation, not alienation. Although they would not have put it this way, they showed that spirituality and religion were not opposites, but integral to each other. I felt that God was uniting my two halves. Because of this conversion experience, I joined the church.

For the first time, I felt whole and grounded, and knew where to satisfy my spiritual thirst. But my questions did not end. I still saw implicit problems both inside and outside religion, especially regarding gender, social, and environmental issues. I still needed a way to unite spiritual and theological satisfaction with prophetic action. Until that point, I had never taken a rigorously intellectual approach to my concerns. But this encounter with the Bible and with a spiritual community dedicated to living it out had helped me see the connection between belief and action, so I returned to North America and enrolled in a Master's degree program in biblical studies to probe further. The relief I found from more intentionally addressing my theological questions made a profound impression on me. I did not have to live in silence, with nagging doubts and unease rumbling around in my head. It was possible to confront these things and resolve them. And such resolutions provided a firm foundation for practical action. All this was deeply liberating.

Finally, in the mid-1980s I found what I needed in mainline Protestantism. Here was a tradition with a rich and complex heritage but also a spirit of open inquiry and ongoing reformation. Questions were welcomed, not bracketed. They pointed to a God who did not expect anyone, including women, to stay stupid or quiet, but who summoned our best efforts and gifts. I learned from feminist theologians that I could find a "useable tradition" and legitimately push it further in the company of others who had similar concerns. Since the tools of theology had proved most liberating, I went on to earn a PhD in this field. The work both grounded and freed me, gave me a sense of connection and transcendence, and the tools to help faith be "reformed and always being reformed." In the late 1980s, I was offered a job teaching theology in a mainline Protestant seminary. I was happy I could now help others find something to stand on and something to reach for. Because I understood this as ministry, I also sought ordination in the Presbyterian Church (USA).

But the irony is that, shortly after I joined mainline Protestantism, it looked like the bottom was dropping out of it. While denominational decline had been observed decades earlier,[4] by the late 1990s, research confirmed that mainline Christianity, both Protestant and Catholic, was in trouble. Earlier warning signs of declining membership, shrinking churches, denominational funding problems, and seminaries' struggles were becoming widespread reality. While I had once felt privileged to board the ship of faith, now I wondered if in my naiveté I had accepted a last-minute officership on the *Titanic*. Had I been deluded, a residual "wannabe" of immigrant roots, needing to become solidly American by becoming mainstream Protestant? Was it just bad luck that I had joined at the same time its hegemonic grip was loosening?

Given all this background, it was understandable that I would be intrigued by the burgeoning "spiritual but not religious" movement which burst upon public consciousness in the 1990s. It was made up of seekers like me, unaffiliated with any religion, trying many things, seemingly in search of something. Although I had eventually committed myself to a particular religion, I remained open-minded, believing that the Spirit would pop up where it desired. Seeing the expanding "SBNR" ferment reconnected me with my own spiritual journey. I identified with and was impressed by the determination and courage of these new spiritual adventurers.

But as I began reading articles on these unaffiliated seekers, something just did not fit what I knew from experience as a seeker and with other seekers. Were they really just commitment phobic, overly self-focused, or salad-bar spiritualists as the media often portrayed them? Weren't there any who had both a spiritual and a theological thirst? I needed to talk with those who might check "no religion" on a survey, often called "nones," yet still claim to be spiritual seekers. Unlike me, they did not mind being "nothing" religiously, but even exulted in it. Surely they had theological questions just like I had. Surely they would be interested in exploring such things.

Rather than simply relying on the research of others, I decided to encounter "spiritual but not religious" people directly, to find out more about their seeking and especially about their beliefs. Being by now an academic, I conceived of a study where I would conduct lengthy face-to-face interviews, inviting SBNRs to speak for themselves. I began my project with great enthusiasm and the help of grants and sabbatical time from my institution. I put out a call for interviewees, traveled around the country to meet them, and spoke with as many as I could. I frequented bookstores, did copious Internet research, and read everything I could find. I also made "site" visits and was a participant observer at spirituality retreats, in yoga and meditation classes, and anywhere else I thought I might find SBNRs. Then I began to analyze the data.

But the personal part of this story does not end there. For just as I began writing this book, I received a medical diagnosis of early-stage breast cancer. Suddenly, the project seemed much less important than getting well. It felt very compelling to focus on a life-or-death issue instead of the vagaries of research and publishing. But the irony was that no matter how I tried, I could not get away from the issues involved in my project. It seemed like wherever I went, the topic pursued me. For with my diagnosis came a free ticket to any number of classes, seminars, and lessons that dealt with the same spiritual practices my interviewees pursued at great expense.

These offerings were not given as an alternative to treatment, but as "complementary" to it. Often provided through the generous funding of nonprofits, these were held free-of-charge at medical centers, hospitals, and ancillary organizations. Because scientific studies have discovered that lowering stress can help in recovery, patients are encouraged to avail themselves of these many options. Some of my SBNR friends and interviewees actually expressed envy that I would get to do for free some of the very same things for which they had to pay—even though I assured them that the price of admission was much too high.

Although the irony was not lost on me, I was very willing—like many patients—to participate in anything that would help my recovery and prevent recurrence. I felt like I had walked through a door into a parallel universe that I, like Barbara Ehrenreich,[5] called "cancer world." It seemed to me that both the caring and the encompassing nature of it were similar to the embrace of the addiction recovery world, something I had studied extensively a decade before. In "cancer world," one could fill nearly every waking hour with a very busy schedule of helpful "adjuncts" to medical treatment.

The classes approached the illness from a variety of perspectives that many would call "spiritual." For instance, one set of classes was based on the healing properties of sound, beauty, and the stress-relief of a singular focus. These included such things as African drumming, acoustic guitar, recorder, journaling, poetry, and art classes. Another set of offerings focused on the healing aspect of community through support groups for nearly every form and stage of the disease. The mind-body connection was addressed in such classes as yoga, mindfulness meditation, qigong, tai chi, visualization, therapeutic touch, energy work, reiki, and any number of similar modalities.

In many of these offerings I encountered the very same SBNR ethos I had been studying. One drumming leader started the class by using a Native American practice of turning to the "four directions." A yoga teacher at a survivors' clinic taught us Buddhist hand positions, or "mudras," to help with various ailments. A qigong teacher, who taught us a set of whole-body meditative exercises, carefully explained about how we needed to improve our "chi" or energy. A therapeutic touch practitioner swept her hands over me, assuring me she was unblocking my energy flow. I knew there were religious roots or theological presuppositions in many of these offerings. But whenever I asked from what tradition or religion this practice originally came, I received the same answer: "Oh, no, this is not religious, it's spiritual. In fact, it's true for all religions; it predates all religion."

I am not saying I disdained their good intentions or spurned their help. I knew they were trying to make their offerings generic so anyone might take them. I appreciated and enjoyed many of these opportunities. I hoped to benefit from them. I liked the teachers. And I definitely felt at one with the participants, since we were all dealing with the same medical problem. But I could not get over the irony of finding this "spiritual but not religious" ethos so deeply embedded in the medical world of cancer care.

After treatment, I returned to writing this book with even more assurance about the value of the investigation. This whole journey has made me even more convinced that a profound spiritual change is going on in America. No matter how organized religions try to ignore, challenge, adapt, or protest it, our society is being deeply changed by this pervasive ethos. Whether this will be the next Great Awakening, a religious Reformation, the launch of a New Age, or our belatedly joining Europe in its increasing secularism, is not clear.

One thing is certain, however; few people have yet studied the beliefs of SBNR participants. Although many surveys have been conducted in recent years, few have attempted an interview-based, or "qualitative," research on this aspect of the religiously unaffiliated. Perhaps a work such as this will give us one more clue to the future. For if we know how people are thinking, perhaps we may more confidently speculate on how they will choose to act. Even though belief and behavior are not always consistent with each other, they do connect. By better understanding the beliefs of a sample of SBNRs, we may also discover how the religiously unaffiliated will live out their beliefs.

Given my own background, this is a project I needed to do. As a former SBNR, I identify with and care about spiritual seekers. As a former journalist, I have an innate curiosity about people and the willingness to listen to them. As a religious professional, I have dedicated my life to making faith relevant, vital, and soul-satisfying. As a theologian, I regularly analyze belief and how it functions synergistically with behavior. And as a researcher, I have spent much of my time studying "lived religion," conversion narratives, cultural change, and the interaction of belief and context. In an age when books are often skimmed rather than devoured, I urge you to take your time reading this work—for I am confident that the cultural changes America is experiencing will deeply impact your own life and the lives of everyone around you.

Acknowledgments

ALTHOUGH I HAVE written four other books and done much stimulating research, this was the most enjoyable project of them all. I am grateful to the generous people who agreed to be interviewed or simply to speak with me about their spiritual journeys and beliefs. I have spent many thoroughly fascinating hours talking, walking, eating with, and listening to this diverse and thought-provoking group of people. So I first want to thank my many interviewees and conversation partners. It was a privilege to be let into your lives and thoughts. I hope I have represented your views well.

I also want to thank the retreat centers, classes, and teachers who allowed me to participate, learn, and meet many interesting people. My special thanks go to Light on the Hill Retreat, Van Etten, NY, and especially director Alice McDowell who encouraged me to start this project and spent much time talking with me about it. As a "retreat center junkie," I have visited a lot of them. The ones I especially want to thank include the Omega Institute in Rhinebeck, NY; Harbin Hot Springs and Heart Consciousness Church, Middletown, CA; Esalen at Big Sur, CA; Findhorn in Scotland; Rowe Camp and Conference Center in Massachusetts; the Iona Community in Scotland; the Soshoni Yoga Retreat, Rollinsville, CO; Degrees of Freedom in Ohio, and many others. I also want to thank the many yoga studios and meditation centers I visited and took classes at, especially Yoga on High in Columbus, OH, and the Shambhala Center in Boulder, CO. The James Care for Life at the Ohio State University Medical Center and the Cancer Support Community also introduced me to many life-enhancing programs that helped me work on my project and recover my health at the same time. I want to especially thank Alejandra Ferrer, who helped me discover drumming as a very powerful and healing practice. And my fellow Victory Drummers, all survivors, especially Maureen Mugavin, Len Fisher, and Marjorie Ebenezer who drum for life.

Initial seed money for this project was provided by an award from the Association of Theological Schools in 2007–08 for my proposal "I'm Spiritual But Not Religious [SBNR]: Addressing the Current 'Cultured Despisers' of Religion." Thank you so much for recognizing this was a project that suited a theologian, even though much other research on this topic has been done by sociologists. I also owe a great deal to the American Academy of Religion, in concert with the Luce Foundation, for their invitation to be part of Cohort II in the two-year project "Theologies of Religious Pluralism." John Thatamanil, and the other leaders, as well as my very fine colleagues from many different religious traditions gave me much opportunity to share my research and learn from all of them. It was an amazing experience which I wish many more scholars, seekers, and religious affiliates could have. I especially want to thank Jeffrey Long who helped me understand Asian religions better and opened my heart to the beauty of Hinduism.

A huge share of my appreciation is directed at the Henry Luce Foundation. I deeply value the confidence they showed by naming me one of six 2010–11 Henry Luce III Fellows in Theology for my project titled "Unfettered Belief, Untethered Practice: Thinking Theologically about 'Spiritual but not Religious.'" Their support allowed me to add an extra semester onto my sabbatical and helped greatly with research expenses. Equally important, their award provided the confidence I needed as I tried to balance theology with the social sciences, something not too common for a theologian to do. The several years I got to present my work and meet with other academics and Luce Scholars have been high points in my career. Their sensitive adjustment of the schedule so I could take some time off for treatment was especially gracious.

Of course, I want to thank my seminary, the Methodist Theological School in Ohio, where I have worked for more than twenty-five years. I deeply appreciate the intellectual freedom and academic trust that I have experienced there. In these days of financial distress for all mainline seminaries, I need to thank the President, Dean, and Trustees for retaining MTSO's sabbatical policy which is a very affirming and generous aspect of our small free-standing seminary. It allows us to do creative research that often only larger institutions can support. Thank you, too, to the library staff, including director Paul Burnam, for scrounging up my most obscure research requests, and doing it with grace and expertise. Thanks are also due to the students in my 2010 Theology and Culture class who foraged for interviewees. I especially thank those whose interviews I referred to, including Chad Parmalee, Deb Bowsher, Kathy Currier, Mark McTrustry, Tracy Temple, Jess Peacock, L. Clevenger, Benjamin Iten, and Joe Ziraldo. I also appreciate the many conversations and feedback I have gotten from the students at MTSO who, as always, listen and care.

I have been encouraged and helped by many scholars. The most accommodating, generous, and supportive has been Stewart M. Hoover, director of Center for Media, Religion and Culture, University of Colorado, Boulder. Our many fascinating conversations, his willingness to meet with me when I have been in Boulder, and his ability to respond to email requests, in spite of his busy schedule, are very much appreciated. I also want to thank other academics including Phyllis Tickle, John Green (Pew Forum); Kenneth Pargament, Michelle Dillon, Patricia Killen, David Heim, Deanna Thompson, Kathy Tanner, Patrick Henry, Judith Simmer-Brown, and so many others who have patiently listened to my forming thoughts and contributed their insights. I also especially appreciate my editor at Oxford University Press, Cynthia Read, for her willingness to take on this somewhat unusual project. I know I have probably left out so many others who helped me as well, so thank you. You know who you are.

Not all institutional support is financial, but it is all supportive. So I need to mention the various types of institutions that helped. I thank the scholars at the Collegeville Institute at St. John's University, Collegeville, MN, as well as the sisters who run the *Studium* Visiting Scholars' Program at St. Benedict's College, MN, for inviting me there, listening to my ideas on the project, and providing me a quiet, peaceful and very blessed place to put my thoughts together. Thanks are due to *The Christian Century* for publishing my initial work on this project: "The Seeker Next Door: What Drives the Spiritual but not Religious?" *The Christian Century* 129, no. 11 (May 30, 2012): 30–33. Thanks are also due to the online publications, radio and television shows, newspapers, and other media which invited me to contribute and have helped me hone this work, including *Open Line with Fred Andrle* and *All Sides with Ann Fisher* (both on WOSU, NPR affiliate); *The SBNR Show with George Lewis*; the *Boulder Daily Camera*; the *United Methodist Reporter;* *The Christian Post; Presbyterian News Service Online*; and others. I especially want to thank Columbus's own Fred Andrle for inviting me many times to speak publically on my topic, his endless interest in this project, and his trust in me.

I owe a lot to the many groups who invited me to give seminars, speeches, and keynotes on this topic. They helped me focus my thoughts and their feedback was invaluable. These groups include the Ohio State University Humanities Institute; Naropa University, Boulder, CO; the Great Lakes Theological Academy, Traverse City, MI; the Missouri State Department of Mental Health Conference; the Indiana Campus Ministries Conference; Thurber House, Columbus, OH; the Ohio Ministries Association; the Goshen College Theology Forum; Erdman Center at Princeton Theological Seminary; the Delaware (OH) Gay-Straight Alliance; the College of Christian Life, Chicago, IL; the Ohio Campus Ministries Association; the Bay View Association, Petoskey, MI; Kansas Conference of Ministers; the Synod of the Covenant, PCUSA; PCUSA denominational headquarters, Louisville, KY; Lakeside Chautauqua, OH; Mennonite National Conference; Call to Action Columbus; Central Ohio Peace Association; Camp Akita; HomeReach Hospice of Ohio Health; Buckeye Ministerial Association; Antioch Writers' Workshop; and many others. Thank you, too, to the Martin Luther King Center in Havana, Cuba, and to the Center for Global Education at Augsburg College for showing me and my students how the church can come alive.

I especially want to thank the churches which invited me to give adult education seminars or retreats on this subject. First United Methodist of Boulder, CO, will always be my "home away from home" church. You helped launch my project. I hope you know how much I appreciate all of you! Special thanks to pastors Claire Childress and Keith Thompson, Patrick Bruns, Joe Agne, and deacon Rosalee Blake. Other inviting churches include First Presbyterian Church, Boulder, CO; Trinity United Methodist, Salina, KS; First Congregational Church, Nantucket, MA; and in Ohio: First Community Church; Broad St. Presbyterian; Overbrook Presbyterian; Indianola Presbyterian; Worthington Presbyterian; Worthington United Methodist; Trinity United Methodist; Columbus Mennonite Church; St. John's Episcopal, Worthington; St. Mark's Episcopal, Upper Arlington; North Unitarian Universalist, Lewis Center; and many others. Thank you, too, to Ian Lawton at the C3 Exchange, Grand Haven, MI (formerly Christ Community Church) for a very engaging conversation and to the Presbyterian Church in Varadero, Cuba, for telling me about Rita Rodriquez. The expressed concerns and needs of all these diverse churches have been taken very seriously in my project.

Of course, the writing was like the penance for all this enjoyment (my sojourn in the Catholic Church is showing here). I liken writing a book to an experience somewhere between house arrest and a long illness. But while it often felt like I was alone, I know I have been supported by many people and institutions, without which this project would never have happened. Great big hugs are sent (will be delivered personally on request) to the people who were willing to read and comment on all or parts of this book in its many iterations. These include: my former fellow journalist Joyce Fargo and husband Mike, Patrick Henry, Susan Bush, Sherry Sauer, Paul Burnam, Jeffrey Long, Paul Numrich, and of course my husband, José Luis Mas (who can get as many reader hugs as he wants). And thanks to friends who listened to me go on endlessly about this work, over several years, and provided very valuable feedback, including Roberta Gerlach, Mary Finke, Barb Middleton, Columbus Mennonite Church pastors Susan Ortman-Goering and Steve Goering, and so many others.

I don't know why people always put their families last because, really, they are the first and most likely to be impacted by all the work it takes to write a book. My son David has lived through four of my five books and someday may actually read them. Perhaps more importantly, though, his amazing sense of humor has always saved my sanity. And although David knows better than to call himself "spiritual but not religious" around his mom, I wonder. Big thanks to my stepdaughters, Emily and Sarah, with husbands Kent and Mike, who are always a welcome distraction from academic work. In addition, they invited me to perform their wedding ceremonies which was not only an honor but also challenged me to think harder about their generation.

Although my parents, Gene and Gerry Mercadante, are gone now, I owe them a great debt for propelling me into being a proto-SBNR without realizing it. I also wish I could thank my brother. He unexpectedly and tragically passed away while I was doing research for this book in Boulder but somehow and non-physically managed to say "good-bye" that night, making me rethink spiritualist claims. Unlike me, Eugene had the advantage of a Catholic education but rejected religion anyway, which confirms my observation that not everyone appreciates the church as much as I do.

And even though it is hackneyed to say the "last but not least" is my husband, it is true. My husband José Luis Mas is the best. In addition to his law practice and extensive pro bono public service work, nevertheless he often cooked, chauffeured, navigated, listened, encouraged, consoled, gardened, repaired, came with me on many of my research trips, and did not complain (well, just enough to know he missed me) when I had to go alone. He did all this and just about everything else so that I could research and write this book. You are amazing and I am so blessed! I dedicate this book to him.

And as for appreciation for the non-human type of support, both of us thank Miss Kitty who in her own *principessa* ways has learned to be the perfect writer's cat. She sat on my lap while I read, seemingly very content to have the book propped up on her hind end. During the writing, she purposely distracted me every hour or so with plaintive meows and invitations to take a break. And while this really helped break up the writing day, Miss Kitty was also polite enough not to walk on my keyboard when I didn't always take her suggestions.

Belief without Borders

I

Introduction

RELIGIOUS CRISIS OR SPIRITUAL REVOLUTION?

"NONES"—THOSE WHO do not claim any particular communal faith identity—are on the rise. Although the term "none" may sound pejorative, it
is simply a shorthand used by sociologists to designate those who might
check "none" on a survey when asked to what particular faith group
they belong. This phenomenon is increasing so rapidly that worldwide
"unbelief" now represents the world's third largest "religion." Even the
United States, historically considered a religious nation, has a significant
and growing share of these religiously unaffiliated. The percentage of
Americans claiming "no religion" has grown dramatically since religion's
heyday in the 1950s. Although the United States has always had a small
percentage of people unaffiliated with any religion, until recent decades
they averaged only around 3% to 5%. A discernible increase in "nones"
began in the 1960s and 1970s as the Baby Boomer generation contributed a small but significant rise. Then, during the 1990s, the number of
"nones" began to rise exponentially until now it is considered the fastest
growing "religious group" in the nation.[1]

Although surveys vary on exactly how many Americans now claim
no religious affiliation, no one disputes the rapid growth in "nones."
Each year during the 1990s, 1.3 million US adults joined the ranks of the
"nones." In the decade from 1990 to 2001, the amount of self-identified
"nones" more than doubled, going from 14.3 million to 29.4 million.[2]
In just the five years from 2008 to 2012, the percentage jumped again,
an impressive 3.2%.[3] By the first decade of 2000, at least 46 million, or
more than one-fifth of all Americans, had no religious affiliation. In fact,

the percentage of "nones" keeps rising by a very significant 0.6% a year. Although that might seem like a small yearly percentage, it adds up. The results of the extensive General Social Survey shows "nones" at 5% in 1972, 7% in 1975, 8% in 1990, 14% in 2000, 18% in 2010, and at least 20% in 2012.[4] There are now more "nones" in America than mainline Protestants.[5]

Although there was also some increase in the number of those identified with non-Christian religion, it was small compared to the rise in the religiously unaffiliated. While it is unclear whether this population will continue to grow at such a fast rate,[6] the numbers of the religiously unaffiliated in America are the largest they have ever been. Even if the United States still contains many religiously affiliated people, continued growth of the unaffiliated seems indicated. This is especially so because the largest percentage of "nones" is among young adults—estimates range from at least one-third to as high as three-quarters. This shows no signs of being a transitional youthful phase but instead indicates a permanent pattern. Young people now are more religiously unaffiliated than earlier generations were at the same age.[7] Thus, although this trend is not yet universally apparent across the country, it seems like a train that will not be stopping anytime soon.

The decline in institutional loyalty has also affected those still within organized religion. Researchers have found much "churn" in religious affiliation, as many people change religious identities at least two or more times in their lifetime.[8] From whatever angle you look, it cannot be denied that growing numbers of Americans have ceased identifying with, contributing to, or remaining devoted to any particular religious tradition or faith community. While the reasons for this are not yet clear (we will explore some of them in the next chapter), this exponential rise is unprecedented in American history.

Depending on where you stand, this profound shift in the American religious landscape can look like a severe crisis or a burgeoning spiritual revolution. Some see this trend of disaffiliation as the triumph of free thinking and individualism. A world without required religious beliefs, moral strictures, or group boundaries could usher in a new era of intellectual and emotional freedom, many say. Others welcome the shift away from religious affiliation, feeling that the blend of religion and politics from the 1980s onward has had divisive and deleterious effects on society. And some insist that one can be "good without God."[9]

Others, however, including many social scientists and religious professionals, worry about the rise in "nones" and not just because their livelihoods are at stake. Many worry because organized religion provides one of the few multigenerational, voluntary, communal meeting places in America offering both social networking and spiritual nurture. Religion has contributed and still supplies many social services to America, from universities to hospitals, soup kitchens to shelters, which need committed backing—financially, emotionally, personally—to continue. Others are concerned that we not abandon or minimize Western religion's intellectual heritage and the important contributions it makes.[10] This seemed to be a danger even in the 1950s—during the height of religious affiliation in America—when Jewish theologian and sociologist Will Herberg warned of a "cut flower culture" where moral principles eventually die once they are cut off from their scriptural and intellectual roots. "Cut flowers retain their original beauty and fragrance, but only so long as they retain the vitality that they have drawn from their now-severed roots; after that is exhausted, they wither and die," he wrote in *Judaism and Modern Man.*[11] Other fields join the worried ranks because it seems that Americans are increasingly separated from each other, segmented, market-driven, virtualized, and specialized in work and leisure. In fact, there are many studies showing the emotional and physical health benefits of religious faith and membership.[12] Social scientists contend that religion, even if not perfect, has always been a strong glue and beneficent presence in American society.[13]

Some take solace in the fact that America has not become the thoroughly secularized nation many had predicted, following the pattern of Europe.[14] Instead, some aspects of religion in America are holding their own in the new millennium. Evangelicalism, Pentecostalism, various forms of Christian orthodoxy, and Mormonism have gained some ground. Roman Catholicism is benefiting by the increase in Latino immigrants. There is an increase in mega-churches, missions, and global networking among religious groups. Islam and Buddhism are growing, albeit slowly, as many immigrants bring their religions with them. And in many religions, such as Judaism, there is a rise in the small but dedicated minority who focus on traditional beliefs and practices. This is not just an American phenomenon, for in other parts of the world, both Christianity and Islam are rapidly growing.[15]

However, the growth rate among "nones" in America—and especially its presence among young adults—surpasses all of this. While this fact may seem to indicate we are becoming more secular in America, something else may be happening instead. Outside organized religion, there is an amazing proliferation of spiritual alternatives which both promote and cultivate the significant proportion of the "nones" who are looking to develop their own spirituality apart from traditional structures, those popularly known as "spiritual but not religious" (SBNR). As Robert Wuthnow says, we have become a nation of "seekers" of spiritual experience, rather than "dwellers" in a firm religious location.[16] So, although America is still considered to be more religious than many other European-based nations, the quality of this ethos may be changing. Given the decline of permanent religious affiliation among growing numbers of Americans, we seem to be moving to a "religion of no religion."[17]

Spirituality versus Religion?

Of course, we must ask what is meant by the terms "religion" and "spirituality." Although this is a common separation, the distinction is not as easy as it seems and the terms can become somewhat fuzzy. In some ways, the concept of "religion" is a social construct, since in other eras religion, culture, and even national identity were often inseparable. And as for "spirituality," this is an old concept with a new usage. Previous to our current era, what people today call "spirituality" was often called "piety." It referred both to one's particular type of spiritual practices and also to the vitality of one's faith. But in no case was it rigidly divorced from communal faith identity. Within Christianity, for instance, there were distinctively Roman Catholic spiritual practices (and distinctions among them, such as Ignatian, Franciscan, Paulist, etc.) as well as Reformed, Wesleyan, Pentecostal, and other Protestant styles. This went hand-in-hand with religion, designating a variety of practices that fostered faith, devotion, and connection with God.

The popular understanding of spirituality, however, is quite wide-ranging. For instance, the Network of Spiritual Progressives include in their meaning of "spiritual":

> All dimensions of life that cannot fit into a scientistic or empiricist frame. We reject the notion that all that is real or all that can be known is that which can be subject to empirical justification or can be measured. On the contrary, we know that love, kindness, generosity, awe and wonder, art, ethics, and music are just some of the obvious parts of life that cannot be understood or adequately captured by scientism and which we value.[18]

An even broader interpretation is given by the website SBNR.org. It simply calls its idea of spirituality "open source," saying the site serves "the global population of individuals who walk a spiritual path outside traditional religion."[19]

As for religion, a working definition is given by scholar Mark C. Taylor in his book *After God*. This statement shows how multifaceted religion is. He says:

> Religion is a complex adaptive network of myths, symbols, rituals and concepts that simultaneously figure patterns of feeling, thinking, and acting and disrupt stable structures of meaning and purpose. When understood in that way, religion not only involves ideas and practices that are manifestly religious but also includes a broad range of cultural phenomenon not ordinarily associated with religion.[20]

The popular contemporary way to express this connection is to say one is both spiritual and religious. Although this seems to go along with the current distinction between the two, many persons keep these factors together. They commonly use the term "spirituality" to refer to the interior life of faith and "religion" to mean the necessary communal and/or organizational component. When examining how religion adds "social capital" to both public and private life, some may define the religious realm as the "what," i.e. "the concrete and tangible actions and resources that faith groups contribute to civil society." And they may see the "spiritual" aspect as the "why," i.e. "that area of belief or faith that actually energises or motivates our ethical and public living."[21] As witness to the importance of the current emphasis on the spiritual life, hardly anyone, except perhaps tongue-in-cheek or regretfully, would insist they were religious but not spiritual.[22] A strong argument can be made that spirituality and religion essentially overlap. In fact, one study shows their closeness by calling spirituality "privatized experienced-oriented religion."[23]

In fact, both spirituality and religion consist of four basic components:

(1) Belief in some kind of larger reality, some transcendent or sacred force, something greater than the individual.
(2) A desire to connect with this larger reality or greater force.
(3) The promotion of rituals and practices as an aid or witness to this connection.

(4) The expectation of particular behaviors (whether called "moral" or not) that foster or demonstrate the desired connection.

Although these can be explained in very different ways, you can find all four elements—beliefs, desire, rituals, and behavioral expectations—in a range of varied practices which today claim a spiritual component, such as twelve-step addiction recovery groups, yoga practices, various forms of meditation, reiki, and others.

Nevertheless, the popular conceptual separation of religion from spirituality is a reality today. Both laypersons and professionals use a variety of ways to perform this amputation. Often a somewhat or highly pejorative color is attached to the "religion" side of the equation. Some make a distinction between the invisible or deeper world of "spirit," versus religion as mundane, material reality. Some use spiritual to describe the vital life of faith versus religion as the institutional container—or hindrance—to this. Others see spirituality as experiential and heart-felt, relegating religion to the dusty world of beliefs, dogmas, rationality, and/or "head-knowledge."[24]

However, this separation is more a rhetorical device than a true divorce. For one thing, it has allowed a proliferation of alternative spiritualities outside religious sponsorship, alternative or complementary health practices outside scientific medicine, and an individualized loosening of social expectations and control. At base, the conceptual amputation of spirituality from religion is a way to get out from under the external constraints of authorities, traditions, or institutional bonds, and personalize one's spiritual quest. For many who promote this divorce, the freedom is so exhilarating that they speculate we are on the verge of a new Reformation or "New Age" where each will forge his or her own spiritual path in an era of peace and cooperation.[25]

For others, the proliferation seems like impending chaos. Some observers worry that this new spiritual ferment is random, unproductive, overly self-focused, and a harbinger of societal breakdown.[26] Instead of religion being a given or "ascribed" identity, some say it has become just one more choice or "achievement" in an often commodified, market-driven society. And as with other consumer products, brand loyalty lasts only until the consumer is no longer satisfied or finds novelty elsewhere. As Rowan Williams, former Archbishop of Canterbury, says, we have become "patrons" rather than "subscribers."[27]

No matter how you evaluate it, however, we are in a time of widespread openness to spiritual things and a new willingness to sacrifice time, money, and effort to find a connection to something larger than ourselves. History shows that these openings come from time to time, sometimes engaging more people, and other times confined to a small minority. In every era, there have been people who set sail through unknown spiritual waters. Spiritual explorers sometimes forge the way ahead of others, finding new routes to God and meaning, such as St. Francis or the Prophet Muhammad did, and other times leading many to destruction, such as in Jonestown or Waco. Although not every journey leads in a productive direction, it is important to stay attentive to the bubbling up of spirit in unexpected places. At the very least, this new higher level of spiritual interest among Americans requires further study.

Why Study Belief?

Many have studied the declining numbers in pews and some have conducted ethnographic studies of the behaviors and practices of alternative spiritualities. Theologians have always studied the core beliefs of their own or other religious groups. But few scholars have focused on the topic of popular belief. Perhaps that is because, for the average person, religious belief is often fuzzy and notoriously hard to pin down. Religious leaders often suspect that the people sitting in front of them have their own reasons for being there. They know that religious adherents can think quite differently about core aspects of their faith than their leaders do. It has been amply proven that few Americans—even religious ones—have much knowledge about the beliefs of their own tradition, and even less knowledge of others' beliefs.[28] And many people of faith prefer to rely on inherited or "embedded" concepts without further reflection. If it is difficult to elicit and understand the beliefs of a congregation and the individuals in it, how much more is it the case with people outside the bounds of a religion?

But, on second thought, maybe we should not concern ourselves with this. After all, it is common to hear today that religious beliefs do not matter, that all religions ultimately believe the same things, or that belief is something best left in the private realm. Even within Christianity—a religion very concerned with belief—there is some movement in this direction. Some say that Protestantism, in particular, is overly cognitive, and they criticize both conservative and mainstream Christians for ranking right belief (orthodoxy) over right action (orthopraxis). Others say that when belief is contested—when a group works to ensure "orthodoxy"—the real issue is control and hegemony.[29]

This debate has led some scholars, like Harvey Cox, to speculate that this change in focus indicates religion is on the verge of renewal. Cox asserts that religion is leaving behind the "Age of Belief," which is characterized as inordinate focus on "right belief," and entering, instead, the "Age of Faith" where dogma is ignored, religious difference is minimized, and spirituality replaces religion.[30] Much of contemporary Christian theology, even in its "neoconservative" manifestation, is affected by this Romantic emphasis away from rational clarity and toward the mystical, primitive, or intuitive.[31] But the change of focus away from belief is not limited to Christianity or even organized religion. For there are researchers interested in non-institutional religious practice who echo these assertions, insisting we should now shift our focus to spiritual practice or "lived religion." And rather than being surprised by or worried about waning belief and loosening tradition, they claim that syncretism and hybridity are nothing new.[32]

It may seem that this desertion of belief accurately describes the situation of the religiously unaffiliated. When I have spoken with SBNRs, they take a decidedly anti-dogmatic stance against religious belief in general. They claim not only that belief is non-essential, but that it is potentially harmful or at least a hindrance to spirituality. In fact, many contend that any insistence on truth claims, religious belief, or conceptual clarity is really the hegemonic thought control of organized religion. They often insist they do not need to believe in anything in particular to grow spiritually, and that it really does not matter what you believe. Instead, they claim that spiritual and/or religious beliefs are personal, individualistic, open-ended, and beyond proof.

In this seemingly live-and-let-live atmosphere, they often contend that the only things that should be prohibited are the exclusivist truth claims of religion. In any case, they say—in a kind of truth claim all its own—all religions, at base, are seeking the same thing or teach the same basic principles. In addition, it is often said, mystics from every tradition transcend such mundane things as intellectual concepts. Given this clear and dominant rhetoric of SBNRs that belief is unimportant, unessential, and even potentially harmful, why study the beliefs of religiously unaffiliated people?

We need to study them for at least one very important reason: the rhetoric conceals more than it reveals. Once we probe below surface claims about the unimportance or even danger of religious belief, we hear another story. Instead of a desertion of belief, we hear the formulation of a new set of principles to guide practice and action. A sea change in belief and an emerging set of core principles is discovered when we listen carefully to the people represented in this book.

It made sense that I heard a change in belief among my interviewees, rather than a desertion of belief. The importance of belief cannot be dismissed easily nor limited to the Christian religion. In fact, as scholars have noted, "For all religions it can be said that theology, or religious belief, is at the heart of religion."[33] To a greater or lesser degree, all religions—including contemporary spiritual alternatives—have certain undergirding principles.[34] Consider that among many types of human groupings there is often wrangling over who is more authentic, whose ideas are more representative, whose practices have more integrity. All human groups delineate boundaries, not simply as power-grabs, but for purposes of identity and viability. Because humans are cognitive animals, these boundaries will inevitably contain a synergy between belief and practice.

Belief, experience, and behavior go together. Most people try to make sense of their faith and hope. Most people look for meaning in life. And most people, eventually, find they need reasons to go on in spite of life's inevitable difficulties. Although this meaning-making is on a continuum—with some making more effort or being more consistent than others—people do think about these things, even if they try not to. Most also agree that, to be authentic, to have integrity, they should be living out what they believe. Religious beliefs are not disembodied, abstract articles, but represent the distilled, contemplated faith and lived experience of an entire community. Sacred scriptures, too, are a testimony to the powerful synergy between compelling beliefs and changed behavior.

An individual's own set of spiritual and religious beliefs are connected to their experience and affect their behavior. We all make choices, whether self-consciously or not, on the basis of cultural, shared, inherited, and/or individually arrived-at beliefs. Scholars who have studied the factor of belief in religious disaffiliation have found it to be a significant factor. In fact, doubt often precedes disaffiliation. Those whose beliefs are weakening often hang on for a time as "ritualists," that is, going through the motions rather than being deeply committed.[35] These may actually be "SBNRs" in the making, especially in a cultural environment where this option is increasingly seen as legitimate and even laudable.

But the connection between belief and behavior is not just about show-ing up for services. One's beliefs make a difference in many ways, both personal and social. Research makes clear that beliefs affect one's civic participation, not just one's religious activities.[36] Studies also show beliefs are directly related to one's vitality, self-image, and sense of wholeness. Secure religious beliefs have a consistent, positive relationship with health and happiness.[37] People who can easily access their religious beliefs seem to have a higher life satisfaction and endure less emotional and cognitive struggle when faced with life stressors.[38] Religiousness, rather than spiri-tual seeking—including both belief and behavior—seems more condu-cive to aging well.[39] And the benefits do not stay at home, for people who are secure in their faith tend to get more involved in their communities, vote more often, and give charitably. All these factors are well documented in social scientific studies.

Theology is lived, not just believed. We must not only speak about "lived religion" (i.e., the practices, rituals, and related behaviors associated with faith) but also about "lived theology." As we will see, many interview-ees do not want a disconnect between belief, experience, and behavior. Many feel it is wrong to join a group unless they can subscribe to all its principles. They want very much to be "authentic" and honest, and to have the integrity to live out their beliefs. Many want their religious beliefs and practices to change them in some way, to affect their experience. In this book, you will hear how they often make choices, join and leave groups, read books, follow teachers, begin and drop spiritual practices, and act in numerous ways on the basis of whether they "make sense," according to their deeply held—or recently adopted—beliefs.

Therefore, no matter how lightly or deeply held, religious and spiritual beliefs are part of one's total being, deeply integrated into our behavior, attitudes, and life journeys. In an age when we are increasingly aware that mind and body are integrally related, this should be no surprise. While less and less people are given the resources for the work[40] of "lived theol-ogy," they still have to deal with the perennial "big" questions about the meaning, value, and trajectory of human life, and whether there is any-thing beyond our mundane reality.

Before we go on, however, let me also be clear about what I am not saying, as well as what I am. I am not saying that the cognitive element is the only important element in religion or spirituality. I am not saying that people, if they claim a religious tradition, must fully agree with it in order to be counted, to be good, to be real practitioners. I am not saying that people cannot conduct their religious and spiritual lives until they get their ideas settled. This has probably never been the case in the history of religions anyway. Nor am I saying that heterogeneity in belief—or hybrid identity—is a new thing, at least in practice if not in overt avowal. Research shows that people's beliefs are not always clear, consistent, and in agreement with their community, but are often a mixture of apparently inconsistent elements.[41]

I am not contending that each person has a fully worked out systematic theology, or that people are always integrated wholes, with belief and behavior totally compatible. We cannot simply assume a deep and consistent "religious congruence" between a person's professed beliefs and their attitudes or behavior.[42] Indeed, it has always been obvious to religious leaders that there are many "fuzzy" faithful sitting in their pews; people who are neither completely clear, completely in agreement, nor completely faithful to the tenets of their religion.[43] If it were otherwise, there would be no need for the regular renewal movements, rousing sermons, or hand-wringing of clergy as they worry about how to awaken even the "faithful" to live in congruence with their faith—or even simply to have faith at all.

I am saying, however, that belief does matter and is an inevitable part of any religious or spiritual life. If we minimize this, insist that people do not take their own beliefs seriously, do not have the resources to do it, or ignore this factor in faith, we may be unconsciously patronizing them.

SBNRs Need to Be Heard

The religiously unaffiliated have not been very much heard, especially in the area of their beliefs. My conversations with them showed over and over again that they have much to say, do not want to be stereotyped or ignored, and are grateful when someone carefully listens. Paying this kind of attention is especially necessary if we want to understand why organized religions, especially Christianity in America, are losing numbers.

Of course, we can look to the social sciences for help here. Scholars in the sociology and psychology of religion carefully study religious behavior, and their data inform this present study greatly. But belief—whether outside or inside religion—has been one especially understudied area within the social sciences.[44] As a result, few have taken seriously the inner structure and internal logic of religion. This is especially true for the beliefs of the religiously unaffiliated. One scholar has admitted that "there are embarrassingly few studies that systematically map the worldviews of the unchurched."[45] So if it is difficult enough to get inside the heads of religious people who worship and practice their faith in community, how much harder is it to learn about the beliefs of the unaffiliated who do not regularly "show up" anywhere definitive, such as a weekly worship service?

It is true that sociological surveys—such as the Gallup Poll and the Pew Forum—do sometimes query "nones" about belief. This information is very helpful, and this book takes it seriously, but sociological surveys are not enough. For a survey method is not "built" to plumb the depths of "lived theology" with all its texture, nuance, and dependence upon context. Only a few researchers have attended closely to the beliefs of the religiously unaffiliated. Among these scholars, several suggest that dramatic changes are underway.[46] Others, however, contend that although many people are becoming unaffiliated, religious beliefs in America have not changed that much. Many "nones," it is said, are "believing without belonging," being simply "unchurched believers."[47] A Gallup poll claims that nine out of ten Americans still believe in God, and many also believe in heaven.[48] Other research contends that although this might be a "distant" or uninvolved God, it is still a recognizable God.[49]

These latter studies can make the rise in "nones" appear simply as an issue of institutional affiliation, with belief largely unaffected. But the SBNRs I met did not conform very well to these theories. After talking with hundreds of them, I realized we cannot console ourselves that most Americans are retaining traditional religious beliefs. My study suggests they are not. And yet even if they believe differently from religious folk, we will see that many SBNRs do retain a concern with belief. Thus we cannot excuse ourselves from the work of listening to SBNRs by postulating that belief is not a vital issue among them. On the contrary, it is a crucial factor that bears much attention.

Through hearing this sample of SBNRs, we may better understand the rise in "nones." As you listen to their voices, you will see that there are various options to ponder. For instance, as some suggest, perhaps nothing much has changed in the area of belief and the problem is more one of institutional commitment and loyalty. On the other hand, perhaps we are witnessing a profound desertion of tradition, replaced instead by hybridity, syncretism, and/or highly individualistic schemas. In effect, will everyone soon be creating their own religion? But let us pause here to ask whether these are the only two options. Could it be, instead, that something else is

happening, something new? Are we witnessing the emergence of a potential theology, perhaps even a new "meta-narrative"? We need to consider
this possibility because, in spite of their surface disavowal, the SBNRs in
this book do hold various discernible beliefs. Even if they are drinking
from a variety of spiritual and religious wells, often unconcerned about
roots or consistency, there are some grounding principles that a majority
of the interviewees agree upon. As you will see, this is what my study of
SBNRs suggests.

But other, more sociological, questions may also be helped by studying this group of SBNRs. For instance, do they fit within the reported
high rate of "churn" in American religion, that is, the frequency of religious switching? Do they understand their seeking as a phase, a journey
on the way from one thing to another? Are they playing with, evaluating,
and cycling through a variety of alternatives, in order to arrive at some
consistent set of beliefs and associated practices? Are they looking for a
permanent spiritual home... or not? And how do these various beliefs get
acquired and play out for people?

Perhaps the question most relevant to the majority of readers is
this: Are the interviewees you will meet here harbingers of changes that
will deeply affect our society? As crucial as this question is, there is no
way we can answer it until we understand SBNR ideas better. Only then
can we attempt to imagine what the changes might be or how they will
affect us. Thus, while many scholars have studied trends in American religion,[50] the main focus of the present work is to open a new window on
"nones." By looking at a sample of SBNRs, we hope to learn something
about changing belief patterns in America. Only then can we speculate on
the effects of these belief changes on society. With this information, too,
religious groups may gain insight on if and how it might be possible to
help SBNRs on their spiritual journeys. Not everyone will automatically
expect that theology is playing a large part in the decline of religious participation, nor that theology could play a part in the development of spirituality. Few assume that SBNRs are discarding religion for specifically
theological reasons or taking alternative routes for theological reasons. Yet
in my conversations with SBNRs, I have heard a theological substrate that
could well justify their hesitation toward or rejection of religious affiliation and their adoption of other practices. Thus, listening carefully to the
religiously unaffiliated, especially those who call themselves "spiritual but
not religious," gives us an important window into American spirituality
and religion today.

The Interviewees and the Interview

I have always been fascinated with "lived religion." It is important to understand how people adopt, integrate, and express their religious beliefs and practices, as well as how this correlates with their lived experience and actions. As a former newspaper reporter—as well as having done other research projects on narrative theology—I have often studied personal expressions of faith and belief. Ever since my research on the addiction recovery movement in the late 1990s,[51] I had been hearing people affirm that they were "spiritual but not religious." Not only did I see increasing references to this term in my Internet searches, but everywhere I went I met people who proudly proclaimed this status. I often found myself talking with them and asking about their spiritual journeys. I was fascinated to learn how they made a distinction between spirituality and religion, why they preferred to remain unaffiliated, how they tried out various spiritual practices and groups, and how they played with disparate spiritual alternatives. I was especially interested because of my own SBNR background.

I soon discovered, however, that there was little research on "nones," "seekers," or "spiritual but not religious" persons, especially in the area of their beliefs. In fact, scholars in the study of religion have called for more in-depth research on this topic.[52] "Qualitative" research—which is used by this present study—is especially suited for this sort of task. Qualitative research, which focuses on individual narratives, is different from quantitative research, which focuses on broader analysis of societal factors. Qualitative analysis goes deep, while quantitative goes broad. Qualitative research has different goals than quantitative research. Rather than being used to generalize or prove causation, its task is to see how larger social trends function in individual lives.

Even though we have a cultural preference for quantification, qualitative research is well-accepted as an adjunct to the broader, representative work of large-scale studies. It handles well such complex issues as ideas on God because—rather than posing a pre-decided set of questions allowing only pre-set choices—the interview format allows respondents to expand, elaborate, and often move in self-chosen directions. Unfortunately, however, not much qualitative work has taken an in-depth look at beliefs.[53] Perhaps this is a reaction against a perceived over-focus on beliefs in a formerly Protestant-tinged American civil religious climate.

While some sociologists blend both quantitative and qualitative, I chose to rely on the well-respected surveys of others for broader trends.

It is essential to the topic we are exploring and I availed myself of this copious data. Then I used the interview approach to enrich, deepen, and perhaps challenge some of those results. While a qualitative project such as this one cannot claim to be representative of the entire population of spiritually oriented "nones," there is merit in digging deep to see how these factors play out in individual lives. The idea that people's real lives, their "lived religion," might differ from what surveys and statistical analysis show is not new.

Some might worry that I, as a theologian, might be imposing artificial categories on the comments of my conversation partners. Of course, this work required me to be especially sensitive to my own predilections and orientations. But from my experience in the SBNR world, I noticed that certain theological categories were already familiar to many Americans. The four themes I chose to examine, the sacred, human nature, community, and afterlife, are based on some major life questions:

(1) Is there anything larger than myself, any sacred or transcendent dimension, any Higher Power?
(2) What does it mean to be human?
(3) Is spiritual growth primarily a solitary process or is it done with others?
(4) What will happen to me, if anything, after death?

Given the European Christian heritage of America, I felt that nearly anyone here would have encountered these questions and spent some time reflecting on them. Since the postmodern era has emerged out of a once hegemonically Protestant and Judeo-Christian nation, we would not be able to lose those themes so rapidly. This was not a value judgment on my part, but an evaluation which was mostly proven true during the conversations. There was little puzzlement with the topics I chose, but often an eagerness to jump right in, demonstrating that my conversation partners had been thinking about many of these topics for a long time.

In order to learn more, I created a semi-structured interview, lasting between one and two hours. Often people would have gone on longer if I had been able to stay. The first part of the interview covered the person's spiritual journey and the second half dealt with their beliefs in the four major areas. No one ever balked when I made clear that my study focused on belief. In fact, the focus on belief intrigued my conversation partners rather than turning them off. They seemed eager to talk about these things and enjoyed the process. I did not set out to evaluate orthodoxy, nor did

I assume that one particular type of belief, such as reincarnation or karma, automatically made the person a Hindu or Buddhist. Instead, I just wanted to know how my conversation partners thought about these things. By conducting interviews as well as informal conversations, I would speak directly to SBNRs myself. Then, after several years of interviews, I would analyze the content and organize the material into themes. As you will see, there is one chapter devoted to interviewees' comments in each of these areas.

It was not difficult to find interviewees. Right from the start, whenever I entered a room and mentioned my desire to speak with "spiritual but not religious" folk, numbers of people would raise both hands in a kind of victory salute and say proudly, "That's me!" Through networking and a "snow-ball" technique, I soon had more volunteers than I could accommodate. Although both men and women responded enthusiastically, somewhat more women contacted me. On one hand, this goes against the statistic that finds more "nones" to be male (in 2012, for instance, 23% of men were unaffiliated compared with 17% of women).[54] Yet it accords with the simple observation that more women are present in the classes and groups exploring alternative spiritualities. Women, once thought to be more religious than men, now seem also to be more interested in spirituality.

Over several years, I formally talked with and recorded the views of about one hundred people—most of them in one-on-one interviews but also through several focus groups. In addition, I had hundreds more informal conversations. I also made many "site" visits and got involved in activities and classes that would attract SBNRs. Many people I met insisted I interview them, saying they had something important to share, something I should not miss. Many would contact me repeatedly until I agreed. If I had not eventually ended the interview process, I could have spoken with hundreds more. Even as this book neared publication, new people were still contacting me and urging me to interview them. I learned much by observing who chose to volunteer and why some types of people were more enthusiastic about the project than others.

The main criteria to be interviewed were that the person self-identify with the phrase "spiritual but not religious" and be willing to discuss their spiritual journey and beliefs. I interviewed all around North America, but focused most of my attention on the Midwest and the West, especially two cities that had quite different profiles. I tried hard to get a fair representation of gender, age groups, sexual orientation, and race/ethnicity. People with and without previous religious backgrounds volunteered, including a number of "spiritual atheists."[55] Some interviewees still maintained loose connections to churches, but many were uninvolved. Most had tried some practices from Eastern religions as well as alternative spiritualities, such as yoga, reiki, meditation. Many were conversant with popular authors who dealt with spiritual topics, such as Eckhart Tolle, Deepak Chopra, and so on.

I did not find this phenomenon outside religion only. Often when I announced my project in churches, asking if congregants could send me their non-religious family members or friends to be interviewed, invariably people from within the congregation would quietly sidle up to me after the service, lower their voices, and assure me that I would surely want to interview them as well, that they had a story to tell, and that they were not really religious, in spite of my finding them inside this particular church. Clergy, too—and I know and have taught many of them—often shared the SBNR ethos, expressed a desire not to be identified as "religious,"[56] and wanted to be interviewed. That so many different types of people volunteered says something about the need of persons today to have their beliefs heard. It may indicate we have not paid enough attention to the theological changes that are happening in America, instead focusing most of our attention on seemingly more tangible, quantifiable things like membership, changes in affiliation, and practices.

I came to the study with some common presuppositions which, early on, proved unfounded. I had anticipated a certain level of hesitation toward me, since I am clearly involved in organized religion and did not try to hide that fact. Earlier research had insisted that SBNRs demonstrated distrust and even hostility toward representatives of organized religion, especially clergy.[57] But rather than finding resistance or enmity, I found warmth and cooperation. My interviewees expressed genuine gratitude that I was taking them seriously and giving them an opportunity to explore things which, most said, they had little chance to talk about with anyone. I felt privileged to be allowed inside the spiritual worldview of each participant. Given that trust, I worked hard to be an interested, compassionate, open-minded listener, not inserting my own beliefs into the conversation.

I also was influenced by the common assumption that multitudes are leaving religion because they have been emotionally or even physically hurt by it, or have experienced rejection, prejudice, or intolerance. Most of the mainline religious people and clergy I know had a sort of "mea culpa"[58] attitude toward "nones," in other words, "What did we do to offend them?" I expected to find examples of "religious distress" in my interviewees' stories, that is, bad experiences, abuse, or direct hurt from rigid, authoritarian, or narrow-minded religious folk. I would have been a likely person with whom to share these stories. I provided plenty of opportunity during the interview and assured them of anonymity. But, as you will see, this is not what I found. Although I did hear a few stories, mostly their objections to religion tended to be conceptual or theological.

At the outset, I had surmised that SBNRs would be unclear about their beliefs or unwilling to discuss them cogently. I thought they would want me to focus instead on their practices and experiences. Instead, rather than being reticent or withholding, people insisted the interview gave them a chance—often for the first time—to articulate their thoughts. They often said they appreciated the focus and the questions, for it gave them an opportunity to learn more about themselves, to see where there were gaps in their thinking. Many times, they said my questions made them realize they had not plumbed very deeply into the core areas of their beliefs, and they promised to think more about it.

The interviewees did not shy away from discussing their beliefs, but seemed to relish these questions, take them seriously, and feel it was important for them to consider. Oftentimes when I asked for clarification or pointed to seeming inconsistencies or undeveloped areas, the interviewee would say with amazement, "I never thought of that!" and end with a hug and a promise: "Now you've given me something to think about!" Almost routinely participants thanked me profusely, saying they wished they could have more opportunities to have discussions like this.

It was clear that interviewees were quite different from each other, representing a diversity of age, occupation, socioeconomic and educational levels, location, ethnicity, gender, and sexual orientation. Using the convenient phrase "spiritual but not religious" does not do justice to their diversity. It may even encourage us to categorize all of them as "seekers" on the way to some spiritual home, when this is not always the case. However, in spite of their diversity, I soon began to hear common themes, an ethos, or a mindset which binds them together. Although their practices may differ, their attitudes toward organized religion and certain theological themes are similar. Thus, rather than belief being outmoded, inconsequential, repressive, or a hindrance, I found among my conversation partners theological reasons for their lack of religious affiliation. (If readers are interested in more specifics about the interview process and methodology, they are encouraged to read the Appendix at the end of the book.)

Before hearing the interviewees' voices, however, we must set the stage. To better appreciate these interviewees and their contexts, we need to understand the great changes that have been happening to religion in America since its heyday in the 1950s. People do not conduct their spiritual lives in isolation but are greatly affected by the trends, ideas, and alternatives around them. In the next chapter we consider what has been going on in American religion and how various researchers explain it. We will consider in what ways contemporary America has provided fertile soil for a rise in the religiously unaffiliated. After that, in the following two chapters, you will be introduced to some of these spiritual voyagers, the "types" they represent, and the themes they share. Then, in the following four chapters we get to the heart of the research, what they actually believe. A chapter is devoted to each of the four main concept areas upon which my interviewees reflected. Finally, in the concluding chapter, we will ponder the possible implications this may have on the American social and religious landscape.

2

Waking from the Dream

THE DREAM OF THE 1950S AND EARLY 1960S

THE 1950S AND early 1960s was a good time for many Americans. The Second World War had been won and the Depression was now mostly a bad memory. The soldiers were home, earning money and shopping for the new two-tone cars with stylish tail-fins. Women, once essential to the war economy, had been edged out of the workforce. Instead, they were encouraged to make babies, cook and clean with modern domestic appliances, and watch a brand-new form of entertainment, television. They could also decorate their tract homes in the growing suburbs, which had been made possible by affordable automobiles and new roads. For many people, and for the first time, there was enough money to do all this. A middle-class couple could support themselves on one income and still afford to have several children.

It was also a very good time for Christianity, especially "mainstream" Protestantism (i.e., those descended from the Reformation).[1] Partly as a response to "godless Communism" and the Cold War, religion was on the rise. Protestantism, in particular, claimed the largest proportion of the population. In fact, a higher percentage attended church than in several decades previously. In the 1950s and early 1960s, the churches were full, making repairs long neglected during the past difficult decades, building new sanctuaries in what were once empty fields, planning to add education wings for all the "Baby Boom" children born after the war. In addition, Protestant clergy were some of the most respected professionals in the land.

The mainstream had decades ago won the fundamentalist-modernist controversy which raged in the 1920s, with the more liberal or modern Protestants gaining control of seminaries and denominations. The defeated conservative evangelicals—who at first had proudly referred to themselves as "fundamentalists"—had decades ago retreated into the background of American religion after the bad press they received during the 1925 Scopes "Monkey" trial.[2] They remembered when their version of Protestant orthodoxy was standard and a bulwark against Enlightenment challenges. But now they felt like the last "defenders of the faith." They purposely distanced themselves from—and condemned as "liberal"—those mainliners who by now had reconciled themselves to modernism, the historical-critical method of biblical interpretation, and science. The mainstream often returned the insult by dismissing them as anti-modern and uneducated. These mainstreamers may not have been the only religious game in town, but they were the most respected and dominant voice. Newspapers would often carry the text of sermons, and the names of theologians such as Paul Tillich and Reinhold Niebuhr were recognized in more places than just seminaries.

The Pentecostal wing of evangelicalism, growing ever since the Azusa St. Mission revival of the early 1900s, was often stereotyped by mainstreamers as too emotional or lower class. The popular picture of them, as depicted in the 1927 Sinclair Lewis novel and 1960 film *Elmer Gantry*, was a bunch of rubes just waiting to be taken advantage of by the next faith healer.[3] Nevertheless, although these assorted evangelicals had retreated, they did not die. Instead, they constructed their own parallel universe, complete with Bible colleges, conservative seminaries, radio preachers, independent churches, and alliances of other biblical literalists.

Mainstream Protestants could still afford to consider their non-Protestant neighbors as somewhat less than fully American. Catholics returned the favor by insisting that only they would reach heaven. However, in the previous decade they had all learned to get along better when they were thrown together in the military and war effort. Many Catholics were still first-generation immigrants from the waves of southern Europeans who flooded into the United States in the late 1800s until legislation closed the door in 1924.[4] By the 1950s prejudice against them had abated somewhat, and they were beginning to think of themselves as mainstream as well. Now they were busy constructing convents, seminaries, and schools for all their native-born children. Hispanic Catholics, many in America for generations, had a long heritage and presence in some places, but experienced marginalization in others. Religiously they closely linked their ethnicity and faith. Although they retained many folk practices, combining them with Catholic devotion, they did not usually create their own denominations.

African-American Protestants, on the other hand, had long had their own thriving denominations, mostly of Protestant and/or Pentecostal lineage. Although still segregated in the South, and often poor in the North, they remembered how integral they had been to the war effort, winning respect and confidence. Increasingly they became emboldened to express their dissatisfaction with their imposed status. And Jews, the ones of German heritage here for generations and others from Eastern Europe who arrived in the immigration waves of late nineteenth and early twentieth century, were shocked and devastated by the brutal picture of the Nazi Holocaust, made real by graphic newsreels and stories. Many found this crisis deeply disturbing to their historic faith in a good God. They were also dismayed by the beginnings of a rise in intermarriage. So they focused their attention on replenishing their numbers, supporting Israel, and insisting "never again."

Other religions, of course, were also present in America in the 1950s. But these Hindus, Buddhists, Muslims, Sikhs, and others were here in much smaller numbers. They were not usually forefront in the minds of Protestants, Catholics, or Jews. Often made up of immigrant communities, for the most part they kept to themselves. Some Christians may have been concerned about their salvation, but generally their presence was not dominant enough in America to cause much concern. The even smaller number of Americans who practiced less well-known spiritualities—spiritualists, Native Americans, mesmerists, yoga practitioners—were almost invisible to the majority of American religious folk.[5] When mainstream Protestants or Catholics did think of them, they probably gave them an even lower rating than they did the evangelicals. And the majority of conservative evangelicals surely thought of these alternative spiritual practitioners as lost, heathen, superstitious, or idol worshippers.

What about "nones?" In fact, there have always been some people in America who remained religiously unaffiliated. Even in the Colonial period, not everyone attended church regularly. Along with those who were simply unable to participate for various reasons (the disabled, the rural, those with language barriers, or socially marginalized), there have always been some who purposely chose to refrain. By the nineteenth century, with Enlightenment thinking influential, everyone knew about the presence of "free-thinkers" and Transcendentalists.[6]

Although surveys were not widely utilized until the mid-twentieth century, still it is estimated that by the 1940s the number of deliberate "nones" was only around 6%. Americans sympathetic to Communism and Socialism, especially during the Depression, were likely part of the mix. But by the 1950s the percentage had gotten even smaller, with less than 2% of Americans saying they had "no religion."[7] During this period, according to sociologist Will Herberg, to be American was to be religious, whether Protestant, Catholic, or Jewish.[8] Given the shrinkage in "none" numbers, it would have been unthinkable to the average person that in a little over fifty years, the percentage of "nones" would represent at least one-fifth of the population and growing.

This dreamy picture of the 1950s is akin to the little television world of perfectly behaved children and perfectly managed towns as portrayed in the film *Pleasantville*.[9] It is the rosy-glowed heritage that many mainstream Christians envision when they look back. Although it is not clear whether the booming religious landscape of the 1950s was numerically representative of previous eras, it can be said that organized religion was always a central feature of life in America. And, since the 1950s was an especially good time, its dream lives on as the gold standard in the memories of many mainstream Protestants and Catholics.

Of course, as with every nostalgic picture, this dreamy vision conceals a lot. It minimizes the many theological, cultural, and ethnic differences even between mainstream Protestants. It conceals the real and often divisive issues among various Roman Catholic groups. It does not take into account the differences within and between religious groups in different parts of the country, or even among churches in the same town. It forgets that the Will Herberg world was made possible, in part, by the restriction in immigration starting in 1924. With fewer new immigrants, the assimilation of their children contributed to this seemingly uniform religious world as many left ethnic churches to join mainstream ones. It burnishes over the still-existing racism, sexism, and economic inequities. It downplays the stress of rapid suburbanization, postwar terrors, the "Cold War," and fears of Communism and nuclear war. It does not include the changes that loomed from the proliferation of cars, televisions, interstate highways, and rock-and-roll. All these things were part of the context in which American religion existed and they all had profound effects inside not just outside the sanctuary. The nostalgic memory of religion in the

1950s leaves these factors out. But it is this dream that lingers in many people's minds when they see the growing diversity in religious America and the increasing numbers who claim to have no religious affiliation at all.

It is no surprise that today many mainstream Christians, both Protestants and Catholics, feel panicky, paralyzed, confused, or depressed. It is easy to hear the pain in their voices when they wonder aloud why their children—including the children of active members, pastors, and seminary professors—no longer attend church. And when even successful, well-trained pastors begin to doubt their own vocations, throw off culturally unpopular theological positions, and feel drawn to alternative spiritualities themselves, it is evident that for many mainstream people the pressure of change feels unrelenting. The changes have been so rapid that many people are still around who have lived through all its phases. The skeletons of mainstream religion's 1950s glory days are visible in the impressive but half-filled urban sanctuaries, convents turned into spiritual retreat centers, down-sized seminaries, and shrinking denominational offices throughout America.

The Change Starting in the 1960s

Although many did not wake up to this dramatic change until the new millennium, it has a longer history. The big change began in the 1960s and 1970s, a period Robert Putnam in his book *American Grace* calls "The Long Sixties."[10] After a decade of riding high, suddenly mainstream religious America had young adult children who did not trust anyone over 30. The parents, many of whom had carefully raised their Baby Boomers in the faith, could not understand why these same children began to disparage the religion of their youth, protested nuclear weapons and the Vietnam War, considered corporate careers suspect, and found alternative spiritualities, liberation movements, and communal living so much more interesting. Many of the changes went against the ethical prescriptions their parents had taught them. These were the inherited prescriptions about gender and race, institutional loyalty, self-sacrifice, self-control, community involvement, and the importance of religion.

It was a true cultural revolution. In light of feminism and more work opportunities, many young women were deciding they did not have to defer to men. In light of the birth control pill and the sexual revolution, married life began to seem constraining. And although many Baby

Boomers still wanted a partner and children, many vowed never to push religion or its old-fashioned values on their own children. With the receding of "Blue Laws" that had restricted Sunday commerce, many found it quite delightful that the old somber Sunday was gone and it was instead a day of leisure, recreation, and shopping. In addition, there was a growing therapeutic mentality that viewed therapy and self-help programs as an equal or better route to personal growth than religion.

Those out in the forefront of change, middle-class mainstream youth, became opinion leaders as magazine articles, film, and television spotlighted them. By the late 1970s, when these Baby Boomers were young adults, the number of those professing "no religion" had started its steep rise, more than tripling from the scant 2%–3% in the 1950s, to nearly 9% only twenty years later.[11] And this did not take into account those who still used the label of a particular religion but no longer ventured inside the sanctuary. Religion now seemed identified with older values that constrained individual freedom and expression.

Of course, cultural change does not happen everywhere at the same time and speed. These attitudes and behaviors may not have been as pervasive in nonwhite, non-mainstream, disadvantaged, and immigrant communities. They were also slower in coming to various parts of the country. But no community was able to completely hold the line against this revolution. Vatican II opened up Catholics to modern trends, as many priests and nuns abandoned their vocations. African American, Hispanic, and Asian Christians also began their own theological revolutions, with Black, Womanist, Latin American, Mujerista, Minjung, and other religious liberation movements developing. Gays and lesbians were beginning to protest society's closeting of them.

Growth of Conservative Evangelicals

Even white evangelical America cracked open a bit. In spite of their better record than mainstreamers of holding onto their young people, a percentage of young evangelicals ventured out of their closed world to attend "secular" colleges in spite of the warnings of their pastors and parents. Cautious but somewhat more open to modernism than their forebears, these young Christians were by the 1970s creating a neo-evangelicalism, which tentatively reconsidered many formerly sacrosanct behaviors and beliefs. Under pressure from the liberated women they met in school and

at work—as well as a growing Christian feminism—they even began paying slightly more attention to the views of evangelical women.[12] Their use
of the Bible also conveyed the encroachment of modernism and science,
as the focus on Scripture was shifted toward proving its accuracy rather
than primarily conveying its call to conversion.

Although elements of modernism did make their way into many sectors of the conservative evangelical world, overall they were not happy with
much of the 1960s and 1970s revolution. Soon they found many others
who agreed with them. So, as Robert Putnam explains, the "Long Sixties"
were followed by an "aftershock." In the 1980s there was a religious revival
of sorts across the generations. While there are many reasons given for
the rise of conservative evangelicalism, Putnam and others see this revival
as a reaction against loosened mores of the 1960s, especially the sexual
revolution. On the surface, the impetus seems more ethical than theological. Conservative evangelicalism shifted its attention toward moral issues
like abortion and homosexuality, rather than its previous core focus on
the experience of conversion. In some ways, Americans seemed to be
returning to their religious roots and the biggest beneficiaries of this were
evangelical churches, which grew dramatically in the 1980s. And, in fact,
this seeming resurgence of religion may well have been, as Charles Taylor
suggests, an aspiration to return America to its theistic roots, its sense of
being "one nation under God."[13]

But another important dimension of this "aftershock" that demands
attention is the specifically political aspect. Previously, the theology of
many fundamentalists was buttressed by a world-suspicious, even apolitical, attitude. Retreat from the world, not the desire to control it, had been a
hallmark of fundamentalism. Along with this was often a siege mentality
and combative attitude. Many of these evangelicals were "premillenialists"
who believed that the worse the world got, the more predictive this was for
the return of Christ. Believers had only to hang on, watch things decline,
wait until they were raptured away from the apocalypse, and then enjoy
the Christ-inaugurated new millennium.[14] Given this ethos, one would
never expect conservative evangelicals to either trust or find a home in
politics.

Nevertheless, conservative politicians reached out to conservative
religious people and found a receptive audience. The alliance proved
strong. Whereas 20-something Baby Boomers had told each other not to
trust anyone over 30, now conservative evangelicals seemed to tell each
other not to fully trust anyone who was not a "born-again" believer. The

logic was that if someone knew Jesus, they were more likely to be doing God's will. Politicians who intimated at this connection did better among evangelicals.[15]

Many mainstream—also known as "old-line"—Christians watched in shock as conservative evangelicalism grew, while their numbers continued to shrink. The mainline decline that began in the 1960s accelerated in the 1980s and 1990s and resulted in some denominations losing up to one-third of their membership. As for Roman Catholicism, it just barely held its own. If it were not for the rise in numbers of Latino immigrants, many of whom bring their religion with them, the Roman Catholic Church would have suffered equal losses. Mainstream Protestants were especially dismayed that their fellow Christians were so eager to align themselves with conservative politics. They could not understand how much of the country seemed to turn away from many of the liberal values—like tolerance, social equality, societal help for the disadvantaged, and appreciation of diversity—which mainstream Christianity had contributed to America. But their voices, values, and advances were drowned out by the media attention and vociferous positions taken by conservative evangelicals.

Thus, the 1980s forced a polarization between conservatives and liberals. As a result, Putnam explains, conservatives became more religious and liberals, as a reaction, became less. He calls this the second "aftershock." All this helps explain why there was such a dramatic decrease in Americans who affirmed that religion is able to "answer all or most of today's problems." For while 82% of Americans had claimed this in 1958, by 2010 this percentage had shrunk to just 58%.[16]

Growth of "Nones"

Although to many people the 1980s and early 1990s seemed like a period of religious revival, something else was also happening: the numbers professing "no religion" began to accelerate. It seems the hyper-conservatives may have been the authors of their own reduction. For evangelical growth began leveling off at the same time the rate of "nones" was increasing. Many of the recent "nones" come from this latter group—turned off to a religion they increasingly identify with conservative politics.[17] This belies the common assumption, even today, that white evangelical, racial-ethnic congregations, and/or at least mega-churches continue to do well. According to an important study, this is not the case. Among all churches, no matter their theology, attendance dropped significantly after 2000. By 2010, "more than 1 in 4 American congregations had fewer than 50 in worship...and just under half had fewer than 100." Even the mega-churches were now only attracting "a bigger slice of a shrinking pie."[18] Many of these church dropouts began populating the burgeoning ranks of "nones."

The growth in the religiously unaffiliated can be charted and it is dramatic. By the start of the 1990s those overtly claiming to be "none" had reached at least 11% and toward the end was at least 14%.[19] By 2008, the surveyed number of "nones" had reached at least 16%.[20] By 2012 the actual number of persons unaffiliated with any organized religion was at least 20% and growing. In actuality, these estimates might be low. When polled, many people identify with something, even if they no longer show up, contribute, or practice. Surveys may also overestimate actual church attendance by half because respondents do not report accurately.[21] Since "showing up" is a good indication of affiliation, it is important to realize that no matter what type of church you consider, attendance has clearly been dropping for decades. Religions cannot survive very well without people showing up regularly, contributing, passing along the tradition, working at common goals, and committing to a shared ethos.

For mainstream Protestants, the rise in "nones" was an additional and especially cruel surprise. In the 1950s, if church decline had been predicted, mainstreamers would never have expected their form of religion to be such a casualty. After all, in many ways they had worked hard to stay relevant and to keep pace with the changes in society. Liberal Protestant denominations promoted the ordination of women. They reconsidered formerly negative attitudes toward divorce, homosexuality, birth control, and abortion. Both Protestants and Catholics adjusted their church operations to the declining numbers of stay-at-home women, formerly the backbone of congregational life. Many recognized the reality of victimization, turned against domestic violence, and championed the rights of workers and immigrants. Many welcomed increased ethnic and cultural diversity. Some even began to reconsider formerly core theological tenets like exclusive salvation, biblical literalism, and original sin. They might be able to understand why "nones" were repelled by conservative Christianity, but they could not understand why their liberal message was not drawing "nones" to their churches.

In fact, there is much we still don't understand about "nones." Interest in them has waxed and waned according to their numbers. During the 1950s the "unchurched" got hardly any attention. When they began to increase during the "Long Sixties," interest rose somewhat, but stayed low probably because the magnitude of the change to come was only dimly perceived. With the huge rise in the 1990s, however, interest in "nones" increased.[22] Now there are many theories that try to explain the "none" growth.

One avenue sometimes overlooked is the popularization of the "postmodern" ethos. Christian Smith describes this particularly well:

The 1980s and 1990s saw the widespread diffusion and powerful influence of the theories of poststructuralism and postmodernism in U.S. culture. These began as arcane academic theories. . . . Soon, however, they spread and were popularized in most of the humanities and some of the social sciences. . . . All that belonged to "the modern" was condemned: epistemological foundations, certainty, reason, universalism, the self, authorial voice, the nation state, colonialism, the Word, etc. (and we think, for the better, in some ways). All that was thought to be postmodern was celebrated: uncertainty, difference, fluidity, ambiguity, multivocality, self-construction, changing identities, particularity, historical finitude, localism, audience reception, perspectivalism, and more. . . . Somehow all of this high theory . . . became democratized and vulgarized in U.S. culture. Simplified versions . . . were now a driving influence. . . . By the time it reached the American hoi polloi, postmodernism had become a simple-minded ideology presupposing the cultural construction of everything, individualistic subjectivism, soft ontological antirealism, and absolute moral relativism.[23]

It is easy to underestimate the impact of this originally academic and philosophical movement. Taking it seriously shows us the power of ideas to change reality. And this power is something we want to keep in mind when we examine the changing beliefs of the "nones" we will soon meet. With its relativizing of all truth claims, postmodernism makes religion a particularly hard sell. It also makes all religious people—but especially conservatives with their clear moral and theological precepts—look retrograde and even dangerous.

Some suggest that a rise in "nones" is just an outcome of our distinctive American way of life, with its emphasis on mobility, minimal life-long ties, and decreasing face-to-face interaction due to technology, bureaucracy, and information overload. Since this often results in loneliness, alienation, and isolation, one might think it would increase religious participation but for some it may have the opposite effect. J. Russell Hale suggests the roots of "unchurchedness may lie outside the religious domain entirely." Studies show those not involved in religion are less involved in any type of organizations. "The marginality of the unchurched...may be a function of marginality of people in the culture generally."[24]

Some worry about the social and emotional effects of a less communal and more self-focused citizenry. Even if we can explain an increasing self-focus among Americans as self-preservation in the face of contemporary anonymity, information overload, and fragmentation, it is still worrisome. While the surge in small support groups may be an effort to ameliorate this alienation, the trend still implies less civic involvement and less loyalty to public institutions. This is quite a change from the behavior the Greatest Generation "joiners" showed in the 1950s.[25]

Some writers claim that a new form of self-expressive "generativity" could emerge from spiritual seeking.[26] We also have to consider how television, Internet, and social media have transformed our sense of community and spirituality. The media world has become a new meeting place with communication becoming more horizontal, less "mediated" by authorities. Religious and spiritual symbols have been appropriated and given new meaning, with religious institutions losing their oversight. A decline in commitment to organized religion seems to go with these changes. Whether new forms of community will arise from these changes is not yet clear.

While the numbers of "nones" may be higher in some parts of the country than others, the trend is sweeping the United States in general. Where once the "none zone" was located primarily in the Pacific Northwest, now it is even more prominent in New England, that former bastion of the American religious heritage. Thus Patricia Killen was correct when she predicted in 2004: "Far from being an aberrant frontier outpost, slow to catch up to the rest of the nation, the Pacific Northwest's religious dynamics throw into relief twenty-first-century, postmodern religious impulses."[27]

Some of the explanation could simply be demographic. Fewer people are raised religiously now. Their numbers tripled between the 1970s and the 1990s.[28] Just the fact that less young people have been raised religiously could explain the rise in "nones." Add that they are maturing, settling down, marrying, and reproducing later in life, and the drift away from religion is increased. Interfaith marriage is part of this. While spouses from two different traditions may have been less religious to begin with, they may also weaken their ties to accommodate the partner. The children of these unions are often less tied to one religious tradition, even if their parents expose them to both or neither. In the past more people were raised in a religion and married "endogamously," that is, within it. Even those few children raised "none" often affiliated with some religion by adulthood.

Already by the 1960s and 1970s, however, Baby Boomers were more likely than previous generations to "disaffiliate" from their religious background. And even though many have become spiritual seekers, they have been less likely to raise religious children.[29] When scholars try to define the "social characteristics" of "nones," they find more of them to be young, male, college-educated, unmarried, and without children.[30] The rise in "nones" may be just a result of all this demographic change. A few theorists speculate that reduced religiousness is just a Baby Boomer blip and, with their aging,[31] the way will be paved for younger people to return to religion. In reality, the increase in "nones" among younger generations seems to contradict that hope.

Even when young adults self-identify as religious, spiritual, or both, they often become "tinkerers" cobbling together an improvised and changeable faith, using whatever lies at hand.[32] And even though young adults may be less hostile to religion than the Baby Boomers,[33] this does not make them any likelier to join. One large survey discovered that 65% of young adults never attend worship services and rarely or never pray with others. About 67% never read any sacred texts, and even when they believe in Jesus and heaven, 68% do not think religion, faith, or spirituality is really important in their lives.[34] None of these factors portends an increase in religious affiliation or loyalty. In fact, it is possible that young adults are actually becoming both less religious and less spiritual than their parents. As one study notes: "The youngest, and the most religiously marginal are much less likely to see themselves as religious and spiritual, slightly more likely to see themselves as spiritual only, and much more likely to see themselves as *neither* religious nor spiritual."[35]

Religious illiteracy is part of this picture. Given the decline in religious upbringing accelerated by Baby Boomers, fewer people understand much about specific religious beliefs than in the past. It is easy to stereotype the religiously "other" when one has little in-depth knowledge of particular religious points of view. Even those raised in the church often come away with a benign "moralistic therapeutic deism" where the chief goal in life is to be happy, to be liked, and to only call upon the combination Divine Butler/Therapist on an as-needed basis. Many both inside and outside organized religion have become religiously illiterate.[36] While religious illiteracy is not the same as secularization, this change has profound effects. Where once America could count on a shared ethos or "meta-narrative," springing from a common theological tradition and related behavior, there is no longer any "sacred canopy" under which all can gather.

In addition, many people today organize their time around leisure activities—sports, hobbies, exercise, media, and travel—and this serves as a distraction from the larger questions which religion asks. There is also the popular therapeutic mentality, and range of self-help techniques, which justify self-focus and make the support of traditional religion now seem less necessary when dealing with inevitable life crises. Finally, the impact of the September 11 attacks on the United States should not be minimized, since they added weight to the argument that religion simply divides, even inspires violence, rather than unites. That event probably played a part in driving more non-religious persons into the open, proud not to be associated with what they saw as organized hatred. Add this to the demographic and social trends that have been building for decades and we can better understand both the gradual rise in "nones" since the 1960s, as well as their dramatic rise from the 1990s onward. Whether you see all the above elements as good news or bad news, they do indicate that the rise in "nones" in America has many significant contributing factors and, in some ways, could have been predicted.

Who Are the "Spiritual but not Religious"?

Many people are not content to be religiously "nothing." Many still seem to be searching for something to believe in. The huge increase in spiritual options, popular books, and entrepreneurial teachers indicates some kind of spiritual ferment. And yet increasing numbers of people do not look to organized religion to satisfy this yearning. When social scientists try to determine if someone is religious, they look at three factors: (1) how often the person attends religious services; (2) the strength and type of beliefs; and (3) how important religion is in his or her life. Many of my conversation partners met two, and sometimes three, of these three criteria. Plenty had beliefs about the matters with which religion deals. There were many for whom their spiritual journey was central. And I also found quite a few who dipped in and out of various religious and spiritual practices, communities, and rituals. Why did they insist on being "spiritual but not religious"?

There were a variety of reasons. Many considered this term more acceptable, enlightened, or "sexy." For many it meant they believed in "something" and were not atheists, a group with a very low popularity rating in America. To a large number of interviewees being "spiritual but not religious" implied they could be moral without the help of religion. Some wanted nothing to do with a Christianity which they saw as politically and socially conservative. And for most of the people with whom I spoke— including those who continued to be involved in organized religion—they used the word to mean they were "alive" spiritually, rather than being confined by arbitrary rules, needless denominational identity, dry dogma, and pointless ritual.[37] Although the term "spiritual but not religious" is notoriously slippery for a variety of reasons which have been well documented,[38] it is noteworthy how many people embrace it. This includes not only liberal or mainline Protestants, but Roman Catholics[39] and even evangelicals, as well. Thus the term "spiritual but not religious" has become part of the common parlance, similar to the word "addiction" after the upsurge in the addiction recovery movement in the 1990s.

But not everyone, even my volunteers, rushes to embrace this term. Even though each interviewee agreed they were a suitable candidate with something to say, a minority bristled at being so labeled. For some interviewees, the term conjured up aging hippies, shallow spiritualists, or someone blithely helping themselves from the salad-bar of American religion, not caring whether fruit gelatin on top of potato salad made for a good "presentation." It reminded me of women who were enjoying the benefits of the 1960s and 1970s cultural revolution but did not want to be known as "feminists." When some volunteers pulled back from the term "spiritual but not religious," they disavowed any negative baggage which this term has. Instead, they wanted to be sure I understood they were serious about their spirituality and seeking. They wanted me to know they had something important to share regarding their beliefs, personal quests, and views on both organized religion and alternative spiritualities.

How can we understand behavior formerly identified with religion, when religious affiliation is now rejected? One scholar suggests spirituality has become "diffused."[40] Another similarly suggests that the sacred has leaked out of religion and into everyday life.[41] Some see this as a sign of hope. They insist that competition is good for religion,[42] and/or that a spiritual renewal of America is taking place.[43] If this ferment will lead to a rebirth for religion, it is not apparent yet. For rather than turning to organized religion, the trajectory is often toward the many non-Western practices, alternative spiritualities, and revolving doors of popular teachers vying to provide a framework of meaning. Seeker "consumers" often find their attention and dollars directed toward semi-spiritual or "quasi-religious" practices—things such as acupuncture, ethical eating regimens, yoga, and meditation—more or less divorced from their religious roots.[44] Some have even returned to a form of magic, possibly as a way to exert control over an environment which feels increasingly chaotic. America's increasing lack of knowledge about religion is likely one reason why our proliferation of competing options has been able to gain more than the foothold it had in earlier generations.

The "spiritual but not religious" movement may not be simply a protest against religion but also a protest against a secular world that brackets the spirit or forces an overreliance on science to answer all problems. This accords with Charles Taylor's assertion in *A Secular Age* that the secularization thesis is unconvincing. For if we look in the right places, he suggests, we will find evidence of the divine. Could it be, then, that we are seeing a "re-enchantment" of the world, rather than a straight-forward secularization process?[45] Or, instead, could this dramatic change in American religion be not so much a desertion but more of a privatization of faith—a "do-it-myself" enterprise? This might be why the few religious groups which have gained ground are often those which focus on personal salvation and private goals, as well as such "postmodern" variants as the "emergent church."[46]

Yet even these are not making significant headway among the SBNRs. In the next chapter, in order to better understand those who do not identify with any particular religious group, I will introduce you to the five types of SBNRs I met, as well as identifying common themes in their beliefs. In this way, you will better appreciate the personal stories and "lived theology" which you will encounter in this book.

3

The Interviewees

PEOPLE FROM ALL age groups came forward to be interviewed. Nearly everyone who volunteered claimed enthusiastically that "spiritual but not religious" was an apt term to describe their current spiritual orientation. Many of them focused on similar things—such as their right to believe as they choose, their reluctance to cede spiritual authority to organized religion, and their prioritizing of personal experience—when they explained why this term fit them.

We met for an hour or two for a semi-structured or "open-ended" interview. I began by inquiring about their occupation, education, and other demographic details. Then we looked at their family background and its religious associations, if any. After that, I asked each person to describe their life-time spiritual journey. I waited to ask them about the four specific concepts under investigation—the sacred, human nature, community, and afterlife—until the second part of the interview. In that way, there was more context for understanding their beliefs.

As I began to hear their stories, it was evident that, although there were many commonalities, each person was inevitably affected by the events and thought patterns of the generation in which they grew up. In addition, no matter what their age, the interviewees clustered into various "types" of SBNRs, based on their reasons and goals. Thus, although my conversation partners often agreed on certain core themes—which we will examine in subsequent chapters—their age group and type colored their sense of being "spiritual but not religious." In this chapter, we will examine some of the generational differences and specific types. By focusing on this sample of people who use the SBNR label for themselves, we may better understand the various ways people become and function as religiously unaffiliated.

Generations

The Greatest Generation (Born 1901–1924)

I got very few volunteers from the "Greatest Generation." This was to be expected. These "joiners," after living through the Great Depression and Second World War, had helped during the 1950s to rebuild the religious infrastructure that had suffered in prior decades. They enlarged the scope and work of their denominations, created and nurtured civic and religious groups, and made sure their children followed suit. This cohort still forms the rapidly withering backbone of many churches today. It is not surprising that very few from this generation wanted to claim the "spiritual but not religious" label. If any who heard my call had ever protested religion, did not believe its teachings, or excluded themselves for other reasons, they may have been hesitant to reveal it. After all, in their day religious identity was just part of being a good American.[1]

There were exceptions, however. I was surprised when a "Greatest Generation" man quietly sidled up to me after church one day. I had just seen him taking up the collection, ushering, and singing in the choir. Even so, he insisted on speaking with me privately. Once we were safely seated in the church library, with door closed, he told me he had come from a long line of highly active Protestants and had continued this tradition. He had been president or chair of almost every religious organization he had joined. In his youth and young adulthood, religious activity was just something you did and no one talked very much about the content of it. Therefore, although he had long harbored doubts and questions, it was not until late adulthood that he felt he could acknowledge them. Even now, however, although he is not at all sure about the existence of God, he continues to be an active member at church.

But most of the many "Greatest Generation" members I met did not volunteer themselves. Instead, they often eagerly suggested I interview their children or grandchildren. They were genuinely puzzled and hurt that these progeny, who had been raised in the church, no longer seemed to consider religion an important part of their lives. When I spoke with people from this generation, it was mostly to help them understand how so many could have turned away from the religions which had been so important to them. As a result, my interviewee pool starts with the Silent Generation.

The Silent Generation (Born 1925–1945)

This generation has always gotten much less "press" than the huge bubble of Baby Boomers which followed them, perhaps because so many toed the line much more willingly. All of these interviewees had some kind of religious training, mostly some form of Christianity or Judaism. Most were raised Protestant, more from mainline churches and a few describing their background as "fundamentalist." Two had a Jewish heritage, but neither had been devout. One, as a child, was made to attend synagogue only on religious holidays and the other had been fostered out as a child, sent to both Protestant and Catholic boarding schools and given extensive religious exposure. One had been raised Hindu. Their stories clearly reflected having been raised in a time when religion was an essential part of personal identity. Just a few of these interviewees were raised by non-religious parents. Even with such parents, however, most of these interviewees became "seekers" as early as middle childhood, soon affiliating with some form of organized religion on their own.

Very few of the Silent Generation interviewees raised religious explicitly rebelled against it when they were young. At most, some admitted to being a little bored with or just acquiescent to the religious training they received. Yet in spite of all this religious background, none of these Silent Generation interviewees now identify themselves as religious. In telling their stories, they often describe profound emotional upheaval in this area, demonstrating that stepping outside their religious backgrounds had been a very costly thing. For many, however, it was also an exhilarating one. In total, Silent Generation people were a bit harder to find, representing somewhat less than 10% of the total. After all, they would have been those brave or rebellious enough to break out of the accepted mold.

The Silent Generation people I met represented an interesting combination of previous religious ethical formation and current lack of affiliation. Each of them had cast off the very religious structures that taught them the values by which they still live. They no longer felt the need for authoritative voices, the ritual, community, or the services of organized religion. They had cast them off even though, many admitted, once these same things had fed their spirits. Mostly retired, the ones I met have lived rich, productive lives and contributed to society. None of the people were restless seekers, shallow individualists, or selfish loners. They had thought hard about their stance toward religion and had taken belief seriously. Oftentimes, their reasons for leaving were theological. Even so, they could not be categorized as "believing without belonging."

William Willard is a good example. Raised in Appalachia by conservative and devout Anabaptist[2] parents, William never had a problem with religion when he was growing up. As with several of the interviewees, he was a "PK" or "preacher's kid." His father, an active "lay pastor," struggled to support his family. And yet they tithed 10% of their income, practiced extensive hospitality and charity, and made sure their children got what they needed. Not only did William attend the frequent church services, but he met and exceeded all his parents' religious expectations, without complaint or issue. He assured me he had experienced neither religious abuse nor great cataclysms of doubt. Instead, his faith had been secure. "I doubt there was ever a time I didn't feel there was a divine being." William remembers his parents with gratitude and admiration. If anyone had predicted that he would end up non-religious, doubting, and barely agnostic late in life, no one would have believed it.

William studied at a Christian college, went to daily chapel, and took the required religion courses. He met and married a girl with a similar background. As an adult, he got a doctorate in science and held various academic positions at prestigious universities. It was not his scientific studies, however, which disturbed his faith. For everywhere he lived, he was very active in some kind of church, moving from fundamentalist, to evangelical, to Presbyterian, to Episcopal, and finally to Unitarian before leaving church altogether. He described a slow movement toward more and more open-minded theologies and churches until he realized he did not believe any of it anymore. William thus rode the crest of the wave that mainline Protestantism promoted as they worked to stay current with the culture. This educated man has no regrets and still lives just down the road from his conservative Christian and devout church-going relatives. At the end of our time together, he smiled slyly, nodded in their direction, and said with a satisfied chuckle: "I'm an utter disappointment to them."

The Baby Boomers (Born 1946–1964)

By far, the most enthusiastic and insistent volunteers came from the Baby Boomer generation. They amounted to more than one-third of my total group and, if I had the time, I could have interviewed two or three times this number. Reflective of the times, most were raised in some form of Christianity—especially Protestantism—or Judaism. About one-fifth had been Roman Catholic, and some had a conservative Christian upbringing. Like the Silent Generation interviewees, these Baby Boomers had grown up in a very religious America. Many were taken to church regularly. They said such things as Patricia Polk did: "It was the thing to do.... You don't really question those things. If you are a good person, you go." Gail Asher, who we will meet again later, said: "It was kind of the fiber of the family.... They certainly relied on their faith in Jesus and the church when obstacles came up or they were celebrating." A significant number of my SBNR Baby Boomers remembered their time in organized religion fondly, even longingly.

Other interviewees had tried to fit in, but could not always pull it off. Jack Acker was raised in a very conservative Midwestern rural area and had Christian friends all around him who attested to conversion experiences. He lamented, however, that he had never had one. "I never had that chill, that overwhelming emotion." One day as a young teen Jack witnessed an altar call: "You're sitting there in the back and watching all these people go up and they're crying and they're happy.... We get in the car afterwards and.... my mom turns around and says, 'Why didn't you go up?'" So, at the next altar call, he went forward just to please her. "My mother was a wonderful person and she wanted a little bit of a show for her lady friends.... That made her feel good, that I went up, even though it meant nothing [to me]."

Just a few interviewees had only minimal religious background. Some criticized their families for this. Mick Sharp, a Midwestern man said: "I feel my family was hypocritical. They claimed to be believers in Jesus but they rarely went to church." Shelly Trump said: "My parents weren't overtly spiritual. My mother did not agree with organized religion, she thought it was evil.... She had no use for it." However, like many Silent Generation and some Baby Boomer interviewees, she sought out religion on her own, for a time sojourning in Protestant evangelicalism. But here is where age began to make a difference because, unlike the Silent Generation, some of the interviewees who had very little early religious training never did get very involved.

Judy Eberstark, a Baby Boomer Western woman from a mixed faith marriage said: "My mother was really an atheist but was raised a Protestant, so she thought in order to have a proper upbringing you went to church.... I never felt comfortable there." Having a Jewish father was part of it, she remembered. Because of that "my mother didn't really fit in...because she was there without her husband." Many of the interviewees only minimally exposed to religion often said they felt like outsiders even when they did attend church. "All the little Sunday School girls and boys had their attendance badges and I didn't have one because I didn't go every Sunday." Another said: "It seemed awkward, a lot of code words. I couldn't figure out what most of it meant. I got the sense of being an outsider. You don't want to go in the door because you are pretending to be something that you're not."

The Baby Boomers started life in a very religious America. They had no clue that as young adults they would live through a profound cultural revolution. Yet—unlike the Silent Generation interviewees who told stories of deviating even from many of their peers—when these Baby Boomers broke away it was easier and often exhilarating, for they were very much in step with the "question authority" ethos of their generation. Of all the age groups, these Baby Boomers were among the most eager to embrace or experiment with alternative spiritualities. They were also the least likely to question these alternatives the way they questioned organized religion.

Perhaps because of the profound change from one ethos to another, many Baby Boomers insisted their spiritual journey was unique and needed to be heard. The women were especially insistent. This makes sense because they had come to maturity in a time with extraordinary opportunity for change—increased higher education, birth control, the sexual revolution, growth in divorce rate, less employment restrictions, various liberation movements, and so on. Along with this also came the freedom to walk away from their religious backgrounds. This most often happened, for both men and women, when a discordant note was struck—perhaps a doctrine they could not accept, or an awareness of hypocrisy. It was then that many of these Baby Boomer SBNRs felt "honor-bound" to leave religion. For many, this often happened in adolescence or in college when a larger world opened up for them. This reflects their orientation to "authenticity," that one must attend to the inner "guide" and reject any externally imposed views which do not correspond with one's own experience.

Deborah Gilmore is a good example of several of these aspects. Her father was a non-practicing Protestant and her mother an Irish Catholic. Although her parents were not regular church attenders, they sent Deborah and her siblings to Mass, and the boys to parochial school. She had trouble comprehending the Old Testament, but loved the saints, angels, and Jesus

Christ. Around 9 or 10 years old, however, Deborah began to question. She could find no one at home or church to help her. Taking matters into her own hands, she began to attend a Methodist church within walking distance of her home. Her mother did not object, but was pleased that Deborah was "following some kind of spiritual path" and had chosen a good church.

Deborah remembers her time there fondly. "I found that a lot of their ideas were beautiful.... It was a wonderful group of people. I enjoyed being there." She added, "I was very impressed that they actually taught us about other religions...rather than saying: 'Other religions are bad.'" She also visited her friends' churches, attended Vacation Bible School, and even maintained her connections with Catholicism by singing in the choir each Christmas Eve. Yet though her church had a "great youth pastor," her questions lingered. She remembers: "They were doing that wonderful Jonathan Livingston Segal stuff that they were doing in the 1970s. You sit in a circle and you tell each other something honestly positive.... In a way, it wasn't so much religion; it was personal growth and feeling comfortable in your own skin.... To me that didn't have much to do with the fact that this was happening in a church."

Although Deborah remained a very active member all the way through high school, college changed everything. I heard this often from Baby Boomers. For Deborah, it was a course in Cultural Anthropology. She learned that "every culture develops some sort of belief system in order to explain things they can't explain and help structure and guide their society.... I found it very disconcerting that when we studied ancient religions they were called mythologies and our own religion was chiseled in stone. That to me was ludicrous." This ended her religious involvement. To this day, however, she believes that church is a good thing, providing many benefits for people. "I very much admire religion. I like to study it as a study of culture. I'm not against anybody who is religious. I'm not an angry atheist." Now, to nurture her own spirit, she does yoga and t'ai chi. She believes in the benefits of these practices and would call them "spiritual," but she tries to ignore any religious undertones.

Gen X (Born 1965–1981)

Gen Xers were born in the midst of the cultural and spiritual revolution of the 1960s and 1970s. Not only was ferment the norm for them, but they were born into an America that was in many ways much less religious than ever before. Mostly gone were the Sunday "Blue Laws." Instead shops and youth sports now commonly used Sunday morning as prime time, churches were emptying out, denominational structures had started to weaken, and so on. For many of the Gen Xers I met, "spiritual but not religious" was not only an acceptable, but a superior and praiseworthy, label.

Gen X represents the second largest pool of interviewees, about two-thirds the size of the Baby Boomer cohort. While not as insistent as the Baby Boomers—or as convinced that their stories were particularly unique—nevertheless these interviewees were eager to share their stories. The Gen Xers I met often had Baby Boomer parents who had made a conscious decision not to "impose" any kind of religion on their children. Unlike their own spiritual formation, Baby Boomer parents often wanted to give their children the freedom to choose what they wanted to believe and whether or not to affiliate with any organized religion. When you hear Gen X stories, you can hear echoes of their parents' generation. Unlike the two earlier cohorts, significantly less than half of this group had a consistent, traditional religious upbringing, nor did as many live in traditional two-parent families. With weekend visitation, shared parenting, or increased demands on the single parent, interviewees often reported a much less consistent spiritual formation.

Of those few raised religiously, two-thirds of them were involved in mainline Protestantism, with a few raised conservative Christian or Roman Catholic. Those raised mainline Protestant reflect a very different religious environment than previous cohorts. For them religion was no longer a clear-cut cultural expectation, or set of beliefs. Instead, they were left to make their own decisions about whether to attend or affiliate. Many of them chose to abstain. I also met a small number raised conservative Christian. This mirrored both the rise of evangelicalism and the decline in denominational identity during this period. These people described a more "generic Christian" identity. Nick Jones, a Midwestern man, said his upbringing "mostly revolved around the church and God and Jesus and do good and stuff." But as for denominations, they were all the same to him: "I didn't think Catholicism and other religions. I didn't think Baptist or Protestant. I didn't think of the different religions. It was just going to church and thinking about the same God. There was no division, really."

But the largest group of interviewees was those who had grown up with a mixed exposure to religion. A few had purposely been raised hybridly by their parents. On one of many visits to a non-religious spiritual retreat center, I met Tamara Birnbaum, a biracial woman who had worked there only a few months. She was enthusiastic about finally being part of a "spiritual community." Unlike the other workers, however, she did not live "on the property." Instead, she chose to live in town where she could also participate in the local synagogue. She told me she had an Asian Buddhist mother who had converted to Judaism for her husband. My interviewee explained that, growing up, she had practiced Judaism with a Buddhist influence. She saw no conflict in the two religions. "Home was very open.... My mother felt I needed at least a strong foundation... so I was Bat Mitzvah'd... [but] it wasn't ever pushed upon me." Instead, she was told "to continue in whatever path I wanted."

I met Maria Falcone volunteering at a sports facility out West for people with disabilities. Her story was particularly striking. She had been born to Native Americans but was adopted as an infant into a Christian family. She praised her adoptive parents for exposing her to various traditions, rather than baptizing her into one. She attended Catholic Mass with the Italian side of her family, Baptist services with her Protestant grandmother, and was sent to a summer camp which focused on Native American spirituality. Her parents, she said, "felt that my calling was more with my culture... [but] they also wanted me to have a really strong connection to God and know that I could pray." They told her "the way I should go would become clear to me."

There were a number of interviewees who had a rather eclectic religious exposure, rather than a purposeful hybridity. Jenny Buchan was raised in the Midwest. Her single mother was a Wiccan with interest in Native American spiritual practices. She thoroughly exposed Jenny to all this until Jenny was 10, when she was adopted by her grandparents. They occasionally brought her to church. When I met Jenny, she was working as an administrator for a Midwestern organization promoting spiritual dance. Definitely a spiritual "explorer"—one of the five types we will soon discuss—Jenny has enjoyed classes in massage therapy, shamanism, and other spiritual alternatives. She said of her upbringing: "It was just more free. It was not one set thing.... The most important thing was prayer, talking about it, being in amongst friends... in the loving environment." Her mother told her to follow "what you feel is right in your heart.... She never had me baptized because she wanted for me to search and find my own way."

Mark Sage had a different journey but one that led to the same place. This Midwestern Gen Xer grew up in the suburbs of a large city. His parents exposed him to so many religious things, he said, that he just ended up confused.

> To the best of my knowledge, I was baptized Catholic.... Before I was able to take Communion...we were pulled out....We went and joined another church organization and also got pulled out of that and then went to another one. I went to Catholic, Unitarian, United Methodist....I don't want to sound like I'm blaming anybody, but my mother and father would get mad at the church and pull us all out and I was too young to have a voice in the matter....We did so much jumping around that I would not say they were religious at all.

Finally, a much higher percentage of the Gen X interviewees than previous cohorts had virtually no family exposure to religion at all. Those without any religion represented almost one in five of my Gen X interviewees. When I asked, "How was spirituality expressed in the environment you grew up in?" several said simply, "It wasn't." Jennifer Babcock grew up near a large Midwestern city. Even though her town was filled with churches, Jenny was given almost no exposure to religion at all. Her mother, widowed when Jenny was quite young, was too busy making a living for her three children. But she also developed a grudge against both God and religion. Jennifer reported that she and her mother never attended services of any kind: "My mom didn't have any kind of religious or spiritual connection to anything....If she ever did believe anything...I don't know....There's nothing at all."

Another, Lisette Marshall, had a very succinct way of describing her lack of religious background. She explained that her Dad was an atheist and her mother a "recovering Catholic," so "they did not do any kind of church, not anything....Zero. I have no memory of any religious anything in my life." Unlike earlier generations who often sought out religion on their own, this and many other Gen X interviewees raised "none" did not seem to feel the lack. When I asked how this woman felt about being raised "none" she said: "Not bad...the whole religious realm, it just didn't even exist to me....Churches were just pretty buildings. I didn't know that they had any real purpose, other than possibly a town meeting hall. It was just not a part of my consciousness."

The theme of religious freedom underlies many of the Gen X stories, no matter what the interviewee's background. However, unlike earlier generations, there was not just less denominational identity but also a loss of theological depth and nuance. The inability of religious people to answer serious theological questions is often reported as the reason they leave religion or fail to connect with any one tradition. Overall, among the Gen Xers I heard a strong desire to live life with intellectual integrity, as well as a hesitation to believe in anything half-heartedly. But there was also a real reluctance to do what most religious people have always done, that is, sustain a mixture of faith and doubt. As a result, many of them stood on the sidelines, dipping a toe in now and then, out of curiosity, need, or desire, without ever fully getting wet.

Given their minimal or random exposure, these Gen Xers had few stories of struggles with organized religion. While it is difficult sometimes to decide what should count as "religious distress," I heard no accounts of physical abuse, emotional angst, or trauma connected with religion. Instead, the most common difficulties among my respondents emerged in the area of belief. From Gen Xers, I heard a striking amount of theological qualms and doubts among those exposed not just to traditional religion, but also to alternative spiritualities, and/or eclectic mixes where they had plenty of freedom to make up their own minds.

The flip side of all this, however, is that for some of the Gen Xers, Christianity has become as valid a choice as any other. Raised without much exposure to it, some can now come to Christianity with more realistic expectations and a more open-minded attitude than earlier cohorts, especially Baby Boomers. In fact, some interviewees had included Christianity among the spiritual options they considered. Gordon Hance was a Western interviewee who had a mother determinedly involved in the "new spirituality." He related how she had pinned her hopes on Gordon's flourishing career as psychic and "New Age" musician. His mother was devastated when Gordon got involved a charismatic Christian church. He remembered: "My mother thought I had been in a religious cult, she tried to de-program me.... It was very offensive to her. She lost the son...she was really pouring her heart into." Rebellion and personal choice can obviously work in favor, as well as against, organized religion.

Jennifer Babcock, whose widowed mother leaned toward an angry atheism, is quite representative of the new less-religious America. Jenny says she was a lonely and unhappy child to whom no one reached out. Her only connection with the sacred, she says, came when she was alone in the ravines behind her house. There she felt "just a sense of peace and order and...feeling like I belonged somewhere....There was...[a] fulfilling and rejuvenating kind of silence. I spent a lot of time down there." When in her teens she started having more clear-cut spiritual questions and longings, Jenny's mother simply told her: "Do whatever feels right to you. I don't know what to tell you." But in the midst of her personal anguish, Jenny also developed an addiction problem and eventually checked herself into a treatment center. There, for the first time, she was introduced to prayer and meditation. This started Jenny on a spiritual pilgrimage outside organized religion. Jenny was one of many of my interviewees who were first introduced to spirituality through Alcoholics Anonymous and related twelve-step programs. Once launched, she worked hard at it. She went through a period where she read books on Eastern spirituality, tried many alternative spiritual practices like reiki and yoga, and explored widely. Yet by the time I met her, Jenny had finished with all this. Now, with a supportive boyfriend and a good job, she told me she was less in need of any of them.

Millennials (born after 1981)

I had fewer volunteers from the Millennial Generation than any of the others. They constituted about half as many interviewees as from the Silent Generation. Although I worked hard to get them, I did not find the same level of enthusiasm for this project as in other cohorts. This could, of course, simply be due to the transitional nature of life at this age. People in their twenties are demographically less involved in religion. Sometimes they are still students, not yet settled down, and often unmarried without children. Religious congregations often see this as a predictable but temporary hiatus from involvement. But I did not get the sense these Millennials would eventually "return" to the religion of their youth, at least in part because many of them never had one. Indeed, the young people with whom I spoke illustrated well the widespread declining involvement in and authority of organized religion in the United States.

A greater percentage of the Millennials—more than even the Gen X interviewees—had divorced parents. In fact, true to statistics, more than half of them grew up this way. Many Millennials with single parents or living in shared parenting arrangements were never taken to any religious services. Even the two-thirds of them with some contact with religion had a much more minimalist exposure than earlier generations. For many it had been, at most, "holiday" attendance. Unlike Silent Generation or Baby Boomer interviewees—and even more so than Gen Xers—hardly any of these people sought out conventional religion on their own after that. Yet neither did many of these seek out spiritual alternatives either. This, too, was quite different from earlier generations.

For this generation, they took for granted that they could affiliate or not, believe or practice whatever they wanted, or nothing at all, with little or no repercussions. Even more than Gen Xers, most Millennial interviewees had parents who themselves self-consciously chose when and if to follow religious strictures. Thus, they served as roles models for their children. I met Rebecca Henderson out West. She had grown up with a Catholic mother and anti-Catholic nominally Protestant father. Her mother wanted a Catholic wedding ceremony and so, as required, promised the priest to raise the children Catholic. When it was time to baptize this girl, however, the mother took matters into her own hands. "My mother baptized us herself because in the church that requires classes which would involve my Dad. He is only religious when you ask him about Catholicism and then he is very anti-papist. My mom didn't want to deal with it. She was struggling with the church and the rules." After this, they continued going to church for a few more years, without going up for communion—a crucial aspect of Catholicism—and then dropped out.

Even the rare interviewee with religious parents was encouraged in the same ethos. Ian Hanby's story was memorable. He reported that his Dad liked to attend church, having been raised a "missionary brat." However, Ian's parents moved frequently and had no particular denominational loyalty. "The brand mostly fluctuated between Methodists and Presbyterians depending on who had the most liberal and passionate preacher.... I got to experience a lot of different preaching and church styles.... From...rural New York to the Bible belt of South Carolina."

Ian's father granted little authority to these pastors and taught his son to do the same. "My dad and I used [to]...pick apart the sermons on little scrap paper while they were being given and afterwards, too. Saying what we agreed with, what we didn't." Then "when I started asking questions and not being satisfied, they encouraged me....As long as I was asking questions, they didn't care what I was believing....They encouraged me in my own meaning-making and not to follow theirs." Ian's parents also blended alternative spiritualities along with more conventional religion. His mother "was very into New Age kind of stuff and very open with sharing that...with me." She practiced Reiki, did her "energy work" with him, taught him how to meditate, and traveled around doing exorcisms with "a Scottish witch who was married to some sort of minister." When I met

Ian he was studying at a Buddhist school to be an interfaith chaplain. This openness to alternative spirituality, blending it with more traditional religion, was something I heard frequently from the younger interviewees.

Alexandra Heim was a Millennial interviewee whose father had been raised Christian Scientist. She said he was "very, very dedicated to giving me a very diverse platter of choices, which I appreciate a lot." When Alexandra was little, her father would take her to the library and read her stories from various religions. "My father had a very strong belief in mythologies created by different cultures and the similarities between them." He told her: "It's not about what you believe. It's about what energizes you, which story inspires you." After a brief foray attending Christian Science church, the family stopped attending. After that, her mother would watch "positive thinker's Christianity" on television every Sunday "instead of going somewhere" and her father would download Christian Science sermons over the Internet. This young woman became interested in paganism as a teen. But, similar to her parents, she minimized group involvement. Alexandra gave many reasons for non-participation. "I wish I could celebrate them [pagan rites], but I don't have a group here and they're in Denver and I don't make time for it anyway." In general, then, when Millennial interviewees took the label "spiritual but not religious," neither religion nor alternative spiritualities made a compelling claim on them.

Yet sometimes these younger interviewees raised nascent theological issues when contemplating existential questions about meaning, life, and death, the questions that religions regularly tackle head on. Unlike earlier generations, however, many younger interviewees did not have the theological or spiritual resources to draw upon or guide them in the search. It often seemed difficult for them to move forward. Brendan Potter's divorced parents gave him some scanty exposure to religion. But those times when he attended Sunday School, he said, "I never really felt like I learned a lot...[they] just taught me how to color and do the pamphlet that the lady told me to do." He decided that you have to "teach yourself to be spiritual and to understand that there is something bigger than yourself." This basic approach failed him, however, when three very close friends in high school died in car accidents, a child he was tutoring drowned, and especially when his grandmother lingered for seven years with a terminal illness.

He wondered, "If there is a God and he is good, why would he do that to a human being?" That was a "milestone" for him, he says. "I questioned my faith and questioned other people that had faith in that God and it led me into a lot of trouble really." He misbehaved, got into drugs and alcohol, and did "anything that would keep my mind off of the world around me." Like many others, this man was implicitly struggling with core theological issues like God's will, providence, sovereignty, and the reality of suffering, in other words, the "theodicy" problem. In this "valley...rock bottom" place, he says, "[I] not only questioned my faith, but...was disgusted with whoever was up there and pulling the strings." In the absence of help and answers, he left religion behind. "That is...why I am spiritual and not religious. I haven't had that epiphany moment when I'm, like, 'I get it now.'"

Kimberly Takahashi is a good example of a Millennial with a religious heritage but little religious exposure. From a Western state, Kim has a Buddhist legacy through her Japanese American parents and grandparents. Her grandparents had been placed in a US internment camp during the Second World War and this impacted their religious and social views. Kim explained her grandmother had "a very positive outlook" on the experience. "It kind of got her...out of the house, and maybe gave her a different opportunity than had she just stayed at home....She got involved in...the work that they gave her there." Perhaps this loosening of her grandparents' inherited tradition, as a result of war and social change, also affected how the children were raised, for Kim explained that her parents neither practiced nor discussed their inherited religion. Although she observed some aspects of it in her grandmother's and aunt's homes, her only real exposure was when she visited "a Buddhist temple...for...a memorial where you...celebrate the life of someone who's dead." The bulk of what she knows about Buddhism is what she has learned in school.

Growing up, however, Kim got some opportunity to learn more about other religions. She had some Christian friends who invited her to church. She knew they were "trying to be really friendly," she says, but it bothered her. In addition, a young Christian neighbor "would ask me all these questions, like, why haven't you accepted Jesus Christ as your savior, and don't you believe in this, or that....I felt so pressured, like if I didn't believe this, then something was wrong." All of this gave her a "weird sort of fear of going to churches." Thus, her experience of religion has been limited to weddings, musical events, and a friend's Bar Mitzvah. These, she says, "are the only functions I have ever gone [to in]...places of worship."

Having little religious formation, Kim was left on her own. "I'm kind of unsure of where a lot of my beliefs came from....Probably I was more influenced...by my peers....I [didn't] start developing my own spirituality until at least...middle school." A major turning point for her spirituality came in a high school biology class when she refused to dissect animals because she believed they had been raised cruelly. This prompted her to become a vegetarian for ethical reasons. In college Kim found reasons to stay away from religion. "Understanding my own sexual identity...shaped a lot of my spirituality....A lot of traditional religion has so much of a focus on sex and gender." Thus, she said, studying "oppression and misogyny...definitely has changed my outlook." Trying to stay spiritually open, she also took some college classes in Buddhism, as well as in alternatives such as witchcraft, magic, voodoo, yoga, and meditation.

Now a young adult, most of Kim's friends are non-religious. But even with the few who identify as "Catholic, Jewish, or Christian...it doesn't really seem to affect our friendship." A commercial graphic design and media arts major, she has "mixed feelings" about her career path. She feels torn between a fear of being "materialistic" yet she has a strong attraction to the lucrative multi-media world. She says: "I'd like to work with some sort of non-profit that works towards social change...whether it's environmentalism, animal rights, [or] civil liberties....But on the other side I have a passion for art and maybe working in the entertainment industry." Facing the future, Kim is left with her own tentative value system and the influence of friends as she makes major life decisions.

Types

Although these interviewees showed generational differences, they also clustered into a number of distinctive "types" that cut across all the generations. Often, there was an almost formulaic pattern to many of the stories. In this, they are similar to the "testimonies of faith" one can hear in religious settings, or the "drunkalogs" one can hear in Alcoholics Anonymous. This should not be surprising. People often form their stories in the presence of receptive others, in a particular spiritual milieu, or influenced by others' journeys they have heard and read.[3] Therefore, although each of my conversation partners is unique, their stories reveal certain common experiences, choices, and reactions that cluster into categories, no matter what their age.

Given the importance of religion in North America, scholars—noting the decline in membership in recent decades—have sometimes tried to categorize people regarding their religious affiliation. For example, in 1993, Brinkerhoff and Mackie looked at a sample of both Americans and Canadians. They divided up the sample into "Stalwarts" (those who stay in their childhood faith or lack of it), "Switchers" (those who shift religious affiliations), "Converts" (those who move from no religion to religious), and "Apostates" (those who leave their religion and do not affiliate anywhere else).[4] In 2001, Robert C. Fuller, in his *Spiritual but not Religious: Understanding Unchurched America,* noted three types: (1) the totally indifferent; (2) those with an ambiguous relationship with organized religion; and (3) the "spiritual but not religious."[5] Another researcher, George Barna, divided up the American religious world this way: (a) Unattached (no personal involvement in religious community, 23%); (b) Intermittents (the "under-churched," 15%); (c) Homebodies (house-church attenders, 3%); (d) Blenders (attending both conventional and house churches, 3%); and (e) Conventionals (attending a congregational-style local church, 56%). He predicts "fastest growth in Homebody and Blender niches, moderate growth in the Intermittent and Unattached segments; and rather significant decline in numbers for the Conventional category."[6]

The unaffiliated are still an under-studied group, however, and only a few have worked to arrange them into types. One of the first is the work of J. Russell Hale who in the 1970s interviewed many. In his *The Unchurched: Who They Are and Why They Stay Away* he identified ten types: (1) The Anti-institutionalists; (2) The Boxed In; (3) The Burned Out; (4) The Floaters; (5) The Hedonists; (6) The Locked Out; (7) The Nomads; (8) The Pilgrims; (9) The Publicans; and (10) The True Unbelievers.[7] Nancy Ammerman, however, takes a different approach. Arguing that we should, in fact, go "beyond binary choices," which separate those actively involved in religion and those outside of it, she instead finds different spirituality "packages." The "theistic package" includes those who say spirituality is about God and practices meant to develop one's relationship with God. More of these adherents would be found in organized religion. The second is the "extra-theistic package," where spirituality is located in the core of the self, in community, in transcendence beyond self. This "immanent" transcendence does not really focus on a personal God but instead on finding one's own "spark of the divine." Finally, adherents in both "packages" often find a common denominator in the "ethical spirituality" package since most seem to agree that "real spirituality is about living a virtuous life."[8] From my own research, I have discovered that people in all three "packages" can be found both within and outside religion.

In my study, I have grouped interviewees into five types depending on their reasons, formative experiences, and goals. Since many within organized religion are concerned with reaching out to SBNRs, it is helpful to see the possible avenues these people travel and rationales they hold for their SBNR status. I have categorized them into (a) Dissenters, (b) Casuals, (c) Explorers, (d) Seekers, and (e) Immigrants. Recognizing there are different types of SBNRs is critical because it helps us avoid homogenizing them and/or characterizing them in ways that do not do them justice. For instance, assuming all have been "hurt by religion" or that all are "seekers" are just two of the misconceptions that we often have. By seeing how my conversation partners cluster into quite different types, readers will better understand SBNRs and recognize some common patterns in themselves or others. While no one fits exhaustively into or stays forever in one type, these patterns nevertheless lend more texture to the SBNR stories.

Among all categories, however, some things were common. First, it is often a life crisis that gets the person's attention, making them attentive to their own spiritual core, sometimes for the first time. Second, often there is much experimentation. My conversation partners frequently talk about looking for a practice or group that "feels right," a teacher who captivates them, or a fellow seeker who seems to possess what they lack and pulls them along. Third, this group or practice often does not last. Many find the satisfaction ephemeral and move on, while others ultimately find the whole search frustrating and quit it. Fourth, it was often beliefs that played a part in their leaving and moving on. While I heard criticisms of the theology and the communities of organized religion, just as often I heard parallel criticisms of spiritual alternatives. It happened repeatedly that my conversation partners would find a tenet with which they disagreed, or they became disappointed with the all-too-human qualities of the average congregation, spiritual group, leader, or participant. Either they found the beliefs ultimately unbelievable, or felt that members were not living up to them. This would cause them to step back and reconsider. Fifth, rather than feeling hesitant to move on, instead, my conversation partners seemed to feel they were "honor-bound" to leave their current affiliation in order to maintain their integrity or remain authentic. Thus, the people I met wanted to be free to believe what they chose, and free to change their minds, but they also wanted a group that generally had the same beliefs they did. The most poignant stories came from the SBNRs who kept moving on because they never quite "got it"—that is, could not affirm the requisite beliefs, or conform to the "ideal" practitioner, and/or experience what others seem to come by naturally—even though they would have liked to do so. From these stories and categories, we can see that belief does matter to a large percentage of SBNRs.

Dissenters

"Dissenters" are the people I met who largely stay away from institutional religion. Some are *"protesting dissenters"* who have gotten hurt, offended, or become angry about some experience or aspect of organized religion. Theology is often in play here. More Silent Generation and Baby Boomer interviewees were in this type than other generations, people who were raised with religion but now have specific issues with it. Many people are convinced this is the most common type of SBNR but, in my sample, it was only a small percentage. Others I found were *"drifted dissenters,"* those who simply drift out of organized religion and never go back. They do not seem to have any particular axe to grind with religion, but simply got out of the habit or could see no reason to attend anymore. They sometimes justified this through theological positions they are rejecting.

A few dissenters were more like *"conscientious objector dissenters."* Although the ones I met were usually not atheist—since few committed atheists volunteered for my study—they insisted they have always had some suspicion toward religious institutions. Some grant that religion may be useful for the weak, but ultimately believe it is not necessary for one's spiritual life. Against popular expectation, I found that most of the dissenters, but especially the protesting ones, listed theological concerns among their reasons for leaving. Against the popular stereotype of Baby Boomers as perpetual questioners of authority, only one interviewee maintained a "dissenter" stance rather than moving on to new spiritual territory. However, there were far more "dissenters" among the Silent Generation than in any other. Clearly, they took religion seriously, whether to protest an old "home" or to seek a new one. More of them than those in any other age group spoke of specific theological positions in religion with which they disagreed.

William Willard, the Silent Generation man we met earlier, is a good example of a "drifted dissenter." He never had a problem with religion when he was growing up, except for the term itself. His family and church considered "religion" to be a dirty word, a dry-bones scrupulosity without fervency, the kind you would find in churches they dismissed as "liberal" or denominational. And yet, as we saw, he himself drifted from conservative to liberal, by stages, until he no longer found religion or church compelling.

A much younger dissenter is Justin Cooper, a Millennial who is more a "protesting" than simply "drifting" or "conscientious objector" dissenter. Justin's background is different from many of the other Millennials I met. He comes from a large two-parent family, with whom he still lives, and was raised Methodist in the Midwest. Unlike many of the Gen X and Millennial interviewees, Justin's parents are not divorced nor have they moved more than a few miles from where he grew up. Also somewhat exceptional, his parents were careful to give their four children a consistent religious upbringing, and one with a more mainline than conservative orientation. "My parents wanted all of us to have...a knowledge of God and Jesus and everything....They just took us to the church, got us baptized and everything." Justin claimed he had no bad experiences with religion and still gets along well with his family. One might expect Jason to have little reason to protest, dissent, or explore. One might expect him to have a conventional spiritual outlook or even take for granted his religious upbringing.

Yet Justin is a different sort of Millennial in two ways, first, his consistent religious exposure and second, his status as a "dissenter." I did not find many dissenters among younger interviewees. Unlike older interviewees, few of them had much theological or spiritual formation in traditional religions. Few understood the theological positions that the SBNR ethos implicitly rejects. They have encountered less repressive religious structures and have grown up with the results of the cultural revolution already in place. In this way, Jason is more like his generation. For, different from the kind of rebellion I found among Silent Generation or Baby Boomers, Justin does not protest specific ethics or ecclesial structures as earlier dissenting interviewees did. Instead, he takes his dissent right to the source, God.

What made him pay attention to his own spirituality was a life crisis, the death of several close relatives and friends. Justin's inherited theology caused him lay the blame directly on God. "God took away some of my friends....He cut their lives too short." Justin did not stop believing in God, but decided that God was both "distant" and "a bully." As a result, Justin dissented from God. He said, "I just felt like he [God] needed to kinda leave me alone because he was hurting me." Rather than turning to alternative spiritual practices or philosophies, Justin came up with his own personal theology, shorn of the aspects he rejects from organized religion. Unlike William, he did not turn agnostic, or atheist. Instead, he says: "I honestly do believe in a god. Like...I don't believe in The God, how society makes it like you have to follow God and Jesus Christ and everything." Instead, Justin speaks of the Green Man. It is unclear where Justin got this idea, but he did not invent it. The vine-covered image has existed in folklore, other cultures, and even iconography in churches. But Justin does not identify with any particular alternative tradition like paganism, Wicca, or others which focus on nature. Although the Green Man is often identified with nature, for Jason the Green Man seems like the benevolent side of the bully God which Justin pushed away. When he is out in nature, he says, "I honestly feel like there is something watching over me—something or someone."

Justin has also created his own eschatology, thus rejecting the Christian idea of judgment day and an apocalyptic end to world history that he was taught. "I believe that the world is not going to end...[But]...the only things that are going to roam this world are animals and trees....The Green Man is going to place each person [in]to a certain animal." In this fully natural world, where humans no longer exist, there will be no worries. Although Justin finds peace in nature and his personal theology, he is not completely satisfied. He says, "I want to at least find a religion where people don't look at me like I'm crazy."

Unlike my older interviewees, Justin's dissent does not spring so much from rebellion as from existential questions for which he's received inadequate answers. In the end, he still respects his family's religion and practices. At mealtimes when they pray, he says, "I sit there and...kind of hold my hands...to try to make them feel good, you know." And he still goes to church with them on holidays because: "My mom wants us all to be there as a family." Even so, it seems unlikely that Justin will return to the religion of his youth.

Casuals

I termed a number of interviewees "casuals," because, for them, religious or spiritual practices are primarily functional. Of course, spiritual practices perform important functions for many interviewees. But "casuals" were different in that spirituality is something that neither captures their full attention nor serves as an organizing principle for their lives. They may read books on spirituality, seek out a teacher, or attend services and rituals occasionally, but only on an "as needed" basis. They drop these things when no longer applicable. The main thing is whether a given practice, teaching, or guide helps them feel better. Many whose primary brush with spirituality comes from complementary and alternative health practices fit into this category. For "casuals," spiritual practices are used primarily as a way toward better health, stress relief, or emotional support. This is, thus, a "therapeutic" spirituality focused on personal well-being.[9] Among the younger two cohorts, I found many SBNRs who fit into this type. Among the older two cohorts, there were comparatively fewer. Less than a quarter of the Baby Boomer interviewees were "casuals," perhaps reflecting the importance of spirituality when they were maturing during the "Long Sixties." And among the Silent Generation interviewees, there were even less.

Today it is very common to create "generic" spiritual disciplines (like yoga, reiki, tai chi, mindfulness meditation, etc.) by minimizing, denying, or trying to scrub away the traditions and dogmas of their religious roots. It was relatively easy to find SBNRs in such classes at fitness facilities, community centers, cancer treatment centers, churches, in for-profit businesses, and nonprofit organizations. Theological concerns were not prominent for this group and many did not recognize, ignored, or were not concerned by conflicting beliefs. In this, they were unlike many of the other types of interviewees. For the "casual" SBNRs did not find that particular beliefs or theology created either problems or opportunities. The pragmatic "casuals" do not seem troubled by theological dilemmas or inconsistencies in the many alternatives with which they experiment. Their SBNR status is mostly a loose, open kind of thing, used for psychological health and happiness, serving its purpose and then receding into the background.

Nearly half of the Millennials I met were "casual" about both religion and spirituality. I found a couple of "immigrants" and a couple of "dissenters," but no one I could categorize as a "seeker" or even an "explorer." It was striking to me how much less interest I found among this age group in both religion and spiritual alternatives. This does not imply that Millennials lacked ethical values, dreams for their futures, or a positive outlook on life. But with this cohort, I did not hear their mix involving as many specifically religious aspects—whether negatively reactive or positively formative—as in my earlier cohorts.

Two interviewees we met earlier, Gen Xer Jennifer Babcock and Millennial Kimberly Takahashi, are good examples of "casuals." As we saw, Jenny had no religious background at all, but was introduced to spiritual alternatives through the twelve steps for addiction recovery. With a group of women friends from her Alcoholics Anonymous group, she started delving into many healing modalities, books, and spiritual alternatives. She, like most of the other women, also was having ongoing psychotherapy. Out of need and a push from a non-religious spiritual program, Jenny and her friends went from being troubled persons to being spiritual "casuals." As many SBNRs do, they focused largely on self-help and psychological healing. "Our lives were almost always about what was wrong with us, and how we were going to make it better, so a lot of our spirituality was around figuring [that] out."

Jenny tried many things, practicing "all kinds of reiki, polarity, cranial sacral, different kinds of therapy." But rather than joining any particular group or following a specific teaching, she decided to keep her options open and use or drop spiritual practices and ideas as needed. In fact, when I met Jenny she was not doing any of the spiritual practices she had previously benefited from. She proudly proclaimed: "I don't do any of that anymore. I feel like what's happened in the last five years is that all those little things I've tried along the road...worked or didn't. And those that worked are kind of integrated into my life. I don't have to...go chasing things anymore. I feel like now I know that all the resources I need are, were, already all there." I met Jenny at a remarkably stable time in her life. One can imagine that if and when new crises emerge, she may again reach out to the many self-helpful spiritual trends widely available in our culture.

As we saw earlier, Kimberly Takahashi had very little exposure to organized religion, although she briefly experimented with it, and what she learned in college confirmed that she wanted to abstain. Now occasionally, friends lend her books and videos on spirituality, positive thinking, and other such things, but Kim feels no compulsion. Although they may discuss them, Kim says: "I guess I'm more interested in studying it than actually trying it." Still, she has experimented with alternative spiritualities. The courses in yoga and meditation that she took for their "health benefits," she says, have helped her deal with stress. They have also, she says, "had some sort of influence on me....The yoga class...showed [how] negative thoughts...affected the speaker as well as the people it was directed to." One of the books she has read on spirituality also impressed her, confirming that she has to decide things for herself. She explained: "The author says 'I am not your teacher. Do not follow.'...It's a little confusing because it asks you these questions and...doesn't quite answer....You're supposed to kind of discover it on your own." In going forward, Kim says: "I think it's useful to look at other religions and figure out what works for you."

Explorers

Those interviewees I call "explorers" seem to have a spiritual "wander-lust." They described trying one thing and then another, moving on as much from unsatisfied curiosity and the desire for novelty, as from disappointment. They found this destination-less, almost touristic, journey fun, stimulating, exciting, and/or a welcome antidote to a crass secular world. Many presented their stance as open-minded, progressive, cosmopolitan, and/or non-prejudicial, similar to "casuals," but they were more intentional about their explorations. "Explorers" are often confused with "seekers," but I found them to be two distinct types. Although both seem to be in search of "liminal" experience, explorers are like spiritual tourists who enjoy the journey but do not plan to settle anywhere. Some explorers occasionally attend traditional or alternative services, but do not make an ultimate commitment. A large number of Baby Boomer interviewees were "explorers." In fact, this cohort had a higher percentage of "explorers" than any other.

Theologically, some may call explorers "syncretists," since they are willing to mix and match seemingly disparate beliefs, techniques, and spiritual practices. They might also be called "hybrid" as they try to have a foot in two or more spiritual traditions. Although these titles might seem demeaning (implying doctrinal "impurity" or confusion), I found many SBNRs types who were happy to embrace them, especially the "explorers." Unlike the "casuals," oftentimes the explorers were aware of the theological differences between the various spiritual options they tried. Rather than finding this unsettling or difficult, however, they often felt exhilarated by the challenge. I found many "explorers" in the Baby Boomer and Gen X cohorts, but relatively fewer among the Millennials I met. While I noticed that Baby Boomer interviewees sometimes found it liberating to become explorers, they tended to stay longer in alternative groups than younger interviewees, especially when they found something that spoke to them. Still, eventually "explorers" move on or add on. Unlike "seekers," a type we will shortly discuss, "explorers" are not really looking for a spiritual home.

David Kaplan is a Baby Boomer and an avid spiritual "explorer" who shows all the marks of having lived through the spiritual and cultural revolution of the 1970s. He started out as an atheistic Jew. "I thought all

Jews were atheists. I certainly didn't believe in God and I didn't know anyone that did except for a couple of people." Even so, as with many barely religious cultural Jews, his parents decided to have David make his Bar Mitzvah. Even when he studied Hebrew and attended the required services, however, he "thought it was just a social club." Instead, David found ultimate meaning in his award-winning math abilities. In fact, in his Bar Mitzvah speech: "The only thing I had to say was about how to teach math better. . . . I delighted in supposed mathematical proofs that God didn't exist. I delighted in that because anyone who believed in God was crazy. That was basically my attitude." When in 1966 the cover of *Time* magazine heralded "God Is Dead," David felt very current and in step with the times.

Even so, in high school, David took a leadership role in the Jewish student organization. He valued his Jewish heritage, he said, because rather than allowing people to "sleepwalk through life," it promoted "creativity from within." But it was a very this-worldly creativity. "The sacred was me doing a mathematics problem. . . . That was how I expressed my creativity because I didn't know what spirituality meant back then." Everything changed when David started college just as the late 1960s cultural revolution was roaring to life. Depressed over a break-up with a girlfriend, David tried to pull himself out of despair by focusing on the arts. Through this he began having "hundreds of dozens of out of body experiences."

Once he was in graduate school in mathematics, he explored more widely, taking classes in the arts, yoga, and meditation at a "free university," all focused on "getting in touch with your creative potential." Soon, even though he had very little training, he began teaching these classes himself. Ultimately David gave up his math fellowship to focus entirely on spiritual exploration. In talking about his influences, David mentions the well-known cast of characters and themes from the 1960s and 1970s: Timothy Leary, Ram Das, Herman Hesse, Allen Watts, theosophical writings, and self-realization fellowship. "I bought a bunch of those books and those were my teachers and I shared with people out of those books." David, thus, was not only an explorer, but a leader, as were many during this period—people who became exhilarated by new ideas, practices, and philosophies and began disseminating them to others.

Finally, the coin dropped, and David became aware that what he was doing was about God. "I was reading a book by Allen Watts . . . *The Taboo Against Knowing Who You Are*. He said this thing that you are touching and experiencing is what they call spirit and God. . . . I had found the secret of life but I had never associated it with God." Now he did, and his spiritual explorations continued more earnestly. But anything even remotely related to organized religion he "avoided like the plague.... I came into this world anti-religion and mainly anti-Christianity" and he planned to stay that way.

But soon his attitude changed. Several of his teachers and readings took an eclectic approach. One told him "that the Eastern teachings had their limitations. Before... I was pro-East, anti-West. He was the one that softened that. He would quote thousands of books and Christian saints. When I was seeking, I didn't want to read anyone unless... they had touched that core of universal truth within them, and were beyond belief systems. He helped dissolve some of that." But David largely goes his own way now. He owns a store specializing in books and products for the alternative spiritual and health communities. His "explorer" orientation has suited him very well for this.

Seekers

These interviewees are actually looking for a spiritual home. That cannot be said for all SBNRs. Some "seekers" contemplate reclaiming earlier religious identities, moving on to something slightly different, or joining a completely new religion or alternative spiritual group. Some may attend traditional religious services, but also continue to "shop."[10] At the point I met these seekers, they were still in process. Their restlessness is shown by their eagerness to claim the "spiritual but not religious" label. Among some of my younger interviewees with no religious home to react against, I heard a spiritual longing they could just barely define or articulate.

Some research insists that there are, in fact, very few "nones" who qualify as "seekers"[11] while others make a distinction between "seeking" and "dwelling" spirituality, finding a recent increase in the former.[12] Religious leaders often assume that everyone experimenting with spiritual practices is a "seeker." In my work, I found fewer "seekers" than religious leaders hope for but more than some research might predict. Seekers were more common among the interviewees with a positive past religious experience, or for those longing to finally belong. There was also a higher percentage of seekers in the Baby Boomer (one in four) and Gen X (one in five) cohorts. In their search, they often looked for "believable" beliefs, rituals that consistently provide "liminality," a trustworthy group, and good personal "fit." With such high standards, few I met had permanently settled anywhere; that is, few became either a "returnee" to their native tradition or what I call an "immigrant." Unlike "explorers," however, many of the "seekers" seemed troubled by this inability to land somewhere.

When Gen Xer Jason Van Buren was growing up in the Midwest, there was not much religion in his home. His only exposure was when his mother took him occasionally to the local Methodist church, while his father stayed home. When he was a young teen, his parents divorced and this began Jason's searching. Since his father's new home was surrounded by churches, he decided to visit them. He finally settled on the Church of God, saying, "It was a spiritual turning point in many ways." He started attending church four times a week, plus "lots of camps." He says he "accepted Jesus Christ as my personal Lord and Savior."

But "it all came kind of crashing one day" when he went to a youth revival. He related: "Someone was doing the Holy Spirit thing where everyone runs up....I ran up...so excited to feel that emotion of God in me....I wanted to feel what it was like to be overwhelmed with the Spirit like everyone else....When he got to me, he hit me on the forehead and there was nothing. He went on to the next guy and I laid down, not to fake it but not to look like I had failed."

This experience threw Jason into a time of intense doubt about motivation, meaning, perception, and even reality. He asked himself: "Why would I fake it? How many people were faking it? What was the point of it? Why was my salvation my only concern?" Jason decided that "there had to be something more than the emotional aspect." So, "little by little" he stopped going to church. He started studying the Bible, history, and politics, and began "wondering why there were some inconsistencies." Another existential crisis was the death of his young uncle who was also his best friend. "I remembered being so shocked and closing my math book. Why would I be doing my homework when Uncle Mike just died?....That was a pitiful time because it started this chain reaction...I couldn't figure out why things were important."

He is a seeker, however, because in spite of all this, he keeps on with the search. He wistfully remembers feeling a holy presence in the Methodist church. He is interested in theater as a form of spiritual expression. He pays attention to "auspicious" events in his life. And, for a time, he thought he could find his identity in "non-spiritual identification." Now he is taking a degree in religious studies at a school with a Buddhist orientation and trying the recommended spiritual practices. But even though he is among religious people, Jason does not believe it is possible for him to land anywhere. He says he has "bouts of envy, jealousy and sympathy" when he sees religious people. He says, "I now respect people for being in a tradition.... I can see the depths of it, but I... I can't do it. I can't. I've tried." Instead, he says, "There is something in me that cannot choose a path because I'm still searching."

Above all, he doubts his own ability to choose or settle down. He says: "I want to make sure that it's not a consumerist point of view.... I have to make sure.... I'm not just going around and filling my own boat up with my own wants and needs. I have to make sure it's a legitimate search." Like many seekers, Jason wants to pick and choose at will. He says honestly: "My religious identification right now would be that of religious syncretist. I'm taking bits and pieces of my own path, my own world and experience.... Very salad bar, very a la carte." It is unclear whether Jason will ever move on to becoming an "immigrant" in any particular tradition. His deep concern to maintain his integrity and be clear about his motives is mixed with doubts about meaning and perception. With little societal pressure to join anything, Jason could stay a perpetual seeker.

Not every seeker keeps on the search, however. A good example is Carole Bradford. This Silent Generation interviewee tried hard for most of her life to find a spiritual home. Her parents had both been raised in "hellfire and damnation southern churches," but rebelled and gave their daughter very little religious exposure. About all she got was her mother reading the Christmas story and an occasional prayer said at dinner, when there was company. Still, from that little bit, she said, "Somehow I came to feel this presence."

Carole was also occasionally taken to church by relatives when she visited them in the South. Her impressions were so positive that when, at about age 8, she noticed a Gospel Tabernacle on her way to elementary school, she asked her parents if she could attend. "My parents, being good liberals, let me go." Carole became very involved there. Her father was favorable toward this, but her mother was not so happy. She became "terrified that I would become a fundamentalist." So her mother "went out and found a nice liberal Protestant church for the whole family to go to." Carole loved it there and was especially gratified at the "tremendous influence" it had on her parents' lives. During their frequent moves, she attended a variety of mainline churches and took an interest in theology.

All of this helped Carole come to terms with her father's alcoholism. One night Carole prayed that if "God would make my father stop drinking, I would give my life to God. That really stayed with me." When her father did, in fact, quit drinking, she said: "I felt I had this obligation." She decided she was called to become a minister. Being a young woman in the 1950s, this was not so simple. "In the churches I saw...all a woman could be was a director of religious education [but] I wasn't going to play second fiddle." In addition, Carole also came out as a lesbian during this process. "It turned my world upside down.... Honor, truth, justice, I learned from the Bible.... None of this made a difference.... If I was gay, I was condemned." As a result, "all that I had, my whole world system, was destroyed."

But Carole did not give up her search. Instead, she was drawn to Roman Catholicism. "Suddenly I felt I had been liberated from the bread and water of Protestantism to the great riches of Catholic theology and ritual." She felt fed by much of their theology but could not accept all of it. Carole's sexual orientation also kept her from joining. "I never participated. I never took communion. I sat in the church and enjoyed it and took in the spirituality knowing that they would condemn me if they knew who I really was."

Still searching, Carole became interested in Eastern religions. She even moved to a progressive Western city so she could become part of a Buddhist community. Although satisfied for a time, eventually she had a profound disillusionment there, too. For, one time, a revered lama visited the community. "The shrine room was just filled with people. It was a very big event...[the lama was] seated on his throne...[but] when they were going to leave and everybody started kissing his ring, I thought: 'This is it, I've done this before.'" She was not ready to accept "the Roman Catholic church of Buddhism." Now, after a lifetime of searching, Carole has largely given up seeking a spiritual home. She occasionally practices solo meditation and speaks with Buddhists she respects. But she does not participate in religious communities any more. The lack of theological answers and vocational opportunities has combined with disappointment and prejudice against women and gays to end her seeking.

Immigrants

I call "immigrants" those interviewees who had moved to a new spiritual "land" and were trying to adjust to this new identity and community. They may have started out as "casuals," "explorers," or "seekers," but when I met them, they were trying to live in a new spiritual home. Often it is one very different from their "native" affiliation, if they had one. These interviewees were usually newcomers "trying on" the new environment, but were not completely at home there. They have not fully "immigrated" but are hoping to become permanent residents. Just like immigrants to a new culture, these interviewees often find it difficult or disconcerting to adjust to the new community. If they had become fully integrated, chances are they would not have responded to a call for "spiritual but not religious" interviewees but would now instead be defining themselves by their new religious identity.

I found very few "immigrants" among any of the generations. One might expect Silent Generation or Baby Boomers—especially those raised within organized religion—to be looking for a new religious home in which to settle. Many from these two cohorts had left organized religion for various reasons, often theological, but were nevertheless enthusiastic about trying alternative spiritual practices. Yet although many became "explorers" or "seekers," only a few actually became "immigrants" to a new spiritual or religious group. As for younger generations, there were even fewer "immigrants." I came across more "casuals" and "explorers" in the Gen X cohort and many less "seekers" looking for a permanent spiritual home. And even when I heard a desire among younger people to become "immigrants," they realized it would be very difficult to accomplish and even questioned if it would be worth the effort.

There may be something inherent in the SBNR designation that makes spiritual "immigration" particularly difficult. Adopting a new religion requires commitment, constancy, and group loyalty, characteristics that vie with those highlighted in the SBNR ethos (i.e., independence, freedom, non-dogmatism, and an open and questing attitude). Often, those I termed "immigrants," still saw themselves primarily as SBNR, even though their new religious compatriots might have thought of them as full members. But these SBNRs' long-standing tendency of non-affiliation seemed to make them very hesitant to fully commit.

I heard many stories of people who could not take the strong disjuncture from their native upbringing and eventually dropped out. Surprisingly often, the source of their discomfort was theological. A religious or spiritual group often makes certain belief assumptions these newcomers found difficult to fully embrace, even with much effort. Like many geographic immigrants, although they tried hard to be committed to the new home they could not block out the echoes of their past. I found only a few who took a fully "hybrid" route and stayed committed to both their "native" and their new spiritual homes. While it might be possible live "hybridly" at the level of performed ritual or spiritual practices, for those who thought deeply about their faith, theological dilemmas were almost inevitable.

Patty Hoffman is a former "seeker" who is trying to settle down in a new spiritual land. She was born in the Midwest. The only thing religious about her father were the hymns he asked his daughter to play on the piano. But her mother was very devout, making sure they attended church and Sunday school weekly. Patty was fine with this. "I liked the choir. I liked to sing. I loved my church. I had very fond memories of my childhood." Indeed, for a time, she became "very religious," even setting up an altar in the basement, with flowers, candles, and her Bible. "I would go down there and read and talk to God," she remembered. This was something I heard from many seekers (i.e., a quiet longing to commune with something Ultimate, starting in childhood and continuing into adulthood).

Even though Patty was also a normal teen, slipping out of church with the other kids and "going to the drug store to get a coke," nevertheless, her spirit was still nurtured by religion. She remembers sitting in the back of the church while her mother helped set up the altar for communion. It was very "dark, very quiet. There were only a couple of lights on... and I remember thinking a lot about God." Nevertheless, Patty began an emotional, if not physical, withdrawal from church at about age 13. Problems with exclusivism and hypocrisy especially pushed her along this path. In spite of her doubts, however, she continued to attend church, putting herself through college by playing the organ there.

During this time, however, Patty entered a "period of darkness" lasting from about age 19 until nearly 30, eventually avoiding organized religion altogether. Like many seekers, though, a "significant other" brought her back in. Her husband was a Unitarian. "The particular group we were in had no spirituality. It was a very nice group of people exploring things. That allowed me to ease back in." In the meantime, her husband's aborted effort to get a Master of Divinity degree, plus two children, took up most of her energy. She had hoped to attend seminary herself, after he was done, but her desire was put on hold.

Instead, she got involved in the quasi-sectarian self-improvement program of "est" having heard about it from another Unitarian. A typical seeker, she "dived into that just as much as I dived into anything else of religion. I did workshops and volunteered." Although this made her very happy at first, believing she had found her answer, eventually she became disillusioned. She especially had difficulty with the requirement to recruit others. "That was part of my job. I was not very good at it. You actually had to call people that you knew personally and invite them in...it was very traumatic."

Nevertheless, she kept seeking a permanent spiritual home. One year she asked her husband for a course in meditation as a birthday gift, attracted by an ad from a prominent Buddhist temple in the large East Coast city where they lived. "I was scared to death that it was going to be religious. I was afraid there were going to be monks in robes. So when he told me it was Buddhist, I was very tentative about going. But there were no monks or Buddhists with shaved heads. There was nothing weird." She "fell in love" with meditation immediately and quickly completed all the levels. Her dedication had a cost, however, for her long marriage ended in divorce. "It's one of the casualties of spiritual growth I think," Patty reflected.

When I met Patty she was living in a Western city and studying in a Buddhist school. No longer a seeker, she is settling down and finally fulfilling her dream of pursuing a divinity degree. This time she has edged closer to religion, becoming a tentative immigrant, not quite a Buddhist, no longer a Methodist. But she's not entirely happy. The biggest disappointment, she says, is the lack of community in her school as compared with her previous temple. "One of my motivating factors for coming to [school here], was ultimately I would like to work with religious communities.... [The lack of community] has been a big disappointment for me.... I really did expect that it would be there for me."

She also struggles with belief, going back and forth between what she believes is a correct Buddhist view, over against her own inclinations and experience. This was especially evident as she tried to reconcile her former belief in the personal God, to whom she used to pray, with the more impersonal divine or "emptiness" which she has imbibed here. Her degree program, she said, teaches "a lot about sacredness.... But to me I think I would say sacred is having some direct communication with something." When she meditates now, she feels the same presence as when she was in church. "Whatever that presence was, that was available sitting in that church, was exactly the same thing that came to me in meditation. That sense of sacredness.... I've reflected on that a lot." But in her new environment, she no longer feels free to call this "God." "Not anymore, because that is such a loaded word." She does not feel comfortable anywhere now, although she hopes, "Someday maybe I'll be a good Buddhist."

In spite of the differences among the interviewees, based on both age and typology, nevertheless, there were striking commonalities of belief among all of them. Certain broad impulses and themes kept recurring in their stories, no matter how diverse their backgrounds, ages, or reasons and goals for being SBNR. In the next chapter we will learn what themes they hold in common.

4

Common Themes

WHEN I BEGAN to talk with people who consider themselves "spiritual but not religious," I heard many different spiritual journeys. Some people had been highly religious as young people, while others had hardly any religious background at all. A few never felt they fit into any religious setting, while others mourned the loss of a faith community. Some debated religious beliefs and finally abandoned them, but others felt free to roam around, taking what they liked, and moving on. One thing they agreed on, however, was that everyone should and does have the freedom to decide one's own beliefs and spiritual practices. Indeed, each interviewee affirmed they felt very free to adopt, adapt, discard, and change any spiritual or religious beliefs they encountered. Among the majority, there was no felt need to adhere to any teacher's or group's set of beliefs.

Some see this as a profound spiritual sea-change. But before deciding we are on the brink of a spiritual revolution, we should consider a less dramatic possibility: Could this simply be a move toward greater individualism? Robert Bellah predicted this spiritual individualism in 1985 when he wrote *Habits of the Heart*. He called it "Sheilaism," from the comment of one young interviewee, named "Sheila," who said she simply listens to "just my own little voice."[1] It is not much of a leap to imagine that this retreat from the constraints of communal belief into private practices and personal philosophies could someday cause the United States to be home to millions of "personal religions." Could this be the likely outcome of the SBNR insistence that belief is not a crucial factor in spirituality?

We have to dig below the surface to get any answers. For the idea that belief is private, non-essential, and non-constraining is more surface claim, more rhetoric, more strategy, than deeper message. Rather than being merely individualism or eclecticism, there was an undercurrent of similar beliefs among the SBNRs I met. Certain recurrent patterns or "organizing principles" were voiced by nearly all of the interviewees. They all had certain ideas in common which prompted them to castigate, disdain, or simply ignore organized religion. In addition, they held in common certain other beliefs which helped them explain, justify, and organize their alternative spirituality and practices. This happened in spite of differences in age, different spiritual journeys, and different reasons for adopting the "spiritual but not religious" label. It did not matter where in the United States they lived, or what their educational and income levels were, or whether or not they had a religious background. I heard the same themes among all types of interviewees, no matter whether they approached spirituality on an "as-needed" casual basis or were seekers looking for a new spiritual home. These common themes suggest that the rise in "nones" is not simply greater individualism but also a kind of loosely cohesive cultural or intellectual movement. In fact, it may well be a sea-change for both religion and spiritual practices.

Added to this is that, especially for younger interviewees, less people are having much exposure to organized religion. Even for those with a religious background, a strain of anti-traditionalism often runs underneath. Along with this, we live in a world where religious difference is downplayed. And today, even among those more regularly exposed to religion, most are encouraged by their parents to think for themselves rather than buy into a collective system of doctrine and worship. But all this does not mean belief is unimportant to my conversation partners. Instead, belief often served as the motivating factor in people becoming "spiritual but not religious." Like a "back-handed compliment," some intentionally opposed what they thought religion, especially Christianity, teaches. And instead of abandoning belief, most also worked to come up with other answers. As we will see in this and following chapters, the interviewees, no matter what their age or type, hold certain beliefs and/or themes in common.

Is This "New Age"?

There was an underlying cohesion to interviewees' various views. The majority of them voiced a widespread opposition to distinctly Western religious concepts, whether or not they explicitly articulated it. Wouter J. Hanegraaff and many others group the ethos under the rubric "New

Age." Hanegraaff says, "New Age thinking is essentially a reaction to the ideas and values which are perceived as having dominated western culture during the last two thousand years." In other words, this movement is essentially a "culture criticism."[2]

New Age spirituality has long historical roots in the philosophies of such things as Swedenborgianism, Transcendentalism, Romanticism, mesmerism, occultism, spiritualism, esotericism, Theosophy, New Thought, "ancient" cosmologies, European mysticism, and aspects of Asian religions. In addition, there is a dialectic between consciousness and energy, a re-envisioning of the mind–body interaction with a focus on the mind's power, a selective synthesis of mysticism and science, psychology elevated to religious proportion, and a modernizing of magic and the paranormal.[3] One author sums up New Age as a "broad term encompassing many diverse belief systems that overlap with interests in transformative powers emanating from nature, from individual beings—humans, animals, plants, spirits—and sometimes from beyond the planet."[4]

Unlike followers in the nineteenth to mid-twentieth centuries, today the currents of thought formerly identified with the "New Age" movement are no longer restricted to elites, communes, cults, or esoteric associations. Revived and processed during the "Long Sixties," they have been shaken, stirred, and blended together with such distinctly American values as: "self-realization, freedom, transforming relationships, getting in touch with one's experience, living more fully in the moment or the world, healing, and so forth."[5] Robert C. Fuller summarizes the resulting mix as:

> A pantheistic understanding of God; continuity of the self with this ever-present divine reality; our innate susceptibility to subtle spiritual energies that reinvigorate our physical and emotional systems; experience and personal reflection as the crucial criteria for arriving at religious beliefs; and the need to develop a personal spiritual outlook that builds on, rather than repudiates, scientific understandings of our universe.[6]

This is not exactly a systematic theology, however, nor is it very specific. Instead, this loose agreement includes such abstract features as a "sacralization of the self," the idea of a "perennial wisdom" at the root of all religions and spiritualities, a syncretistic tendency, and the idea of interconnectedness or "holism." This eclectic conglomeration makes everything available as a potential site for spiritual reinterpretation. One study reviewed the literature on this consensus and claimed: "The very fact that an underlying unity can only be described on a high level of abstraction makes it easy to call many things 'spiritual' just to evoke a vague association with this meta-ideology." Obviously, it is also ripe for commercialization and marketing usage.[7] In recent years, according to Paul Heelas, the "diffusion has become considerably more pronounced."[8] In fact, "contrary to predictions that New Age would go mainstream, it's as if the mainstream is going New Age."[9]

All this adds up to a new way for people to separate from religious tradition and external authority. The focus on spiritual practice, meditation, mind/body techniques, and other experience-altering exercises is the practical arm of a general "de-traditioning." Thus, as Robert Fuller says about the trail-blazing retreat center Esalen, their widely copied efforts showed "how altered states provided the experiential template for a new, countercultural epistemology...[and] an instantaneous 'deconditioning agent.' These techniques dismantled the whole cognitive universe constructed by both the scientific and religious wings of American culture."[10]

Post-Christian Spirituality

Even though I heard many of the above themes from them, most interviewees did not want to be called "New Age." They often identified this term with older generations or with a marginalized, non-serious, or aberrant approach to spirituality. Instead, many of them felt they were in the majority, the mainstream, or on the cutting-edge of inevitable and quickly approaching change. By using the term "New Age," many felt their spiritual efforts would not be taken seriously. Nor did those interviewees practicing Wicca, Paganism, and Native American spirituality want to be considered "New Age."[11] What is common among the diversity of interviewees, however, is their nearly universal criticism of theological positions and views they identified with the Western religious heritage. Therefore, this new spirituality might be more accurately described as "post-Christian spirituality." This is a "spirituality standing on its own two feet and broken from the moorings of Christian tradition."[12]

Although, as we will shortly see, much interviewee thinking was deeply influenced by earlier "New Age" thought, and embedded in those larger themes were specific theological doctrines and concepts which they reacted against. Rather than the surface claim, then, that belief is unimportant, instead, their focus was very much on belief. This makes sense, for it is not possible to simply skip over the theological heritage of the Western world. As Mark C. Taylor says in *After God*, "You cannot understand the world today if you do not understand religion." And essential to religion is, of course, belief. Although religion's profound influence is often hidden, "to the tutored eye, religion is often most influential where it is least obvious." Not just any belief, but theology of a particular kind forms a core part of that influence. In fact "modernity as well as postmodernity is inseparably bound up with Protestantism," and "the world as we know it would not have come about without Protestantism."[13] As we will continue to see, the doctrines and themes most often rejected stem from a certain, albeit sometimes stereotyped and misrepresented, version of Christianity often identified with conservative Protestantism.

Yet the interviewees, whether knowingly or not, do not represent an absolute or total departure from Western religious thinking. Instead, many aspects of interviewees' beliefs assume, celebrate, and/or benefit from the Western and European stream of thought, including the "Protestant principle." This principle affirms that one must refrain from idolatry, not absolutize the relative, and allow criticism to be part of faith. Because of this, one has both the freedom and obligation to continually reform belief and practice. While the SBNR ethos is nevertheless very far from "believing without belonging," neither is it really a "turn to the East." Instead, it is a truly American blending of elements, resulting in an eclectic mixture which often produces an internally inconsistent schema. Yet although the pieces do not always fit together very well, many interviewees were either not aware of or not bothered by that fact. In fact, diffuse, diverse, even idiosyncratic beliefs—and the freedom to select from this cafeteria of options—is one hallmark of this new spirituality.

This ethos is not simply a phenomenon of the United States. I found my conversation partners from other countries conversant with the same themes I found in the United States. Whether in Canada, Mexico, or Scotland, I found lively SBNR communities which echoed themes very similar to those I heard in the United States. Other researchers have discovered the same thing.

When a team surveyed spiritual "questers" in Canada, they found a familiar ethos, commenting that this "spiritual questing is a personally significant process, open-ended and anchored by personal turning points." Core themes from the stories they heard included a "desire for profound spiritual connection," a search for "transcendence in daily life," a belief in "questing as identity shaping" and an inclination for "growing beyond traditions." Another study has mapped out the "indicators for affinity" with this alternative spirituality as it is practiced in fourteen Western countries. Someone with this affinity would agree with several of the following characteristics: (a) believes in the existence of a spirit or life force; (b) believes in a life after death, but thinks the churches do not give adequate answers to people's spiritual needs; (c) believes in reincarnation, but does not believe in God; (d) does not belong to a religious denomination, but does not consider oneself an atheist either; and (e) does not consider oneself a convinced atheist, but has not very much or no confidence in the churches.[14]

What holds all this together? What common glue makes the ideas of a blue-collar rural Midwesterner sound similar to those of a young, female yoga teacher from a progressive Western city? Two core factors are surely an increase in individualism and a "detraditioning" or shift in the "locus of authority." People, freed by Western individualism, have claimed for themselves the authority formerly given to others. This does not necessarily imply a rejection of the social order, nor even a call for radical social change. But it does include a taking back of authority over what beliefs to accept and to reject, what to have faith in, how to practice one's faith, and what criteria by which to judge the self. One, therefore, does not need to believe in spiritualism, esotericism, magic, or theosophy in order to be deeply influenced by this new or "post-Christian" spirituality.

Paul Heelas calls the crux of the new thought-world a *"self-spirituality"* and says it is the "essential *lingua franca*" of this movement. It starts with an assertion that the person's life "does not work." However, it is immediately asserted, this situation is fixable. Since the person is held to be essentially spiritual, "to experience the 'Self' itself is to experience 'God.'" This inner realm can then serve as the source for developing the authentic qualities of the perfect life. But something is in the way of moving from "exile to authentic experience." It is the ego, which represents external, yet internalized and inauthentic, tradition. The Self must be liberated from this tyranny. A host of psychotherapeutic, artistic, and spiritual practices are called into service to make this happen.[15] As we will see from the interviewees, personal well-being becomes the way to measure one's success.

The resulting "unmediated individualism," or sacralization of the self, means that each person is now his or her own spiritual authority. As one author aptly put it, this new spirituality is an experience of "the miracle of my own presence."[16] Many interviewees were thus comfortable in what

Nancy Ammerman defines as the "extra-theistic package" of spirituality. In this combination of belief and practice, spirituality is not "anchored in theistic images and religious participation," but instead "spirituality is located in the core of the self, in connection to community, in the sense of awe engendered by the natural world and various forms of beauty, and in the life philosophies crafted by an individual seeking life's meaning."[17]

Once religious authority is deserted, one is left with one's own intuition, inner voice, or "alignment" to serve as the guide. Finally, in this ethos each person is responsible for his or her own liberation. To make this happen, each must tap into their own intuition, "magical" power, or energy. The result is freedom to live one's life as one pleases. And even though "New Agers are averse to traditions, with their dogmas, doctrines and moralities," they paradoxically assert that a hidden wisdom lies at the heart of all religions, causing them to dismiss apparent differences which are just the product of "historical contingencies and ego-operations."[18]

In their openness to all religions, says Leigh Schmidt, many contemporary people have inherited the nineteenth-century ethos of certain elite seekers, which he calls "cosmopolitanism." In other words, "seekers deeply want to appreciate religious variety. They're not content...to have one religion. They want to have a little bit of all religions. They want the piety of the world. They want the gems of sacred wisdom wherever they can gather those gems. But even as they're appreciating that diversity, there's also a sense that they're looking for the underlying unity in all religious traditions."[19] This desire becomes especially tricky when one wants to blend seemingly disparate elements of various religious traditions.

Although the interviewees were conversant with many of the above themes, they were often more "mainstream" and also more theological than the term "New Age" implies. Most significant, I heard specific emphases from them, demonstrating a consensus on what in Western religion they are rejecting. As we will see, they virtually all rejected religious or salvationary exclusivism and championed an internal rather than transcendent "locus of authority." Many took this further, into a questioning of both perception and reality. Almost all embraced a liberative ethos—especially in gender and sexual orientation issues—rather than accepting older role-restrictive teachings. Most had a belief in "Universal Truth" as well as affirming the essential similarity of all religions. Most downplayed religious commitment. Many had a decidedly therapeutic orientation to spiritual practices, rather than one which focused on ethics or morals. They also demonstrated a positive-thinking ethos or conviction that one's ideas create one's reality. Most soundly rejected the idea of "sin." The vast majority used spiritual experience as a touchstone and often saw nature as a source or mediator of spiritual feelings.

These and other themes identified with the growing trend of non-religious spirituality were present among interviewees. In the remainder of this chapter, we will explore the specific themes most common in interviewees' comments. Then, in subsequent chapters, we will more closely examine the specific theological positions they adopted, pertaining to the sacred, human nature, community, and after-life.

Rejecting Exclusivism

Many interviewees, especially Baby Boomers and those raised Roman Catholic, questioned the all-or-nothing attitude they said characterized religion. Becky Samuels had a very devout immigrant Catholic maternal background. From her mother she got the impression: "You have to buy this whole package, you can't be picking and choosing...otherwise it's no good....[So]...I said okay, if that's the way you feel then I won't have any of it." The related theme of salvationary exclusivism—a decidedly theological stance which speculates on who will be saved by God for eternal life—was an important issue, especially for those raised either Catholic or Protestant. Baby Boomer Patty Hoffman developed doubts when, at about age 13, she began to "question whether this was the only church." But those with minimal to no religious exposure also rejected exclusivism.

Mark Sage, the Gen X "casual" who simply got confused when his parents took him to so many different services, ended up believing in God through an addiction recovery program. Common to that form of spirituality, he firmly rejected exclusivism. "The biggest problem I have with various religions is that one religion says: 'If you don't believe what we believe then you are going to hell.' Then another religion says: 'If you don't believe what we believe then you are going to hell.' If that is true, then everybody is going to hell and I don't want anything to do with it." Another interviewee had non-religious parents who had rebelled against their strict sectarian background. Yet her grandparents tried to expose her to their religion. She liked a lot of it, including, she said, the church people who gave her the love and attention she did not get at home. But this one doctrine upset her. "My grandfather thought that everyone else [in the family] was going to hell...so he cried a lot whenever my parents were not there." At age 14, she finally blurted out: "Grandpa, this can't be right, I don't want to hear it anymore...my parents aren't going to hell."

"Dissenter" William Willard gave a more thorough explanation. He described a liberation from exclusivism through his informal study of theology. As a child raised in a conservative Christian environment, he had never questioned what he had been taught and had no problems with its exclusivism. He was taught that true believers, such as those in his parents' denomination, were the only ones who would inherit eternal life. His experience in mainline Protestantism changed that. But William did not simply abandon the church. Instead, during his frequent moves William always joined a church, even becoming ordained as an elder at one point. He also looked for churches with good youth programs for his children, eventually volunteering to take over the Junior High class, which he found "a wonderful experience."

The curriculum he was given was "very well thought," he said. In the process he said he "read everything that came to my attention and started really seriously questioning orthodoxy." The theologians he read, such as Hans Kung and Karl Barth, championed a more open orthodoxy. William exclaimed: "It was like discovering a new country. It was just wonderful." In his readings, William said, he found a more "eloquent expression of orthodoxy," which was a change from his more narrow upbringing where they were "so blasted convinced that they are the right ones that everyone else must be somewhat wrong." But rather than staying with a more open approach to other religions and salvation, William eventually moved away from religion altogether.

Even those interviewees with little religious background protested exclusivism. I met a young Midwestern Millennial who had a brief exposure to Protestantism before his parents divorced. He said he never understood that religion. "There was no conversation in our family really about spirituality....that might be part of the reason why I fell out....I wasn't quite sure of the reasoning behind it....that was the missing link." When his parents divorced, that clinched his withdrawal from church, but in college he reconsidered briefly. There he was approached by Campus Crusade, an evangelical student group which focuses on salvation. He was open-minded at first, but their explicit message and methods turned him off. "They were very pushy...they kind of stalked me....Finally I sat down and talked with them....They asked me about my fellowship to God." Then "they pulled out graphs and charts...'Here are you and here is where you could be'...and I was overwhelmed." Taking this focus on the "saved" versus "unsaved" to be representative of Christianity, he concluded, "I think that's why I'm very hesitant towards conventional [religion]."

Ethical Objections

Exclusivism was not the only reason interviewees stayed away from orga-nized religion. "Seeker" Patty Hoffman began separating spirituality from religious commitment by juxtaposing behavior to belief. This was spurred by disappointment that religious people were not always exemplary exam-ples. She became aware of those who actually lived out their spiritual beliefs, being drawn to people who, by their integrity—a favorite minister, the mother of a friend, and especially her grandmother—gave her a dawn-ing sense that "religion was not about church." Patty is unclear why she eventually decided "religion was to be avoided." Rather than being based on a bad experience, she speculates instead, it was "a general disappoint-ment in religious communities. Living up to what they said they were standing for, the difference between doctrine and the ability to live it out, was something that struck me as an ideal, I suppose."

The issues that troubled "dissenter" Carole Bradford had to do with the teaching about the divinity of Jesus Christ, but it was sexism that clinched her rejection of religion. While she felt spiritually enriched by her adult experience with Catholicism, she said: "With Jesus being a male, as the central symbol, it's still so excluding." Although a Silent Generation per-son with a higher view of authority than younger interviewees, Carole was still contemporary enough to take matters into her own hands, reject church authority, and continue her spiritual quest elsewhere. When she found similar problems with the Eastern religions she explored, in the end she gave up all spiritual seeking.

Not Tradition but Personal Choice

Many interviewees found great social support for distancing themselves from religious tradition. Jon Farmer, a Western man, said that even though his family went to church often, "most spiritual topics, however, were discussed in a more philosophical manner. I don't believe my par-ents were ever very rhetorical on the subject and allowed me to remain fairly open-minded on spiritual topics." Sandra Dick, a Midwestern Gen X woman, remembered as a child that: "My mother was responsible for

taking us kids to Lutheran church, baptism, and Christian ed[ucation].
She willingly talked about church at home...[and we had] prayer at
meal time." When, however, this child asked why her father "zoned out,
and did not participate," her mother calmly explained "It's his choice."
A woman raised mainline Protestant remembered her parents saying
about church: "If you don't want to go, you don't have to.... We want you
to form your own opinion." So she realized: "You don't have to be in a
church to be spiritual. That's basically how we were raised."

Some interviewees reported that even their religious leaders stressed
religion as a personal choice. Tammy Kalini related how, as a young teen,
she considered joining the Episcopal Church. But she was also studying
world religions in school. When she learned that Hinduism and Buddhism
"want all sentient beings to be free from suffering.... That was enough
for me to know that I shouldn't be confirmed.... There was something
else out there." She immediately consulted her minister and she reported
him saying: "I don't think you are Hindu, but I think you should look
at Buddhism." Then she added approvingly: "He was a very cool minister." In the end, this interviewee joined neither the Episcopalians nor the
Buddhists.

Sometimes this went further. Gordon Hance was raised out West and
explicitly taught to forswear any particular beliefs at all. His formerly
Mormon mother had found her adult spirituality nurtured by "New Age"
philosophies, while his father joined the Unitarians. Gordon remembered
that "most everything was accepted, people's ideas or dreams, no matter how strange or eccentric.... The only things that were wrong—even
though there was no right or wrong in my family—[was that] if you believed
something and held it to be true, it was thought to be narrow-minded.
If somebody was dogmatic, even if they weren't pressing that dogma on
somebody else, they were looked down upon.... The worst thing was propagating ignorance."

Detraditioning and Shift in the Locus of Authority

Among the majority of interviewees, there was a strong bent toward
"detraditioning." This was more an unhooking from all religious tradition, rather than a turn in another religious direction. As we will see in
the next chapter, one of the clearer manifestations of the "detraditioning"
element in the SBNR ethos is the interviewees' various efforts to abandon

Western theism.[20] Some observers celebrate or bemoan this as the West turning towards the East. Other observers champion or worry about a turn away from the organized religions which have developed along with civilizations, and the turn towards earlier, more elemental, tribal, or folk beliefs. But, in fact, in my experience with interviewees, I found few who fully embraced Eastern religions or their beliefs. Nor did I meet any who had deserted Western lifestyles, values, or the fruits of science to live fully "in touch" with nature as they imagined earlier, more pristine tribal cultures had done. Even when interviewees tried to live within alternative thought-worlds, they reported difficulty adapting. Instead, as we have seen above, many live with syncretic and frequently inconsistent beliefs, creative amalgams which were often unique and changing.

For many interviewees, withdrawing from an external source of authority happened early in their lives. Angela Roman had a strict Catholic upbringing. But at age 10 she told her parents she had "graduated" from catechism and was not going to take the confirmation classes. "What they were telling me didn't sound true." She objected when they started "instilling fear [and]...dogmatic remarks," noting in particular that "they were against homosexuality." She made her own decision to leave church at this early age and never went back.

David Kaplan, Baby Boomer and atheistic Jew, reacted against a religious ethos that he identified with Christianity. As a child and young person, he said, "There were three words...I just hated....the word 'wrong,' the word 'sin,' and the word 'Christ.' Those three words would almost send me into a fury." When I asked him why, he said "because they smack of negativity, control, hypocrisy and outright lies, the opposite of spirituality." For David, then, his American positive-thinking ethos and latent fear of anti-Semitism combined with his feeling that organized religion, while it might do some good, was nevertheless expendable. Although David practiced Judaism as a child, as an adult he has never settled down into a particular religion, nor even to an alternative philosophy or group. His problem came, as with so many SBNRs, in the area of belief. Although he has an outward allegiance to a small alternative spiritual movement, he says, mostly he "does his own thing," because he is "not in total agreement with the way they communicate the teachings." Clearly, theological disagreement happens not just in organized or traditional religions.

"Dissenter" Justin Cooper was raised religiously but felt a new world opened up—one which he had a right and even a duty to explore—when he started learning about spiritual alternatives. He says he started out bowing to external authority, even if not enthusiastically, but soon felt free to desert it. "I was religious in middle school...because that is what society wanted me to do. But I felt like there was something better out there." Then he "started...hearing about the Big Bang and Buddha and Hindus and...Wiccans and all these other religions and cults." Unlike many other interviewees, however, Jason did not do much experimentation with these things. Instead, his freedom from authority and trust in his own intuition gave Justin "permission" to construct, as we saw, his own alternative theology of "The Green Man." Although the Green Man is often identified with nature, for Jason he is a created power who mostly helps him maintain his individuality and "not to fear anything."

Going forward, Justin is not so much interested in staying in a perpetual argument with religion as in creating a new way to look at things, mediated through nature. He spoke warmly about the power he feels outdoors. "I, honestly, kind of sit out in nature and let everything speak to me." In nature, he gets away from the "cold city" where "there is so much weight and burden you have to carry around with you. But when I get out into the woods, I feel like I can be myself." On the surface, no one would know Justin has created an alternative belief system. In fact, during the interview, Justin checked several times to make sure no one was overhearing his unconventional views. But, unlike some of my older interviewees, Justin's views do not spring so much from outright rebellion as from existential questions for which he has received an inadequacy of answers.

Jason Van Buren, a younger interviewee, shows another side of the popular SBNR withdrawal of authority from exterior and religious sources. While some SBNRs place more trust in their own perceptions, for Jason—like many other younger interviewees—this withdrawal from external authority has made him doubt his own internal perceptions as well. As you may remember, Jason went forward for an "altar call" and pretended to be "slain in the spirit" (i.e., to be so moved by the pastor's touch and message that a divine energy caused him to fall backward). The fact that Jason feigned this experience yet convinced others that it was real threw Jason into a time of intense doubt about motivation, meaning, perception, and even reality. "I thought about why would I do that? Why would I fake it? How many people were faking it? What was the point of it? Why was my salvation my only concern? And so after that I stopped going, little by little."

This discovery led him into stage-acting, an alternative place where he said he could explore his questions of "identification, who I was, and how easily I could become other things. What was my soul and how could it change and be so seemingly altered?...Lots of different things unfolded from that point." But Jason has taken this rude awakening very far. Now he does not trust either external or internal authority. In this lack of trust in reality or his perception of it, he is like many of my younger interviewees. Although he continues to have existential questions about the meaning of life, he has determined not only that answers cannot come from outside you, but that, actually, there are no answers. His journey has shown him "It's not going to come from anywhere. It's not going to come from belonging to a group. It's not going to come from accepting Jesus into my heart. It's not there. There is nothing but the search. It's coming to the point where the search is the answer."

"It's All Good"—Perennialism and Universal Truth

Among most interviewees, I heard the assertion that all religions are essentially the same at their core. This "perennialism" assumes that mystical experiences of "Ultimate Reality" are valid encounters with something objective, something not part of one's own subjectivity or personal perspective. The interviewees implicitly rejected any "constructivist" view that considered mystical experiences culture-bound and produced. However, underlying their "perennialism" was the assumption that no one religion gets it completely right. In fact, many felt that disagreement between religions or promoting the truth of any particular doctrine is a sure sign of "getting it wrong." We might call this the "theology of Universal Truth." It is expressed well by one Midwestern woman: "If you really look at all the simplicity in all the religions, they talk about the same things, being there for your brothers—ah, for your neighbors—caring, compassion...love and understanding and not being judgmental....I won't say one religion is right and one religion is wrong....We are all trying to get to the same place, really."

An overwhelming percentage of my conversation partners—perhaps as much as 80% or 90%—felt that they and other SBNRs were in the unique position of realizing the essence of true spirituality. They viewed traditional religion as exclusivist and unable to see beyond its own boundaries. They reiterated this frequently, even though surveys say just the opposite (i.e., that there is very little exclusivism anymore in American religion).[21] Nevertheless, interviewees were able to oppose a stereotyped "exclusivism" to their understanding of "Universal Truth." It was as if they imagined themselves standing on a higher plane, able to discern the similar core nuggets in each religion, rather than getting bogged down in "dogmas," rituals, or structures. Some allowed that mystics from all the world's religions, too, discerned and sought this truth.

The idea that SBNRs have access to a higher truth is very common. The majority of the interviewees claimed that they could discern the similarities in all religions. This claim was made irrespective of what type of spirituality they were practicing and included those SBNRs I found inside organized religion. The apparent differences between religions they simply ascribed to human error, institutional exclusivism, non-essential teachings, or down-right manipulation. The monistic perspective unobtrusively undergirded this claim. For if "all is one" and differences are only apparent, not real, this means that ultimately everything—including religions—blends into an undefinable essence without properties.

Amy Legrand was actively working to change the views she inherited from her very conservative Christian environment. She said she had found the "universal truth" idea a helpful vehicle for her journey. She said: "There's a fundamental core to all faiths and religions.... They're all very similar.... I still believe in one God and that one God is the same God for all religions and faiths. I didn't believe that as a child.... We have no business trying to restrict what that should look like for each individual person.... That's what religion does." I asked her why she was still exploring religions, then, since she was considering attending a liberal mainstream seminary. She told me: "Because I feel like I threw out the dogma bath water but I still kept God.... Religion has harmed the idea and the concept of God or the Divine.... Religion has screwed up God, but that's not God's fault."

In spite of the reality that interviewees spent an hour or more with me freely expressing their beliefs, many still blamed the problem with religion on the fact that religions have certain core beliefs. Anne Heimlich, Baby Boomer and spiritual "explorer," echoed a common theme, equating the dark side of religion with belief itself, or with faulty beliefs. I found many interviewees who, like her, made a sharp distinction between personal experience and the beliefs taught by religious traditions. She said firmly: "I feel like so many religions have gotten too into: 'Believe this and you'll be fine.' People have gotten away from their own truth through their own personal experience. We have this ability to get caught up in beliefs that lead us astray." Penny Watson, also a Baby Boomer, expressed a similar sentiment, except that she tried to separate practice from belief. Clearly rejecting the exclusivism and "boundaries" which she associated with religion, she nevertheless appealed to truth and preaching. Like several other interviewees, she had no particular trouble with the teachings of Christ, indicating they might be a good enough "guide for living." She said:

> Once you start naming something, you put boundaries around it. That's one reason so many people are hostile to the idea of God because too many people have put boxes around it and built flying buttresses around God and said: "This is what you have to say and believe about God and if you don't you are excommunicated and you are damned." Well that's not what God is. If you strip away Christianity, or any of these other religions you may have, and get back to the truth that was preached by Christ, for example, you're getting back to a guide for living. That to me is what matters in religion, and if you don't feel you need that guide, but you just listen to those spirits out there, then that's fine too.

For many interviewees, they are first introduced to the perennialist and/or "Universal Truth" orientation by the therapeutic foci of many spiritual alternatives. Oftentimes, in trying to open the experience up to the greatest number, teachers of spiritual practices stress the "generic" and non-religious nature of their classes. For "casual" Jennifer Babcock, as we saw earlier, it was her need for healing and her therapeutic orientation that prompted her spiritual journey, starting with AA, then psychotherapy, and finally experimenting with all sorts of spiritual alternatives before outgrowing the whole enterprise. She illustrates well the idea pervasive in this milieu, namely, that all religions are similar, potential dispensers of wisdom and good for therapeutic purposes, but ultimately non-essential. She explained that although for a while she had read widely in Eastern-influenced literature, she never discriminated between different teachings. Nor did she ever consider joining any particular religious group. She felt justified in this when she heard a yoga teacher promoting spirituality over religion.

She explained her feelings in a way I heard often from SBNRs: "I completely respect all religions, and all the reasons why people have religion....I think that religious people are spiritual people...I'm a spiritual person....I see things in all...different religions that work for me. But

I don't want to belong to any one thing cause I feel like I'll put myself in a box.... I want to expand in this life.... I want to be open to whatever is supposed to be happening." Like most of my interviewees, Jennifer sees religion as constricting, closing off options, unnecessary for spiritual development. But she also illustrates what Heelas calls "self-spirituality." Jennifer, like many of the interviewees, simply takes for granted that the self is the only true or reliable source of authority. "Now... spirituality is just natural to me.... I think my intuition is the Divine and... I just follow that.... The result... is I have a really beautiful life. I mean, things happen that make me sad and stuff, but I still think my life is perfect.... I don't feel like I have to have any specific practice because... it's every moment of my life, you know?" The only spiritual activities she could now identify were playing music and being out in nature.

Kimberly Takahashi agrees with this view of religion. Raised with very little exposure to it, as we saw in the previous chapter, she insists that although she rejects much of religions' ethical injunctions, she "can agree with most of... the core beliefs of a lot of religions." In addition, she says that "no belief system should be labeled as savage, or lesser, than any other religion." But they do not represent authority for her. None of them, she says, can be wrong or right. Instead, "they all have their own sort of right." Kim has made a conscious decision to rely on science as a guide. Science shows the grey, she says, while religion makes things "black and white." It is "really unclear... what is moral and what isn't."

At this point, she is not able to trust any one system. "I've always questioned the structure of traditional religions," she says, and finds the stories "mentioned in holy scriptures... really unbelievable." Now with "most structured religions or belief systems, I look at it critically and always question." Like so many others, she is turned off by exclusivism and totally rejects any position that claims "this is the only thing that's right." In going forward, Kim says: "I think it's useful to look at other religions and figure out what works for you." Her non-religious milieu, hesitation about any kind of spiritual authority, and willingness to entertain various ideas without committing to any is a common aspect of the SBNR ethos among interviewees, especially the younger ones.

What facilitates the belief in the essential similarity of all religions for many younger people is that they grew up in minimalist or looser religious environments. Their lack of religious knowledge is combined with their strong desire to keep their spiritual options open indefinitely. This helps explain their lower level of dissent than earlier generations and high tolerance for "using" or enjoying spirituality without feeling an obligation to commit. Not only did many of my younger interviewees find it difficult, if not impossible, to settle down in any one tradition, but they did not see the point nor experience much external compulsion, as previous cohorts felt.

Hybridity, Syncretism, Poaching

Many of the SBNRs I met, especially "seekers" and "explorers," found the rise of spiritual alternatives exhilarating and liberating. To this day, many continue to experiment with new spiritual trends and have few qualms about mixing disparate elements. The idea that it is inauthentic to "poach" elements from a wide variety of traditions—in effect, divorcing these beliefs and practices from their roots and community—struck many interviewees as absurd. Their contention that all religions and spiritualities are, at bottom, essentially similar made them comfortable in choosing diverse elements to add to their own spiritual tool-belt of beliefs and practices. This "self-spirituality" made them feel they had the right—and ability—to distinguish those beliefs which derived from deep, common wisdom and those which were simply cultural-accretions or products of ego. They seemed to see their SBNR posture as a higher platform, as it were, from which to view people and groups they felt were confined within or limited to individual religions.

Many interviewees, but especially younger ones, had trouble understanding the reason for shared worship, tradition, or commitment. Instead, they promoted the idea of some Universal Truth that was clearly accessible to everyone, without the need of any collective heritage or any intermediary or interpreter, whether communal or clerical. Many saw this as a peaceful, open-minded approach. Yet in practice it often worked to exacerbate their hesitancy to fully commit to anything spiritual or religious, especially for the more thoughtful participants. They often expressed an underlying suspicion that when someone promoted their own group's grasp on some kind of distinctive truth, this would be when they were most in error. This could make them call into question the very nature of truth, belief, and perception. Instead, most interviewees kept their distance from group commitment, and instead chose, mixed, adopted, and adapted religious beliefs and spiritual practices on their own. Being their own "locus of authority" facilitated this stance.

Not everyone could blithely mix and match, however. A few interviewees became uneasy with this eclecticism. One spiritual "explorer," Tony Ricci, was raised Catholic in the urban East and enjoyed his time as an altar boy. His mother, however, he said, was a "woo woo New Ager." Since he was open to spiritual alternatives himself, Tony moved to the West to attend a progressive college and then lived in California for many years. He described with appreciation the many spiritual practices to which he had been exposed. But his hesitancy to commit to or fully believe in anything was also evident. Many times he would be attracted to a group, get close to it, and then be disillusioned. Often for him, as for many interviewees, it was the issue of religious authority which proved his undoing. In his effort to commit to Buddhism, for instance, he saw people gravitating away from Western religion to Eastern teachers. But Tony felt they were simply "transferring [their] Judaic, Christian guilt and shame onto these teachers...making them into the Godhead." The issue of discernment also came up for him. "There's people who are very authentic in what they're doing, but there are people who are using the same language, the same vocabulary [and]...just hurting people."

Unlike many of the older interviewees, Tony was struggling as well with the underlying tension of conflicting philosophies, clearly a theological problem. He said that, ultimately, it was the "conglomeration of spirituality in the New Age that bothered me." He warned others: "We need to question this stuff. We need to not separate our critical thinking from our intuition, from our faith, from these systems." He seems stymied in this task, however, because his theological dilemma has made him doubt his own perceptions and ability to believe anything, something we saw earlier with Jason. In this self-identified "spiritual crisis," this young man said: "I've...really wondered why, what's real, what's not, what do I believe, why I believe what I believe?" When I met him, Tony Ricci had pulled back from nearly everything spiritual or religious. Although he might perform an occasional spiritual practice, like meditating, mostly he "drifts." "I connect with my dog...I connect with trees, I connect with nature...and that's good."

In each age cohort and group, I occasionally had someone who suggested it is better to go deep than broad. This is not the same as "exclusivism," since it maintains both a functional and universalistic view of religion. These people were not making truth claims but instead asserting that a clear-cut theology and/or set of practices is more beneficial to an individual's spiritual formation than cutting a broad shallow swath through alternative spiritualities. One biracial Midwestern woman was once a Protestant pastor before digging deep into her Native heritage. She said: "For a while when I was a minister, I had a Catholic spiritual director and sometimes people would get intrigued with Native American spiritual [tradition] and try to combine the two. When you try to bring in two completely diverse traditions, you wind up basically losing the integrity of both of them.... Christian and Indian spirituality come from totally opposite ways of thinking... I know some people... can mesh the two, but I can't."

I began to see a spirit of discernment and questioning in my younger interviewees. The older cohorts often simply felt liberated by leaving religion behind and were often uncritical of the many spiritual alternatives with which they experimented. But some younger interviewees, especially Millennials, raised nascent or explicit theological critiques. Surrounded by many spiritual alternatives with no compulsion to adhere to anything in particular, they often turned a critical eye upon them. This sometimes happened even among those immersed in an SBNR environment. One very articulate Millennial interviewee from the West, Rebecca Henderson, was in the process of moving from "explorer" to tentative "immigrant." She questioned the "blissy blissy" quality of "New Age" spirituality where people work at "blocking out all the pain and suffering. If your practice is geared toward [that]... that's where you'll go. [But] eventually you fall out of that." This became evident to her while serving as a hospital chaplain. She noticed social workers promoting the widespread view that your beliefs or intentions create your reality. "It's really hard to have social workers... telling you that you have cancer because you are a resentful person."

Rebecca also criticized the common presuppositions that religious practice is merely functional, that religions are ultimately the same, and they can be blended at will. "People who start mixing Hindu and Buddhism or New Age stuff... those people are the most aggressive.... I would rather talk to somebody who is very exclusivist and says you are going to hell if you don't believe in God, than somebody who says you're really a Hindu, and it's all the same thing, and if you just get in touch with your chakras, everything will be okay." Not surprisingly, this young woman is now seriously studying Buddhism.

The interviewee who had been taught by his parents to question while attending a variety of Protestant churches began to explore spiritual alternatives while in high school. But he soon got bored with the "totally pop culture fluff stuff" which is all he could find in his small Southern town. At his Midwestern state university a professor gave him a copy of *Zen-mind,*

Beginners Mind. "That was really cool and really fit for where I was." He switched his major to philosophy and was guided by another professor in meditation practice. In retrospect, he realizes what he really needed was something which combined "existential questions...philosophical rigor and meditative practice."

Nature and Experience

Since religion is often not considered as a source of spiritual experience, a large number of interviewees, especially younger ones, reported turning to nature as the resource for their spirituality, either blended with or in place of specific spiritual alternatives. Some consider nature the prime "sacred" dimension, which is a very this-worldly or "immanent" perspective, theologically. One scholar defines it this way:

> Nature-based spirituality seems to be an attempt to make a *personal* meaning out of one particular manifestation of the "really real," namely an overwhelming sense of awe and wonder in the presence of the natural world, accompanied by a loosening of the grip of ego and a new sense of belonging, acceptance and union with the divine. Nature-based spirituality also offers a certain kind of comfort—not the comfort that comes from hope of heaven, or from collective worship of an agreed-upon deity in an agreed-upon way, but the comfort that comes from laying down the restless search for meaning, from finding a touchstone against which to measure one's individual life.[22]

Nature-based spirituality is especially prevalent in the Pacific Northwest, also called "The None Zone,"[23] but I found this theme in other geographic locations as well. Among the various age groups, the Millennial interviewees seemed most comfortable with it. Nature spirituality is behind the archetypal claim many SBNRs make when they assert that they can find plenty of spirituality in a sunset and do not need organized religion. This assertion is also part of the rhetorical strategy we have been tracing, since it ignores the fact that plenty of religious people also find the divine presence in nature, especially since it is seen as God's creation.

Some interviewees held out the hope that this type of spirituality might attune us more creatively and appreciatively to our natural environment.

I found many interviewees who were able to "lose themselves" when out in nature and some who tried to be ecologically sensitive recyclers, eaters, and buyers. Few, however, seemed aware of the inherent limitations in this form of spirituality, perhaps because these limitations were the flip side of the core affirmations of the SBNR ethos. Researcher Gail Wells, who appreciates the potential contributions of nature spirituality, also sums up some of the disadvantages. For one thing, the radical emphasis on self may offer "solace and comfort" but it comes "at the risk of self-absorption and disconnection from the larger community." This thus works against the vision of connectedness that the SBNR ethos claims. Also, "in its embrace of a mythical landscape, nature-based spirituality is by and large ahistorical," for instance, romanticizing the attitudes and practices of indigenous peoples towards the natural environment. In addition, by sacralizing places where humans are not present, "nature-based spirituality has a frankly imperialist dimension" and can lead to "moral absolutism." Also, this spirituality often fails to appreciate how science "practiced in the right spirit, is an ally of environmental activism, not the enemy." Finally, nature-based spirituality can be more faddish than functional, feeding "into the nihilism of disaffected people."[24]

One young interviewee insisted she was an atheist throughout her moderate Catholic upbringing. Nevertheless, she found spiritual meaning in her Western mountain environment. "There's always been this really strong and deep relationship with sacredness, and sacredness in the mundane. Just being outside or doing the dishes or that sort of thing." Even so, she longs for the contemplative aspects that religion has historically provided, but she has trouble reconciling them with her lack of belief in God. Another interviewee inherited a reverence for nature from his parents, along with both Protestant and "New Age" practices. Rather than in these traditional or alternative practices, however, he first experienced the sacred as a child on hikes with his father. "Being out in nature is one of the places where I would experience. . . . dropping into something bigger."

Many interviewees went out into nature in search of spiritual experience. Yet, for most of them, spiritual experience—wherever they found it—was not only sought after for its own sake, but seen as a confirmation of any belief or group's validity. For many interviewees, having a heightened spiritual experience justified mixing and matching, borrowing, or using whatever touched them. But this insistence on experience as a marker of "truth" also led some interviewees to try things only briefly and then move on or even give up. Kimberly Takahashi remembers a friend who was "pressurizing" her and gave her "one of those pocket Bibles.... I remember trying to read through it, just trying to understand what she was telling me." She was told that "all you have to do basically is believe in this and ask him [Jesus]. I tried that and I...don't know if I was expecting someone to actually answer me, but...I didn't feel anything at all." This lack of immediate experience led her to discard religion. She said: "I would definitely consider that an important discovery, [the] lack of [an] answer, or any spiritual response. I got nothing from that."

For some interviewees, experience had to be accompanied by careful and adequate theology as well. Rebecca Henderson is a good example. She had some exposure to Catholicism growing up, but decided she was an atheist in high school. She enjoyed arguing theology with the many evangelical students in this conservative town and resented the favorable treatment she thought they got in school. When it was time for college, her parents pushed her towards a Catholic university. Although she started out angry and defensive, to her surprise, it was a good fit. Most amazing, Mass provided the experience Rebecca had missed. "Church was right there on the campus. I loved the bells, the incense. I really wanted to be Catholic." She added: "I went to Mass and I cried a lot. It was sort of my second big push to decide what really worked for me and how I could really fit." She added, "If there was any possible way that I could...work with it, I would definitely be Catholic, but I just can't do it." Although she tried dialoguing with her Catholic professors around inter-religious topics, in the end, she rejected Catholicism for theological reasons. The things she could not accept included: "personification of the divine, that's a huge one; the salvific role of Jesus. I have no issues with Jesus personally, but the whole salvific issue. The internal contradictions within theology." The last I heard, Rebecca is still trying to find answers in Buddhism.

While it might be fascinating to try to trace out the theological or philosophical roots of each trend represented here—and several authors have done that[25]—for the purposes of this study it is beside the point. Most interviewees had little idea where the theological trends they echo came from. Rarely could they point to specific books, authors, or traditions. Nor did they have much interest in finding out. Instead, many assume and insist that these are generic truths, taught by all religions or, alternatively, represent wisdom more ancient and authentic than any religion. Rather than identifying the various strands of their thought—and, even less, being aware of or concerned with potential inconsistencies—my interviewees seemed content to be in the middle of a contemporary and popular stream of thought. The SBNR ethos they imbibe is simply "in the air," creating a very American brand of spirituality which instinctively, rather than consciously, combines elements of Eastern and Western religious thought, folk religion, spiritualism, "free-thinking," as well as popular versions of scientific and psychological theories. And this spirituality is one strongly shaped by certain American values—often derived from Western religious roots, especially mainstream Protestantism—like progressivism, egalitarianism, free choice, pragmatism, and individualism.[26]

But this is not simply an amorphous ethos without concepts. As we will see in greater detail soon, theology plays an integral part in interviewees' deliberations over spirituality and religion. Theological issues are more explicit for older generations and those with religious exposure. But even for younger participants, these issues are nascent, although less explicitly identified with clear-cut religious positions. In any case, there is an undercurrent of protest against the Western religious heritage. But at least among younger interviewees, there is also a critique of spiritual alternatives. In the following four chapters, we will now explore interviewees' beliefs in the major areas I queried: the sacred, human nature, life-after-death, and community. We will learn not only what the interviewees believe in these specific areas, but how the more generic themes we have just explored influence their thinking.

5

Transcendence

IS IT STILL true that most Americans believe in God? That is what various credible surveys have reported ever since this data began to be collected in the 1940s.[1] Even though the rates of non-affiliated and non-attenders has risen dramatically since the 1950s, are we still a fairly "religious" country after all? Religious people comfort themselves with the Gallup statistic, many considering this almost "etched in stone."[2] Survey numbers like this are not only comforting, but convenient. When reported briefly in the media, they give us a sense of confidence, assuring us that nothing much has changed.

But the percentages that surveys report, as useful as they seem, can also obscure much important information.[3] In the interests of efficient questions and straight-forward answers, they can conflate the different meanings that people attach to the word "God" and miss the nuances involved in people's beliefs. When people claim they believe in God, what do they really mean? Is this the stereotypical "old white man in the sky" interventionist God? Is this God personal and available to any believer? Is it the Creator-God of Deism, who did "his" job and then left us to our own devices? Is this a more "process" oriented deity, growing and changing with the world? Or is this some kind of impersonal "universal spirit" or cosmic force? These would all be very different meanings for the word "God."

Recently, Gallup broke apart the questions, separating out those who believed in God, from those who could only affirm a "universal spirit." Things looked quite different once they did this. Now only 80% could affirm a belief in God, with 12% simply affirming a "universal spirit."[4] Other surveys have found even lower percentages for belief in God. In fact, the percentage of Americans who are completely confident about the existence of God has dropped dramatically since the 1960s. Analysis of the very credible General Social Survey shows that in 1965 certain belief in God was 77%, in 1991 64%, and by 2012 it was down to 59%.[5] The International Social Survey found that only 62.8% of the total population believes in God.[6]

When surveys poll only those unaffiliated with any religion, the drop is even more dramatic. When the Pew Forum asked who in the "none" group could affirm their belief in God with certainty, only 36% of the unaffiliated, many of whom would identify with the term SBNR, could say "yes." Another Pew Survey found only 28% of the unaffiliated said they believed in a personal God, with another 35% understanding some kind of impersonal force.[7] This seems to represent a dramatic change in American religion. For, as we have seen, the number of "nones" represents a rapidly increasing percentage of our population. In fact, it is going up some 0.6% annually with no indication of a slow-down.[8] Yet, like Gallup, books meant for a general audience[9] still promote the idea that most Americans believe in the standard Christian idea of God—that is, one who is personal, loving, active, intentional, good, just, sovereign, and involved with, yet distinct from, the universe.

When my interviewees and conversation partners insisted that they "believed in *something*," I was curious to know what they meant. I soon learned I could not assume that when they spoke of the "sacred," a transcendent reality, a divine dimension, or even used the word "God," that they meant a "personal" God, an "Almighty" who created the world, hears prayers, takes an active part in earthly affairs, and—even if an eternal non-bodily Presence—is nevertheless someone with whom they can "have a relationship." When I opened with the fairly broad and standard spiritual-inventory question "How was spirituality expressed in the environment you grew up in?", as we have seen, many of my younger interviewees said simply, without elaboration, "It wasn't." And many others, with some level of religious background, often just described their movement away from religion.

Yet few, if any, of the interviewees of all ages considered themselves outright atheists. In fact, the percentage of atheists in the United States has remained only around 2–3% for decades. So my conversation partners did believe in something and that something was usually greater than their individual selves. One might think this would divide up along age-cohort lines. After all, my older interviewees had significantly more exposure to organized religion than my younger ones. But, this was not the case. Rather than falling along age-cohort lines, instead the ideas of transcendence or "the sacred" divided up into several core themes, which we will explore below.

When we investigate people's relationship to a "transcendent" sphere, we need to become clear on what they mean. For there is both a "horizontal" and a "vertical" dimension to transcendence. Although these spatial terms are simply metaphors, they have important meaning. A "horizontal" transcendence can mean one is reaching beyond one's limited ego, out to others, the world, community, nature, and so on. This is often what "spiritual" means from a psychological perspective. A "vertical" transcendence, however, implies one is reaching out towards God, Higher Power, the cosmos, the "Ultimate," or some other way of conceptualizing an ontological reality beyond the material world. This is where a philosophical or theological perspective adds another dimension to the term "spiritual." Since these interviewees considered themselves "spiritual," it implied they were interested in some kind of "transcending," but was this, for them, mostly horizontal or also vertical? Did they simply want to have a healthier ego which was joined to a larger world? Or were they aiming for an even greater goal? Towards what goal were they "transcending?" Was there anything "out there" which could be called God?[10]

In the interview, I encouraged people to talk about whatever they felt was essential to their belief in the area of transcendence and "the sacred." I aimed to discern toward what "higher goal" they might be aiming. Was their view of the "greater than" personal or impersonal? Was this "higher power" someone or something with which they could communicate, or from which they could feel guidance, or feel loved or cared for? Or was it an impersonal force, energy, source, or power? And how much separation did they see between themselves and the "greater than"? Did this higher power have an individual consciousness, apart from their own? How did they see themselves in relationship to this greater than? Were they like it in any way, or completely different from it? Did they see a need to cooperate with this "higher power," or were they, instead, helping to form its identity, or bring it to fruition? Answers to these questions quickly dispel the idea that SBNRs are simply "unchurched believers," that they "believe without belonging," or that they hold traditional ideas about God while simply being critical of organized religion.

No More "Clown in the Clouds"

Masculine Imagery

We might guess SBNRs would want to overhaul the idea of God. Surveys report that they often turn up on the moderate or liberal side of social and political issues.[11] And—being contemporary people with progressive values—surely they would insist on moving away from the stereotype of a male God, and one who is demanding, authoritarian, or punitive. We could assume they would move instead toward a kinder, gentler, perhaps female version. In fact, many interviewees—both men and women, and from all age cohorts—did specifically reject a male image of God.

Susan Cashman was a Silent Generation "seeker" I spoke with who still regularly attended a mainstream Protestant church in her small Western city. It was clear that she was appreciated, active, and happy there. She had been raised Eastern Orthodox, which is where she had first learned of female imagery for the divine. She said of her childhood faith: "I thought that God was Jesus and since Mary was the mother of God, she was God, too. [This was] a real female essence even though the church itself was very patriarchal." As an adult, she moved to liberal Protestantism and was gratified to find a receptive audience when she worked to bring female imagery for God into her church. But she had also long been drawn to many SBNR sites, practices, and themes. In fact, the main room in her home contained altars to many female deities from various traditions. Her beliefs, too, combined elements from psychology, shamanism, nature worship, and other aspects of New Age philosophy. It appeared clear that her guiding principle was to bring back female symbolism. She explained, "I bring a lot of females because I think we are lacking that in our spiritual energy." As with many of the interviewees, regardless of whether they attended traditional services, her identity was hybrid or syncretistic. She told me proudly, "I'm a Druid-Celtic-Native American-Judeo-Christian."

Many interviewees did not like the idea or term "God" because they connected it with negative masculine stereotypes, such as the demanding, difficult-to-satisfy father, or the capricious king who could just as well smite you as help you. When I met Becky Samuels, a Baby Boomer, in a progressive Western city, she was a yoga instructor and "casual" SBNR who used yoga as her main spiritual practice. This was a big departure from her upbringing, since she was raised in a Midwestern Polish enclave as a strict Catholic. She remembered that as a child, when she thought of

God: "It was the guy on the Sistine Chapel, sort of a stern dad. Like us, but powerful, like a superhero.... If he befriended you because you were being good, that was good for you. But if you were being bad, he had it in for you. It was hard for me to know [which he would be]." Laurie Hanson was a Baby Boomer spiritual "explorer" who no longer had any use for church. She saw the word "God" itself as gendered. "The God word is very masculine and it's very rigid in my mind."

Jim Haag, another "casual" SBNR and Baby Boomer, grew up in a Midwestern city and attended a large, very liberal mainstream Protestant church. Although his family consistently showed up on Sundays, there was not much religion the rest of the week. He remembered church services as "very formal, very dry and unrelated to anything that meant very much to me." When, at age 13, he decided to officially become a church member, he "came out" to the minister that he was an agnostic. As he remembers it, the minister simply said, "That's fine." Although his ideas of God were formed in this milieu, now: "When I hear the word God I think of the old white man with a beard that I don't believe in. I hear the word Jesus and I think of a younger white man with a beard that I don't believe in."

Matt Adler, Gen X "seeker," was raised in a conservative Midwestern church where he participated willingly until young adulthood. Although doubts and questions eventually distanced him from church, they did not stop him from wanting to grow spiritually. Eventually, as a young adult, he joined a Buddhist spiritual assembly. He was very dedicated and involved, progressing rapidly through the stages, working on more and more advanced spiritual techniques. Although he gained significant benefits from his sojourn with Buddhism, by the time I had met him he had left to join a liberal mainstream Protestant church and was considering the ministry. He says he withdrew from the Buddhist group because it did not put its principles of compassion and concern into practice. The journey taught him much, though, especially about God. He says he has learned: "There is no deity with wrath that's going to come after you if you don't believe. Coming back to Christianity, the God of my faith was no longer the angry grandfather who said, 'This is what you need to believe or else your life will be miserable.' God is very open and accepting and wanting to be in relationship with you."

Not everyone understood traditional male imagery for God to be oppressive. Yet they, too, felt compelled to leave it behind. Baby Boomer Don Blum had had a profound conversion experience of God through his addiction recovery process. Though now involved with a church, he still saw himself as an SBNR. He struggled to explain his new understanding without using either New Age or what he saw as antiquated Christian imagery. He said: "It's a very personal relationship that I have with God...God is more than just a force. I don't have a vision of God being a kindly old man sitting on the throne some place, but I don't know any other way to say it than it's a very personal relationship." Although he rejected male imagery, this man's focus on an intense personal relationship with God was unusual among interviewees.

Margie Mason is a spiritual "explorer" who grew up in a conservative Christian church in Western Canada. A Baby Boomer, she is of mixed parentage, First Nation (Ojibwa) and English. She insisted she did not have negative childhood impressions of the male imagery from her conservative background, even though she grew up "with a very patriarchal God." Instead, she said: "My experience of God was not...[a] punishing, mean father. For one it was consistent with my understanding of [my] father...very loving, nurturing, kind to us." Nevertheless, she left her childhood church, as well as the male imagery for God, finding a "glorious expansion of understanding" in the "Mother Goddess" concept she discovered in an alternative spirituality.

Although I heard the critique across the generations, focusing on male imagery for God was most common among my Silent Generation and Baby Boomer interviewees. It is not surprising that these age groups might focus on male imagery, since they have lived through the profound change in gender roles that took place mid-twentieth-century. Far fewer Gen Xers and Millennials brought this up and even among those who did, few had problems with it. However, many presented a masculine image of God as an immature view which they had outgrown or a vestige of the past. Becky Stryker is a Gen X woman and popular clairvoyant in a large Midwestern city. She is known locally for "channeling" beings from other galaxies. Her current work, however, does not spring from bad experiences with traditional religion, for she had pleasant memories of her youth in the Presbyterian Church. As for her childhood idea of God: "It was a supreme being that was male that could hear me, could see me, created me, and was like the governor of the whole universe, as I understood it." But she now thought of the sacred as largely impersonal, a view that became increasingly common among the younger interviewees.

Jenny Buchan, a Gen Xer raised by a Wiccan mother and "holiday" Christian grandparents, is definitely a spiritual "explorer." Since her grandparents occasionally brought her to church, she remembers a God image from her childhood: "I kind of really just pictured Him as a man, just sitting up there, just making things happen, creating things. [I] never really put too much thought into it.... It was more just, 'OK, yeah, He's there.' You know, religion, spirituality, it's all good." Amy Legrand is the Gen X woman with a very conservative Christian background. When I met her, she was consciously trying to change the views she had inherited and clearly felt proud of the progress she had made. She said, "[My] Sunday school version has always been, you know, the Wizard of Oz running the show." But now—as many interviewees did—she has stripped away both masculine and personal imagery, seeing God more as a "metaphysical non-embodied entity beyond definition."

Younger interviewees, although they were not as bothered by exclusively male imagery for God, were true to their generational stress on tolerance. Many said they didn't mind if others needed to retain the masculine-stereotype-tinged view of God. Alexandra Heim, a Western Millennial, had a nominally Christian Scientist father who tried to expose her to many religious traditions. As a "casual," she had a live-and-let-live attitude to God imagery. It is fine, she said, "If you want to think about it as a big god reigning down on the sky." As for her, thoroughly immersed in alternative spiritualities, the divine image changes depending upon her needs. "Some days I only have one Goddess. Some days I have only one God who is male. Some days it's [an] androgynous, non-human thing. It's kind of [a] dynamic system. It's never the same, but they have similarities and threads that remain throughout my life." About one thing she was clear, however: "I don't believe that there is this man in the sky with a big beard who is going to strike me down if I don't do things right. That is a very remote idea to me." In the end, she said, it "depends on what faith-based mood I'm in.... As long as I'm ... being in alignment with who I am ... who cares if you believe in some clown that exists in the clouds?"

If backing away from a male image of God—and its more egregious stereotypes—was the only adjustment SBNRs wanted to make, they would be able to find a home in many mainstream liberal, especially Protestant, churches. For many of these churches have been working for several decades to use less male imagery for God in their benedictions, baptismal formulas, and personal references. Nor is this simply a change of apparel, for many have also worked to scrub away much of what Brian Wren called "Kingafap" [meaning King, Almighty Father, and Protector] imagery[12]—that is, the hegemonic, demanding, unquestionable sovereign God who expects obedience, gratitude, and submission. Instead, many mainstream churches now emphasize instead a benevolent, kindly God who very much wants to be involved in everyone's life, to be kept in touch with, to be consulted. In other words, many churches have emphasized the "Cosmic Butler and Divine Therapist" God, which is the view heard by sociologist Christian Smith and team when they surveyed and interviewed thousands of young people from mostly mainline churches.[13] But that updated and scaled-down version of God did not go far enough for most of the interviewees.

Divine Involvement

Along with a rejection of masculine imagery came, for many interviewees, a rejection of a personal God who could or would intervene in human affairs. This included many things, such as the idea that God cares about individual persons, could save persons from trouble, hears prayer, notices human actions, and even that God would want to get involved with humans at all. Intervention, whether as punishment or help, was often rejected by people from all age groups.

Even though Tony Ricci, an East Coast Gen Xer, had been raised in an ethnic enclave as a Catholic—including an enjoyable stint as an altar boy—in his young adult years he extensively experimented with, and even led seminars in, alternative spiritualities. By the time I met him, he had become disillusioned by the all-too-human qualities of other participants and had pulled back from these activities. Now, as we saw, he had few spiritual practices beyond enjoying nature and his dog. Yet this young man retained much of what he had learned from his explorations. In particular, he rejected the word "God" for its interventionist connotations. "I don't like the word God because it's so loaded.... Although ... I do believe that there is something that is, that we are all connected to ... something bigger than us ... [But is this] something outside of us, controlling what we're doing? No. Not into it, not down with it."

Similar to interviewees' rejection of male imagery for God, many saw the idea of an involved, personal God as childish. I spoke with Shirley Stein, a Silent Generation woman who had clearly been a "seeker" for years, trying out many traditional and alternative spiritualities, and who was now working at a New Age retreat center in the West. She insisted that the idea of a personal, involved God was immature. "I think we're on our own. I don't think it's rooting for us or pulling strings for us or anything. I think that's a childlike vision of reality." Yoga instructor Becky

Samuels told me that God was not at all like she had been led to believe as a Polish-American Catholic child. Now, she said, although she still used the word "God," "I don't know exactly what I mean by that. I always get a little uncomfortable when I use it because I think the other person might think I mean that guy on the Sistine Ceiling and I don't."

Others put a somewhat more open-minded spin on the idea of a personal God by "psychologizing" it.[14] While they themselves felt beyond this need, they allowed that others might not be. Joyce Moffatt, Silent Generation religious "dissenter," summed up this view well: "Some need to know that there is a personal god and some people don't need that." She reported that when she was a conservative Christian she was in the former category. But now she no longer had this need and was an "agnostic." She believed that, while there "is a spiritual place.... I don't put that in as personal. No, I don't plug in.... I don't believe *per se* in a personal God." Millennial Kimberly Takahashi had a similar psychological approach, stating, "I wouldn't say there's a higher being, because I tend to think that people prescribe humanistic qualities to the things that we can't control." Mary Johansen, another older interviewee, followed suit: "I know [I] think of God symbolically whereas once I thought of it literally. It's a human way to describe a mysterious but real experience of life."

Some interviewees simply did not think God would single out people for individual care. Laurie Hanson put it succinctly, "It is really hard for me to believe that there is any external spirit that has any investment in us." Jim Haag, who even at 13 was already agnostic, insisted he did not believe in traditional notions of a caring God because: "It doesn't have a self.... It's not a being to be prayed to for your leg to heal or for Aunt Molly to recover from heart disease. It's nothing like that." Barbara Axel, a Baby Boomer, was mixing shamanism with Roman Catholicism. She said: "I think we are each part of the mass.... Are we each important to God? Yeah, as we contribute to the whole. God wants each part of the whole to become its own best self so that the whole can become its own best self."

Many found it liberating to reject the idea of a personal God. They seemed to consider that giving up divine involvement in their lives was a small price to pay for their freedom from any external personalized oversight. For one thing, it removed a human obligation to please or appeal to an observing, divine agent. Thus, Baby Boomer and spiritual "casual" Connie Buchholz asserted: "My God is probably more transcendent than personal.... I don't do things because I need God's approval or empathy." Withdrawing from an involved interventionist view of God also did away with the fear that when bad things happened, they were specifically being sent by God to punish one.

Becky Samuels, yoga instructor, described her movement away from more Western understandings of God, in effect replacing her Catholic God with Shiva—a complex Hindu God-figure who destroys illusion as well as creates. Although she retained a concept of God, it appeared to be for her more symbolic than actual. Most striking, she conceptualized its actions as cold, impersonal, or generic. Now, she said, when bad things happen, it is not because a God is angry with her. Instead, "I would say the dark side is that dance.... The yin and the yang.... I look at Shiva and I almost hear Shiva say to me: 'It's nothing personal. This is what I do and you and your loved ones get swept up in that and we all will eventually and, yes, that hurt you a lot.'" The idea of a divine dimension detached from, even though aware of, human suffering, and creating rather than containing chaos, was one I heard often.[15]

Like Becky, there were many interviewees who, while they did not deny the reality of harm, often pulled back from making a moral judgment on it. They seemed not to want to call anything "evil" or to imply that a divine judge would, in the end, "balance the books." Given the inherited Western religious emphasis on ethical principles and moral judgment, this is note-worthy.[16] But it was not just the negative aspect of divine intervention that my respondents abandoned. When interviewees rejected a personal inter-ventionist view of God, it did not matter whether this was a God who loves and saves or one who punishes and condemns.

Ron Richmond, a Silent Generation spiritual "casual," was raised in a large Midwestern progressive mainline Protestant church. As he remem-bers it, going to church was just something everyone did. "The word spir-ituality, the word religion, they didn't mean anything. We just went to church.... We never had family prayers at the table. We didn't have devo-tions or anything, none of that." However, the family was especially active, he remembers fondly, at the church's summer camp. His memories of church were fairly positive. But he also remembered the idea of God he got from this experience, a God that sent Jesus to die for his sins and the possibility of hell should he reject this gift. His sarcastic tone was evident as he summed up his spiritual journey, as a child and young man, away from traditional views:

> I thought that God existed and...that I was okay because everyone was going to heaven. [But] the rules made no sense. One thing that

sent me up a wall was the Apostle's Creed. I wanted to throw up every time I heard it.... Tell me about a God who loves us unless we do something we shouldn't and then we burn in hell. Oh, and I'll send my son and get him killed and make it all better for you. It made no logical sense. As I got older and into college and into debates in philosophy, I just thought, I can't imagine [a] God saying "Okay, that's it, I'll dump ya."

Alex Johnson was raised a Roman Catholic in a gritty urban ethnic East Coast neighborhood. Both sides of his mixed West Indian and European parentage were life-long Catholics, and Alex had few complaints about his growing up in the church. But when I met him, he was working at a generic spiritual retreat center in the West where he held an important managerial position, enthusiastically rising through the ranks over a period of many years. In spite of his upbringing, this Gen X spiritual "explorer" echoed even less of the traditional theological narrative. He called the divine the "Big What" or the "Big Woo." He saw it "manifesting" in various ephemeral things that came and then dissolved, with no caring or intentional involvement in human life. He explained it like this: "The inherent quality of the Big What, the Big Woo...is not necessarily caring. It just is.... So it's kind of like, we're on this road and I see a guy down the road. He's a better biker than I am. I know to follow him....I draft him. But the road itself has no...care whether I make it to my destination or whether I fall off the bike."

When interviewees pulled back from an interventionist, involved God, it made sense that the idea of a savior, of needing someone from outside the self to redeem, also should drop away. Carole Bradford left space for the reality of an external, though rather impersonal, transcendent, but she still saw no need for this divine dimension to intervene in any kind of saving way. She said: "It's up to us. The sacred is always there and is continually creating and there is a process that creates and destroys and it's up to us to bring about our own salvation....It may not happen."

Millennial Rebecca Henderson stated it quite succinctly. When asked why she stayed away from organized religion, she said: "Personification of the divine, that's a huge one. The salvific role of Jesus. I have no issues with Jesus personally, but the whole salvific issue." In the end, no matter how they explained it, most interviewees seemed to blithely abandon the idea of a personal God who is deeply involved in each individual life—a core tenet of much traditional Western religion. This is striking, especially because it challenges the findings that insist most Americans hold on to a belief in a transcendent and loving God who intervenes in human affairs.[17]

However, I did meet a few interviewees who found it difficult to leave behind the belief in a God who personally cares and is involved, even though they felt they should divest themselves of this view. This was especially the case among the Baby Boomers with whom I spoke. On one hand, many clearly felt that giving up a belief in a personal, engaged God was the more contemporary or "evolved" thing to do, and so they acquiesced to it. Yet I could hear the struggle in their stories.

Patty Hoffman illustrated this in a poignant way. A former Methodist, she was trying with only moderate success to be an "immigrant" to Buddhism, but finding it particularly painful to change her ideas of divinity. Talking about her previous interventionist view of God, she said: "I equate it with believing in Santa Claus. That was my first big disappointment. That was my version of God. Something bigger than me that would grant wishes if I was good enough." Patty had started her spiritual journey as a married woman involved in a Unitarian Universalist church, simply interested in the inner calm she could get from a meditation class.

She explained, sadly, that her journey had resulted in getting divorced, moving across country, and now feeling unable to become a "good Buddhist." With a sense of resignation in her voice, she said she had learned that spiritual growth inevitably required multiple disappointments. Even though she was trying, Patty was clearly having trouble giving up her earlier sensibility of a personal God. While she said she "sort of buy(s)" into the idea that no one is "out there manipulating the universe," nevertheless "at the same time my experience is that there are things that evolve that look like some manipulation is taking place." In reflecting on her current situation, she said: "It really was a calling... I didn't know why, but I felt very strongly that I needed to be here. It feels strongly implanted. I'm not sure it has [been], but it feels that way."

The Sacred Power Is Always On

Guide or Realized Master

Some interviewees did mention Jesus, Buddha, or other important religious figures. But these figures were seen not as saviors but as special human beings, "realized masters," more fully evolved, or role models for spiritual growth rather than supernatural beings who could intervene, redeem, save, rescue, liberate, or reconcile. Some also took these figures as "spiritual guides." Jenny Buchan, the Gen X woman with a Wiccan mother, has reconciled her explorations into various non-traditional spiritual practices this way. Her accommodation was one I noted in several interviewees. Using Christianity as another spiritual practice among many, Jenny says that she has taken Jesus as her gentle, benevolent, but not very demanding, "spiritual guide." He is not any kind of savior or transformer and she insists she could have chosen anyone to perform this guiding function. Thus, she said: "Your spiritual guides can be anybody, from any religion. I just happen to choose Jesus as mine.... Not being raised Christian...I think that kind of helped...[be]cause most people I talk to my age, they turn away from Christianity....The way I see Jesus, he's open and understanding and caring for everybody and whatever that person wants to do, that's on them, you know. It's not for me to say 'Oh, you're going to hell.'"

A few interviewees reported an experience of Jesus as a mediator, or permission giver, validating their hybridity. Judy Eberstark has teetered between "seeker" and spiritual "immigrant" for many years. She was one of the most articulate and thoughtful of all my interviewees. We spent much time together on each of my trips to her city exploring her beliefs and her interesting spiritual journey. A Baby Boomer, with a mainline Protestant heritage, Judy had spent many adult years practicing Hindu and Buddhist forms of meditation. But even after all this time, she was still troubled that many of her fellow meditators were atheist. She found it hard to leave behind the more personal view of God she received through earlier spiritual formation. Her struggle was palpable, as was her attempt to live hybridly.

> I still have a little bit of trouble using the word God....I had established a practice [of] the repetition of mantras and I realized that I was praying. I thought, "Now that I know how to pray...I don't have to be Buddhist anymore." During this time I started to understand the power of faith and I started to experience a sense of presence in my sitting meditation. [Before] there was a sense of stillness and acceptance [but]....it was very impersonal.

She found herself praying to Jesus, which was clearly at odds with her current spiritual orientation. She tried to explain this by enculturation, but was not entirely successful denying her own experience. "We are finite beings that grow up in a certain culture and family and for some reason I feel more comfortable praying to Jesus. When I read these really profound [Christian] commentaries or the Bible, somehow I feel that it goes more to the roots of the being that I am in this lifetime than in reading Buddhist scriptures." Each time I visited this intelligent woman, I was struck by her insights and self-awareness. On one visit she told me she was returning to her roots, that she had found a liberal Protestant congregation she really liked. She said she appreciated their openness, sense of inquiry and worship, as well as the pastor's willingness to discuss theology with her. She was excited to have opened a new door in her spirituality.[18]

> The only thing that has come to me, which is kind of freaking me out at this point, is this has been a very big change for me. I thought I was going to be sitting in a cabin at a Buddhist retreat center for the rest of my life. There is a contemplative part of me, but I don't think that's all of who I am.... I've realized, I want to be around healthy people of faith. Not fanatics, but healthy, open-minded people of faith. I don't want to feel like I have to make an excuse to somebody because I have faith or because I'm inspired by things that happen during prayer. I don't want to feel like that's something you don't talk about.

Edging back to a somewhat more interventionist view of divinity, she said, "I'm developing trust that there is a plan. Or there are plans. That there is a way for me and even if I don't know it today, tomorrow or next year, it's still there." However, the next year I visited her things were different again. She admitted that her many years of Buddhist practice had made a strong imprint on her. Since we last visited, she had stopped attending the liberal church and was planning on finding a Buddhist group with which to meditate. As for her hybrid beliefs, she had resolved to keep them to herself.

Spiritual "explorer" Jack Campbell was another especially articulate interviewee. As a child he had been a very active and conservative Catholic. But now he was trying to live "hybridly," considering himself "a decent Buddhist" but also involved in a United Methodist Church. When he told the pastor about his dual allegiance, the pastor told him it did not matter, saying, "It's a broad tent, and you decide. I don't decide." When it looked like his marriage might end in divorce, this man dealt with the stress by increasing his meditation practice. Through this, he reported he "had a series of visions... [where] The windows fell out, the doors fell down. The paths led out in all directions... I was just in tears... [it was the] very strongest emotional experience I'd ever had." Eventually, this Baby Boomer had an experience of Jesus coming to him in meditation, affirming his eclectic spiritual path. He remembered he saw "a figure walking towards me and saying 'It's okay, what you're doing is okay.' The figure turned out to be Jesus." I asked him if he interpreted this as approval for the divorce or for his path away from the church. The man reported: "The path I'm taking is okay. The breakup wasn't totally decided, but the meditation path [was]... I needed to be different.... So the tradition doesn't matter that much to me."

A Plug-In God

Some interviewees did not see the divine as personal to them in particular. Nor did they see Jesus as a personal element in an otherwise impersonal dimension. Yet there was a personalist aspect to their idea of the sacred. For they understood the sacred as an impersonal force behind everything, but one that was available to particular humans, on-call, and benevolent. Many called it "The Universe."[19] I thought of it as the "plug-in God," available on an as-needed basis, generating power but not specific to anyone in particular. From another perspective, having this kind of on-call transcendent dimension meant they could, in effect, "screen their calls." With this arrangement, there would be no unwanted contact, no judgment, no punishment, no unasked-for personal attention. Instead, they simply posited a generalized, non-demanding, benevolence they could tap into when necessary. Yet no matter how much they insisted this was impersonal, it seemed to be a force that, in a way, cared. They would say such things as "The Universe is telling you something," or "The Universe will take care of you." This conceptualization spanned gender, generations, and geography.

Connie Buchholz was a Baby Boomer who had very little religious training in her childhood. Bad memories of religion had prompted her Roman Catholic mother and Christian Science father to each abandon their religious backgrounds. They told Connie that she could decide for herself. Like many of my older interviewees, Connie periodically chose to be involved in various churches throughout her life, going to them more as a spiritual "casual" looking for short-term sustenance, rather than as a "seeker" looking for a permanent spiritual home. Difficult life circumstances, she said, left her with what she describes as a spiritual "chip on my shoulder." It was not against religion or people so much but, she said, "The traditional white God was where I focused my anger." Her experience in church was one of approach-avoidance. She associated the word "God" with judgment, but deeply wanted to believe in some kind of universal benevolence that she could access. She told me:

> I have trouble with the concept of God. But if you talk about a universal presence or a resonating energy at a certain frequency, the result of that is quietude or peace, or the harmonics within you are quieted. I get that resonating harmonic when I am doing self-growth and self-knowledge work and I don't think I need a God to do that. I don't think I need a God to be peaceful or happy. I do think I need to tap into that resonating energy, but I don't know what that is and I'm okay with that.... I think it's there and you access it. It's always there, always running and always available.

When I asked if this was a personal force, one deliberately involved with her, she forcibly insisted it was not. But she also questioned her understanding and sometimes went back to personalizing the sacred.

> I have read and heard things from people and read books about people who say they had this voice in their head saying, "Don't do this, don't do that." For me, I've never experienced that that I can remember, but I often get a feeling about something. I don't know if that's a force speaking to me or the undigested radish. I don't know and right now I have a tendency to think that it's my "Higher Power." I don't know.

She also reflected other aspects of traditional Western religion. "The Universe always was," she insisted, similar to the idea of an eternal, uncreated God. And when reflecting on her spiritual journey, how she was often given the things and people she needed, she summed up with: "The Universe is good." Rather than this goodness being directed personally at her, some kind of unearned divine grace, instead she saw human initiative as the determining factor. She said: "This stream or flow that is always there, you can make the choice to tap into it or not. If it gives you a sense of peace, [if] it's inspiring at whatever level, I think that's a choice." This view does away with the need to believe in specific, personalized or intentional divine intervention, while still providing the assurance that one is not in an entirely meaningless, chaotic, or uncharted world. Many interviewees echoed another Baby Boomer woman who explained how to have "guidance" without a "Guide": "I rely more on synchronicity for direction.... Who is in charge of synchronicity? I don't know, God? Angels? The Universe? I don't think that I've tried to label it."

This sense of obligation to give up the belief in an involved, personal God was not restricted to older interviewees, however. Amy Legrand, a Gen Xer, frankly admitted she is still "in process." One could see her struggling to reconcile her "Sunday school version of God" with what she felt was a more progressive understanding, partly imbibed from her much more liberal husband. "Marrying someone who didn't believe exactly like me, that's eye opening," she said. Previously, she said: "I believed in free will. If we didn't accept Christ as our personal Savior, then we would die and go to hell.... There was the full acceptance of God as the strict judge, but also that he was all loving at the same time, but not really grasping... how could you hold those two belief systems at the same time?" Now, she says, "I take that much less extremely and literally than I used to. It's much more sort of conceptual. I see God more as a Divine presence.... It's evolving as I learn more.... I could come to a place where God might not be a real entity, more of a concept. I'm not sure yet. I'm still working on that." Amy, like several interviewees, wants to have it "both ways," hoping for a God who is present but only in selected, personally defined ways.

God's Therapist or God-in-Training

In an interesting twist on the personal versus impersonal sacred, a significant number of interviewees found a different route through the dilemma by focusing on the development of consciousness within God's own self. This, then, was not a fully impersonal sacred, since consciousness can imply personal awareness. The interviewees did this by tapping into ideas from the human growth or human potential movement combined with a Western expectation of progress and a nod toward evolutionary theory. It was a popular amalgam, seemingly passed by word-of-mouth, rather than being informed by specific texts or writers. Most simply assumed the logic of it but could not explain where it came from. Their use of "evolution" seems a creative switch on Darwinian theory, because it is not humans who are evolving as much as God. I was struck by how many interviewees focused on divine "consciousness." Some explained that while humans were self-conscious, the divine was not necessarily or independently conscious.

This view challenges the traditional view of God's "aseity," that is, God's independence from creation. To claim God's "aseity" means God can be deeply involved in the world, yet not totally dependent upon it. Thus God is free to act and respond, but is not so enmeshed, or "codependent," with the world that the divine vision is totally submerged in and controlled by humankind. These interviewees strikingly depart from this traditional way of describing God. To them, God does not have an individual, developed self-consciousness. Instead, God needs humans in order to experience, feel, or be aware. Rather than a God who transforms human consciousness, we now have humans who transform God's consciousness. Instead of being independent and fully conscious, God needs humans for the divine awakening or simply to have experience. Thus, the onus for the deity's growth, change, or development is on humans. Many interviewees believed that their own growth is what helps God to evolve. This could come about through "working on themselves," finding their right path through life, or various self-help techniques. Given the considerable psychological tone in much of the spirituality I encountered, it sounded as though humans were now in the role of "God's therapist," helping God become more fully the divine self.

This theme was frequently echoed by a number of older male interviewees, ones we could expect to have had some religious enculturation. Jeff Wurtzel, from the Silent Generation, said: "God is just sitting back and letting things happen. I think that we are the way that God experiences the creation." James Wolfe, an older spiritual "explorer," said he thought God was in some way self-conscious, but no more than the man's own knee is. "We all make up God. This little microorganism that is causing my knee to hurt is part of me, it may think of me as God. I don't know if it thinks at all. Everything makes up God." He continued: "I think that God is self-conscious at some level. I don't know that God is self-conscious so that God knows specifically what is going on with me or any individual anymore than I am particularly conscious of what is going on with my body."

Another Silent Generation man reiterated this point: "God experiences himself through us.... We all put off energy.... You could force me to say that's God." But when I asked him if God has any self-consciousness apart from him, this man answered forcefully: "No!" Sam Klein was a Silent Generation man still actively engaged in a liberal Protestant small city church in the West. He was very eager to share his views with me on this issue. Although he could comfortably use the word "God," he avoided personal pronouns and followed the theme of divine consciousness. He said of God: "It's beyond judgment. It's pure isness or pure creation. Its intent is to know or experience." Leaving little separation between the self and God, he said: "Its desire is for me to be conscious of it as myself. When I say myself, I'm talking about…that unique expression of my essence.…It doesn't know separation." David Kaplan, the Baby Boomer "explorer," put it this way: "I have a consciousness [of] God watching everything without doing any judging, in awe and amazement. It's probably just observing and having the time of its life."

Another interviewee, Daniel Nimitz, who was raised Methodist, alternated in his remarks between a God with a "plan," a God who did not communicate, and a God who was so wrapped up in this man's life that his own growth equaled God's growth. He said:

> I don't think I had a good understanding as a child. God was some mysterious something out there up in the sky. It was a big distance between that God and me. Now I don't feel that. I am part of him, he is part of me, he is part of this whole thing.…I think that's why I've been led [on] the path that I've been led. I think his plan for me is to get better and better as a human being and be more conscious as a human being. And we're really all in this together and we have to help each other. So he is not saying anything to me…but there must be a push in this direction for me to be doing these things.

Jeff Wurtzel went further, conflating divinity and the human self. He said simply: "I see myself and everyone else as a god-in-training" adding that it was the same with "Jesus and Buddha and maybe a lot of others.…That's what we're working towards. I believe that we are working to progress."

I was struck by how many of my older male interviewees echoed this theme. Popular thinking might assume that older white males would want to retain a belief in a controlling and independent male-imaged God, even if only as a projection or wish-fulfillment for their own cultural role. Yet these men eagerly discarded such traditional ideas of God. Still, a belief that their own consciousness guided divine consciousness might be another way of envisioning something similar. This focus on consciousness was not restricted to men or any specific generation, however. Maria Falcone is the Gen X woman of Native American roots who was adopted and then raised in both Protestant and Catholic traditions, although her parents gave her the freedom to make her own choices. Her searching was extensive, including a stint as a Christian evangelical. But she gave all this up when she became involved with Western Native American spirituality. In trying to reconcile her past and present, she retained an image of an external divinity, calling it "the mystery." But she now blends that with the Native spirituality she has learned.

She believes that: "The Mystery decided one day that [it] had to understand itself and it, this understanding, created the earth....In its struggle to understand itself, it has attached itself to each person and thing....I think some of my Christianity [is that] sometimes I picture it as a being, I look up and think 'That's God.'" I asked her if there would be an eventual outcome, that is, would the divine reach some final goal? She said: "Its quest may end. It may totally understand itself....I think it's striving for self-consciousness. I think it's striving to understand all of the parts of itself that it doesn't understand....I don't think it plans things out....That's how it gains its understanding." As for her own involvement in its evolution, she said: "I am but one [of] its storylines for understanding and as I go through things in life, if...I pass through them quickly and easily, then it already understands them. If I go through things and struggle with them, it's because it's trying to understand."

Judy Eberstark, the thoughtful and articulate Baby Boomer woman who was trying to reconcile her Protestant and Buddhist experiences, also used this theme. She said of God: "I wouldn't say it's a sentient thing, but it is a consciousness....It's conscious because it manifests itself in Jesus or Buddha." Yoga instructor Becky Samuels framed it similarly: "God is not a separate consciousness to me. I think it's a lot like what Jesus says, especially in the Gospel of Thomas,[20] what Buddha says, what many of the great wise thinkers, the special people in the past, have said, 'The kingdom is within you and it's all around you.' You don't need to go down to the sea, you don't need to go to the sky to find it, to paraphrase one of the sayings of Thomas. You need to be aware of it, that's your practice. To be able to see it."

Baby Boomer and "seeker" Helen Exline had intentionally sought out religious affiliation all her life, even to the point of earning a seminary degree and trying unsuccessfully to get ordained as a Protestant minister. Yet now she was deeply invested in SBNR communities, leading workshops in alternative spiritualities. She still occasionally used the word God but sees it more as a "collective consciousness." According to her, this God does not know itself apart from the humans in which it resides. "In terms of it being aware of itself, I have to anthropomorphize it. [But] if something is all that is, is it aware of itself? I don't know.... It's the collective life, the collective source of life." Becky Stryker, the Gen X "channeler," spoke of "divine consciousness" this way: "It's not a single entity with a conscious-ness. It is a single entity, but it is a single multi-faceted entity. I'm always challenging my beliefs, but I've gotten to the point where I believe that this creator is kind of a divine consciousness that permeates every sub-atomic particle, it's everything and nothing at once."

Emily Orbach, a spiritual "casual," was particularly interested in shar-ing her views with me. This Gen Xer attended one of my lectures and was clearly engaged. Afterward she came up to speak with me, insisting she might have a more nuanced view on these themes than some other interviewees. Emily was a writer with no religious upbringing, but she was nevertheless dedicated to her spiritual search. As an adult she had become an intelligent and avid consumer of alternative spiritualities. She echoed a variation of the impersonal, collective consciousness view—which she called "macro-cosmic consciousness"—along with the "plug-in" guidance aspect. Like some others, she also pulled back from moral judgments, something that seemed to follow when respondents decided there was no longer any divine Judge.

> The notion that we're all God means that we all are microcosms of the macrocosm.... If I were attuned enough, I could connect with all the information in that universal body of intelligence, across time and space.... I think it's impersonal.... This intelligence responds to our individual vibration.... We, as energy vibrations, attract con-ditions of like vibration.... What we attract will serve our spiritual path if we consciously mine it for its spiritual instruction.... "Good" and "bad" are manmade constructs... all of it is consciousness, but of varying degrees/vibrations that depend generally on whether love or fear is the driver.

But then Emily also brought back in an element of personal divine involve-ment, seeming to want it "both ways." To me, she seemed to represent a subset of interviewees for whom the world felt too empty with only "syn-chronicity" and human initiative to count on for meaning and direction. Emily solved that problem for herself in this way:

> At the same time, I believe there's another level of being, which is personal (e.g., spirit guides, angels) and wants each of us to

fulfill our lifetime's calling...guiding...via synchronicities, our dreams...instincts/intuitions....I believe the larger impersonal consciousness is only responding to the collective vibration, but the personal sacred dimension of spirit guides and angels is trying their damnedest to help us wake up. It's said that they only respond when we solicit their guidance.

Exceptions

Although the interventionist, personal, caring God was something many felt they had to leave behind, there were a few exceptions. Emily was verging in that direction but wanting it both ways. However, I found a few younger interviewees who were quite comfortable entertaining the idea of a Higher Power specifically involved in their lives. Perhaps the rise of evangelicalism during their growing up years, having evangelical friends, or the lack of negative associations with religion—due to their scanty exposure to it—made this idea more acceptable.

When Matt Adler left conservative Christianity for Buddhism, he worked hard to be an "immigrant." But ideas of an external deity were a sticking point. I asked him if he had been able to suspend this belief during his years as a Buddhist. He said: "I don't think so. I think I always sort of felt I couldn't. Even to the whole practice of prayer, I never thought of the Buddha who intervened on my behalf. I believed in some kind of God out there. I thought of the Buddha as someone who had been on this earthly plane. I couldn't give it up."

Brendan Potter, a young Millennial man raised with little religion, told me he is very conscious of a Higher Power involved in his daily activities, especially at work. "I feel like God has a plan and a path for me and I'm following it. But that's funny because the only place where [my relationship with God is]...strong is that I feel like I am doing his work daily." For a long time, he said, he was angry with God because of tragedies in his life, but "even then I was 100% sure he was teaching me something and that was part of my anger that I couldn't figure out what. Still to this day I struggle. That is my struggle with why I am spiritual and not religious. I haven't had that epiphany moment when I'm, like, 'I get it now.'"

Even though he finds no reason to be religious, waiting until he "gets it," he tries to stay conscious of "promptings" in his life and says about them: "It's God. It's that thing that makes me text my uncle when he is having a bad day without me knowing he is having a bad day. It's the same. It's Jiminy Cricket. It's the conscience. You know? It's the little thing you can't explain but it gets you through the day. It's the thing that makes you hold the door for the little old lady." Gordon Hance, the Gen Xer raised by a "New Age" mother, came from a family who expected him to become a New Age celebrity. But a difficult period in his life got him to reconsider his spiritual orientation. When he was young, he said, "I thought of God as impersonal [but]…now God is really the reason why I'm alive, it's like oxygen."

Lisa Grollen is another good example. I met her at a stable time in her life, but the journey there had been difficult. She had walked away from a nurturing church background, came out as gay, and gotten involved in addictions. Eventually she found herself turned around through a recovery program. Although she still considered herself "spiritual but not religious," she, like the young men above, had no problem with an involved God. Speaking about her experience of encountering God through "hitting bottom" in self-destructive behavior, she said: "It wasn't anything that I sought out or registered, or analyzed or tapped into. I could just see that there were moments when I was being protected by something outside of myself because the choices I was making were putting me in harm's way. Some people just say, 'That's just luck'.…[But] nobody is that lucky." Now, as with the young men above, she finds God directing her life:

> God wants me to do the things that make me a better person and that help the people that I love and care for and do the positive things as opposed to the selfish things that I do. Those things don't feel right anymore. That's part of how I know God is real because there was a time when I couldn't imagine being good or doing good and being healthy. That didn't feel right to me. But now I am okay like this. I came to that by myself.

Another Gen Xer, Kit Partin, frankly talked about his addiction and recovery as well as his trust in a personal God, yet with some qualifications. "I am a recovering alcoholic so I've been sober…three years.…I've been trying to get sober probably since 2001.…A big part of that was me giving my will over to a Higher Power of my understanding.…I've been sober ever since." Along with the routine addiction recovery program focus on a "God of your own understanding," he, too, felt compelled to specifically distance his understanding of God from traditional religious conceptions, as well as from conservative believers. He said:

> I do believe in a higher power. I don't call it God. I don't call it Jesus Christ or anything like that. But I know that there is something out there that is looking out for me and I can give over all my problems to and they will all be taken care of....I try and pray every day and you know church is a little bit of a place I haven't gone to yet....I believe that people that are healthy spiritually are happier, they seem to be more at peace, more guided. I'm not talking about the born-again Christians.

Mark Sage told a similar story. This Gen Xer explained that his parents had taken him to so many different churches that, in the end, he just ended up confused. Whether because of or in spite of this very sporadic exposure to religion, Mark seemed to have a bias against traditional notions of God. Yet when I met him he had recently "found God" and become sober in a recovery program. He said:

> Previous to a month ago, any time the word God would come up, I would throw up my little defenses and I don't want to hear none of that. And I would so much as walk away because I was so worried about what everybody else's definition of what God was. I'm not really for sure what happened. I was driving home in my car one night and it came over me that it doesn't matter what anyone else thinks that God is. It matters what I think God is. What do I want my God to be? My God should complete me. If I am lacking in love one day, he helps me to be more loving. If I am lacking in understanding, he helps me understand me. That is my definition and that's what I choose to believe in today.

Mark was comfortable interpreting "the God of your understanding" into the God of his creation and choice. But he also hesitated before fully committing to the reality of an external divine being. When I asked him if God was self-conscious, he said: "No, God to me is an idea....I still refrain from saying that I pray....For today, just me believing in the idea is enough. If I get caught up in: 'Is it real or is it fake?' then the wheels start spinning and the smoke...It's good enough for now that the idea is there."

These interviewees are like others in that some had no experience of religion and some had exposure, whether scanty or intense. They are like others in that they seemed compelled to distance themselves from the traditional notions of God that can be found in organized Western religion. But they are unlike others in that they speak positively about a personal and an intervening God. Interestingly, three of these younger interviewees also represent a small subset of all respondents (just under 10%) who became "spiritual but not religious" and also involved in a personal relationship with an interventionist God through participation in a twelve-step addiction recovery program.[21]

All Is One

Monism

Apart from the interviewees above, who kept remnants of an involved divine while also moving toward an impersonal view, there were many who went much farther. A significant number put forward a view that was one variation or another of "monism." Although most SBNR interviewees toyed with monism in some way, few were aware of its theological roots or various meanings. Some, however, more specifically referred to "non-dualism" or the ultimate interconnectedness of everything, a philosophy with many variants, especially in Eastern religions. A substantial number of interviewees did not simply entertain the monistic view, but clearly adopted it.

Monism is a philosophical position that posits all reality as one, that there are no real distinctions, only apparent ones. Ultimately, there is neither a separate God nor a separate universe. Monism can be a confusing term in theology because it may sound superficially like "monotheism" (i.e., one God). While there have been monistic tinges in some Western religious thinkers,[22] true monism is resisted because it seems to deny God's freedom and ultimate sovereignty. A popular misconception I found among interviewees was the idea that a belief in theism implied God is distant from and external to the world. In fact, the Western Abrahamic religious traditions (Judaism, Christianity, and Islam) affirm that God not only created the universe but is also deeply present, invested, and involved in it (i.e., immanent as well as transcendent).

Even with this deep divine involvement, though, Western religious traditions are clear that God and creation are distinct from each other. This is another perspective on the "aseity" of God which we considered earlier. In this type of theology, God is said to be unchanging, unlimited, and eternal, whereas humans are finite, subject to change, time, and mortality. Against the stereotype of a cold, uninvolved God, this focus on God's independence affirms God's dependability rather than any lack of responsiveness. In effect, God is fully able to freely act rather than being a captive of the world. This is where the idea of "divine intervention" comes in. Even though that idea seems to posit a universe which God needs to "break into" in order to act—seemingly denying that God is immanent in it—its real point is that God is free. Thus God is not identical with the world, even though God's loving maintenance keeps the world from devolving into chaos. And even if humans are ultimately designed to become "partners" with God, to live together eternally, or to become more and more like God, the distinction between them is maintained.[23] In this theological perspective, God is independent of the world—which ensures God's ability to act—but the world is dependent upon God—ensuring that its origin, well-being, and ultimate goal are included in God's care and plan.

My interviewees' version of monism does not see it this way. Their monism would not break reality into two "sectors," but instead sees them as ultimately indistinguishable. This can be indicated by the frequently repeated statement "all is one." This view of ultimate unity is not completely alien to Western tradition, however. For many in it can affirm that God is "all in all" or will ultimately reconcile everything with the Divine Self. The theological variant panentheism, in fact, does posit that all is in God.[24] In addition, some interpretation of non-dualism might be acceptable, in that God created, guides, and is part of everything. But according to Western religions, carrying this too far is problematic, since it seems to "tie the hands" of God and subsumes God to the world. This was of no concern to many interviewees since ruling out any transcendent reality which has control over the world may, in fact, be a key theme in their protest against Abrahamic religions. Thus theirs is often a more "materialistic monism" which rules out the existence of any ontological reality greater than the whole of this material reality.

Theologically, and certainly in the way the interviewees used it, "monism" is quite different from Western "theism." Many respondents sketched out a reality in which there are no distinctions between an impersonal divine dimension and its cosmic, worldly or human dimension. Either they saw "God" and the universe as one, or explained that what we perceive as reality is an illusion. If they saw a divine "dimension," it was simply a manifestation of some essentially impersonal form of cosmic energy, force, or power.

Understanding the monistic tinge of much contemporary popular spirituality helps explain what we heard from my discussion partners earlier. For it is this monistic bent in alternative spiritualities that made many interviewees resist the idea of an external, transcendent deity who was free to intervene, or not, a divine "Someone" outside human control. Ron Richmond, from the Silent Generation, put his finger on why many of my SBNR interviewees shied away from an interventionist God: "I don't sense a need for the transcendent. I would argue that most of the people that say that [they] are 'spiritual but not religious' are disagreeing [with] that very thing." Indeed, I found the monistic tinge nearly everywhere I went.

One day, I visited an Episcopalian retreat center in the upper Midwest. They held weekly meditation sessions and invited me to join them. Since they advertised this as a distinctly Christian style of meditation, I was anxious to see how it differed from the many Eastern style meditation groups I had attended. Before entering the circular meditation room, we were asked to remove our shoes and then cover up our street clothes with identical brown robes. When I asked about this, the leader explained that this would help erase our outward distinctions. Once we entered, we took our places on cushions placed in a circle. There were Christian icons placed around the perimeter, but the chants we used came from the sayings of mystics from various religions, both East and West. Overall, the emphasis was on uniting with the Oneness. In the end, the hour finished with the claim "We are all God."

Many interviewees stated the monistic view in a fairly uncomplicated way. Jennifer Babcock, whose widowed mother gave her no religious exposure, summarized it succinctly: "I don't think I see it like a person.... It's just like a force or something...I mean, it's everywhere. That's what I feel like. It's behind everything we see in the normal life here but I can't see it. That's what it seems like to me." Baby Boomer Shelly Trump used the whole/part analogy. "We are all part of that source as this little cell is part of me. These little dots on my hand are all part of me. We all make up one."

Others got more elaborate when explaining their monistic views. Rebecca Henderson was especially thoughtful and articulate. As we saw earlier, she was raised with some minimal Catholic training but was now trying to adapt to Buddhism. She told me that Buddhism's lack of "reification" (i.e., personification of the divine) was the most compelling aspect. Since Rebecca had only been exposed to one form of Buddhism, she seemed unaware she was over-simplifying that tradition. But that was not especially relevant for her because she used a non-reified Buddhism "rhetorically," that is, for purposes of argumentation. Against a Christian or even Hindu "reification" of God, she offered an impersonal, monistic view. She explained it suited her because:

It's the most truthful way of looking at divinity in my experience. It's not a solid thing. It's not a permanently existing, abiding phenomenon. It's not one thing separate from anything else. It's not a thing.... Part of it is ineffable and I can't describe it and part of it is the whole package. The part of the package with Buddhism that fits for me is the lack of reification. Whereas in Christianity and in Hinduism, I just feel this withdrawing in myself from that.

The monistic bent in much alternative spirituality was indicated by how often the word "energy" came up in interviews. Partly a signal indicating their spirituality was "scientific," the word was also used monistically. Many interviewees felt that seeing the transcendent dimension as "energy" was the contemporary way to go. Even for those who had a hard time transitioning, most felt it was a necessary adjustment. Courtney Szabo, Gen X "explorer" who had a religious background, realized she was having trouble adapting to this popular view but nevertheless affirmed it. She said: "I do see the transcendent as this energy force. But yet, I don't know if it's my roots in Christianity or what, but I just have this feeling that there is something out there that is concerned with me and cares for me."

Unlike her, the majority of interviewees who embraced the monistic perspective—and a large percentage did—were enthusiastic about it. Anne Heimlich even refrained from using the word "sacred," much less the word "God" as she described her views. "I'm having trouble [with the word] because 'sacred' means it's something that I have to detect.... It's this formless energy that is present in all of life.... I would call it spiritual energy. It's definitely not a single being. It's an energy.... It's just there. It's a life force. Self-consciousness would be giving it some attribute of a god somewhere. It's a formless energy that is behind what keeps my heart beating.... It's the energy behind everything. It's not any consciousness that's dictating anything."

When Jim Haag "came out" as an agnostic at age 13, to the approval of his minister, he says from then on: "I started feeling a connection to something universal. It was not the God or Jesus I didn't believe in. It was universal. It was not a person. It was light...it was like energy. It was quite different from the God that I was familiar with....I was thinking about it like radio waves. There are radio waves going through each of us right now. There is digital TV going through us. Electromagnetic whatever, it's a sense of connection between us."

Lisette Marshall, Gen X "casual," succinctly described her childhood exposure to religion as "zero." Still, she actually tried to be involved in mainstream Protestantism because of her husband's interest in it. She had made a great effort to become an active participant but, by the time I met her, was back in the "none zone," specifically because she could not buy their concept of God.

> I think of the higher power as God, but not necessarily the God of anyone else's understanding. I think of God as more of an ele- mental energy, the life force that flows through everything that is alive, or the great unknowable that the human mind cannot com- prehend. Perhaps to do with electricity and chemicals, electrons and neurons and scientific things that are just as much beyond my comprehension as spiritual things seem to be. Sometimes it seems a mix of so many images I've gotten from my readings of magic, stories, fables, creation stories from other cultures and my own. All striving to know what is possibly unknowable for human beings.

Another Gen X "casual," Nick Jones, felt confident in his belief in "energy" but had difficulty explaining the connection between this energy and himself. It seemed he was struggling to use the "all is illu- sion" version of monism. He said: "[It's] a force, like the 'Star Wars' force.... Everything is just energy. Everything is composed of littler things. It's...electrical, neurological, physiology. It's an energy....I am just here living in this body but...the body and the physical are in my head because everything is mental." Millennial Ian Hanby was taught by his "missionary brat" father and "New Age" mother to critique ser- mons and decide his own beliefs. Now, studying at a Buddhist school to be an interfaith chaplain, he needs to think about the language he uses in his work. To him, this sacred energy is simply "life." But since his chaplaincy internship requires him to provide spiritual comfort and guidance to a wide variety of people, he will use the word "God" when necessary. He said: "The word God has relevance to me, but that's because I am a chaplain and use it quite often.... For me it's the felt sense of being alive and connected to other people. That's what's sacred."

While some interviewees used scientific analogies about sacred "energy," even more referred to alternative health practices for credence. Many of the people with whom I spoke knew of or had been involved in what is called "energy work," where a practitioner tries to "realign" the body's inherent vital powers. This was a common phenomenon among my SBNR interviewees, not just among the "nones" but also among respondents affiliated with organized religion. A pastor in a mainstream church went to considerable lengths to get trained in one such technique, known as "reiki." She often used this technique during pastoral visits with hospital patients. She explained it to me by saying confidently: "We know that everything is made up of energy." Another pastor was diagnosed with cancer. She assured her congregation that she was frequently practicing reiki on herself to harness her body's healing powers. A Catholic sister I visited worshipped Jesus and prayed to God four times a day in the traditional "liturgy of the hours" along with her fellow nuns in the convent. But she was also a "reiki master," doing "energy work" on nuns and laypersons. During the sessions, she assured her clients that "The Universe" was working in them and that they already had all the healing power they needed inside.

Many interviewees also explained that this force was something with which they, ultimately, were identical. The last statement from the Episcopal meditation group (i.e., "We are all God") verged in that direction, although they frankly admitted that some visitors to their group objected to it. Outside of organized religion, however, I often found people who enthusiastically embraced this view. Millennial Alexandra Heim, whose Christian Science father exposed her to many religions, used the idea of "universe" when asked about God. But unlike some earlier interviewees we met, she saw herself coterminous with it. "I think of it as a universe, as an orchestrator in my own head...drawing things to myself.... We're part of this collective oneness. There's not [a] separate conscious being that's separate from us.... There is this intelligence that you can get inside your own brain." We will explore this further in the next chapter on Human Nature.

Pantheism and Gnosticism

Given the critiques I had heard of "New Age" philosophy, I had expected to find many who embraced "pantheism." In simple terms, pantheism is often thought of as a form of nature worship and/or a philosophy where the earth is divine or sacred. In fact, pantheism is a form of monism, but not all monism is necessarily pantheistic. Like monism, pantheism proposes that all is one, but those who hold it often focus more attention on the natural world and its sacred quality. The popular stereotype of the "tree hugger" is a short-hand way to group those who find their spirituality primarily in nature. Pantheism and panentheism are not the same thing since the latter term implies a divine reality greater than the material world, although encompassing it. We became introduced to the theme of nature spirituality in a previous chapter, and it is a common stereotype of New Age spirituality. But few of my interviewees were actually nature worshippers. Although I found many interviewees who felt "more spiritual" in nature—particularly those who lived in the West—I found few who actually deified nature itself. Even Millennial Justin Cooper, who earlier proposed his "Green Man" theology, actually saw a power beyond nature itself. He explained it this way:

> I kind of feel like my body is more comfortable in nature. So I tend to the Green Man....Have you ever seen "The Lord of the Rings"?...The trees would walk and talk....That is kind of like what the Green Man was....[The] Green Man was over them in character. But...he actually took care of the earth. It was not like Mother Nature or anything. It was the Man....If there was a plant dying all he would have to do is touch it and it would stay healthy for years and years. And that's pretty much what I started to realize. I don't need to start surrounding myself [with] Bibles and stuff, even though that's what society wants me to. I feel more happy, I feel more closer to everything when I am out in nature....When I am out in the middle of the woods I can actually feel...the presence in my body....I am like the Green Man.

I found some interviewees who edged closer to pantheism among those who practiced variations of shamanism, Wicca, magic, and/or efforts to harness natural powers to guide or effect change. Some of these spoke of their "earth-based spirituality." Margie Mason, the former Christian conservative with Canadian Ojibwa roots, was one of the few who frankly said her spirituality was "pantheist." While she did not worship nature, she saw a male and female principle in all of nature which disclosed a likeness in the spiritual realm. She said:

[In] a lot of earth-based spirituality, there's a balance between a patriarchal, a male aspect and a female aspect....It was just a glorious expansion of understanding to understand the Mother Goddess....connecting fully with the Mother aspect allowed me an understanding of my own potential divinity, and also to be able to relax that image of God....Through that connection I came to understand a male aspect of God that fits a lot better for my life as well....I would define my spirituality as...pantheist: God in everything, everything in God....I am very comfortable with the earth-based conception of Spirit, which is that understanding [of] a myriad of Gods and Goddesses and animal forms....Not that God has necessarily ten thousand forms, but rather each gives us a further understanding of the nature of Creator....We understand that unity of all of those things, most of all as God and Goddess who...are material, are matter and spirits. The masculine, feminine, all the things that are apparently [in] opposition in creation are in fact not a duality, but are joined and, for a lot of it, the metaphor is sexual congress.

Apart from the popular idea that SBNRs are mostly pantheist, some observers also assume that SBNRs might fall into the philosophy known as Gnosticism. Gnosticism proposes that there is "gnosis," or secret knowledge, which is only revealed to the adept by others already so initiated. This hidden knowledge is crucial, for it is the sole way to save oneself from the degraded natural world. In this philosophy, the natural world is seen as a prison rather than the home of the sacred. Some versions of Gnosticism understand an actual divine dimension, from which emanations devolve downward, creating spirits with less and less divine qualities. Humans come at the end of this devolution, but are able also to rise up through gnosis. Gnosticism has deep roots in history and there have been many variations of it, even within Western religion itself. But it is not a philosophy inherent to the Abrahamic traditions, for their tendency is to focus on divine revelation which is available to all who seek it.

It is not surprising that I found few actual "Gnostics," among my interviewees because the SBNR ethos is a distinctly American brand of spirituality, emphasizing such values as democracy, equality, inclusivity, progress, and freedom. But some interviewees specifically tried to include Gnostic elements within their monistic understanding of the divine. James Wolfe told me: "I do think that there is a hierarchy of souls from the lowest going all the way up to God and some of those may be more personal than God itself. We all make up God."

Michael Blade is a Baby Boomer and almost archetypal spiritual "explorer." He explained how he had experimented with much traditional and alternative spirituality, including paganism, Wicca, and various forms of Christian orthodoxy and heterodoxy. He framed his Gnostic perspective like this:

> I don't view God as this sort of monolithic Father, Son, Holy Spirit concept but a culmination of an infinite number. . . . I would say the further you go away from humanity—if you look at God as sort of a trickledown effect, and I look at God as sort of an emanationist and a series of emanations—the further you go, you remove yourself from humanity, the less like humans God is. So you are using human language to define something that is not human like. . . . My concept of God would be that the further away from humanity you go the less like us God is.

Michael used the metaphor of a wheel to emphasize what he saw as the huge distance between conservative and mystical strains of religion.

> I kind of look at it like there are spokes in a wheel. On the outside where the spokes touch the tire you have . . . [the] more rigid, dogmatic, fundamentalist type belief systems. But as you [get] closer inward you get the more mystical strains of Islam, of Judaism, of Christianity, of Hinduism and all sorts of isms and religions. And as you look at the mystics, they are very close to one another no matter what their dogmas. And so that's been my focus, tapping into what are the similarities versus what are the differences.

Other interviewees, similar to Alexandra, moved to a fluidity in all references to the sacred, blending masculine, feminine, and impersonal. In this, Silent Generation and Baby Boomer interviewees differed from younger cohorts. Most Gen Xer and especially Millennial interviewees I met had less memories of oppressive male imagery for God and seemed less concerned with it than older interviewees. It is possible that for these younger interviewees, the stereotype of the demanding male God was diminished in religion by the time they experienced it, or they had less religious upbringing in which to hear it.

In summary, the interviewees were not satisfied to simply clothe God in a more contemporary wardrobe, making the divine more feminine, more accessible, nicer, with less wrath and more love. While male imagery was often their jumping-off point, many went on to abandon all personal references to God. As a result, out went concomitant features like individualized care, intervention, responsiveness to prayer, and so on. Most felt that it was more correct, contemporary, and even more mature to give up the idea of the God they identified with Western religions (i.e., one who creates, controls, intervenes, judges, responds, and is personally involved).

But for some this was not an entirely cold "Ultimate Reality." A few interviewees found it hard to give up the comforting images of a God who guided and cared personally for them. Some wanted to have it both ways, getting guidance but not unwanted attention. Thus a variety of adjustments were made to their image of the sacred. One common result was a kind of "plug-in God," like a power-strip constantly generating energy, ready to be accessed at any time. Another variation was to apply a human growth perspective. This meant that as humans become more "conscious," God would be swept up in the evolution and awaken. Most interviewees, however, voiced some form of "monism," where "all is one"—whether that be energy, consciousness, or some other form. Within this framework, the individual's goal would be to unite with this larger reality, whether that be only resident in the world (a "materialistic monism"), or of some ontologically higher reality. In the view of many interviewees, this Ultimate Reality—whether it was simply material or also transcendent—was neither aware of nor involved in individual human lives.

6

Human Nature

WHILE MY INTERVIEWEES may have labored a bit to come up with their definitions of the "sacred," I expected them to eagerly address the topic of human nature. After all, they have first-hand experience. Yet even though we are each personally involved in the topic, human nature is more difficult to define than it seems. Before hearing from the interviewees, we need to briefly consider the extent of this significant subject, because when we think about what it means to be human, many questions immediately arise. For instance, what is the "self"? Is it some fixed entity or a fluid, changing phenomenon, even illusory? Is it something to enhance and firm up, or, conversely, something to minimize or even eliminate? Is there some ideal standard or external referent by which we measure and/or pattern ourselves? Are we prone to "messing up" or is human nature essentially good?

Another important facet is the issue of freedom. To what extent is human nature malleable and can be changed? How much do we shape our own situation and how much affects us without our consent, intention, or even knowledge? In addition, even if we can desire or pursue certain ends for ourselves, how much are we able to act without hindrance to bring these about? And if we are pre-determined, what of this is internal (nature) and what is external (nurture)? Thus, the debate between "free will" and "determinism" underlies much of the study of human nature. When we consider human nature, the debate often takes place between two poles. On one hand, we celebrate the potentiality of human nature and wonder how we can enhance that. But, at the same time, we puzzle over and often lament the way we can be our own worst enemies.

What Does Religion Say?

Because my interviewees tend to draw from existing ideas, whether or not they are aware of that, it is helpful to overview what religious traditions say on this important topic. Indeed, the pervasiveness and inevitability of these questions is one reason why religion has long been such an important part of human culture. Religion observes the human condition, hypothesizes about it, notices problems, diagnoses them, and proposes remedies. While the social sciences may also do these things, religion is different in that it does all this with reference to some transcendent "other" which puts these issues into a larger perspective than just our individual lives, social structures, and preferences.

It is important to realize that most of the major historic religions note something is out of order for us humans. And in spite of the internal diversity within each particular religion, each religion nevertheless has a core theme about the human condition. Because the religions of Asia are attractive to many SBNRs, it is important to consider them. Although Hinduism is diverse, there is agreement in seeing ignorance as the core problem. This does not simply mean a lack of education but a much more fundamental problem. For it is claimed that humans are ignorant of the illusory and ephemeral nature of all reality. This ignorance is what causes suffering. To solve this, Hinduism teaches that one must give up a personal identification with the human, phenomenal self and instead seek union with the ultimate, a state which has been obscured by spiritual ignorance.

Buddhism posits that suffering is the core problem but goes further. In order to be liberated from the problem, one must realize there is no unchanging, essential or real "self" at all. Personal existence itself is an illusion. Without a self, there is no suffering. Confucianism takes a different approach. It sees societal disorder as the core problem, focusing its attentions on human duty. Elevating self over against the group would be wrong. Taoism also sees disorder in human society, but teaches we must conform more to nature. These Eastern traditions, at least as understood by Westerners,[1] are generally more monistic, pantheistic, or at least less theistic than Western religions. Understanding one's connection with the Ultimate is important in the East, but it is best achieved by transcending, not enhancing, the solitary self. It seems, then, that elevating the self would be anathema in these religions.

The three Abrahamic traditions, Judaism, Christianity, and Islam take a different approach. Since they are profoundly theistic, a strong God-focus sets the tone for any discussion of human nature. All teach that God created humans—and created them good. Thus God is the ultimate source of human personhood. This reality alone gives humans their value, dignity, integrity, and destiny. Thus the ideal and standard for human nature is not self-chosen, but set by its creator. Most important, God means for humans to be in relationship with the Divine Self and each other. But humans and God, although connected through divine action and intention, are distinct from each other. According to these religions, here is where the core problem lies. Our failure to recognize the difference between God and humans—and the concomitant failure to orient ourselves accordingly—constitutes a major source of alienation and lack of abundant life.

For these traditions, there is no need to divest oneself of the "self," but only to reorient it. According to Judaism, human nature has the ability to turn toward or away from God, to choose good or evil. It is the divine Law which guides the path and makes it straight. In Christianity, too, the problem is one of positioning or alignment. Is one faced toward or away from one's Maker? Is one alienated or reconciled? The unfortunate fact is that humans tend to disregard their intended God-orientation, even though human well-being consists in this. So God's grace, best exemplified in Jesus the Christ, makes restoration possible. In Islam, humans are out of order when they are not submitted to God. They are capable of this, but need to profess and recognize it.

What Do the "Spiritual but not Religious" Say?

These diagnoses of and solutions for the human condition represent well-trod, although different, paths. It is hard to avoid some of these traditional schemas, since they have long track-records of dealing with the inevitable questions that arise from being human. Even so, my interviewees generally shun the diagnoses and solutions laid out by religion. Most see religious beliefs as externally imposed standards, even damaging or antithetical to one's own best interests. Yet clearly my interviewees are intimately concerned with the same questions about the human condition as are religions. In fact, many of their spiritual practices involve programs to improve their lives, live abundantly, help them aspire to an optimum condition, promote wellness and holism, and deal with the inevitable difficulties all humans face. The sticking point, however, as we will see, is that without an external referent or tradition, the main measure available to gauge success is the ephemeral "personal well-being."

When we discussed their views on human nature, I did not ask my interviewees for a philosophical disquisition on the topic. Instead, in keeping with the informal approach of qualitative research, we focused on lived reality rather than disconnected theories. I also avoided theological terminology or framing questions in religious ways. Instead, I asked them open-endedly for their views on human nature, assuming that many of the logical issues would be raised. The assumption held true because, although not everyone raised each vital question, in the aggregate many of the important issues were addressed.

My interviewees were willing to speculate about the extent and causes of human problems, how free or determined we are, and the inherent state of humankind. But in doing so, they did not look to an external standard, ideal, or authority figure for any of this. True to the shift in "locus of authority" which we identified earlier, almost all of them felt it was their own determinations that had the final word. And almost all of them agreed that well-being, comfort, or happiness was the standard by which to measure. In today's world, looking inward for answers seems like common sense.

One reason for this is that we live in the midst of "the triumph of the therapeutic."[2] According to incisive observer, Philip Rieff, our culture has produced "Psychological Man" who takes his or her own inner state as determinative rather than also looking outward toward certain agreed-upon authoritative or society-wide standards. In this milieu, "self-fulfillment" becomes one's main organizing principle rather than age-old values such as such as obedience, sacrifice, or duty. As we will see, many of my interviewees tried to restrict their comments and especially their evaluations to their own situations and selves. A large majority of them stepped back when it came to answering many of these questions in a more global way. They indicated that each person must decide such things for him or herself and that no one should presume to judge another or set up a standard.

Humans Are Inherently Good

The one thing nearly everyone said—the one thing they most often started their comments with—is that human nature is inherently good. Even without specifically articulating it, this seemed a veiled reaction to their impression that Christianity, and perhaps other religions, deem humans inherently "depraved." In opposition to this, many said that each human possesses some inner core that was invincibly positive. This pair of assertions was so universal among my interviewees that it seemed to represent another aspect of the common rhetoric.

Susan Cashman, church-going Silent Generation "seeker," put it this way: "I think we're born all good in terms of spirit." Joyce Moffatt, after moving from conservative Christian to agnostic, reflected: "I think that people have incredible potential [for] unbelievable good. I think that the little child is born in goodness." A Baby Boomer man said: "I believe in essential goodness.... Basically we're very good. We want good for ourselves and others." A woman about the same age posited, "We are good and doing wrong is out of character." Another woman from this cohort reiterated this theme: "I think people are essentially good. Each one of us has a nugget of basic goodness."

Younger generations did not depart from this primary assertion. In fact, it was striking how many across the age cohorts used very similar words. One Millennial man said, "I feel like every person is born pure and innocent, good all the way around." Lisette Marshall, the Gen X "casual" with no religious background who tried for a while to be a mainline Protestant, said, "I think people are good at their core." In spite of early difficulties in her life, she said she held onto this assertion "stubbornly," saying: "I think people are basically good. Even though I've had a lot of evidence to the contrary!"

Sometimes, however, this assertion was more of a hope or a decision, rather than an evidence-based observation. One Millennial woman said: "I think we are good. I don't think we're evil. I hope not." Another Millennial man stressed this as a decision: "I think we are essentially good, because that is what I want to think." And even when one Gen X man wavered, he returned to this assertion of some essential goodness: "I think [people] are essentially good at their core. I wouldn't necessarily want to say pure and some of those other words. Well, maybe at the core."

But what does this essential goodness look like? How would we recognize it? Although many did not tackle this issue, relying instead on simply affirming this nearly programmatic assertion, some interviewees did give it more content. For a few, it was primarily about relating to others. Shelly Trump said it was "the ability to love." Some equated it with being able to see the goodness in others. Several mentioned compassion, as did Rebecca

Henderson, the Millennial interviewee who was studying Buddhism. She affirmed that our basic nature is "compassion and not aggression." Baby Boomer "casual" Mick Sharp said optimistically, "Most of the time when you need something, someone will help you." Jack Campbell, the Buddhist-Methodist who saw Jesus in his meditation, saw it as a two-way street. Once the self is served, generosity naturally flows: "Basically we're very good. We want good for ourselves and others and we wouldn't limit it to ourselves if we had enough.... Some people don't have enough, but most of us Americans do. If you recognize it, then we tend to be very generous and loving."

But many more interviewees who tried to describe human "goodness" saw it not as reaching out to others, but essentially in service to the self. These comments show the influence of the "therapeutic" character of our age. Deborah Wright, "seeker" from the Silent Generation, saw it as having "a strong sense of your own self-interest." Several saw it as primarily inner peace or an internal state of harmony and well-being. Susan Heinz, Baby Boomer spiritual "explorer," used "happiness" as the standard. Our inherent goodness is best served, she said, when we choose "the path that makes us happiest, the path that makes us vibrate the highest." The idea of "vibrating"—something I heard more than once—referred to the sacred as the "ultimate energy source," as we saw in the previous chapter. She indicated that when one is happy, one is in tune with one's source.

"Casual" Jennifer Babcock, the Gen Xer whose widowed mother gave her no religious exposure at all, asserted that this state of well-being is always latent throughout life. She said: "When I'm born I'm more like my true self, and I move away from it and then I move back into it.... I'm...more aligned and more integrated and more pleasant and at peace in the beginning and the ends of my life. I think that everyone is like that.... I think that we're all good people." A Millennial man also defined the inner goodness psychologically, but this time as self-approval, "I think deep down everyone wants to feel good about themselves." The idea of self-esteem as the highest human value—very common in popular psychology and spirituality—can be heard behind this comment. Another Millennial man, influenced by Buddhism, understood the essential goodness as individuals being "awake" to their pristine internal state. He said: "I believe in basic goodness...that is human nature. That is that awake spark, that is within each of us, that we just need to remember that it's there.... We are inherently awake."

Religion Does Not Teach Inherent Goodness

Over the course of these conversations, it became clear that underlying many comments about essential goodness was an assumption—and stance against—what many interviewees perceived as a traditional Western religious view. In the next chapter we will more thoroughly examine SBNRs attitudes toward religion in general, but a key aspect of their objection is the idea that certain religious teachings are off-base. In other words, this contention was more than an objection to religion for ethical or personal injury reasons. Instead, it added an often unrecognized theological element to the rhetorical strategy, implicit in the SBNR ethos, of detraditioning and separating spirituality from religion.

This is especially striking in relation to interviewees' insistence on humanity's inherent goodness. Indeed, many understood Christianity in particular to teach that humans are inherently bad, created that way and, what's worse, eternally condemned for it. James Wolfe alluded to this as he affirmed inherent goodness. Although he wanted to concede that good people sometimes do "evil things," he immediately countered this by saying: "Does that mean their soul is doomed? I don't think so. The soul itself can never be doomed."

These oppositional stances came from different angles but showed a consistent underlying argument which was also deeply "therapeutic." The assumption was that organized religion had led people astray, teaching them to doubt their own inherent goodness, go against their own self-interest, disturb their latent internal harmony, distrust their "own truth" and feel condemned for their problematic behavior. Deborah Wright insisted that Christianity teaches one must always sacrifice oneself for others. She countered this vehemently, "I think there is nothing wrong with having a strong sense of your own self-interest, but I do think it should not be at the expense of other people." Then she added with much emotion, "Self-sacrifice I don't believe in." Ian Handy, the Millennial man whose "missionary brat" father taught him to critique sermons, contended that religion teaches the essential selfishness of human beings. He purposely opposed this, saying: "I don't think that selfishness is part of being human. I think generosity is more a part of what it means to be human."

Carole Bradford is the Silent Generation religious "dissenter" who was also a determined seeker until giving up in frustration. She claimed she had moved away from her Christian roots and toward a more Eastern view when she decided humans were inherently good. Although she was not practicing any religion when I met her, she had been influenced by her search. She said, "I like the Buddhist approach...which is there is a basic assumption that human beings are good." She was not the first to juxtapose what they saw as a positive Buddhist approach versus what they claimed was a negative Christian approach. Gen Xer Bethany Storm said, "If I were to respond to human nature, what comes up for me is the Buddhist view of Buddha nature and that all beings are benevolent and that our view becomes obscured and that even the most brash, aggressive, violent actions underneath are benevolent intentions."

Whether this is an adequate rendering of Buddhist theology—and one could claim it is not—this interviewee clearly felt she was standing in opposition to Western, in particular Christian, views on human nature. In fact, it was almost universal among interviewees to counter the supposed negative Christian evaluation of humans with a supposed much more positive view from Eastern religion, particularly Buddhism. It did not matter—or they were not aware—that Asian religions do not have such a diametrically opposite view to Christianity when considering human wrong-doing.[3] Instead, this was the Americanization of a theme used for "rhetorical" purposes.

During the interviews, I tried to stay away from theological terms and certainly never used the words "original sin" in the interview. Even so, most interviewees assumed that Christianity teaches people are born evil. Although this is not an accurate rendering of the original sin tradition, I did not challenge their assumption. Instead, I observed how many, without any leading whatsoever, spontaneously inserted this assumption into our conversation. They did this in a number of ways, but the most obvious was by stressing the purity or innocence of newborns.

An especially interesting Baby Boomer was Babs Chapman. She had tried everything from Roman Catholicism to Unitarian Universalism. At each church, she would disagree with something the leadership said and would move on. Eventually she settled on Wicca as her spirituality. Even Wicca, though, ended up disappointing her since—ironically—she could not maintain any authority over the women she initiated into it. She put forth this psychological theme about inherent goodness but also the dangers of human control: "I've never seen a guilty baby. Guilt is man-made and it's used to control people."

Tonya Bond was a black woman I met in an alternative spiritual retreat center where she worked. She had been raised Anglican by her devout and very socially active parents. Nevertheless, she was now a priestess of an American style of African spirituality. She alluded to the popular idea that original sin means people are born evil, and purposely refuted it by saying: "Our human nature is that we are really born innocent." Darlene Schultz, a Midwestern Baby Boomer, was raised Roman Catholic. Although she did not attend church anymore, neither did she disavow her roots. Nevertheless, she addressed this contention more explicitly. "I don't know what I believe about the concept of original sin. I understand it, but I think that human beings are essentially born good." Even Matt Adler, the young man who had tried for years to be a devout Buddhist but eventually reconsidered Christianity, set himself in opposition. His time as a Buddhist, he said, gave him something different from what he thought were Christian teachings. "One thing I...let go of is identifying myself as a sinner.... [This] means that I am this person that is never going to make it. As if God's always there as a judgmental God. I'm always incomplete in some way." Instead, he said, "Now I think, 'I've stumbled.'"

Anne Heimlich, the spiritual "explorer" who we have heard from before, came at this same underlying assumption from a different direction. She felt the idea of humans as inherently good was in tension with externally imposed religious and cultural beliefs. This fit the therapeutic ethos, for the lodestar was internal and unique to each person. Although the "fundamental nature" of people is "basically good," she said, "It's hard to see because we get caught up in our belief structures....A lot of them that are out there are harmful because they aren't allowing people to find out what's true for them."

Not Only Good, but Divine

Some interviewees went beyond claiming the inherent goodness of human beings and claimed humans are perfect and even divine. In this theological assertion, they carried over the monistic understanding of divinity, seen in the previous chapter, by extending it to humans. Bruce Carter, Baby Boomer spiritual "explorer," linked this theme with the common refutation of original sin by saying that babies are "a perfect perfection of the creator when they are born." A woman from the same generation clearly drew upon this by saying: "We are all unique expressions of the oneness."

Becky Stryker, the Gen X woman who claimed to "channel" beings from other planets, said it most strongly: "'We're all divine....We're all masters....We're all perfect and all we have to do is remember that." To illustrate her contention that "we are God," she used the metaphor of a "power strip." She explained: "My inner guidance....would have to come from my divine self....I think of it as a power strip. My divine self is the power strip. There are individual lives plugged into that and the prongs are the higher power....So the divine self is that part of me that knows everything....God could not not be involved, because we are God." The image was unclear as to where the divine and the person began and ended, but it was reflective of other comments I received as people tried to explain how they were human in appearance and yet divine in essence.

Emily Orbach, the Gen X writer with no religious background, said similarly, "The notion that we're all God means that we all are microcosms of the macrocosm, that if I were attuned enough, I could connect with all the information in that universal body of intelligence, across time and space." David Kaplan, the Baby Boomer and health store owner, said simply, "Each soul is the essence of God, a ball of love." He tied together this theme with our earlier exploration of "consciousness" saying: "I'm an individualized unit in the body of God and the experiences that I get, God assimilates. God uses all of us souls to experience more and more of itself consciously."

I spoke many times with Gail Asher, a Baby Boomer woman who worked in the office of a very progressive mainline Protestant church in a mid-sized Western city. Her family had been devoutly Protestant, such that religion was "kind of the fiber of the family....They certainly relied on their faith in Jesus and the church," she said. In fact, Gail had been quite active at church, attended a Protestant college, and seriously considered the ministry. She insisted there had been no "dark side" to the religion of her youth. Yet now she freely admitted she had trouble accepting the theism of the congregants. She set herself apart from them by insisting, "I don't use the word God...I don't separate anything from the sacred." Sam Klein was a Silent Generation man active in that same congregation. He did use the word "God" but in a non-personal monistic way. Like Gail, he saw no separation between God and himself. He explained: "Its desire is for me to be conscious of it as myself. When I say myself, I'm talking about my essence, meaning that unique expression of my essence. My temporal self." This view was not restricted to those with Christian experience.

I spent a long time talking with Rachel Abramowitz, a Jewish woman who had received a holiday-only exposure to her religion as a child. She related to me that after a bout with cancer, which led her to explore many spiritual options, she decided to come back to Judaism. She was soon a leader at her synagogue, responsible for congregational management and training of youth. But Rachel was also an avid reiki practitioner with views that reflected that philosophy. When she described her view, she called it "panentheism." One definition for this theological term—which is sometimes used within religion—is that God is eternal, creator of, and greater than the universe, but interpenetrates or encompasses it. This woman, however, used the term much more monistically, demonstrating that the monistic theme, for many interviewees, extended over into their views of human nature. Rachel was aware that her "we are all God" interpretation was something to which her rabbi would object, but she affirmed it anyway: "I'm a panentheist. Everything is in God...God is in one unity. We are all God. I don't know that [my] rabbi would get that. It is not traditional Judaism."

Jack Campbell, the spiritual "explorer" who described his meditative experience of Jesus giving him permission to depart from his Christian background, said it another way: "I'm not different from what's out there. You breathe in with God, you breathe out with God. It's a connection to everything and I'm just part of it." Jennifer Babcock tried to explain how she and the larger force are one: "I have this feeling that I'm connected to it and that that connection...expresses itself through my mind. Like, my mind is a computer and that's the electricity....[The force] wouldn't have a mind." Finally, Millennial Alexandra Heim, whose Christian Science father exposed her to many religions, gave this intriguing image to illustrate her sense of divinity:

> It's like a story. [There's a] big non-physical space, existing as the cosmos...a blob....In this blob is all the existence of everything that's living and feeling. When someone is born, or when life is created...it's a vessel. There's a little bit of this blob that is pinched off and pours into this vessel, then we walk around in physical as part of this big blob that has been poured into this vessel. My whole theory that I've come up with about life is that love, in all its forms is our desire to reconnect ourselves with ourselves. I think it relates to the Native Americans or the Buddhist "we all are one," it's like that. So romantic love, caring love, friendship love, wanting to cuddle with somebody, wanting to connect with others [is]...trying to get back to that spirit, that energy, that blobness. When we die, it's the opposite of birth, it goes back to that blob and it may go back into a vessel, but when we are in the vessel we are not separate, we are all part of that one blob.

What about When Things Go "Wrong"?

Avoiding Value Judgments: No "Good" and "Bad"

Even if people are inherently good or even divine, many interviewees nevertheless admitted that things sometimes go "wrong." To deal with this, many took a common path by making a distinction between good people and their problematic behavior. One Silent Generation man who blended Buddhist, Christian, and alternative paths covered all his bases by saying: "I think of people as essentially good and that activities which are 'evil', i.e. harmful to themselves or others, are the result of their separation from God, or in Buddhist terms, behind unconsciousness and lost in cravings and aversion. I also believe that evil/sin is just losing our connection with the present, or God, the source."

Susan Cashman, the Silent Generation "seeker" who regularly supplements her church attendance with alternative spiritualities, said of human nature: "It's good stuff and when it's bad, it's not bad stuff, it's just not what was needed to hold that kind of space. The concept of sin and evil doesn't [apply], although I think of times when I have said that that person is terribly evil. I think that the behavior is evil." The idea of something being necessary to "hold a space" came up in several interviewees' comments. They seemed to be suggesting that people did not always behave in a way that would create optimum conditions for the universe, but that did not make them bad. This is one way interviewees struggled to categorize people's behavior without actually making moral evaluations of them.

In fact, it was clear that many struggled with the labels "good" and "bad." Without any agreed-upon standard, such as religion might impose, and purposely eschewing values they associated with religion, many interviewees were clearly in a quandary. A significant number of interviewees took the seemingly clear-cut path of disavowing "good" and "bad" altogether. Thus they did not just eliminate value judgments upon persons' inherent state but also refrained from labeling their questionable behavior as "bad." Gail Asher, the Baby Boomer woman who worked in a church office, showed the difficulty of this position, yet held to it anyway. Gail was clear that she did not want to label behavior. Nevertheless, she still tried to evaluate it: "It's not good, it's not bad. People just do things that are not always beneficial for everyone that they are with, so in that regard that could be defined as good or bad. My preference is to try to not put those definitions on people."

We met Barbara Axel previously. She is the Baby Boomer woman who leads shamanic workshops along with some participation in church. Barbara used the word God but did not see God as the creator of moral standards. Her view tended toward the monistic even while she kept some traditional terminology. Thus, she said, "Our creation of good and evil doesn't affect God and doesn't affect God's non-dualistic nature." Ron Richmond, the Silent Generation man raised in a large progressive mainline church, gave an example with the concept of selfishness. He insisted this label is an arbitrary social sanction, rather than an enduring moral standard. "The only selfishness is when I make a judgment about it or we get together as a society and make a law [about it]....There is only selfishness when we use words to make a judgment on the actions of somebody else."

Babs Chapman, the Baby Boomer who had tried many churches before committing to Wicca, clearly struggled between avoiding value judgments and yet wanting to set out demarcations. She said:

> We have that seed of perfection in us. It's like light and dark, up and down, I try to stay away from the good and bad concept, but the best way I know how to explain it is in this little magazine called *Highlights for Children*. They had the "Goofus" and "Gallant" [characters]. The Gallant guy had this little angel on his shoulder telling him what to do and the Goofus had this little devil on his shoulder. I think we have those opposing forces within us but it's up us to choose. Many people, because of my belief, think it is devil worship. In the Wicca faith there is no devil....A long time ago I committed myself to the light. I have no desire to study about negativity or demons or power over because what I teach in what I practice is power from within, not power over someone.

For some the problem was immaturity or lack of development, whether individually or societally. Margie Mason, the Canadian Baby Boomer of mixed Ojibwa and English parentage, said her "stance is that not that somebody is bad, but they haven't learned." Jason Van Buren, the Gen X student studying to be an interfaith chaplain, spoke about humans as creators and our need today to not be "stuck in our technological adolescence." In our progress from agrarian, to industrial, to technological, he said, we have "a very confused outlook." Thus, "rather than saying good, bad or evil, I would say we love creating but are very confused about how we do it." Dana Dove is a Baby Boomer woman from a strict Southern Baptist background, but now heavily involved in alternative spirituality. She went so far in avoiding value terms that she denied anything was wrong at all. "There isn't anything wrong. It's our illusion that something's wrong, even with the horror of the planet changing." Humans could go the way of the dinosaur, she said, and we, like them, would not be mourned. This attitude seemed to be a denial of the reality of evil but, at the same time, a sanguine acceptance of the consequences.

Becky Stryker, the channeller, emphasized trusting one's feelings. She, like many others, set an internal standard. Yet whether external or internal, this standard came without long-term implications. Thus she focused on the inevitability of the evolution of one's "soul" no matter how heinous one's behavior. Like many others, she also strenuously avoided value judgments. Even though she spoke of what "you are supposed to do," she made this standard wholly internal, with each person their own arbiter. "I don't think that doing good in the human sense evolves your soul. I think that it means doing what you feel you're supposed to do. Because what someone else might say is good, might not be what I am supposed to do. . . . If someone thinks they are right, then they are."

In our "lawic" society, she said, there are standards, but they have no inherent value. Obeying or not is a pragmatic choice. And although breaking the law has consequences, she refused to put a value judgment on what society has declared bad behavior. "I'm not going to say it's wrong for someone to kill someone. They choose to do it. It's not going to serve their soul's evolution. It's not going to put them on the fast track. . . . but they can get there no matter how many detours they're going to take." This complex quote plays on several themes: free choice, avoiding value judgments, American pragmatism, and the ultimacy of one's personal evaluation of one's own behavior. Her view on the inevitable progress of the soul shows an underlying rejection of any kind of eternal condemnation, even as the result of human choice.

Shelly Trump added a measure of intentionality to this explanation, indicating that sometimes difficult situations were "meant to be." Thus she said: "We are all here to have unique experiences. I think we're born with the ability to love and things happen. Our experiences shape us and some end up on a path that is destructive to them and others. Is that evil? I don't like to think of it that way." Quite a few other interviewees tried to wring meaning out of life's problems by declaring them necessary for one's evolution, chosen before birth, and/or painful but advantageous learning experiences. This was another way they avoided calling the problems or the people "bad."

Some of these interviewees were on the more radical end of a very common strategy. While the larger percentage of interviewees did in fact make moral judgments, almost all leaned hard toward the positive end. While these few tried to scrupulously avoid all labeling of "good" and "bad," most allowed for a good evaluation, but sought for extenuating circumstances to avoid a "bad" evaluation.

Determinism and Free Will

Quite a number of interviewees did more than simply assert that people are inherently good even if they unfortunately do less-than-optimum things. They wanted to go further, and took several theological, ethical, or philosophical paths in this effort. Most people tried out either environmental, physiological, or "free will" arguments, and some chose a combination. The most common contention was that a bad environment regrettably pushes good people in the "wrong" direction, something for which they might suffer and even be punished by society, but for which they should not be held morally responsible. In many ways this rehashes the traditional theological argument within Christianity about whether sin is inherited, whether guilt is attached to it, and whether there are inevitable consequences.

Even though interviewees often implicitly refuted the idea of "original sin," ironically many still made a similar move in their efforts at alternative explanations. The idea of "original sin" has been presented in various ways, but one common contemporary theological explanation is that people—although created good—are born into a distorted or "fallen" world and cannot help but be affected by it even without, or before, being consciously complicit. My interviewees often took a similar path. Although leaning heavily on psychological explanations, they nevertheless saw bad behavior as something transmitted down through the generations, whether poor child rearing, deprivation, or something environmental, perhaps equivalent to "poor soil." Joyce Moffatt, the Silent Generation woman who had moved from fundamentalist Christian to agnostic, said, "I think it is the adults in their lives that warp the child and then in the long run people do stuff…[causing] interpersonal pain." Even Carole Bradford, the Silent Generation seeker who had finally given up the search, took a similar approach: "I like the Buddhist approach to psychotherapy which is, there is a basic assumption that human beings are good and the goal of therapy is to clear away the obstacles to that being expressed. I feel that it's possible and very hard to overcome things that have been coming down through the generations."

The idea of deprivation warping a person was a common theme. Jack Campbell, the meditator who had a vision of Jesus, speculated that "if you're not safe or if you don't have your basic needs met then you're so busy trying to make yourself safe—then you don't have a lot of opportunity." Jenny Buchan, the Gen X spiritual "explorer" raised by a Wiccan mother and "holiday Christian" grandparents, felt that bad circumstances could deeply change a person. "That energy, evil or whatever it is, just kind of changes them completely. I mean, makes them something that they are not. I think it's a very powerful thing."

Connie Buchholz used incarcerated individuals as an example. "My husband works in a prison for the mentally ill. He comes home with these stories and how they were abused in the past. It's no wonder that they lost their perspective." Beverly Bosch, from the same generation, took the same approach:

> I don't think anyone—even people sitting on death row—I don't think that they meant to do some of the things that they did. I think some people react out of feelings, they re-act. If they grow up with violence, they're going to catch themselves being violent. Does that make them inherently evil? A bad person? It makes them toxic to society, to a board of people. But you know, I think every baby comes into the world with a clean slate.

Tony Ricci, the Gen X former East Coast altar boy, said: "I guess human nature is this nurture thing, and our environment has a huge, huge way of influencing who we are and how we are in the world. But I think that we come in with pure innocence and so it's very important how people are parented and brought up and how they kind of turn out." Millennial Brendan Potter stressed the lack-of-control aspect but did not avoid naming situations—although not people—as "evil." He said, "Maybe we all start pure and innocent but in a really bad situation that we couldn't control, we learned evil, and we learned to find joy from evil."

Jon Farmer, a Gen X "dissenter" we have already heard from, added the element of group influence:

> I think that we learn hate and fear at a very young age. I also think that we learn moral responsibility the same way. I think that what

starts as curiosity in children can quickly become cruelty if not corrected. I think most people are fine as individuals but have the potential to become thoughtless droning automatons when in the presence of large groups. We are programmed to want to be connected to something larger than ourselves because we are social animals. I think that this need makes people lose their sense of rational thought at times. I know I have been subject to that.

Therefore, many of these answers were similar to one interpretation of "original sin," that although humans are created good, we are born into a "fallen" or warped world and cannot help but be affected by it.

Drawing from Science

Although most interviewees mentioned the environmental issue, some added an element of brain chemistry, genetics, or other physiological abnormalities—things over which a human might have little control—as a way to account for problematic behavior. So, ironically, in a culture that celebrates freedom—and something the SBNR ethos normally affirms—many of my interviewees were fairly deterministic about human nature. Susan Cashman thought this might happen in the womb: "I think that there can be anomalies in the birth process where things are missing which can make people [not] be as cooperative with themselves and the world." James Wolfe speculated: "Something got in their system that caused them to do something bad. A poison of some kind that has poisoned their mind."

Several Gen X women gave the most full-orbed array of uncontrollable extenuating circumstances. Perhaps this should not be surprising, given that they have grown up during a psychological age, when more attention is being paid to the deep-seated, pervasive effects of deprivation and trauma. One said: "I think external circumstances shape people into something, sometimes, that they might not want to be. But I guess that gets into the whole issue of mental challenges, things like that, that you can't necessarily help."

Lisette Marshall, who still believed in essential human goodness in spite of her difficult childhood, tried to cover many bases: "You might be abused. You might be born into major deprivation that brings out the worst in you—things your parents do to you that are horrible. I mean, any number of things can happen that can just ruin a human being....I believe in a mix of environment and genetics. I believe that people have innate, inherited characteristics that they are born with, that they inherit from their parents, and the environment works on that."

Jennifer Babcock agreed that the problem was largely physiological. "I think that along the way what can happen is…when either there is something wrong with your brain or you learn something differently. Or…something really traumatic happens to you.…I think things change along the way and I think it's mostly that's a physical world issue." She similarly struggled with labeling even a murderer as "bad," adding: "I think that we're all good people. I hate to say good but I hate to, like, label.…Even, like, people that have murdered people. I just feel like that's something wrong with their brain, you know?"

She went further than others, for her difficulty with labeling went so far as to make her suggest maybe there was some impersonal cosmic scheme that justified the violence. If it isn't bad brain chemistry, she postulated: "[Maybe] there's some weird divine order and they needed to get rid of some part of the population. I don't know! (laughs) I mean, if you look at it from a science point of view, it could be like that, you know, there's some excess in some area."

Tammy Kalini was the only woman out of this younger group who tentatively ventured a moral evaluation: "I have this assumption that people are good in a basic sort of way. But I hate even saying that because of the vast amounts of pain and suffering going on because of people making choices to create it. I can find compassion. I can always see that there is a cause that preceded that condition. That makes [sense] to me. If this dad is beating his kid, it makes sense that he was beaten as a kid. But I'm not okay with that. I always hold that in a great deal of feistiness and anger because I want it to be right." The idea of "holding" here was a somewhat common one among my interviewees. It seemed to allow them to evaluate something from their own perspective, without extending the evaluation beyond the personal.

Perhaps because Baby Boomers were raised prior to the explosion of psychological explanations, a few more of these interviewees skated closer to making a moral evaluation. One rural Midwestern male interviewee who had a hard, working-class life and found alternative spiritualities a welcome respite, said, "I think there are some people that get so chemically imbalanced that they could be termed evil." Mick Sharp tried to stay with the external damage argument, but indicated some few might inherently be defective: "I think that most people are good and start out that way. I think the ones that aren't good, probably had circumstances that convinced them to go another way. Maybe a bad seed here and there, but I think most people are good." The "bad seed" argument ensconced in the more positive framework reminded me of the same concept put forth in the Big Book of Alcoholics Anonymous. For there it says that nearly anyone who wants to change can do it, except for those unfortunate few who are "constitutionally unable to be honest with themselves."[4]

Wanda French was a Baby Boomer and Canadian who was running a rural animal shelter when I met her. She spoke at length on this theme. She tried to advance the nonjudgmental argument but also subverted it, even though she allowed for mental illness and environment as extenuating circumstances. This lengthy quote shows her struggle. She starts with the typical environmental and mental illness suppositions, but then suddenly veers off in a different direction, comparing some people to "bad dogs," "biters."

> There certainly are bad people and you get that "eek" sense. And some of them, like Charles Manson—but you wonder if that's mentalism. I think that people are inherently good—I hope. But you're back to nature versus nurture. It goes back to how people were raised. You really can't judge people until you understand fully. When that Reverend Wright thing blew up, Michael Moore was the smartest person I ever heard on TV. And when Larry King asked him what he thought he said, 'You're asking me? I'm a white guy.' That says it all right there. How would you know unless you've been black, been oppressed. You don't know why he's got a hate on. So I say, you've gotta walk a mile in people's shoes before you judge people and I don't think most people are bad. But some are. There are bad dogs too. No matter how well they were raised, they're biters. There's something lacking in them and it's the same with people. Dog trainers fight all the time about nature versus nurture. [They say] 'You can take any dog and make them a good dog.' I'm sorry, no you can't. There are dogs you will never be able to trust.... Something didn't come out in the genetic math. There's not going to be any redemption there. Some of them are just plain bad.

Brendan Potter, a spiritual "casual," was the only Millennial man to venture out into negative territory with his comment, mixing a moral evaluation with extenuating, uncontrollable circumstances: "I think that there are bad people out there but they are products of their environment and they are evil because they have been taught to be evil and that evil feels good. I think everybody is born pure and becomes tainted." However, these people who made moral judgments on the negative side were very unusual among my interviewees.

Even so, all these arguments worked to color the interviewees' earlier adamant assertions that people are inherently good. They seemed to struggle with the same issues that have plagued world religions, in particular Christianity. For there the debate over how much sin pervades human nature, how free we are to avoid this under our own power, and how much we are responsible for our inherited condition have been topics of discussion for hundreds of years.

It Is Their Choice

While many interviewees focused on problems over which humans have little or no control, as a way to explain problematic behavior, a few saw more freedom. Still avoiding moral judgment, many of these interviewees argued that personal choice was the key issue. Positing that although people may operate under certain environmental or physiological handicaps, nevertheless, everyone is free enough to choose their "best" behavior. They thus claimed that humans had the free ability to choose between problematic and life-enhancing behavior, even as they avoided labeling any of it good or bad. This is part of the repertoire of Western arguments about problem behavior. It is reminiscent of the Pelagian view (from Pelagius, a contemporary of St. Augustine) which claims each person operates from a neutral place, having the free will to choose good or bad behavior. In this scenario, external circumstances do not weaken one's ability to freely act and divine grace is not necessary to propel right choice.

Baby Boomer "seeker" Helen Exline blended reiki, alternative spirituality, and some church attendance. She said about choice: "I think that humans are potential. The potential manifests itself within a certain set of circumstances in which all of us are born. In that sense we come into a world that is very difficult, but I believe that we have ongoing choices of responses. I would not say humans are inherently selfish or loving; I would say they have choices."

Babs Chapman, who had become Wiccan after trying out many churches, drew upon prior theological understandings acquired from her forays into organized religion. She refers to a Creator and uses "good-ness," yet you can also see her mixing in her current understandings as well. Thus the "Creator" is more "creative force" rather than personal God, she chooses "light" and "dark" more than "good" and "evil." Explaining her earlier mention of "Goofus" and "Gallant," she said:

> The Gallant guy had this little angel on his shoulder telling him what to do and the Goofus had this little devil on his shoulder. I think we have those opposing forces within us, but it's up us to choose....I think that 98% of the people do practice that goodness, but that is [not] so easy. By the time children get to kindergarten, kids learn to distinguish between different things. They learn to be self-ish; they learn to throw temper tantrums to get their way. Because of our culture—I can't speak for other cultures—but people get into lack and they don't trust the creator to provide. Years ago I heard the Quakers had a saying, "Pray while moving your feet." I can trust the creator to provide but I have to go and do my part. That's why we are co-creators with the creative force. Wasn't it Paul that said, 'I die daily'? You have to die to the negative part of you and this day I choose to walk with the light, to serve the light and to make wise choices.

Michael Blade is the Baby Boomer "explorer" who had experimented with much traditional and alternative spirituality, including paganism, Wicca, and various forms of Christian orthodoxy and heterodoxy. In his explana-tion, he tried to blend choice and determinism, indicating that persons choose what they let control them:

> We are condemned to be free, to use a Sartrien term....What that means is that we are free to choose our own determinism. If we decide that we want to be controlled by alcohol, we will be. If we want to be controlled by our spouse, we will be. If we want to be controlled by our church, we will be. If we want to be controlled by this concept of original sin and think that whatever we do is tainted by that, well then, that's gonna happen....I don't subscribe to any sort of strict determinist philosophy. Even when they make sense, I resist them because, if anything, I like the idea of being the master of my own destiny, even when it's not a reality.

Many others were less ironic than Michael about the reality of choice, yet expressed something similar but in a much stronger way. They insisted that people attract or draw things to themselves based on their thoughts, mindset, or inner disposition. Tonya Bond, the Baby Boomer who moved from Anglicanism to an African spirituality, combined the "alignment" idea with the theme that you draw things to yourself. She related that in college she experienced depression until she realized she had no power over anything but herself, "So it was an 'ah ha' moment when I decided to work on my internal experience." Common to many SBNRs I interviewed, she did this with a bodily focus. "I started cleansing, fasting, eliminating certain things from my diet." Out of this, and her experience in alternative spirituality, she came up with a theory about choice. She explained to me that "the universe" is simply "giving you what you are putting in, you know, what you're aligning yourself with.... You are experiencing...[the] result of what your ingredients are. I call that alignment.... So that is the kind of expression that I'm talking about as a result of your will, your intention."

Jane Ransom was a Baby Boomer with seminary training who had served as a pastor in a mainline denomination. When she found out she had some percentage of Native American heritage, however, she left Christianity and aligned herself instead with a form of native spirituality. She clearly rejected the deterministic argument in favor of free choice: "We still believe in free will. When they talk about gruesome murderers and then you discover that they were treated gruesomely, but then there are people who were abused who don't become killers."

Lisette Marshall, the Gen X "casual" who said she "stubbornly" held to the view that people are inherently good in spite of "a lot of evidence to the contrary," gave herself as an example of the power of choice, along with a smidgen of that uncontrollable factor "luck." Earlier she had told about parental abuse and neglect, alcohol and drug problems, and trauma. Thus, she said she understood that although people "start out good.... sometimes they encounter things like what happened to me that might cause them to go in a different direction." Yet even this was not totally deterministic. "I've chosen to go in a positive—but maybe someone could choose to go in a negative—[direction]." Then she reflected: "Well, I did go in a very negative direction with it for a while. I'm not really sure how that changed for me, but [I was] lucky."

A Gen X man added to this argument by stressing human weakness. "I believe we're good, but mostly because of our free will and possibly a desire in some people to wield that 'whatever' or their inability to recognize signs or feelings or things like that, they fall prey more to the more weak sides. They become weakened and they stray from being a good down-to-earth person, even if at the core they are a good person. Then they do the things that they do." Gen Xer Jenny Buchan allowed herself a moral judgment of a sort, but focused on choice: "The only hell that I believe in is here on earth.... There's always that hope of turning it around. If they choose, you know, they want to stay evil, then that's their choice."

Millennial Brendan Potter, who insisted that everyone is a product of their environment, nevertheless focused on choice. "I think that everyone has a chance to be good and pure and everyone has a chance to be evil and weak and I think there is [sic] times in your life when you can switch from one role to the next. I don't think that every human being is the same either." Kimberly Takahashi, the Millennial of Asian heritage who had almost no religious background, tried to stay optimistic and positive, but seemed less loath to make value judgments. Nevertheless, she relied, as these others, on choice: "People have good intentions and they believe what they are doing is right. But at the same time there are definitely people that know what they are doing is wrong...and still do it, but...I guess I'm optimistic that most people act on good intentions.... But...there are times when you know what you are doing probably isn't right."

A number of interviewees took the issue of choice further, positing that people draw to themselves what happens to them in life. Some attributed this dynamic to the fairly impersonal "Universe." Jack Acker was introduced earlier. This Baby Boomer, struggling to make a living, was trying hard to give himself "affirmations" about his impending monetary success and good health, but admitted it was not working. He took responsibility for it, though, by saying: "I'm also sending mixed messages to the universe.... Any time you send conflicting messages, you are going to get conflicting results."

Alexandra Heim was the Millennial "casual" who said her nominally Christian Science father had been "very, very dedicated to giving me a very diverse platter of [spiritual] choices, which I appreciate a lot." Although she felt drawn to paganism, she admitted she was not motivated enough to attend any kind of gatherings. Still, she was especially talkative on the issue of choice and agreed with the above theory. In her comments you also can see the implied opposition to views she associates with organized religion and a reluctance to make value judgments:

I don't believe that there is a good and bad or a bad river or a good river, or a heaven and a hell.... There's one river that you set forth. If you turn around and let it beat you up...that's your source of anger and hate.... It's okay to feel anger or hopelessness. But you can choose to feel better and you can choose to feel worse.... You make choices in your life.... I don't think you have to struggle through things and have a hard time with it. When you hold some- thing strongly in your mind and have positive associations with that thought then you will draw things to you, and I have many, many proofs on that. It's really a good system.... This is a very pagan belief. You have to have a strong, strong sense of responsibility for every situation that you are in.... You have ultimate control. A lot of people think they are victims of their situation, but you draw to yourself that which you are most like.

Then Alexandra reiterated what I heard from many interviewees, that is, your personal well-being—especially as judged by your feelings of happi- ness—is the standard upon which you should base your choices:

Ultimately, if you don't go into alignment with what your true self feels then you're going to feel some grossness, because you are going upstream and going against your own personal desires as a spiritual being. Some people get very good at paddling upstream and they spend their entire lives wondering why they are unhappy. That would be what people call being corrupted because you're turning against your own whatever.

Alluding again to the strictures of religion—or any organized group— which have the potential to go against one's own self-interests, she said:

I rely on my own intuition a lot.... I don't like people telling me what to believe or what to do to be in alignment. It would be like a witch saying, "You need to get a hound and boil it," or saying "You need to go to church on Sunday and pray just like this and this is how I pray." Sorry, I pray differently and you can't know what's inside me and what's in alignment for me. You're not in my head and I'm not in your head, so maybe you need to do this and I need to do this.... Alignment is positive feeling, not nega- tive, by definition. If you are feeling aligned and you're feeling like that's what is inspiring you, what makes your heart jump, then by golly do it.

A few interviewees took human choice even further. The ones who believed in past lives, reincarnation, and so on—a topic we will explore in the chapter on "after-life"—explained that we chose to be born into our particular situation because we have "lessons to learn" from it. They explained that although difficult things may happen to us, we have charge of how to respond or even use these experiences. Gen X writer Emily Orbach commented extensively on this. Playing upon themes we have seen earlier, you can see her understanding of the sacred as impersonal energy and vibration as a form of connection. Like many other interviewees, Emily posits that we attract the things that happen to us, which gives us a certain core responsibility for them. And, like so many, she strenuously avoids moral evaluations. She is somewhat different from many others by seeing the main choice being between "fear" and "love."

> I think it's impersonal... this intelligence responds to our individual vibration... we, as energy vibrations, attract conditions of like vibration—but not in a black-and-white, simplistic, cause-and-effect way.... What we attract will serve our spiritual path, if we consciously mine it for its spiritual instruction.... "Good" and 'bad" are manmade constructs.... All of it is consciousness, but of varying degrees/vibrations that depend generally on whether love or fear is the driver.

The Self and Its Problems

Given the clear emphasis on the "sacralization of the self," or "self spirituality," it was striking to find some interviewees who saw the self as the problem, not the solution. For some, it was human rationality that caused problems. Others saw the human ego in general as a handicap. Several considered the "unconscious" or "unawakened" self the real issue, and a few simply mentioned their own personal self-limiting problems.

Jeff Wurtzel, from the Silent Generation, had a "philosophical" attitude to what he saw as natural self-centeredness, and he avoided judging it. He said: "Most of the time, most of the people only think about the good of themselves. If they do good to you and you think that was really nice, they didn't mean that. Just like if they do something that you think is really nasty, they didn't mean that either. They just weren't focused on you. They are focused on themselves. That's a large number of people." Against this natural tendency, he put in a good word for the training that religion and spirituality provides. "People that are serious about living their religion, they take a different view than that and that's one of the main benefits of religion and spirituality is it gets people thinking about others besides themselves." Still, true to the widespread nonjudgmental ethos, he said about the first group: "They are doing the best that they can with what they've got at the time. I don't think it's negative. I don't think the ego is negative either. It's just part of what we are."

But some others were not so sanguine about it. Rachel Abramowitz, the Baby Boomer who blended Jewish practice with many alternative spiritualities, said: "I feel that we should be able to do what is right, but there are a number of things in our way.... I believe people basically want to be good and we are our own worst enemies. Who stands in my way? I do." Gail Asher, church secretary, attributed her views to Eastern religion. "My belief is that if people stepped away from their egos, they would be really good people. I'm sure a lot of that came from Buddhism, because they try to influence you to step away from the ego." Penny Watson, also a Baby Boomer, seemed rather pessimistic about human progress. This was unusual since a belief in positive human evolution is a fairly common tenet of the SBNR ethos. She said: "I think humans are mostly selfish, but most animals are. I like to think that people, through education or through greater understanding of the world around them, will try to make things better than they found them, but I don't think most people are that way."

Anne Heimlich likened the personal ego to a "little mind" which was cut off from or not recognizing the "bigger wisdom." The goal, then, was to overcome one's identification with this personal self.

Whenever I get really caught up in my thinking and not feeling so great, I stop and I recognize that I'm caught up in my little mind and I just get quiet and I orient that to a bigger wisdom that I'm not tapped into right now and I would like to be....It brings me peace and helps me be a better person in the world....[Then] I am not caught up in the small mind, personal mind kind of thinking of the world that causes so many problems. People get so identified with these identities, these roles....I can [be] more helpful in the world if I am coming from this universe place as opposed to believing all my little thoughts about who I am in the world. It helps me see the goodness in people that's underneath, because I see that they are caught up in their conditioning and their habits.

Some other interviewees called this "monkey mind"—a phrase many said they picked up from meditation instruction.

This view was not limited to Baby Boomers. Amy Legrand, the Gen X woman who was actively trying to change the views she inherited from her conservative Christian background, said: "I think it's human nature to sort of be wrapped up in our ego, and do selfish things unless otherwise convinced through negative consequences of those choices to alter that behavior.... Ego blocks compassion." Unlike most other interviewees, one Gen X man took a very harsh view of himself and others, forcibly rejecting the religious view that "we are made in the image of God." About that view he said: "I don't see that.... There is no way that I can believe that.... That is really an egocentric kind of thought for me.... I think people are evil, weak and selfish because I am.... I am motivated by survival.... You don't do anything that makes you sad. I mean you don't forcefully do negative things to yourself. I believe that I am guided to make myself happy. I am [a] hedonist."

Tammy Kalini, a Gen Xer, took her spiritual quest so seriously that she lived in a Zen monastery in Japan for several years. While there, she learned that her mind was not necessarily her friend and that it gave her a false sense of self. During her lengthy meditation sessions: "I got to meet myself and notice how fantastically busy my mind was chatting constantly. Judging this or that and making everything good or bad to this ridiculous degree." Some interviewees carried this theme further, seeing "thinking" itself as the problem. Susan Cashman stated it bluntly: "The thing that separates us is that we think, instead of really feeling.... Thinking separates us from ourselves, each other and God.... When we can feel with another person, we can connect."

As a young adult, formerly Roman Catholic Tony Ricci had turned to New Age religion and Buddhism with much enthusiasm. But after seeing shortcomings in the groups he joined, he retreated from most spiritualities. Nevertheless, he had held onto some views about the human ego, saying: "I think that there is something bigger than us that we need to be in awe of in order to get beyond our own self [and] selfish motivation." He echoed the views of others, but focused on the body as well as on feeling. "I have these conversations with my heart, and I ask my heart questions because I feel like my heart can give me information that I can't just get from my head. So it's kind of dropping down into the body more....The body has a lot of information....We're a very mental culture, so getting into the body is really important."

Alexandra Heim echoed another version of the critique of rationality. I heard this often, that is, that logic and consistency are not essential virtues when dealing with spirituality. "As long as I am in sync and in harmony, I'm in alignment. That's important. But making...sense to other people, that's not important....If somebody else says, 'well first you said this and now you're saying this.' I would say, 'Yeah, that's the same thing.' To someone else if I'm inconsistent, that's fine....I rely on my own intuition a lot....I don't like people telling me what to believe or what to do to be in alignment."

In summary, we have seen a general agreement on inherent goodness. Many suggest that Eastern religions teach that humans are essentially good, while Western ones teach that humans are essentially depraved. This simplistic, but false, dichotomy does not really indicate a "turn to the East," so much as part of the rhetorical strategy to "detradition." The interviewees also considered the issue of human choice in their actions. Many strongly believed in human freedom to choose one's own actions. However, they hesitated to make any kind of widespread value judgments about these choices. This led them to forego much comment on human wrong-doing, even to the extent of claiming that good and bad are arbitrary value judgments with which we should dispense.

Nevertheless, a significant majority of interviewees turned out to be fairly accepting about the strong effects of environmental and physiological influences on the individual. Thus, even though freedom is a hallmark of SBNRs, their revulsion at making moral judgments seems to push them to the side of determinism in the free will versus determinism question. Some interviewees say this deterministic influence comes from nature and some say nurture, but the striking result is that they have less hope for human freedom. Sometimes interviewees held both views—determinism and freedom—at the same time. They posited that, in spite of everything, humans have free choice over how we behave. When freedom is championed, it is a freedom of choice, a personal freedom unaffected by others. But many interviewees went further, claiming that we have a choice or even some form of control over what happens to us.

No matter where they stood on the freedom/determinism question, there was a fairly large consensus that took personal well-being and happiness as the gold standard for assessing individual human action and spiritual achievement. Although putting the self at the center is to be expected in a "therapeutic" culture, it was more than simply self-centeredness. Instead, a romantic idealization of the self, the assumption that deep within the self, apart from societal influence, was purity, even divinity. There was confidence that one could in fact peel away the influence of tradition in order to uncover this pristine self. And yet, perhaps echoing religious themes, for a few interviewees, the problem was the ego or the self. Rather than being overly self-judgmental, however, for many it was not so much the self per se that was the problem, but the "unconscious" or "unawakened" self.

7

Community

ACCORDING TO MOST Americans, community is a good thing; we do not have enough of it and we need more. As Paul Morris says, "Everyone, but everyone, is for community."[1] Perhaps that is one reason people try to label all sorts of contemporary human groupings as community, such as the "Internet community," the "corporate community," even the "iPod community." The SBNR interviewees were no different in affirming community, but they took the concept even further. Most of them insisted that humans are already interconnected, that "we are all one," and that our biggest problem is that we do not realize it. Many also nurtured the hope that a new age is coming when all beings will recognize and celebrate their unity.

However, when it came to the form of community known as religion, interviewees often became highly critical. As we have seen earlier, they make a sharp distinction between spirituality and religion, often equating religion with external organizational structure, and spirituality with deep personal experience. Many can only see problems and excesses in religion as they decry such things as dogmatism, rigidity, hypocrisy, or repression. They often insist their personal integrity requires them to emotionally and/ or physically detach from organized religion. In order to better understand their specific concerns, we need first to set them in context, understanding more about the nature of community and its relationship to religion.

Perspectives on Community

What Is It?

Humans are social animals. We need each other, we are interdependent, and we group together. Some of these groupings are simply individuals coming together out of self-interest, exercising their "rational choice." This type of association, or "society," may share geographic proximity, common risks or needs, or other factors promoting some kind of social cohesion. But the participants do not necessarily share deep common values, enduring emotional bonds, nor does the group produce a loyalty more lasting than each individual's personal welfare. Of course, a form of community may result, almost as a "byproduct," in order to facilitate the joint enterprise. However, that is not the primary goal. Especially in contemporary society, individuals come and go from these groupings based on their own needs. One may work today for a corporation that manufactures medical instruments, but tomorrow take one's skills to a company that sells auto parts. We must also distinguish between institution and community. Although there are many definitions of institution, Paul Heclo says that "experts seem to agree that institutions have to do with creating and enforcing rules."[2]

While all these factors, such as self-interest and rules, may be part of a genuine community, something else exists as well, that is, a deeper form of association. Full-orbed communities are based on common beliefs and values, responsibility for one another, shared and enduring emotional bonds, and a loyalty to the larger whole rather than just to the self. One can be born into a community—such as a family, religion, or ethnic culture—but one can also become part of a community by embracing the shared values. Therefore, even though social cohesion, self-interest, preservation, and organization are involved in genuine communities, there is more going on.

Community can be a very good thing. Humans need it and they often long for it when it is absent. People are both healthier and happier when they are part of a well-functioning community. Not only does genuine community provide value, roots, connectedness, and stability for each individual, but community is also good for society. Communities provide a glue that holds society together, and those communities oriented toward a "common good" can create an ethos that extends out in ripple fashion. This "social capital"[3] reaches beyond the community itself, promoting collaborative networks, productivity, cooperation, mutual welfare, and individual well-being. There are many positive results that effective communities can add to society.

What Are Some Problems?

Of course, living in community is not all sweetness and light. Something serious has been lost when creating and enforcing rules or institutional

preservation becomes primary. Not all communities are focused on societal transformation or individual well-being but may be more concerned
with their organizational welfare or survival. Internal problems are
always a potential, too, such things as abuse of power, an insider-outsider
dynamic, or creating a hierarchy even among "insiders."

But there is also a perennial tension between self and group which
does not inherently qualify as "dysfunctional." It is just the way things
are when humans get together. Although this tension is endemic to all
human associations, communities must take special care when dealing
with it. Since a community expects some loyalty to a greater good, community members must recognize that not all individual preferences can
be honored or all needs always met. In a community with deep bonds,
simply walking away is not the first or best strategy when problems arise.
Indeed, for many societies in the past, group allegiance was far more
important than individual identity or personal well-being.

To these perennial issues, America adds its own factors that create
unique problems for community survival. With our historic focus on individual freedom—which is, in part, a byproduct of America's Protestant
heritage and its emphasis on the direct relationship between the individual and God—the tension between self and group becomes even more
acute. Additionally, the proliferation of a "therapeutic ethos" in the last
few decades causes difficulty as this orientation supports personal healing
much more than group welfare. And our mobile, transient, and bureaucratic society adds more pitfalls to community stability as geographic,
ethnic, and family roots are constantly disrupted. Another recent factor
is the growing cynicism toward and distrust of human institutions in general. So while America seems to protect individual freedom against group
hegemony, the downside is that it is more difficult for communities to
flourish or endure.

Committing to community requires a balancing act between personal self-interest and group welfare. But this can only work when it is
undergirded by some level of trust. The irony is that, as Heclo says, "We
are disposed to distrust institutions. That is the basic fact of life we share
as modern people." The tension comes because we must live with them
anyway. "Of course, not everyone is actively distrustful of every institution all the time. If that were the case, we would not have a functioning
society.... [So] we are compelled to live in a thick tangle of institutions
while believing that they do not have our best interests at heart."[4] It is no
surprise that, in this cynical age, people are often wary of handing over

any more of their own self-determination. When it comes to community, we can end up confusing community and institution and thus distrusting the very thing that we need to survive in our complex world. Finally, all human groupings, whether association, institution, society, community, or family—being made up of finite, limited, and mortal beings—always have and will continue to make mistakes. Therefore, while a distrust of human associations can be both warranted and protective of individual freedom, it can also verge on the unrealistic as people expect to find a group more perfect than they are. While it is perhaps correct to hold spiritual communities up to higher standards—after all, their goal is to orient one to the sacred—one cannot deny their human character. Therefore, disappointment is especially endemic to spiritual community, since people seem to expect more from them than other sorts of groupings.

All of this adds up to a very difficult environment for community in contemporary America. Yet, in spite of its inherent and contemporary difficulties, there is a decided wistfulness, especially among the middle class, about contemporary society's "loss of community." This is not just nostalgia, for research suggests that both the reality and the sense of community may, in fact, be diminishing in America.[5] All of these factors provide the soil in which the SBNR ethos grows. When we hear interviewee voices later, we may well ask whether this social climate makes SBNRs long for and create more community, or instead pushes them further in an individualistic direction. One thing is clear, however; religious community would not be their primary route to address relational needs. But why, since religious community has historically been a provider in this area? Have they been hurt by religion, or is there something more ideological at stake? Is religious community inherently defective, or have the interviewees abandoned it for other reasons?

What Is Religious Community?

The culture which has fostered the SBNR ethos is broader than any problems within religion itself. And yet, as hinted above, there are nevertheless some religious roots—especially theological ones—to our current situation. The Protestant heritage sowed seeds which have bloomed in unexpected ways, especially regarding community. In its reaction against the hegemony of the Roman Catholic Church, the Protestant Reformers liberated believers from dependence upon an intermediary between self and God. They returned primary authority to Scripture rather than tradition and gave people the right and the tools to read the Bible for themselves, guided by the Spirit. The Protestant Reformers did not go as far as promoting individualistic spirituality, however. Instead, they countered that potential reaction by focusing on the church as the community of gathered believers, a group meant to help each other understand and live out their commitment to God. Still, the stage was set. With this wrenching away from church authority centuries ago, the current individualistic climate became one unintended consequence.

Even with this heritage of individualism, however, religious community endures. So what kind of human association is it? Is religion just an external, even hollow, organization—all rules and requirements and survival mechanisms? Even worse, is this religious structure largely the vestige of a hegemonic past, a struggling entity desperate to retain a semblance of its influence over people and a "market share" of public participation? Is religion anything more than an association of convenience, control, or influence? Of course, religions organize. All human institutions need some kind of infrastructure and economic base to endure and flourish, so religion must have that.

But religion is significantly more. As Keith Ward says, religion is both an attempt to apprehend, as well as respond to, transcendent reality. Since these attempts develop over time, reflecting their particular historical and social contexts, religions are different from each other.[6] Human association is basic to religion for "it is part of the belief-structure of most religions that there should be a particular society which protects and sustains their basic values and beliefs, within which one may pursue the ideal human goal, as defined within the society."[7]

Religion thus fits the criteria for community. Religions are composed of people with a common orientation to the sacred, common goals, common methods for reaching those goals, and an enduring commitment to one another based on this shared bond. Both social cohesion and emotional bonds are part of religion. Religion also makes truth claims which members feel are enduring, compelling, and authoritative. Religion provides the values and stability of community for individuals and also provides much of the "social capital" upon which society depends. The irony is that although interviewees often spurn religious community, they sometimes unknowingly draw upon traditional ideas of spiritual community. Thus, it is useful to briefly consider how various religions see community.

Judaism, Christianity, and Islam on Community

Although all of the world's major faiths promote community in one way or another, each puts a different emphasis on it. The major Abrahamic traditions—Judaism, Christianity, and Islam—are all deeply concerned with their relationship to the wider society. Community is crucial for these groups. The natural self/group dilemma is resolved by members being oriented in the proper direction, toward God. All are optimistic that this can happen. And they base their assertions on sacred texts. Judaism sees itself as a set-apart, strongly bonded community charged with obeying God's law. Rather than trying to convert others, it works to set a good example to the wider world.

Islam is also a community concerned with obeying God's law and is likewise optimistic about that possibility. But rather than being set-apart, it aims for a global society or universal *umma*, living under God's law, with everyone potentially Muslim once they recognize their obligation. Christianity is very much a communal religion with a strong emphasis on social transformation. Although also attentive to God's law, Christians expect this transformation will happen through God's grace, with the goal to release the good potential inherent in the created order. Anyone can become a part of this mission, with the church serving as the embryonic realm and community of God empowered by the Spirit of Christ. Ward writes that "the duty of a Christian is to co-operate with others and with the Creator in the actualization of goodness. It is to bring into being a community of justice, peace, kindness, and happiness."[8] All three religions within the Abrahamic tradition agree on this goal and that "human beings have the responsibility of forming a society which will enable that purpose to be realized."[9]

Hinduism and Buddhism on Community

The major Eastern traditions of Hinduism and Buddhism provide community but take a different approach to the self/group dilemma. Both are convinced of the ephemeral, transient nature of material reality, including human community. Neither one believes that human society has the potential to realize any ideal goal. Thus, there is no overarching goal to change society as a whole. Neither the world nor the body claims a high value. The individual soul, however, does have a higher possibility. The goal of the various forms of Hinduism is to help the person realize the divinity within. This must be experienced by each person individually and those who attain this goal can leave the world, or stay to help others achieve this state.

Although Hinduism and India can seem to be one cultural entity, in practice Hindus do not see themselves as forming one religious community. Instead there co-exist a diverse set of schools or *sampradaya*, sometimes formed around a particular *guru*. This leader is often seen as a manifestation of the divine, and thus receives both reverence and obedience. While each school or lineage may be different, and one can choose one's own *guru*, within the community there is tradition and authority rather than simply individualistic spirituality.

Even though Buddhism emerged in close dialogue with Hinduism, Buddhism is often more inclined to emphasize the idea that the world is a place of suffering, sorrow, hopeless desire, and illusion.[10] Ward says: "For most Buddhists, the whole structure of human society is doomed to failure, to endless suffering and frustrated desire. Buddhists do not seek to bring the world under the rule of the laws of God. There is no Creator God, and if there were, a God who could create such a world of suffering as this would not be entitled to obedience as an ultimate moral authority."[11] Instead, the goal for the individual is to leave this world of suffering and merge with the oneness that is the true "reality" as well as to help others do the same.

Traditional Buddhist spiritual community is not for everyone. "Buddhists theoretically form a Community of monks and nuns who renounce the world and its concerns, and pursue the path of final liberation from sorrow."[12] In the many iterations of American Buddhism, there can be different styles. A community or *sangha* can be traditionally monastic, yet have associates who are free to take part in meditation or other services while conducting their everyday lives. Or an American Buddhist spiritual assembly can be the entire community of practitioners.

The goal of the *sangha* is to help individuals on their personal journey of world renunciation, transcendence, and attainment of nirvana. Leading by example, showing compassion to the wider world, and reducing the harm one causes are also important. Yet while the goal of helping self and others transcend ego might also result in societal transformation, within both of these Eastern religions the goal is not to transform society, but to transcend it. On the other hand, Taoism and Confucianism may be seen as somewhat more this worldly, since both focus on an ordered and harmonious, perhaps even utopian, society. All these influences show up in various interviewees' reflections on community.

Indigenous Religion and Community

The SBNRs often turn to indigenous spirituality as an alternative to organized religion. They may feel that indigenous religions are somehow truer or better because they are more "natural" or older, less organized, and/or without dogma or creed. They are often careful to specify that these faiths are not religions. But there is no clear reason to call these types of faiths "spirituality" while reserving the term "religion" for other world faiths. If anything, these rudimentary or primal forms of faith serve to highlight the essentially religious nature of human beings. These localized forms of religion—called by such names as shamanism, native, indigenous, tribal, primitive, aboriginal—do have some similarities, often being oral, ritualistic, animistic, totemic, henotheistic [loyalty to one god among many], and focused on gaining some control over the natural world.

Yet there appears to be no one common primal form of spirituality apart from particular groups. For geographic, cultural and racial diversity, historical differences, and inter-group conflict and contact all have led to diverse forms and responses over time. And far from being individualistic, purely experiential, and anti-traditional, native religions are very group oriented and concerned to preserve their own spiritual outlook. While individual personalities and contributions might be recognized, group loyalty, standards, and traditions are crucial, built into the fabric of the community and geared toward survival.

From this quick survey, we can see that all religions combine beliefs, organization, spiritual practices, and transcendent goals. They have also been a prime social bearer of community. Given the decline and changes in America's sense of community, why do these interviewees reject this important source? Have they had bad experiences with religion? Is their turning away from religion a minimizing of community, or is it simply part of the rhetorical strategy? Does this turn away simply allow for alternative communities, or does it further individualize and privatize spirituality as personal quest?[13] To consider these issues, we need to hear interviewees talk about community.

As we do this, we will ask several questions: How do they prioritize the tension between self and community? Has their distancing from religion come in reaction to personal experiences of harm or abuse? Are their objections to religion more ethical, or more conceptual? If conceptual, what are the core principles that make them "allergic" to religion? All of this should help clarify why—even if they might participate in religious services at times—interviewees see themselves as emotionally, spiritually, and/or intellectually detached from religious community.

Interviewees on Self and Community

I have spent years talking with SBNRs and can say with some confidence that the common stereotypes of them are misguided. The interviewees do not come across as particularly selfish, hyper-individualistic, commitment-phobic, or libertarian, and certainly not narcissistic, anti-social, or anarchic—at least not any more than the average American. They function normally within contemporary society, taking care of their families, enjoying their friends, going to work, pragmatically following procedures and obeying rules. Indeed, some could be called especially "public spirited" because they directly work in human services, such as chaplaincy, nursing, teaching, hospice work, and so on. I have also met many who work more directly with spiritual alternatives, contributing to others through their efforts as yoga instructors, massage therapists, reiki practitioners, retreat center employees, New Age store managers, and so on.

Thus, in their workaday and domestic worlds, the interviewees were contributing, productive members of groups. When it came to spirituality, however, the situation was often different. Although a large percentage of interviewees dipped in and out of groups that promoted spirituality, I found few who maintained any long-term identification with any one entity. When I asked interviewees who their primary spiritual support was, many said immediately "I am." America has certainly become a place of religion-switching and church-shopping, offering a plethora of spiritual options. Unlike in the past, today there is no economic advantage (unlike employment) and no societal compulsion to be part of any religious or spiritual group. Thus the interviewees—like most Americans—could revel in their right to refrain from or leave spiritual or religious groups with which they disagreed, when troubles arose, or when the group did not meet their needs. Fear and distrust sometimes colored their conversations about community.

Mary Johansen, a Silent Generation "dissenter" who worked as a therapist, said: "When I think of going to a community, I think of them making demands on me and my work and my family and my marriage life. It's life-draining. I haven't found a community that nourishes." Beverly Bosh was a well-educated Baby Boomer, and spiritual "casual," with very limited experience of church. She worried about such things as financial obligations, power struggles, and scrutiny. "I get weird about organizations. They collect money. And if I don't put money in, are they going to talk about me?...And they want you to be on committees....They all sit there and fight....That's the sad thing about things that get organized: People!"

A few others were afraid of the potential for more serious problems. They worried about not just "narrow-mindedness and judgmentalism," as one person put it, but also about group-think, manipulation, isolation, repression, or even abuse. Many felt these problems were especially endemic to spiritual communities. Penny Watson, a Baby Boomer "seeker," had been warned by her father to stay away from religion altogether. She said: "There has been an awful lot of evil done in the world in the name of religion and playing on this desire of people to be saved....Certainly there have been a lot of movements to wipe out people who have the wrong beliefs....There have been too many preachers through time who have used people for their own power."

The Righteousness of Not Belonging

But it was not just fear, inconvenience, or distrust that kept them away. Instead, there was a deeper philosophy at work as well. What distinguishes these interviewees is their firm belief in the rightness—even righteousness—of this lack of loyalty to any particular spiritual group. While they might be a contributing member, for a time, of a class formed around a particular spiritual teacher, or show up regularly for an ongoing meditation or yoga class, participate in a coven, or put on a solstice event, nevertheless, the reality was more "revolving door" than lifetime commitment. There was no "once a yogini, always a yogini" attitude as in "once a Catholic, always a Catholic."

This philosophy seems to be endemic to the SBNR identity and it has several facets. The first facet, as we have seen, is the assumption that spirituality is an individualistic pursuit, one that is not necessarily supported—and may even be hindered—by group membership. Mick Sharp, who we have heard from before, summed this up: "I don't think you have to be in a church to be spiritual. You can have your own relationship with God, or higher power...that is more important than anything else you believe....I am more spiritual than religious because I don't really need to go to somebody's service and have people's rules." Seeker Angela Roman went further, actually feeling obligated not to identify herself with any particular group. She said emphatically: "I'm not supposed to label myself. I'm supposed to be … more of a free spirit, kind of walk in all kinds of spiritual circles yet not necessarily become one of them." Brendan Potter put a twist on the same theme: "What is the difference between spiritual and religious? In my mind, there is no difference. I am my own church. I am my own congregation.… I personally don't feel like I need help. I know God is there. If I need to talk to him, I can."

Beverly Bosch, who was especially worried about religion's demands, followed up by saying: "I'll just do my own religion in my own way … I have to take care of myself. Part of my spiritual practice is that I have to get in touch with my own breathing … work on my trust issues, work on all those things." In all my interviews, Susan Heinz, a spiritual "explorer," was the only interviewee who wondered if her lack of long-term commitment was anything but laudable. After recounting her many efforts at spiritual community she said, seeming a bit embarrassed: "I don't know if I'm eclectic or undisciplined or crazy, but I just can't seem to stick with one thing."

Jennifer Babcock, a Gen Xer with virtually no experience of religion, expressed what a significant number of my younger interviewees said—they just did not want to join or identify with any religious group at all, ever. They felt it would limit their options. "I don't want to belong to any one thing [be]cause I feel like I'll put myself in a box. You know, I want to expand in this life, and I want to be open to whatever is supposed to be happening." Lisette Marshall explained: " 'Spiritual' has less 'you-gottas' to it than 'religion.' My experience with religion has been a lot of: 'This is what we believe and we would like you to believe it, too. And if you don't yet, it's okay. You will.' " This attitude horrified her, she said, adding: "I want to retain my freedom of thought and … make my own decisions and not believe. [Just] because the church says it's right, I must believe it? I don't buy that. I believe I should be able to question."

The second facet to this ethos is the overwhelming agreement among interviewees that their primary spiritual commitment was to themselves and their own growth. For some this meant pursuing their own personal happiness without regard for others. But many other interviewees were, in fact, concerned with others' well-being. Their route to living that out, however, was not self-sacrifice, group loyalty, or putting the needs of others first. Instead, they were passionately convinced that by pursuing their own personal growth, they would naturally contribute to the wider world. The best way they could act in the world was to become, as one person said "the best, truest expression of my deepest self." Most also asserted that it was everyone's individual job to discover their own true nature although they might help others by "modeling authenticity" or allowing them enough "space to do their own work."

Interviewees often indicated that following their own instincts would result in a personal happiness which would automatically radiate out to the world. Jennifer Babcock said she "find[s] peace and love and satisfaction in life by doing what feels right to me. . . . I also want to . . . do whatever I can do to help in the world. . . . And for me that just means I'm doing what feels right, you know?" A great many held this assumption. Several, however, nuanced this view, pointing to the difficulties the ego sometimes inserted as one searched for one's truest self. Shirley Stein, the Silent Generation spiritual "seeker" who works in a retreat center, said about her goal: "What I want is to be an expression of my true nature. More and more expressing of my true nature and less and less expressing of the obstacles of my egoic nature."

The third facet of the SBNR philosophical stance was the goal. The ideal state many said they would like to achieve was internal, expressed variously as joy, happiness, and peace. Very few interviewees had a larger ideal of changing the world, reforming society, or improving people's material situation. Such changes to the world as were possible they felt would naturally come as they "worked on themselves." Meditator Jack Campbell summed it up by saying he hoped to make "little changes in myself. . . . That's how you change the world." Mark Sage, the Gen Xer who found his spirituality born in twelve-step groups, suggested that being in a better mood was his contribution to the wider world. "If I feel better then I make the world about me better because I'm not grumpy and focusing on internal stuff."

Deborah Wright, from the Silent Generation, worked part-time as a teacher. She said her goal was "trying to do as little damage as possible to others . . . I would like to extend to people as much love and kindness as I can without sacrificing myself." One interviewee took it very seriously when her guru said she could do the most good for the world by sitting in meditation. These various interviewees may reflect an Americanizing of an already generic Eastern spirituality, with their common goal being personal spiritual growth, even self-transcendence, rather than the direct improvement of society.

Doing Good in the World

When Emily Orbach heard me lecture, this spiritual "casual" had a strong reaction to my comment that many interviewees have prioritized personal growth. She jumped up during the presentation, insisting passionately that she and her SBNR friends all want to do good in the world. Afterwards, she wrote me a long email. In it, she said: "I think there are plenty of individuals practicing solo spirituality in ways that are narcissistic and negatively self-reinforcing/justifying. I believe the most healthy spirituality is a combo of personal and group practices." Nevertheless, she made it clear that priority must be given to self-development. "My goal as a human being is to be the best human I can be....I urgently want to express my calling, which I'm still discerning. In the meantime...I'm expressing aspects of it...by...encouraging inquiry toward authenticity/truth-telling." She feared I was making too sharp a dichotomy between self-development and the common good. She insisted instead that "everyone's true calling supports the common good, and it would actually be a good thing if they invested their resources into developing that calling." The choice to prioritize self-development over social action is many interviewees' resolution of the self/group dilemma.

Nevertheless, perhaps reflecting the American "can-do" ethos, I did meet a few who wanted to work for the common good directly. Millennial college student Kimberly Takahashi was conflicted about this. She said: "I'd like to work with some sort of non-profit that works towards social change in some capacity, whether it's environmentalism, animal rights, civil rights and liberties....I'm not sure at this point." But the problem came, she said, because "On the other side, I have a passion for art and maybe working in the entertainment industry." Unlike many of the older SBNRs I spoke with, she saw her choices as more vocational than spiritual and confessed she had no standard by which to make this important decision.

I also met several Millennial persons who were training to be chaplains or pastoral counselors in an interfaith program that emphasized Eastern spiritual values. They focused on helping people accept suffering. Ian Hanby was doing a student internship in a cancer unit. He felt that trying to change difficult situations was not as effective as simply accepting them. He said, with a mixture of resignation and acceptance: "Being at peace doesn't mean everything's peachy keen. It means that I accept things the way they are....It means accepting that I was abused as a child.

It means accepting all of these things. But when I accept them and stop struggling against them, then they're not a problem." When I asked him how this affected his work with patients, he said he was "helping other people wake up in that same kind of way. It's saying, 'Sweetie, I'm sorry, I know it hurts a lot but this is also the way things are right now.'" While compassionate and empathetic, this comment still echoes in my mind. It seems quite a change from the typical American "can-do," change- and progress-oriented attitude that has fueled various communal efforts to improve society.

Experiences in Spiritual Communities

Many people assume that SBNRs have been hurt by religion, especially Christianity, and this is what fuels their avoidance. However I heard few, if any, stories of confrontation, violence, isolation, or abuse from my hundreds of conversation partners. Of course, problems with religion do not necessarily have to involve such serious incidents. Also troubling are problems with religion that are emotional or cognitive, or involving some synergy between the two. On the emotional level, a person might experience interpersonal discord or strain. This could erupt because of disagreements or failure to cooperate. Individuals can also have difficulty living up to the standards of the group, or they may disagree with these standards. These factors interfere with the beneficial social support provided by religion. Also emotional is a failure to benefit from such religious coping behavior as prayer and worship, or the possibility that such religious coping could become something harmful if, for example, relied on to the exclusion of other aids. The influence of other people can also play a part in disaffiliating from religion. While the emotional level has its pitfalls, the cognitive level is no less fraught with potential difficulties. Doubt plays a very large role. One may doubt the beliefs being taught by the group, yet feel ashamed to reveal them. One may have doubts about the reality, presence, or nurture of God and feel one's faith is ineffective or insufficient. Or one may simply have trouble understanding the sacred texts or beliefs. Whether emotional, cognitive, or both, such problems can lead a religious participant to depart abruptly or simply drift away from their group's beliefs and behaviors, until they eventually leave.[14]

But nonbelievers were not spared "religious distress" by being disaffiliated. Equally difficult, if different, problems plagued them as well. These can also be both emotional and cognitive. Some nonbelievers feel alienated from religious "others," especially those related to them. Negative public perceptions about nonbelievers, especially atheists, may be uncomfortable. Doubt itself can cause psychological stress, since studies demonstrate that certainty in belief lends itself to better psychological health. Ironically, nonbelievers experience more anger toward God and have more trouble forgiving God than religious participants. Death anxiety can also cause problems when the nonbeliever is unsure if there is any kind of afterlife.[15]

Among the people I met during this research project, by far the most common problems were the cognitive ones. Whether or not they had ever belonged to a religious group, there were many people who had trouble believing what they did hear from religious people, some who once believed but then doubted, and a great many who had never found adequate answers to their pressing theological and existential questions. However, although the numbers were small, I did hear some stories of distressful experiences in spiritual communities beyond strictly theological ones. What was most intriguing, however, since it disturbs popular stereotypes about SBNRs is that—far from being limited to churches—these stories spanned the range of spirituality groups, both alternative and more traditional.

On one hand, I did hear the expected stories of people who, as children, had been raised in repressive, isolated, often sexist, religious communities. Some interviewees told of the hypocrisy they had witnessed in religious groups. A few recounted how they had asked spiritual leaders for help only to be brushed off or blamed for their own or a family member's problems. Some of the women interviewees spoke about being prevented from exercising their gifts, being directed into secondary roles, or being simply ignored. And I heard stories of GLBT persons who had to stay closeted in order to participate or were actively prejudiced against.

But I also heard stories from another angle, both non-religious and alternative. For instance, many interviewees complained of families and friends who prevented them from pursuing their interest in religion or spirituality. A large number told me stories of having atheist, non-religious, or "New Age" parents who were deeply upset when the interviewee wanted to become part of traditional religious groups. Some interviewees spoke of sexual excesses promoted by the guru or leader, within the inner circle of an alternative spiritual group. Some recounted being ignored, neglected, or not taken seriously by spiritual leaders and groups. Many mentioned the lack of community they found in non-religious spiritual groups. And a significant minority objected that they had to recruit outsiders as a condition of their spirituality-group membership.

A large number of interviewees were critical of other members in the alternative spiritual groups they had tried. Many complained that group members were weak, sheep-like, or too willing to give over authority to a leader. Others observed that group members uncritically participated in what seemed—to these interviewees—like meaningless rituals. Some felt that the leadership was arbitrary, too controlling, or condescending. A few told stories of dissident members who disrupted the entire group. While I do not want to minimize the emotional impact of these bad experiences, it was striking how quintessentially American these complaints were. Many people seemed upset that they had landed in a non-democratic group, which neglected some participants but focused on others, with an authoritarian leadership, uncritical followers, and/or excesses without any built-in mechanism for redress.

We need to be clear, therefore, when considering reports of negative experiences, to make a distinction between a community that abused and a community that disappointed. People have high expectations of religious communities and it is common that they often do not live up to a seeker's ideal. When I heard stories of disappointment, they often had to do with group dynamics or leadership styles. Again, these stories ranged across the board, from churches, to meditation groups, *sanghas*, guru-focused communities, est, sweat lodges, covens, and other types of alternative spiritual groups.

But I also heard about positive experiences with spiritual communities. These often centered on overcoming a fear of commitment and being positively surprised by finding any kind of group cohesion. More common were stories that showed a longing for community but the difficulty of achieving it. These stories, too, spanned the range from Christian churches to Eastern-inspired groups and alternative spiritualities. Bethany Storm, a Gen X "seeker," tried a Buddhist study group, even though she had always been "so anti-membership. I think it's because it lets people not think for themselves, which is a pet-peeve of mine. I heard the word *sangha* and I was so cynical about it." But she took a chance and happily reported: "What I have found [are]...people being really committed to expressing themselves as honestly as possible....interested in engaging in the questions...instead of 'Let me have the answer so I can get on with other things.'"...[I] am finding community here to be...something I am very thankful for." In keeping with our therapeutic age, she was most impressed with the members' self-expression, honesty, and open inquiry, and did not mention if they also helped each other in practical ways. It is not clear, however, if she will make a commitment to Buddhism.

A Gen X woman, who had been raised Catholic, had not realized how much she lacked community as an adult until she inadvertently found it in a martial arts group. "I felt very comfortable with the people there and I could tell it was definitely filling a hole that...I had forgotten existed....[But it] was just a patch over a hole that I needed to try to fill spiritually." Although she wanted "to get back into some sort of religious community," she hesitated. News stories and scandals involving religious groups, and perhaps some personal experience, made her afraid to take a chance. "I don't want to be disappointed, or find out that someone I grow to respect has betrayed a trust....That is why I am having trouble."

Mark Adler tried Buddhism for a time before moving to a more liberal Protestant denomination than the one in which he was raised. He had a complicated story about his experience with spiritual community. As a child he had been taken to church regularly but never got much out of it. His first good experience of community came when this church took him on a youth-group mission trip to an impoverished area. "Trying to help those people, I've never felt so close to God being close to the people in our worship in the evening after we had been busy building houses during the day....That was when I first discovered that God is in community." As so often happens, when he went away to college, he did not participate in any spiritual community. Eventually, he realized something was missing. He decided to take a meditation class at a temple and ended up being part of that community.

For a time, he advanced in spiritual practices and became integrated into the group. But as he participated in the rituals, he became uneasy: "There would be so much stress on these outward signs. Am I doing this right with the oil? Is my *mudra* [hand position] right?...These outward ceremonies at first attracted me....The philosophy is beautiful, but it seemed to break down in so many of these practices." He complained of having to pay fees for trainings and of spiritual elitism among the more advanced. But his discomfort climaxed around the issue of self-development versus mutual responsibility within the community. One day, at a community gathering, he observed the plight of an elderly couple. "There was a lady who had to move. Her and her husband had a lot of medical conditions and no one really stood up to help her." He continued: "What's the point of me getting over myself if I'm not going to use that? The whole benefit is to benefit others." In the end, he left this community and found a church more liberal than his childhood one but also one with an ethic of mutual help.

One of the more complex stories I heard came from Maria Falcone, the woman with Native American roots who was adopted by Christian parents. She was proud of her maternal native heritage but also of the spiritual formation her Catholic and Baptist adoptive family had given her. "If I only acknowledged that I am Cheyenne, then I am throwing away...everything my mother and father that raised me gave me." Since she did not have enough "blood" to be registered with a native community, she saw her mission to create a "mixed lodge" where anyone was welcome. Even though she welcomed people from any and all religious backgrounds, some people criticized her. "There is a definite distrust of all things Christian or they'll say to you, 'That's all good but you have a lot of *washtelos*—You have a lot of white people.'" Maria tried to bring an egalitarian and inclusive SBNR ethos to a spirituality more oriented to authority and roots. At first she used a strong leadership style, as she had been taught by some Native elders who were willing to work with her. But she felt she could not always rise to the spiritual heights necessary. "When I'm out of harmony...I'm nobody's way to the light." Instead, she told participants: "Everybody is a leader. Everybody is a conduit for the spirit. Everyone has a time when they have to step up and lead."

This did not work out the way she had planned. One day, on my way to participate in one of her sweat lodges, I called to see if there were any last minute things I could bring. She said, "Oh, I'm sorry, don't even bother coming. We're not having it. My sweat lodge is gone." A fire had destroyed it the night before. She related how she had told a group member he could not "come on" to the boys there, that she would not allow this on her property. "Well," she said sadly, "last night that guy came and burned down my sweat lodge." Clearly no one type of spiritual group has the corner on the market of difficult group dynamics, boundary-setting, leadership struggles, and dysfunctional members.

Some interviewees, even though they longed for community, found the SBNR ethos and/or their personal histories held them back. Jason Van Buren, a Gen X "seeker," had always felt the SBNR title had more integrity than any one religious identification. Although he found evidence to the contrary, he still found it hard to commit.

> I was on a huge bent of non-spiritual identification...[but] I now respect people for being in a tradition....I can see the depths of it

but... I can't do it.... My religious identification right now would be that of religious syncretist. I'm taking bits and pieces of my own path, my own world and experience.... very salad bar, very *a la carte*, because I want to make sure that it's not a consumerist point of view.... I have to make sure that I'm not just purchasing... going around and filling my own boat up with my own wants and needs. I have to make sure it's a legitimate search.

But even when people had a strong longing, positive experiences, or active involvement in a community, my discussion partners often held their group commitment very lightly. Tamara Birnbaum was the Asian-Jewish young woman who had just started to work at a New Age-style retreat center when I met her. Growing up, she had been part of a synagogue, but said: "I came from a community that wasn't awake, and I was just so thirsty for a community that could give each other spiritual support in that way.... So I came here. It was a huge contrast, and I found exactly what I was looking for.... It's amazing.... It's like I'm weaving my little web into this community.... I feel like it's a gift to be here." When I visited her three years later, she had risen to an important administrative position at the center. Yet when I asked her if she would be staying on indefinitely as an integral part of this community, she said, with pride: "Oh no, I'm always open to new directions. I don't identify myself with any one thing."

Addiction Recovery Groups as Spiritual Community

One type of group I heard mentioned often was the addiction recovery model, such as one finds in Alcoholics Anonymous (AA). Nearly one-third of my SBNRs told me they had some experience with a twelve-step addiction recovery group. This is an unusually high percentage of any population (although statistics are not kept or obtainable for twelve-step groups because of their insistence on anonymity). It was striking how many of my interviewees had been exposed to this philosophy, even though when I met them, most reported being only minimally involved, if at all. For many, however, this had been the alternative community that helped them deal with personal problems and where they got introduced to the idea of spirituality without religion. While the group did not really push them to work for the common good or changes in society—such as fighting the societal causes of addiction—many said the twelve steps opened them up to the spiritual dimension of life, helped them "meet God," and/

or got them comfortable relating to others. In fact, many had their first taste of spiritual community here. The community ethos is integral to all twelve-step programs because of two interlocking principles. First, because addiction is not just a biological or psychological problem but also a spiritual one, this is seen as a spiritual program. Second, in order to be successful in the program, one must make a commitment to continue attending meetings. In other words, one must make a commitment to the twelve-step community.[16]

One reason recovery groups have flourished in the last few decades is that they ameliorate the emotional isolation so endemic to our society. Although the AA style does not work for everyone, many people find help for addiction problems when they join a community where they can honestly reveal themselves, weaknesses and all. Dedicated twelve steppers will usually have a "home" group which they attend faithfully, although they may also visit other meetings on occasion. The connection between the SBNR ethos and the addiction recovery movement is often overlooked. Yet there is actually a historical connection between the twelve-step philosophy and alternative spiritualities.[17] Thus, when I realized that many of the interviewees' first or most successful experience of spiritual community came through the twelve steps, I listened carefully.

Jennifer Babcock had something to say on this topic. As a Gen Xer with little prior experience of religion or spiritual community, she learned how to pray and meditate, as well as being introduced to New Age books, through friends she met in AA. She felt that "the basis of the whole thing...was teaching people how to get just a really simple spiritual practice going. Find out what works for you....It helped me so much....I got really excited about spirituality." But when the group tried to have her share in their mission to help other alcoholics, she balked. "People in AA used to say that...in order to be fulfilling your purpose, you had to help other people that had drug or alcohol problems...I realized that wasn't true for me." Instead, she stopped attending meetings and instead formed a discussion group with other like-minded women because "I'm doing what feels right, you know?" Given the "take what you like and leave the rest" aspect of AA, she felt no compunction about departing from its standard of communal behavior.

Lisette Marshall, the Gen Xer with no religious upbringing, found it was AA that got her thinking more positively about religion, even though she was not actually an alcoholic. "It probably brought me closer to being able to accept anything religious than I had been...because of that whole higher power thing.... [They said] people could think of it as they wished...that was the freedom that I needed to be able to say: 'Okay then, as long as you aren't going to tell me exactly what and how to believe, then maybe we can deal.'" In fact, being young, lonely, and from a dysfunctional family, she needed community more than she needed recovery. "At the time, I just knew that these were a bunch of friendly people who were kind to me.... I never really actually did have an alcohol problem. I just made one up [be]cause I needed a place to be...so I thought: 'Whatever I have to do to get in, that's what I'm gonna do.'" For a time, the community functioned well for her. "I stayed in AA until I was 16 or so. So it probably kept me out of great deal of trouble."

For several young men brought low by addiction, AA was the one thing that changed their minds about spirituality and community. Kit Partin, a Millennial, said: "I love the Alcoholics Anonymous people.... it has taught me so much. It's really guided me [and] got me stronger spiritually.... Honestly, the program is what I look up to. And I can tell you those words coming out of my mouth are amazing.... [Once] I thought it was...brainwashing.... But now I have seen how life has changed for me." Mark Sage, Gen Xer, said earnestly: "I found a group of people that helped me find a power greater than myself.... [Previously] any time the word God would come up, I would throw up my little defenses.... After my problem got out of hand as it did and I found this group of people that solved that problem.... It's nice to have the help. Today I'm okay with saying the word 'God.' I've stopped fighting it." Both of these men have made a commitment to the recovery community.

Brendan Potter had also struggled with addiction as a teenager. He found the AA model actually moved him away from religion. Part of his rehabilitation program was "sitting in group with other peers who at the same time were questioning their faith.... We had all hit rock bottom and were working our way back out of it.... Everybody had to tell what their higher power was and there were some people that didn't choose God.... I think it helped boost me into understanding that not everyone feels the same way.... I was naive to the fact that not everybody just believed in God." He now sees himself as SBNR, never returned to his church background, and has also stopped his twelve-step participation.

Some prefer the AA community to the religious communities they have experienced. Lisa Grollen, the Gen Xer with parents who were religious professionals, had gotten caught up with drugs and alcohol. "I had to have something bigger than alcoholism to crush that, and that's what

AA did for me. That's when I became spiritual. . . . It definitely was born there." Carole Bradford, Silent Generation "seeker," felt AA worked better than church community. "I have found more profound spirituality there than in most churches. There are all different kinds of people. Such a sense of striving and acceptance. In fact, I took . . . a Buddhist monk to an AA meeting and he said 'Gee, if there were only as much honesty upstairs as there is downstairs.' The meetings were held in the basement."

Yet, ironically, some others found recovery groups too religious, even "too Christian." Susan Heinz, Baby Boomer spiritual "explorer," complained, "They were saying too much God and Jesus and it was just too Christian for me. I started to feel uncomfortable." Dana Dove had left a conservative Christian upbringing when she came out as a lesbian. But her drinking problems led her to AA. "I went once, it was too Christian sounding. I was so pissed off." Her partner, however, begged her to return. "So I found a group. I didn't like the group, but I was going to do whatever they told me. All I heard was Christian ideas and also fed this unworthiness and connection to a higher power. . . . that was like an acid flashback to my Southern Baptist heritage."

It is important to understand what characteristics made the twelve-step recovery model function well—at least for a time—as spiritual community for many of the interviewees, especially when nothing else worked for them. As we have seen, the twelve-step program does not only attract SBNRs; it also helps create them. It does this either by introducing spirituality to people with no religious experience or by offering a more generic spirituality for people with prior religious affiliation. For many, AA is the archetype of a "spiritual but not religious" community and yet ironically contains factors that make it function like religion.

First, AA has always refused to identify itself with any religious group. While this makes it ostensibly "nondenominational," it is also ironic since its historical roots—as well many of its practices—are in a Christian para-church organization, the Oxford Group. Indeed, as we have seen, some interviewees—for better or worse—hear echoes of Christianity in the program. Yet for others, AA offers the shared goals, emotional bonds, and core values common to religious community. Second, AA's "take what you like and leave the rest" anti-dogmatic stance seems to run counter to the popular impression that religion insists on belief control. This, too, is ironic, because certain unwritten but core tenets—especially the "disease model" of addiction—are orthodox for the program. Third, its apparently non-hierarchical and loose organizational style is attractive to many people. Here is another irony because an informal authority structure does exist. The "Big Book" of AA functions as "scripture." Meetings have ritualistic elements repeated no matter which one you attend. There is a central publishing organization which tightly controls approved reading materials. Members with "more recovery" exert important influence. And the admonition for newcomers to take and obey a "sponsor" operates to guide and condition them.[18]

So part of the success of the AA model is that it functions in some ways quite like a religious community, incorporating such elements as strong emotional bonds, commitment, a common focus, common beliefs, ritual, and mutual responsibility. In any case, the twelve-step promotion of a generic "live and let live" spirituality has become very familiar and comfortable to great numbers of Americans, including many of the interviewees. In the 1990s, a proliferation of recovery groups treating a wide range of human problems likely gave the SBNR ethos its biggest boost. Creating a "perfect storm," however, was also the fact that the recovery trend coincided with the rise of evangelical Christianity and its linking with conservative politics. This gave another boost to the SBNR ethos, as people began to associate Christianity with right-wing, authoritarian or oppressive attitudes and practices. For many interviewees, a twelve-step group was the closest they were willing to come to spiritual community.

Hunger for Experience

Positive experiences of community were not enough for many interviewees. Something more than a functional community of "nice people" was necessary for many of the "seeker" interviewees. Just filling the community gap was not going to be enough for them. Many SBNRs I met often complained that the spiritual groups they tried did not facilitate, live out, or convey what interviewees thought of as true spiritual experience. Many said this about Christianity. Ron Richmond was quite blunt about it: "The thing that I didn't have was an 'ah-ha' moment and...I blame that on the church." Baby Boomer Pamela Ames said about her previous church experience: "They were sweet people. It was an experience in community...it wasn't an experience in spirituality." Her longing was palpable. "That was why I was so damned angry at the church at times....I would look at some of the conservative fundamental people...and say 'That's not me, but I wish I could be that'.... I believed that other people had that experience, but not me.... It made me sad."

Mick Sharp, a GLBT Baby Boomer, kept trying: "I wanted to find an open and affirming church. I wanted to experience faith a little more." And Dana Dove, the GLBT Baby Boomer woman raised in a conservative Baptist church, did not leave so much because of homophobia, but because her needs for spiritual experience were not met. She speculated: "Religion is about the safety of a group, and the norm and fitting in with a group.... There's not really a lot of spiritual experience in that." Patricia Hoffman, who had very little religious experience, became a Unitarian Universalist because her husband was a member. While it did "ease her" into religion, she said: "The particular group we were in had no spirituality. It was a very nice group of people exploring things."

Even those with positive memories of church as children often still felt something was missing. This complaint was made by people in every age group. Sheryl Best, a Baby Boomer "dissenter," was part of a youth group in a liberal Protestant church. "You sit in a circle and you tell each other something honestly positive. You learn to trust other people. In a way, it wasn't so much religion; it was personal growth and feeling comfortable in your own skin." Gen Xer Kit Partin said something similar. "I did get involved in the youth group and I did have friends at church, but it was more of a social outlet for me and not a spiritual one...I never really got what...all the fuss was about." Millennial Brendan Potter found that Sunday School, although pleasant enough, did not give him what he really needed. "I learned simple little tales of David and Goliath...but even that didn't teach me spirituality. That just taught me how to color and do the pamphlet that the lady told me to do."

This lack of spiritual experience was not restricted to stories about the Christian church, however. Amit Singh from the Silent Generation had grown up in a family that maintained a Hindu temple. He said: "We...brothers went and led services. We all learned to do that, but otherwise they were more mechanical. From my study of the Sanskrit, I learned that there was something deep that I was not grasping, but I had no big desire to grasp it either." Shirley Stein related how, as a child, she had been taken to the synagogue on holidays: "To me it was very awful that my mother would dress us up on the High Holy Days and parade us around. It just didn't feel spiritual to me." James Wolfe had left the church to try a meditation group but still did not get results. "It's a nice group of people. I like them. But as far as talking about spiritual things, some people have these experiences and....I don't disbelieve them. It's hard sometimes when you don't have your own experiences, to understand somebody else's experiences."

Even so, I heard many stories of interviewees who had deep spiritual experiences in both church and alternative communities. Dana Dove had been a devout Christian as a child and even had a powerful experience of being "saved." As an adult, she took a meditation class at a temple and found a similar "total religious experience." She said, "To be able to go to the *stupa* and sit and be in the room with the remains of a guru and the statue of the Buddha, it's just a most powerful place." Although many took away good memories of their experiences, few of these interviewees maintained a deep commitment to the spiritual communities they did find.

What sense can we make of this? Even though I met many interviewees who longed to understand "what the fuss is all about" and to have deep spiritual experiences of their own, I found that even among those who clearly had them, there was still a predilection not to identify too closely with a religious or spiritual entity. Even the addiction recovery groups, although attractive to SBNRs, did not have staying power for many interviewees. If we do not find multiple or overwhelmingly horrid experiences in religious communities among the interviewees and if the seemingly straightforward issue of spiritual experience is not enough to explain their attitudes toward religion, there must be something deeper, something conceptual or inbuilt to the SBNR ethos that impedes commitment.

Religious Authority Does Not Count

There were two very dominant themes undergirding interviewees' views on religion and both of them go far in explaining why they often have trouble committing to any one particular religious community. The first theme has to do with authority: Who has it? Where does it come from? What is it allowed to decide? The key question for many interviewees was this: Is there any value in following a distinctive religious tradition or is spiritual authority simply something one finds by "going inside?" The second theme has to do with the nature of religion. All religions make truth claims about the nature of reality and realms beyond the material. They orient one to a sacred or transcendent dimension from which authority proceeds or is derived. Essential to religion is the idea that truth is "one," that it conforms to reality. So, if all religions claim truth, are religions essentially the same, with just different outward styles? Are we all simply going up different paths on the same mountain? And if so, why do you need religion at all?

Any objective study shows that each religion presents a unique interpretation of reality. Each one does not just have different practices and outward forms, but different beliefs, goals, values, and standards. If so, how does one know which religion to embrace? These issues have been debated by scholars and practitioners throughout history. The interviewees may not have consciously been debating these questions, but the apprehensions they had about religion demonstrated they were concerned with them, even if on an inchoate level.

Although I rarely heard the word "authority," many of the indictments interviewees made of religion ranged around this critical issue. The authority issue is what they were raising when they leveled charges of "dogmatism," "judgmentalism," and "exclusivism." In other words, many of the interviewees saw religions as claiming the corner on the truth market, which they called being "dogmatic." They believed that religions felt qualified to decide who was living according to higher standards, in other words to be "judgmental." They felt that religions appropriated to themselves the right to say who is "in" and who is "out," and that each group put its own above all others, in other words, that religions practiced "exclusivism." A significant majority of my SBNR interviewees found these views offensive, no matter what spiritual group or religion was promulgating them. "They have no right" would be a succinct summary of their feelings about this.

Some interviewees reduced the whole problem to a psychological mechanism, seeing religious belief and assurance as simply "self-soothing" in a chaotic world. Nick Jones, Gen X "casual," suggested claiming to know truth is a comforting, even enviable, delusion. "So maybe it is good to be closed minded.... As long as they understand things, they feel good and they gain pleasure because it's not mystery. It's known." But many more interviewees made a harsher judgment, being suspicious of, or offended by, others with strong beliefs. The word "dogmatic" was the short-hand term for this certitude. Some focused on the harm—even if unintended— that conviction can cause. Brendan Potter had, at age 7, attended a church Sunday School class the day after his pet had died. "We were discussing how it was okay because the cat went to heaven. And the lady said 'Animals don't go to heaven, honey'.... It's those kinds of things that I wish didn't happen, where people are so set in their own beliefs that they...weren't open to other people's."

Others focused on the power issues behind certitude. Courtney Szabo, a Gen X spiritual "explorer," used this view to rebel against her conservative Christian background while attending a religious college.

> I fell in with a group of sort of rebellious people. It doesn't take much to be rebellious on a Nazarene campus.... We played Dungeons and Dragons and that got banned from the campus.... I thought, 'This is supposed to be an institution of higher learning. We are supposed to be seeking ultimate truth and they've already decided what that truth is....' They have their Truth with a capital T and they are going to cram it down your throats. It's their way or the highway.

Becky Samuels, former Roman Catholic, remembered "the little book we got as kids in catechism with all the lists of the mortal sins and the [*sic*] menial sins"[19] and the fear "if you died with one of these zillions of mortal sins on your soul, which seemed pretty minor to me, like [not] having eaten fish on Friday." There were no loopholes. Instead, "it was all that orthodoxy and.... it was presented as you have to buy this whole package, otherwise it's no good." As an adult she got deeply involved with yoga, as an alternative spirituality. "I was finding my own spiritual sustenance that was not dogmatic."

The irony of the objection to dogmatism is that it was not confined to conservative Protestantism or Roman Catholicism, but could be turned inside-out and function just as well in a very liberal context. Gordon Hance, the Gen X man raised by Unitarian parents, struggled to explain how his family was dogmatically against dogmatism.

> It was basically that most everything was accepted, people's ideas or dreams, no matter how strange or eccentric, they were accepted. The only things that were wrong, even though there was no right or wrong in my family, there were social taboos that were, like, they wouldn't use the word sin in the Unitarian church. That was not an okay word. If you believed something and held it to be true, it was thought to be narrow-minded. If somebody was dogmatic, even if they weren't pressing that dogma on somebody else, they were looked down upon because they seemed dogmatic. The worst thing was propagating ignorance.

Ironically, Gordon had become a Christian and was scorned by his family for it. I asked him what they would consider "propagating ignorance," and he said: "I suppose the belief system I have now. Really believing the Bible and teaching the Bible and teaching Christ as being uniquely God would be propagating ignorance. So for me growing up that way, I naturally rebelled and wanted to find out if there was something such as an absolute truth." Gordon's comments are instructive about the nature of authority, because authority assumes some higher standard, which has inherent validity, or truth. Yet, for many interviewees, the truth claims that are inherent in the various religions are seen as hubris, over-reaching, ludicrous, or offensive.

Some took that further. Emily Orbach, the Gen Xer who objected to some comments in my lecture, wrote me a long email afterward and spent considerable time on this point. She judged negatively any religion that departed from the "simplicity of God's message" and became "exclusionary, politicized versions." Indeed, she said, "I believe all fundamental and guru-based spiritual/religious groups are harmful because they believe their way is *the* way, and use dogma/manipulate the sacred texts to claim a spiritual superiority and to exclude others." In fact, like Emily, a significant percentage of interviewees made an almost "moral" judgment against those who claimed to know truth at all. In other words, they believed that it is wrong to think you are right.

For Tony Ricci, as with many of my younger interviewees, there was more value in admitting ignorance than in claiming truth. Tony said: "I find that to be one of the strongest traits of credibility is being able to say 'I have no idea. I don't have the answer to that.' I think that is just one of the most brilliant things that a person can say…'I don't know. I have no idea.'" But for many interviewees something deeper undergirded this objection to the authority claimed by religion and religious beliefs, going beyond harm, hubris, and power plays. Instead, many believed that any community-held beliefs or "dogmas" got in the way of personal spiritual experience. Angela Roman, the Baby Boomer "seeker" with some childhood Roman Catholic experience, said: "Religion is definitely very organized and very controlled and, you know, you can only hear from the priest. You can't have your own direct experience with God. You need to get it through the priest."

By claiming one needed to have spiritual experience unencumbered by religious beliefs, many interviewees were not denying the authority issue, but simply relocating it. In other words, by objecting to the "external authority" they associated with religion, they instead wanted to "take back" authority. Authority is thus not seen as derived from community, but from the self. They were assuming that spiritual authority resides within the individual, in the privacy and self-deliberation of their own soul. This might seem a simple "take" on the Protestant idea of the "priesthood of all believers" and the contention that each individual is made in God's image with, potentially, God's spirit residing within. In fact, many religions, including Christianity, do put value on personal religious experience. However, it is assumed that the claims of the religion will be verified in this way. But interviewees often went further, turning the Protestant principle back upon itself, using it not only to critique Christianity but all religions.

Many people spoke about not finding "the" truth, but finding "your" truth, indicating that truth is something relative and personal. When I asked James Wolfe whether a person could distinguish the truth from individual inclination, he said "everybody has the ability to do that." But rather than finding some essential truth, it was a relative truth. Thus, James said, "What I think is true, may not be true to everybody else." Truth, then, becomes reduced to personal preference. Truth is whatever is true "for you." This is quite a movement away from the usual sense of the concept. Yet the proliferation and attraction of this view is understandable. In this age of postmodern "deconstructionism" we are all suspicious of truth claims, suspecting that they spring more from personal interest than any kind of universal standpoint. If we are honest, we may even be suspicious of our own beliefs, worrying that we have been influenced by sources outside our inherent selves. This fear of forces alien to our own best interests—as we understand those interests—is one factor that fuels the shift in "locus of authority."

Yet most interviewees do not go so far as to profoundly distrust themselves. Although many fight a continual battle to adhere to their "own" truth, what keeps them away from this precipice is their belief in the inherent goodness of each person. Thus, many affirm that we can trust that "personal truth," the "truth" that comes from inside our selves. This fits well with our discoveries in the chapter on transcendence (i.e., the SBNR view that divinity lies within). Anne Heimlich, who qualifies as spiritual "explorer," well reflected the ethos when she said:

> I think people are basically good. That's our fundamental nature. It's hard to see because we get caught up in our belief structures and

insecurities....A lot of them that are out there are harmful because they aren't allowing people to find out what's true for them. Maybe they can have them through having a belief structure that's been given to them, but a lot of times that's constricting. For myself, I keep uncovering layer after layer of my own beliefs, not religion, but culturally imposed beliefs. I think there is the full spectrum. There are beliefs that are simple, that encourages you to get your understanding. Then there are others that say you have to do "this and this" to get "here and here." That's where religious wars come from. To me it's crazy that we let all these belief structures get in our way to lead us to fighting with each other. Religious wars or a war with your spouse, it's the same thing. You can have fights with your spouse because of beliefs that you are hanging on to about how things should be.

This is the process of "detraditionalization," discussed in earlier chapters. Paul Heelas, who is an authority on alternative spiritualities, explains it like this:

> As a working definition, detraditionalization involves a shift of authority from "without" to "within." It entails the decline of belief in pre-given or natural order of things. Individual subjects are themselves called upon to exercise authority in the face of the disorder and contingency which is thereby generated. "Voice" is displaced from established sources, coming to rest with the self.[20]

Given this, it made sense that the overall critique of religious authority was not limited solely to Christianity. Judy Eberstark, formerly an avid Buddhist practitioner, stopped being part of a community attached to a particularly famous temple.

> I was unhappy with several things in the community...I couldn't buy that structure imposed by the teacher, who I loved for his community and wisdom. But to act certain ways and dress certain ways and automatically be interested in certain things, is how I experienced it. I also didn't like the hierarchy in the community. There was definitely an elite in the community and other people would back me up on that.

Bonnie Doolan was another spiritual "explorer" who was willing to listen to what visiting gurus had to say, and she attended many of their lectures. Nevertheless, she was particularly offended by a famous female spiritual teacher who seemed to undercut her devotees' self-knowledge. "I went to these talks and there were people asking their questions of the teacher. One I went to really turned me off.... It was almost like she was making fun of people for their human experiences. And she sort of laughed. Her tone was that I know better who you are."

Other interviewees set Eastern against Western traditions and implied that Eastern religions, in particular Buddhism, had a lighter hold on truth and less of a focus on belief.[21] Rather than for purposes of conversion, however, this shift was more for the sake of detraditioning. For interviewees were using their interpretation of non-Western religions as permission to unhook themselves from external religious authority which, for most of them, meant the Abrahamic traditions. Some focused on Hindu-derived practices, particularly yoga, and meditation, but insisted it was more primal than religious.

Angela Roman blended the withdrawal from religious authority and lack of certitude together. She had studied yoga intensively, as much as eight hours a day for nearly five years. When I asked her about the Hindu roots of this practice, she said it was not essentially religious but "universal." She added: "Hinduism isn't even religion. Hinduism is a way of life.... The world has made it into a religion.... I guess yoga has its roots in Hinduism.... [but] I prefer not to associate with any particular [religion]. I just want to be open. I don't want to stick to one thing or think that I know something when I really don't know." Since this interviewee neglected to mention, as many did, that all religions are a "way of life," she demonstrated the "rhetoric" of championing one tradition for the sake of argument, rather than affiliation.

Several interviewees linked their withdrawal from religious authority to Buddhism, which they said encouraged them to test out the religion's assertions to see if they worked. Dana Dove said she had been taught: "The basic principle of Buddhism was trust your own mind. If something doesn't make sense to you... then don't do it." Matt Adler, the Gen Xer from a conservative Christian background, had been initially attracted to Buddhism for the same reason. Although he eventually returned to Christianity, his sojourn into Buddhism had made him take a new look at the beliefs of his childhood.

The Buddha...said "Don't take my teachings at face value. Take them and put them into practice and see for yourself." There is no deity with wrath that's going to come after you if you don't believe. Coming back to Christianity, the God of my faith was no longer the angry grandfather, who said, "This is what you need to believe or else your life will be miserable." God is very open and accepting and wanting to be in relationship with you, not only in worship but also in community. There is a reason why "Love your neighbor as yourself" immediately follows "Love God with all your heart, soul, mind and strength."

Thus, many interviewees did much more than just "question authority"—the slogan of the "Long Sixties." Instead, they relocated it within, relativized it to each person, and detached it from any particular spiritual community. And yet, ironically, many of them claimed that—deep down, at heart, at their core—all religions in fact believed and taught the same things.

All Religions Teach the Same Thing

The second issue with religious community is that interviewees felt either they all taught the same thing, or they were all equally fallible. The widespread rejection of exclusivism among these interviewees was not simply about tolerance and mutual acceptance, although there were many comments on that. Indeed, the view that no one religion is better than any other, that no religion has more truth than any other, was asserted as a key ethical stance by most of the interviewees. Deborah Wright put it very viscerally: "It almost makes my skin crawl to narrow it down to Christianity and think that it is the...only way."

According to nearly all the interviewees, there was something deeper or truer than any religion could discern, or had a right to claim as its exclusive property. Darlene Schultz wanted to maintain her connection with the Roman Catholic Church, but on her own terms. She said: "I think I'm religious but not particularly dogmatic. I've never bought into the idea that there is only one true belief system. I don't think God is that way." Amy Legrand, a Gen X "seeker" who had also grown up in a conservative Christian community, echoed the same theme: "God reveals God's self in God's own way, in God's own time, and that we have no business trying to restrict what that should look like for each individual person, and that's what religion does....Religion has screwed up God, but that's not God's fault."

The relocation of authority to within also meant that when people interacted with various religious traditions, there was very much of an

AA-type attitude of "Take what you like and leave the rest." One Gen Xer felt it was arrogant to identify with any one religion. He said: "I know certain groups always say our way is the only way...[but] I like to kind of layer one tradition or practice on top of the other." Scotty Wallace, who I met in a United Methodist church, was of the Silent Generation. To the outside observer, he might appear to be Protestant Christian. In reality, he roamed around many different religious traditions. He said: "I think of myself as a Buddhist Christian but there is no exclusivity for me. Any things that sound true are part of my path and I find that, at the core level of spirituality, all traditions seem to be the same. Only the gateways are different."

Most important, by abstaining from religious affiliation, interviewees often felt they had a unique vantage point, which helped them discern the universal core common in all religions. In fact, many felt their lack of religious identification gave them an advantage over most "true believers" who might be blinded by their loyalty to their particular religion and its truth claims. Anne Heimlich explained it this way: "My spiritual path has been about seeing the truth in so many different contemporary spiritual paths....The Bible has fundamental truths in it, but yet you have to know how to interpret it to get those fundamental truths. I feel like so many religions have gotten too into, 'Believe this and you'll be fine.' People have gotten away from their own truth through their own personal experience." James Wolfe spoke at even greater length.

> I'm not a student of comparative religions....[but] the differences don't seem to be in the basic beliefs. The differences are in the outer part of the church. A lot of them are cultural. But if you look at the core beliefs, a lot of them are the same. I think no one religion is better than another. I think every religion has value...and any religion can teach you what you need to know....But I don't think that any one religion has all the answers. I maintain that religion is man's interpretation of God. There are as many interpretations as there are people on the planet. What you see on the outside is cultural, and if you delve deeply you can find the truth....I try not to be judgmental of other people's beliefs because deep down I believe there is the same core belief in all of them. I think spirituality has been around much, much longer than religion. Religion is a fairly new concept in the last 2,000 years and I think people get caught up in a personality such as Christ, Muhammad, or Moses, or Buddha, or Krishna and

they lose sight of what they were saying. If you look at their words, many of them were saying the same thing or very similar things.

Jenny Buchan tried to be more specific about what religions hold in common: "If you really look at all the simplicity in all the religions, they talk about the same things: Being there for your brothers, for your neighbors, caring, compassion, and love and understanding and not being judgmental.... I won't say one religion is right and one religion is wrong...[but] opening up to all religions and understanding that we are all trying to get to the same place really." Sheryl Best, who had once faithfully attended Sunday School but now admitted she was barely agnostic, saw these essential truths as evident even without religion. She said: "I do believe that there are universal rights and wrongs. I don't believe you need religion to teach you that. I don't believe that you have to believe.... I think people should do the right thing because it's the right thing." She almost sounded like Immanuel Kant here, with his "categorical imperative," meaning that all humans have internal, almost implanted, categories by which they know certain core truths and, further, that they should do the right thing, regardless of whether or not it benefits them.

The view that all religions, at base, teach the same things is called "perennialism." Some explain it at a cognitive level, that is, that core beliefs reside at the heart of all religions. Others explain it experientially, meaning that mystics of all religious traditions describe and seek the same experience of self-loss, transcendence, or union with the divine. My interviewees usually did not get as detailed as this, but their widespread assumption of perennialism showed an important commonality among them. Nor did the apparent contradiction in their views seem evident or disturbing to them. No one explained how truth can be relative, subjective and personal, when at the same time there exists a discernible set of core truths common to all religions. What they did agree upon and articulate, however, was that because no one religion gets it all right, yet all at base teach certain fundamental principles, there was no need or motivation for them to align with any particular religious group. In fact, most felt it was more authentic, honest, or even safer, to simply go one's own way.

An Ideal Spiritual Community

In the end, I wondered if it was possible to form a spiritual community around this ethos. So I asked each interviewee about his or her ideal spiritual community. What would they want and how would they recognize it? It was striking how similar were their requirements. Many of the first elements commonly mentioned were negatives, reflecting the principles above. They seemed directed at the problems they associated with organized religion. The majority insisted their ideal group would have: no dogma, no written tenets, no labels, no belief systems, no symbols, no pressure, no fixed leadership, and would be entirely non-judgmental.

The rejection of specific beliefs was the most common tenet mentioned. Becky Stryker, the woman who led spiritualist groups, said she wanted her ideal community to be ever-changing. "It would have to be something that was always evolving, always changing, different presenters, different points of view, with the group never saying this is what we believe, this is what we are always going to do." Sam Klein, a Baby Boomer who participated both in non-traditional spiritual groups and in church, said that although none were ideal, he found them good enough. Nevertheless, he was clear that he felt no compulsion to accept any of their particular beliefs or religious identity. "I belong to four or five communities. As far as anything that points to a religious community, I would say I don't belong to any.... If I go to a Christian church, what I feel, is what I would call the fellowship. I'm not interested in the doctrine, because I think it's been edited up the wazoo."

Gail Asher insisted the church members she served as secretary of the congregation were spiritually immature in restricting themselves to Christian beliefs. For her, the ideal spiritual group would be "one that would include people who were open minded, not necessarily labeling themselves as a certain belief system, one that allowed for exploration, growth and maybe some experimentation and one that allowed self-study and study of other's interests and sharing." Several interviewees, like her, simply wanted a community that would enable their own explorations. Kimberly Takahashi fit here, envisioning it providing "more like instructions on how to figure out things on your own." Jim Haag, a gay Baby Boomer, attended services but refused to identify with the Quakers. Still he said he found good-enough community there. He also participated in many other spiritual groups. He especially favored the Quaker group, however, because:

They respect me the way I am and allow...other people to be the way they are....I don't feel that I need to make the pretense that I believe certain things....I can go to Quaker meeting...and say one week that I'm going to a Catholic group and the next week say

I'm going to an atheist speaker and they don't kick me out....No symbols on the wall, an open space that people are not pressured into being something that they are not.

Ironically, although most interviewees agreed that they wanted a group without any belief requirements, pressure, or symbols that indicated a particular tradition, many interviewees also indicated they wanted a group where people had "similar beliefs," where people were like them and agreed with them. Bonnie Doolan, now a spiritual "explorer," had grown up in a small religious enclave, which she had left as a teen. Although she occasionally attended a variety of informal classes focused around particular spiritual teachers, she had not found her ideal group. She speculated, "I think I could be with people who are doing similar practices and have similar values." Brendan Potter showed the tension between the SBNR ethos which champions tolerance and objects to dogmatism, yet the human longing to be part of a like-minded community. His ideal community, he said:

Would all be people that share similar beliefs to myself....When I say similar, I mean similar. I don't mean like their beliefs are exactly like mine....I mean that they kind of have the same concept. They might have different ideas about the concept. But I would want a community where people weren't ostracized or put down for not having the exact same belief. Because I think ultimately we are all entitled to our own beliefs and that's why we have them. I mean, I don't think there is anybody that has a belief that isn't valid.

Rebecca Henderson was a dramatic exception. Her mother had kept her in the Catholic Church until fifth grade. After that, the family never attended again. Even without much religious experience, this young woman was very clear what her ideal spiritual community would look like. She would know it, she said, because it would be:

Orthodox...in this case Buddhist, so that there is some very solid ground of theology. There is strong ethical commitment. There has to be some strong mentorship within the community, an emphasis on spiritual practice and ritual....There has to be a monastic element even if I can't participate in that. And there has to be a householder practitioner element. I think all three of these are important, the monastic, the householder and devotional practice.

Alexandra Heim, spiritual "casual" and Millennial, was different from many others in that she longed for spiritual leadership, although not from an established religious group. She may have been conflating paganism and Wicca, but she was clear what she needed. "I feel I have a potential for a community with a pagan coven.... I think that I will have one. I want to have someone older and wiser and practiced...teach me because I'm self-taught. A lot of pagans are." She ended by saying, "I would really like to find people of similar beliefs."

When talking about their ideal group, interviewees often describe something more therapeutic than specifically spiritual. They insist they want a group that supports them emotionally, is tolerant, welcoming, and allows diversity. It would be a place where each can express their own gifts, find peaceful minds and hearts, and be encouraged to explore, experiment, and grow. Baby Boomer Penny Watson had a completely non-religious background and insisted she did not want to have to start this group herself. "The ideal spiritual group would be a healthy one that I would not have to found myself, and [I could] go and sit and it would be wonderful and I would be home." A Gen Xer said her ideal spiritual community is "just a group of people that, not even necessarily like-minded, because I think diversity is good, just that are there for you, that understand that you need to express who you are, even if your beliefs are different, because I really think that different beliefs are good and challenging. And basically just being there for anything, for campfires, for singing, for anything."

Judy Eberstark was somewhat unusual in that she struggled for years to find a group identity. She had participated faithfully in a number of meditation groups, both Buddhist and Hindu, over the course of her adult life. Yet she felt there were some important aspects of Christianity that she missed, including a belief in a personal transcendent being who cared for humans. For a time, she decided to search in Protestantism for a spiritual community. When I asked what she would look for, she said:

People of faith who are open-minded, who aren't standing on the rooftop with a bugle. They just have a simple, modest, ordinary faith, but profound. They care about each other. They don't feel there are things they have to hide from each other. I don't mean you have to tell your life to everyone, but there is joy and mutual appreciation and something much greater than ourselves that we depend on and draw from it.

The first year I met her, she was not participating in any groups, Eastern or Western, only occasionally joining others for meditation as her family obligations allowed. The next year she was actively trying the Protestants. By the third year, she told me she had decided she was too formed by meditation groups to go back to Christianity and hoped eventually find a *sangha* she could join. The fourth year when I visited her, her family obligations had subsided considerably. Now she had gotten involved with a gentleman, but he did not have the same spiritual thirst she did. So, instead, she determined she would enjoy the outdoor activities he loved rather than continuing to search for a spiritual community.

Many interviewees expressed similar visions of an ideal spiritual community, yet only a few—even with much exploration—admitted to having found one. Even so, interviewees blew apart most of the stereotypes about them. Although there was a range of personality types, personal problems, and histories with spiritual community, I did not find the SBNR interviewees to be essentially narcissistic, commitment phobic, or simply people who have been hurt by religion. Nor did the heart of their critique of organized religion have to do with ethical issues, such as judgmentalism, hypocrisy, prejudice, elitism, or unfriendliness. Nor did I find the crux of their problem with organized religion based on a reaction against the politics of conservative Christian groups. Although this played a part in keeping them away from churches—especially for those with very little religious experience—the prime motivating factor was deeper than this. Instead, the root of their separation of religion from spirituality was more theological than personal or political.

As we have seen, the factors contributing to the SBNR ethos include: a prioritizing of personal growth over group identity, a relocation of authority from external to internal, a belief that all religions teach the same things, and an abhorrence of the triple religious "sins" of judgmentalism, dogmatism, and exclusivism. Even twelve-step groups, which manage to embody many of these features, did not engage many of the interviewees for long. Indeed, the kind of group that would engage them, according to these standards, would have trouble surviving since they would not contain many of the core elements of spiritual communities such as shared belief, mutual responsibility, and common mission. All these various factors, then, go a long way in explaining why my SBNR interviewees were "allergic" to religion and—even if they participate in it at times—often chose to avoid long-term commitment to spiritual communities.

8

Afterlife

DO AMERICANS STILL believe that something lies beyond death? Various surveys say that about two-thirds do.[1] But this widespread belief is not as clear-cut as it may seem. It is no longer a simple choice between believing in a literal heaven and/or hell versus believing that death is the end. The evangelist's common strategy, expressed by the question, "Where will you spend eternity?" does not makes sense to as many Americans as it once did.

Still, we cannot avoid the topic of death. It is not only personal and visceral, but it is highly theological. The question of what, if anything, comes "next"—also known as eschatology—has been a perennial concern upon which most religions have speculated. How can we grow, mature, and learn, only to decline, wither, and disappear? Why do we spend time on relationships knowing they will inevitably and irrevocably end at some point? Is that all there is? Especially if there is a God who created us and desires our affection, or a loving force, or intentionality in the universe, how could this terrible waste of resources be part of the program?

Various religions take different approaches. For Judaism, death is not necessarily the end of human existence. Given that the religion focuses on this life, however, it allows adherents to hold various opinions on life after death. More specific views on life after death may have arisen late in Jewish history, but the fact that there is not much dogma around it is possibly one reason that Jews sometimes feel free to align with religions that believe in reincarnation.[2] Christianity, however, takes a strong stand that death is not the end of human existence. Because a loving and infinite God created us for relationship, it would make no sense for this to end at death. Leaning on the various indications given by Jesus, much of

Christianity teaches that after death we maintain our identity, but receive a new resurrected body, come into the presence of God, and become part of a holy community. There is a diversity of teachings about those who reject this gift. They may linger in a limbo, may go to a permanent netherworld, or may disappear. For Islam death is a natural process leading humans on to the next stage of existence. Life after death is a core aspect of their beliefs. A last judgment, a final end, and physical and spiritual resurrection are all taught. As a result of God's ultimate judgment, individuals will find themselves either in paradise or hell.

Various Eastern religions do not ignore death but teach that the merging into the One, or the dissolving of the ego, is the ultimate goal of human existence. Resurrection of the body would be antithetical to this goal. But reincarnation exists as the vehicle toward that goal. It is the path toward losing or transcending the self, rather than an endless process of second chances for improving the self. Those who achieve enlightenment in this life may skip that process. Folk or indigenous religions have a diversity of views on life after death, including such things as envisioning a mystical community of ancestors waiting to greet the recently departed. In any case, death is such a dramatic feature of life that few, if any, religions can afford to ignore it. One might even say that the human need to address death is one reason religions exist.

Still, death and afterlife are admittedly difficult topics, and a few interviewees did not want to talk about them at all. Even when I asked about it directly, they skated around the issue, insisting that the subject is distressing, unknowable, and something they intentionally avoid. A small number frankly rejected the whole idea of an afterlife, seeing this belief as simply an egoistic wish for survival, or a religious fear tactic to keep people in line. They seemed content with, or resigned to, the fact that people are part of the earth and they simply get recycled like everything else.

But the vast majority of my conversation partners insisted there is "something" after this life. One might assume that they would embrace a simple heaven/hell dichotomy. After all, studies have shown that many Americans still hold to these views. One study found 67% of Americans "absolutely sure" there is a heaven and another 17% "probably" sure, totaling a high 84%. As for hell, this same survey found 59% of those questioned were "absolutely sure" about hell and another 20% "probably," totaling a substantial 79%.[3] But the interviewees' views diverged widely from these results. Their beliefs in an afterlife were very diverse, suggesting everything from reincarnation and past lives, to alternate universes, to an "open house" with spirit guides. Although most interviewees did not buy the heaven/hell schema, most had thought extensively about this topic and were not at a loss to describe alternatives. In fact, many presented as clear an idea of the journey as one can have without having yet made the trip.

Rejecting Heaven and Hell

Whether or not they believed in an afterlife, and as much as they differed on the details, most of my conversation partners made one thing very clear. They outright rejected the idea of a static heaven and a torturous hell. Most also rejected any kind of "winnowing" process where some would go to a better place and some to a worse one. This rejection came from those with no religious roots and from those with religious backgrounds. It came from those who avoided religious services and those who attended. It turned out that the traditional heaven/hell image was one of the main topics with which nearly everyone agreed to disagree—not with each other, but with organized religion. In fact, the issue of life-after-death was often one of their main theological sticking points, especially with Christianity. The near universality of this view among interviewees is, in part, an influence of the liberalizing of Christian views on heaven and hell. More importantly, however, it is part of the rhetorical strategy to distance themselves from Western religions.

Even though it is not the actual case, my interviewees were convinced that almost all church-goers believe that gaining eternal life means "my way or the highway." They felt this way whether they relied on personal experience, or on popular stereotypes, or on the media focus on high-profile religious groups. In reality, statistics do not bear out this stereotype. Reputable studies prove that more than two-thirds of religiously affiliated Americans reject this sort of exclusivism almost as much as SBNRs do. In fact, most Americans already believe that more than one religion can lead to eternal life.[4] In spite of this, my interviewees got much traction for being "spiritual but not religious" from their assumptions about exclusivist religious beliefs regarding heaven and hell.

In examining my interviewees' reasons for rejecting an exclusivist or literal heaven and/or hell, there were some common, underlying rationales. Some considered it psychologically manipulative on the part of religion. A few likened it to a "marketing scheme." Almost everyone thought it was unfair or psychologically "unhealthy." Guiding their judgments, again, were factors like the American ethos of "fair play" and equality, as well as the therapeutic ethos. But there was also an echo here of an earlier theme which cropped up in their beliefs about the sacred. That is, a number felt that believing in heaven and hell, or in any kind of afterlife, was immature, childish, selfish, and/or a vestige of a superstitious past. Several felt almost "honor bound" to reject such seemingly unpopular or unscientific views.

It's Immature, Sick, False Hope, or Manipulative

Mary Johansen, the Silent Generation "dissenter" with a previous religious background, well-illustrated the feeling that a mature theology was one which rejected heaven and hell, even if this loss came at a psychological cost:

> I think one of the hardest parts, one of the most important maturing points in my theology, was in terms of a literal versus a symbolic version in terms of the afterlife.... In the context of science, to believe in an afterlife was seen as a superstition. I had to find some way of reconciling that.... I love life and it's hard to let go of life. It's hard to think that there is nothing after my atoms go back and my cells go back. There is a part of me that would love to have a consciousness after death, but I think I have matured to the point where I can accept that there may not be.

Several other interviewees felt it was simply egotistical to want to live on. When I asked "seeker" Penny Watson about her views on life after death, she said:

> I have no opinions about that. I don't feel that that is something I should be concerned about, because that seems kind of selfish: "Oh, I've got to do these things so I can live forever." I will do what is expected of me, because it is expected of me, not because I think there is any reward or punishment.... I know it's a comforting thought, but I don't think about it. If I think about it, I think about what I need to do to have lived a good life and earn my keep here. I don't think about getting into heaven.... You have to earn your keep for being here.... [Or else] I don't think I would be living in harmony with the cosmos.

Rebecca Henderson, the young woman who is trying to make her personal views more Buddhist, went further. She saw her desire for life-after-death as psychologically sick. "There is a really neurotic part of me that is very paranoid about death, not in a clinical kind of way, but a subtle wanting to live forever...wanting to know what kind of impact I've had. I recognize that is neurotic....It feels sick, like nauseous and tunnel-visioned and closed off and hard and breakable. That brittle feeling. That's where you step back and say that's not good."

Some people actually based their rejection of religion almost entirely on their childhood religion's focus on heaven and hell. Joyce Moffatt, who had once been a devout church-goer and missionary, was a "dissenter" and barely an agnostic by the time I met her. She said: "I don't believe in a heaven or a hell. I think I was raised too much in [the idea of] people being in this world in order to get to heaven. Their whole reason for being was heaven and an afterlife. It doesn't make sense. I love my father dearly but I don't think I need to see him again. The thing for me is what people do with their lives now. That's what's important to me."

Like her, many interviewees saw ideas of life-after-death as false hope. They stressed that now is all we have and that we make our heaven or our hell right here on earth. Echoing the theme that your ideas create your reality, spiritual "explorer" Susan Heinz said: "I think we create our reality based on what we are thinking about. Our thoughts can create our emotions and our emotions can create hell depending on what we are thinking." Amy Legrand, raised a Protestant but now a "seeker," agreed. "I grew up with the Sunday school version.... People who believe in Jesus go to heaven and people who don't go to hell." But now she had a different, more this-worldly view. She said she believed in "a different idea of sin.... Being separated from God or...the Divine presence is its own hell.... Being wrapped up in yourself is its own hell, versus living within compassion. Knowing the Divine presence is its own reward." Jennifer Babcock, the Gen X "casual" with a difficult background, believed that there was enough heaven and hell right here on earth. "I don't know what I believe about afterlife, but I feel that all those things are real now, while we're alive. Because I've experienced both. Like if you call it heaven and hell, I certainly have had both. Definitely in my life."

A few responded wistfully that a form of "immortality" would come through memory. One young person said: "In my eyes I just die, leave this world, and I'll just be a memory. Maybe that's how this whole life continues. It's not the soul that lives on. It's the memory of you. And maybe that's my intention in life...to make my memory carry through. That in fifty years, a hundred years' time, people will remember me. Through that I will have achieved something that, in a sense, [is] immortality." But Laurie Hanson, realizing the limitations of memory, said, "As long as we are remembered, then we have a presence on this earth." Scotty Wallace, the Silent Generation man trying to combine Buddhism and Christianity, actually rejected both traditions' views on afterlife. Unlike the interviewees above, he was not even wistful about it. Scotty told me, "Other than leaving reflections in the people we interact with, and the things and places we touch, I don't have a strong belief or desire about life after death."

Some people rejected the idea of heaven and hell as a ploy by religions to distract people from death or make them behave. Nick Jones speculated: "We don't want to talk about the fact that we are going to die...Ya know?...Going...to heaven...takes over for that fear of death." A few people questioned the idea of heaven and hell as outright intimidation, but wondered if it might nevertheless serve some purpose. One young woman asked why "there needs to be a heaven and a hell and a scare tactic? [Or do] you have these moral guidelines because you need to keep society in check? I don't know." Like her, a few others allowed there might be some usefulness in life-after-death beliefs. They suggested that religious threats of afterlife might serve to control the negative behavior of some weaker people. However, they usually insisted that they themselves were strong enough not to need it. Alternatively, some simply rejected the idea of hell as a ploy that goes a bit too far. Barely agnostic and clearly a "dissenter," Sheryl Best told me:

> I'm not against religion because in some people's life they get the guidance and structure that they need. Without it, who knows what would happen?...[But] I never believe that you have to make people behave because they think they will burn in hell if they don't. That's threatening them to behave, which is negative reinforcement, which I don't ever think is good.

Ron Richmond, who had been reared in a very liberal Protestant congregation, was similar to this woman. He felt all religions overstepped their bounds when they spoke about life-after-death. "I'm not critical of religion because I understand that people have a need for answers and people get paid to give them those answers....They are called the clergy. People strive for it and we have clergy to help us through it. But implied in that statement is that there is an answer." He did not feel there was. Jon Farmer, the interviewee who had never been religious, took a more jaundiced stance: "Death is the one thing we know the least about. Therefore, it is the one thing that gives most religions their influence. No other organization uses death in a more manipulative way, in my opinion."

Popular Descriptions Are a Turn-Off

For others, it was the popular descriptions of heaven and hell which turned them off. Former Christian conservative Amy Legrand remembered: "I grew up with the pearly gates and streets of gold and a mansion and all.... That makes it sound [like] a very capitalistic environment... [It's a] great marketing plan. But I don't think that's what it's all about." She was not the only one who was cynical. Matt Adler, who walked away from his own conservative background, said: "I felt like it was a pyramid scheme. I saved my soul. Don't you want to save your soul? Then you can have them save someone else's soul." Even though this man ended up in a more progressive Protestant church after his serious sojourn into Buddhism, he returned with radically different views of afterlife. When I asked him what he believed now, he said, sounding somewhat monistic:

> I believe we go back to the source. Hell was a development when the Hellenistic culture came in. If you read biblical Judaism, Sheol was an afterlife, but it wasn't punishment.... I believe I will go back to God and we will bask in the glory of God and the love that surrounds you. I think as Christians we focus too much on the afterlife. We've been given a message about how to live now. Let the afterlife take care of itself.

For many interviewees, hell was a bad idea. The idea of endless torture just did not sit right with more socially liberal Americans who rejected "retributive justice" (i.e., that people deserved to be punished according to their transgressions). Even Beverly Bosch, who told me about her abusive childhood, assumed her deceased mother would not "suffer for her sins." "With my mom, I think that she did the best that she could with what she could. I don't think that she went to hell for being suspicious and paranoid. Or for beating us kids up, or anything like that. I don't think she went to hell for that. I think she went to a better place. At least I hope so."

Like several of my interviewees, Courtney Szabo was a religiously raised person who claimed that literal views of heaven moved her away from Christianity and toward Eastern religions. She said:

> I can remember my mother was my Sunday School teacher in ninth grade. We had this three year march through the Bible....After all this time, we are studying Revelation and she is trying to read the passage and interpret it literally....They talk about the city with the gates and she was literally trying to draw this out on a chalkboard....I was mortified. That was probably the point where I decided that I don't think heaven is like they think it is. I think it's something else. I don't know what it is, but I don't think it's this, only better. That's what sparked the interest in Eastern religions and kept me reading and saying, "This is different. This sounds right." [This] was one gap in my Christian upbringing that I found insufficient. Because even now, my husband's family will talk about loved ones and "Oh, they're sitting up there and someday we'll get to sit up there with them." I don't think that it's like that.

For some interviewees, including those without a religious background, the idea of heaven was like a happy dream in which they only barely hoped. Even when they wished to be reunited with loved ones who had died, few had much confidence that this sort of personal afterlife—where one maintains one's individuality—could happen. This was the case for Becky Samuels, who had lost both her husband and her son. When I asked if she ever thought about life after death, she said:

> Yes I do. I thought about that a lot after I lost Carl and Richard. I wanted to see them again, well and whole...not suffering because of their bodies in this lifetime. I wanted to tell them that I was sorry for something in this lifetime that I didn't do. I want to meet them again in another realm that transcends what we can do in this realm. I thought about [this] so much and it's still a hope of mine that I would like to be able to do, but I don't really know what to think.

In fact, regardless of their backgrounds, a large number of my conversation partners had become "spiritual but not religious" as a reaction against popular descriptions of heaven and hell. One Millennial summed it up when he, with a touch of sarcasm, speculated on heaven this way: "Okay, now we are all back together in the afterlife and whether I think we are all dancing around with wings on clouds and playing bocce ball and harps... I don't know.... [But what] if we are all wrong? I guess that is the 'doubt' part of me. [That's] part of the reason I am spiritual and not religious."

There were some exceptions. A small number of interviewees adhered to traditional, even literal, views of heaven and hell. But they seemed to focus on ethical and psychological reasons, rather than strictly theological ones. Some speculated that justice demanded some form of punishment for wrongdoing in life, whether limbo, purgatory, or hell. One young man, a Gen X "casual," said:

> I definitely believe there is a heaven and a hell. I would like to think if you go to either place, for whatever reason, that you do have a consciousness of your identity... that you do understand why you are where you are at because... there's some pretty awful things in the world that have happened over the history of mankind and—however mean-spirited it is—part of me is just hopeful that if someone has done enough to deserve to go to hell, then they ought to understand... what it is they have done... To me, that is part of the justice of it.... God's justice, my justice, whatever.

Several others who believed in hell reiterated the "choice" theme, insisting that hell was an option, although one most would not choose and, even so, a temporary one. Michael Blade, the spiritual "explorer" who had experimented along a wide spectrum of religions and spiritualities, used a film reference to explain:

> I believe in hell as defined in the movie "What Dreams May Come." There's a part in the movie where one of the characters says something along the lines of "Hell is a choice that you make...." [So] if I die in a state of such grandiose despair... that could potentially carry over into the afterlife. That doesn't mean that it will be permanent. That's something that... my soul will have to work through before it can reconstitute itself again.... I don't believe that someone is going to condemn me there. I think I would condemn myself.

The idea of maintaining relationships in heaven was attractive to some interviewees. It made Lisette Marshall, the young woman raised non-religiously, try out Christianity to please her husband. In fact, it was his views on the afterlife which persuaded her. She said about her husband: "It was his sincere love for me and wish to share heaven with me that caused me to give Christianity a real try," she said. Like Lisette, a few interviewees found the idea of a static heaven—enduring relationships, being in God's presence with no further effort or growth needed—restful and pleasant. But, no matter their picture of it, most of the interviewees who believed in a more literal heaven and hell felt fairly confident that they were going "up" rather than "down." In this, they accorded with surveys of Americans' beliefs.[5]

It's Exclusivist and Unfair

What bothered most interviewees more than simplistic depictions of heaven and hell was the seeming unfairness and exclusivism of it. They rejected the idea that only those from your own religion are rewarded with heaven. Even as a child, spiritual "explorer" Jack Acker thought the common evangelistic quandary about "those who have not heard" the Gospel was unfair. He said he could never understand the idea that "all those hundreds of millions of people in China were going to hell because they didn't know Jesus. I could never figure that one out. . . . I never felt it." For a few other interviewees, it got more personal than that. Shelly Trump, the "seeker" with a minimal religious background, had gotten involved in evangelical Christianity as a young person. She stayed with this a long time, but eventually left because of their views on afterlife. She put it this way:

> My first year in university I was at this Baptist church and they believed in predestination. I had a horrible time and I really had a crisis of faith. . . . As I remember it, you've got the select few. I'm going [to heaven], so that means that my parents who aren't professing Christians are doomed to hell because they aren't predestined. I had a really hard time with that.

We have heard from Susan Heinz several times already. This spiritual "explorer" was raised without religion in a chaotic household. Her grandparents, however, were Seventh Day Adventists. She stayed with them often, especially after her parents got divorced. She remembered:

> My grandfather thought that everyone else was going to hell in the family so he cried a lot whenever my parents were not there. I remember one time, he broke down in the driveway because he was so mad at my parents....Mom had left us with my Dad and my Dad was out running around on a motorcycle and just left my sister and myself at the house. That was when I said: "Grandpa, this can't be right. I don't want to hear it anymore. You can't be right. My parents aren't going to hell."

For some, legalism was also a sticking point—the idea that your eternal salvation rested on the following of specific earthly rules. A significant number of Baby Boomer interviewees I met seemed to be reacting to a pre-Vatican II Catholicism with "rules" about who would go to heaven and who to hell. Darlene Schultz had been raised Catholic and still hung on to the Catholic label even though she rarely went to church. She explained how her lack of participation had grown the more she objected to many of the principles she had learned. This included the need for baptism to ensure eternal life. She said:

> I cannot believe that a good person who does not have a spiritual home of some kind, a religious recognizable home of some kind, isn't going to get into heaven. My father...he got baptized at the end, but...I'm not even sure that he believed in God....[But] he was a wonderful, kind man. There'd be no reason to deny him heaven, just because he didn't go through a particular ceremony....I think those are man-made elements.

Others remembered the rules about no meat on Fridays, which seemed particularly illogical to them, especially after they were loosened by Vatican II. Becky Samuels, now a "casual," remembered the "little book we got as kids in catechism with all the lists of the mortal sins and the menial [*sic*] sins. There...[would be] nobody in heaven, if you died with one of these zillions of mortal sins on your souls, which seemed pretty minor to me, like having eaten fish [*sic*] on Friday." In other words, she suggested that the rules were so difficult to follow that no one would make it to heaven.

This reaction was not confined to formerly Catholic interviewees. One young man, once a very devout evangelical Christian, said of his childhood religion:

> The mantra of this church culture—even though I don't think they meant to teach it—was as a kid, if I'm naughty, I'd better ask for forgiveness. I had this mindset that if I was caught doing something, without having a prayer of penance and asking forgiveness of the Lord, then I would be doomed to hell. So every night before I went to bed, [I asked] what have I done wrong today? That created a weird sort of guilt-based experience that I had to walk through later.

But even a spiritual "seeker" with only a minimalist religious background could get caught up in this. Becky Stryker, the Gen X "channeler," for a time was attracted to the warm community of a very sectarian form of religion. She liked it at first, but left when they told her: "If you cut your hair, you're going to go to hell. If you wear makeup, you're going to go to hell. If you wear pants you're going to go to hell."

It was not just Christianity that was deemed exclusivist. Mark Sage, the young man who got his spirituality from Alcoholics Anonymous, said: "The biggest problem I have with various religions is that one religion says, if you don't believe what we believe, then you are going to hell. Then another religion says, if you don't believe what we believe, then you are going to hell. If that is true, then everybody is going to hell and I don't want anything to do with it. I don't want to go there, wherever 'there' is." Whether it was exclusivism, unfairness, or legalism, many of my conversation partners rejected the views they associated with organized religion and used their own ethical ideas as the criteria for whether ideas of afterlife should be believed.

Doing Theology

Only a few interviewees went beyond criticizing unfairness, bad psychology, legalism, or implausible descriptions and into more serious theological arguments. Several people called upon the character of God to dispute the idea of hell. Shelly Trump, the "seeker" raised with no religion, joined InterVarsity Christian Fellowship in college. Once a member, she accepted heaven and hell literally. When she stopped believing in hell, however, she left the group. I asked her what made her stop believing this. She said: "Understanding God's grace. Why would a loving God put us in hell? And if you believe that Jesus died for everyone, then where is there room for hell?" Jack Campbell, who we've heard from several times, had been a devout Catholic growing up but now mostly relied on Buddhist meditation. About his religious background, he said: "It was very important to me as a child.... I really liked the Mass. I served Mass. I was very connected to that until adolescence when my mind kicked in and I started thinking about hell. I thought a loving God doesn't condemn someone to hell forever.... I quit participating in the church at that point."

Darlene Schultz, another theologically reflective person and raised a Catholic, was not sure about hell. She postulated it could be a place without God's presence, yet someplace no one would choose. Instead, she depicted heaven as almost irresistible. "If there is a hell, it is a place where you get to see God and then you are relegated to a place where you don't get to see God anymore. I don't believe in Milton's version of hell. The burning flames and the flaming sea and all that stuff... I cannot believe that if you saw the face of God... you would... want to be anywhere else."

Amy Legrand was a woman who had moved from conservative to a more liberal Christian view largely through contemplating life after death. Although she no longer attended church, she felt "hope" was the core principle of Christian theology. Growing up, she said:

> I didn't like the idea that a person [who] has a terrible life and they go and kill someone... [is] supposed to be in hell forever. I would like to believe that everyone has hope of being redeemed.... I don't have a really good formula other than believing that there is hope for everyone. There is accountability and there is hope. I can't really believe in the traditional hell [where]... there are those that are lost forever.... That's not Christian faith, in my limited understanding of it.

But a few interviewees found something theologically profound in the ideas of heaven and hell. Judy Eberstark, who I spoke with repeatedly over several years, was one of the more theologically reflective interviewees. Raised without religion, she became an intermittent Buddhist while also entertaining the idea of being part of a progressive Protestant church. Instead of finding the idea of hell negative, she found it illustrative and compelling. In college she had been enthralled by reading the archetypal hellfire sermon, "Sinners in the Hand of an Angry God," delivered in 1741 by Jonathan Edwards and part of the Great Awakening. She remembered: "I really got interested in Christianity in a deeper level when I started taking American History courses.... I didn't think [Edwards] was this crazy guy preaching hellfire and damnation. I became interested in the Christian mystics, you know, St. John of the Cross. I started realizing what I had been missing growing up and as a teenager." When I asked her what attracted her about that sermon, she said:

> It had something to do with the way that Jonathan Edwards could express the difference between our utter nothingness and the everythingness of God. Although a modern rational person would say that's some kind of perversion, or trying to impress us with our guilt, I didn't feel that way. I thought, yes, we are nothing and we do sometimes need to...see that, see ourselves as small or insignificant in comparison with the Creator.

It was striking, though, that few of my conversation partners even considered the perennial philosophical and theological dilemmas attached to the afterlife issue. For instance, no one wondered if immortality is inherent to the human condition, or instead is a gift. No one debated whether or not people have an eternal soul or spirit, although some simply assumed it.

Surprisingly, no one speculated about the body. This gap was odd, given the strong focus on the "mind/body connection" in the therapeutic and spiritual circles the interviewees frequented. Even so, no one asked whether or how the soul might endure disembodied. No one wondered if the actual body is resuscitated. No one speculated, alternatively, whether some kind of new creation, some kind of "resurrection body" would result. No one asked whether the body—in some way—was necessary for a holistic human identity, whether some kind of body/soul connection was necessary in order to have a genuinely personal future existence.

Nor did many see death as a hostile force or an enemy. Instead, a large percentage had a much more resigned attitude to it. And when they rejected the idea of afterlife, they often went to the "lowest common denominator" explanations. Few, including those with religious backgrounds, understood the rationale behind the Abrahamic religions' confidence in life after death (i.e., that humans are a divine creation, destined for eternal life and relationship). Even those raised in Christianity did not mention the resurrection of Jesus as an indication of eternal life, or death as the last enemy that only God can conquer. It seems that, even for those with some childhood religious education, many important topics had been neglected. So my interviewees filled in the gaps themselves. Rather than leaving such an important topic blank, they set their sights on other thought worlds to replace the rejected stereotypes they associated with the Abrahamic religions.

Replacing or Supplementing Western Views

Many of my interviewees, in looking for alternatives, experimented with ideas of reincarnation, karma, expanding consciousness, and endless growth. This raised another set of perennial questions, which some interviewees did explore. For instance, if there is some form of eternal life, who decides whether you go and what kind you experience? How much control do you have over your own eternal destiny? If there is some kind of standard, how many chances do you have to "get it right"? Is attaining afterlife universal, or only for some? What about justice? Is there any repentance, penance, or punishment for wrongdoing on earth? Or does everyone simply get what they deserve? And, finally, is there some ultimate goal in the afterlife? Do we retain our individuality or are we simply absorbed into some kind of unity?

As my interviewees explored these questions, they did not adhere to any particular religion's views. Instead, their suggestions were very eclectic. Even though they asserted their right to reject traditional Western religious views, in the end they did not leave them aside entirely. Instead, they often retained selected aspects of Abrahamic views, especially Christian, but blended them with other ideas they had picked up from various books, workshops, films, and spiritual teachers. When all mixed in together, it was a very American perspective on the afterlife.

Reincarnation, American Style

A very large percentage of my interviewees said the kind of afterlife they believed in was reincarnation. While surveys show that about one-quarter of Americans now hold this belief, among my interviewees it was well over two-thirds.[6] This included those who were never religious, those who had left religion, and those who maintained an intermittent relationship with religion. I was likely to find as many church attenders in this group, as people who got their spirituality from self-help groups, spiritual teachers, and/or popular books. A belief in reincarnation was held by the majority of my interviewees, including the many who had had no formal contact with Hinduism or Buddhism. The reasons they chose to believe in reincarnation were very instructive and, again, often related directly to what they were rejecting in Western religion.

Rather than being more Eastern or more Western, a variety of other principles seemed to exert a stronger influence. American values such as independence, self-determination, and freedom of choice prevailed. For instance, most felt their personal choice of where to "end up" should be determinative rather than some impersonal law. They very often believed there should be no "judgment," except perhaps what they leveled on themselves. Many felt progress was inevitable, rather than the possibility one might return at a "lower" level. And, often, increasing "consciousness" or "growth" were important goals.

A Better Option

Again, psychology or ethics seemed to be driving forces, in particular the idea of "fairness." In a land that believes in "second chances," to many interviewees it seemed unreasonable to only have one lifetime to "get it right." Instead, many believed it seemed better to have multiple lives in order to work out their issues, understand their true identity, and/or to become a better person. Rebecca Henderson said: "[Reincarnation] makes more sense to me than we leave this place and go to some other realm and stay there forever and ever. That just seems strange." While many interviewees admitted to being confused about the afterlife, the idea of reincarnation was almost always something they considered. One young woman seemed conflicted when asked about her beliefs in an afterlife. "I know what you're supposed to believe, but it's hard to comprehend.... My faith is a little shaky. I can't wholeheartedly just say 'Okay, I trust...there is such a place as heaven or hell'.... I almost more so believe...how you just keep coming back until what you are meant to fulfill is fulfilled.... That, for me, is a little bit more easy to comprehend."

Several interviewees blended reincarnation with either heaven, hell, or both. "Seeker" Patty Hoffman insisted the idea of reincarnation kept her from committing suicide. She said: "Reincarnation has both the hell and fire and brimstone of my childhood, as well as a hope that you'll be reunited with someone. But I'm not really counting on it. It does stop me from contemplating suicide—not contemplating it, but getting to that point. I come from a history of depression and all of my children have threatened suicide.... In those dark times the need for spirituality is strong. Anyway, reincarnation has kept me from that."

It is not surprising that many interviewees wanted to retain an idea of heaven, given how popular it has been in Western thought.[7] Yet many felt that more than one life was needed to attain it. That way, each person was responsible for his or her ultimate destination. "Dissenter" Carole Bradford had tried numerous spiritual paths and, although she never settled on just one, found the idea of reincarnation a great relief. Like several other interviewees, she retained an idea of heaven, got rid of hell, and blended it all with reincarnation. She said:

> Human beings are basically good, but that doesn't mean that they cannot be diverted for generations. That's why it was such a relief to realize I didn't have to do it all in one life. I remembered thinking in college, now that's a fairer system because I didn't like the idea of anyone going to hell. Everyone gets to heaven, but nobody gets there until they deserve it.

Finally, I ran into several people who saw Christianity as deficient in not having a belief in reincarnation. Bruce Carter, the spiritual "explorer" from a conservative rural environment, insisted that every religion, including Judaism and Islam, taught it. He said: "I believe in reincarnation. Christianity is the only one that doesn't have a reincarnation. Why should that be?"

Several interviewees speculated that reincarnation did not necessarily happen on earth alone. Former Episcopalian and now New Age retreat center teacher Tonya Bond said: "There's a hundred trillion stars in the universe.... I don't think that necessarily you have to come back to this earth. To think that this is the only place that we can...work on our remembering who we truly are.... There's lots of places for us to possibly continue on our education and experience." Spiritual "explorer" David Kaplan, raised a secular Jew, now blended the idea of God, denial of death, and reincarnation on "other planes." He said: "There is no death. When the soul leaves the body, you continue to exist and have consciousness.... Then you die into another life. You die into the astral plane, the causal plane, the mental plane.... It is definitely reincarnation."

Many interviewees went beyond simply adding reincarnation to their views of heaven and/or hell and brought in the idea of karma. Spiritual "seeker" Amit Singh, raised Hindu, explained it: "The theory of reincarnation is based on karma. Karma is like Newton's law of motion. Whatever you do, you will pay for it one way or another. You cannot get out of it." Some interviewees blended Western ideas alongside it. Rather than an impersonal law, some believed that God had created karma originally, but was no longer in control of it. Jeff Wurtzel, raised by conservative Christian parents but now involved in a Spiritualist church, said: "He [God] set up the rules.... The law of karma is absolutely true. The Golden Rule is a more positive way of stating the rules of karma. I believe that's...the way things work. Your fears are answered and your dreams are answered."

Some felt karma was an alternative way to keep people in line, better than the idea of hell. Daniel Nimitz, also involved in a Spiritualist church, said: "There is a continuity. You live. You die. You are reborn. You die. You have karma to work out. That's one of the reasons why it's really important to live the best you can so you don't have to repeat it too much." Angela Roman, the "seeker" whose parents sent her to the Catholic Church until she refused to be confirmed, saw karma as an impersonal force that nevertheless exerted guidance. "You'll totally be guided anyway, so there's nothing to worry about. You don't have to think about anything. It's all happening like it should. If you've got any karma, you're just gonna have to go through that."

Without any belief in a judgment day or a judge, many interviewees substituted the "law of karma." In this scenario, many postulated that evil was a necessity. Gail Asher said she got all the spirituality she needed from reading the Tao Te Ching and explained that doing "atrocious things" was essentially a necessary learning experience for the perpetrator and even for the victim.

Unfortunately...I think in every decade that we've lived, there have been atrocious things that other people have done. There is still genocide going on and it's incredibly difficult to understand how anybody could do that to another person.... I believe that the souls that were a part of that experience can explain how that happened...and how to avoid it in the future. That was the lesson that they carried into the future. I'm hopeful that eventually that will no longer be necessary. But it does seem to be a necessary experience for human beings to understand the preciousness of life, the importance of love, understanding, compassion. There are all

sorts of lessons that should be learned from that kind of experience.... When we experience things that we qualify as suffering,
those are the lessons that we need to learn in this lifetime and carry
into the next lifetime. So that eventually those things don't continue.

Many interviewees, as we have seen earlier, suggested that one's thinking was determinative. It could bring bad experiences, but it could also
change them. "Channeler" Becky Stryker said that while one could not
"cancel" bad karma, one could alter one's perspective of it so it would
not seem so negative. "It's not possible to cancel karma but it's possible
to shift your perception of what it is.... Maybe it's not a universal law as
much as it is a belief which becomes real.

Others suggested that suffering was a choice that God was learning
not to make, with human help. Tonya Bond said: "Whatever energy that is
this spark...sent out from the Godhead...continues to experience itself
until it realizes that it doesn't need to suffer." A few took this further and
postulated that evil is only a perception, not a reality. Spiritual "explorer"
Dana Dove told me: "There isn't anything wrong. It's our illusion that
something's wrong. Even with the horror of the planet changing." Even
for those who recognized evil, however, most optimistically speculated
that progress was inevitable, at least on the human, if not always on the
worldly level, no matter what choices we made. Amit Singh insisted: "The
law of karma says that nothing goes to waste. Even if you have not realized
the Lord, you will still know what is the right thing to do. In that life you
will be doing the right thing."

But for others, choice still ruled. I asked Becky Stryker whether she
believed, as many in Eastern religions do, that one could regress in the next
lifetime, rather than always progress. She said: "Oh, sure...if you choose
it. Nobody's putting that on you." Alexandra Heim gave another illustration
of this idea. First she offered her theory about how your thoughts control
your situation, likening it to a "personal weather pattern" that draws good
or bad to yourself and also contributes to a collective "weather pattern."

You have to have a strong, strong sense of responsibility for every
situation that you are in. That doesn't mean, I was feeling negative
yesterday or eight years ago and that's why the war in Iraq is happening. No, no, no, it's your personal situation. Each person has a
personal weather pattern in their head and the collective weather

pattern is a direct reflection of that. So you have ultimate control. A lot of people think they are victims of their situation, but you draw to yourself that which you are most like.

Since she seemed tentative about the reality of victimization, I asked her how she would apply her theory to the Jews in Nazi concentration camps. She explained that those who had better attitudes survived.

> I would say that the survivors, if you talk to them, are the ones who had some tiny, itsy bitsy speck of hope. There was this man talking about his experience and people asked him why he survived and the others didn't. He said, "I think it was because I offered my soup to people because it made them feel good and I took the bread which had more nutrition in it, because it was watered down".... For some reason that little scrap of information stuck with me.... It's hard to tell people to have faith or hope in those situations. But if you can be like: "If you can find one little thing in your daily life, that you appreciate and feel grateful for, that will make your life better." Regardless of the conditions but you could feel better.

For those who did not survive, however, she said they would get another chance, since "if you go into the oven, you die, and you go back into the blob and you go into another vessel and try again."

Some interviewees felt karma only operates within one's lifetime, rather than being carried over through successive lives. This theory was similar to the idea that heaven and hell were only what you create now. Ian Hanby, the Millennial man trying to adapt to Buddhism, said: "I don't believe in karma from past lives. I believe in karma in the here and now.... In this way...everything that I do has ripple effects that I can't begin to imagine. That's how I live on. The goal becomes living in such a way that the ripple effects help other people wake up. It helps me wake up.... It's waking up together.... That's all there is.

Your Choice, Your Goal, Your Helpers

Although many felt karma was an impersonal force, an inexorable law that could not be evaded, they also expected to exert their own influence on it. Gen X "seeker" Bethany Storm said: "I do not believe in an external anything in the sense of some omnipresent 'whatever'.... I do subscribe to this notion of karma, but again that's not some external something exuding its forces on me." For most interviewees, mixed along with karma and reincarnation was the confident and optimistic belief that each person was in control of their own destiny. This seemed far preferable to the idea of some divine judge determining your fate. This choice theme was reiterated again and again. For most, it seemed to make more sense in a world that emphasizes personal freedom. Apparently, the freedom to choose one's own "lifestyle" extended also to one's "death style," thus taking very far the belief that your ideas create your reality. Many insisted that, like choosing one's religion, one could also choose one's afterlife.

Laurie Hanson believed death was the end, yet she also asserted that there would be an afterlife for those who believed in one. Not only that— but the ultimate in the theory of thought control—this afterlife would be created by their beliefs.

Whatever people think they believe is going to happen is what's going to happen to them. Why not? If you think you're going to be reincarnated, then you go to the reincarnation realm. If you believe in heaven and hell, then that's where you go. If you don't know, maybe you never know.... I don't actually believe in an afterlife. My basic belief is that what we have is what we have on earth. I do think that as long as we are remembered, then we have a presence on this earth. That is my artist self speaking. As long as I leave my quilt behind and the paintings, my poetry, and my children remember me and my grandchildren remember me, that's my immortality. And the trees that I've planted will grow.

Barbara Axel, the spiritual "explorer" who blended Roman Catholicism, Protestantism, and shamanism, allowed some space for God, but basically said the same thing very succinctly: "I think you can choose heaven or choose reincarnation, or choose other realms that God has." Spiritual "explorer" David Kaplan based this same assumption on God's character. "Wouldn't a loving God give choice?...You could become an earth or a Jupiter, if you wish. That's part of our destiny, if we so choose." The idea of personal choice extended also to the details of the next life. Daniel Nimitz told me: "You move on, but you choose people that you know when you come back into this life." Margie Mason, another spiritual "explorer," said that although everyone's lives were "laid out before [human] incarnation, in at least a basic pattern, we make plans with others about the lessons we are all to have in our life time."

I wondered if there was some ultimate goal to all these reincarnations. Most interviewees did not go beyond an afterlife of continuing "second chances." They did not address the idea of some ultimate endpoint unless I specifically asked them. Retreat leader and spiritual "explorer," Tonya Bond, believed in endless progress, explicitly denying there was any endpoint or stable "nirvana" as the ultimate goal, but simply increasing levels of "consciousness." Again, though, it was by choice. She said: "We get to cultivate our consciousness. [If] we want to be at a higher level of consciousness, then it's up to us to do some internal cleansing, align with that, and to invoke it."

A few interviewees did speculate on some kind of endpoint. A woman, who had been raised Jewish, affirmed there was an ultimate goal for one's successive lives. "There is a goal and I feel we're not going to leave this earth until it's complete. I think that's how you get to nirvana. It's completing your purpose, your goal, and until then ... it won't release you." But she also speculated that once someone had dealt with all their "bad karma," they still had a choice of whether to reincarnate again. She said one might "keep coming back because you get it so right that your resources are needed again.... Ultimately we have that choice, to stay or to go. It's not like a punishment ... I don't look at it [like] ... you're gonna be punished, so you're going to be sent to hell. I don't believe in any of that."

Jenny Buchan, the spiritual "explorer" raised by a Wiccan mother and holiday Christian grandparents, felt we had to keep going through successive lives until we "got the point." It seemed she was proposing some external standard. But, like many interviewees, when she got too close to the idea of some external judge or rule, she repeatedly fell back on the idea of choice. "Life is just a big lesson. There's something we have to evolve to, something that we have to learn.... We keep on going through it until we get to that point, where we think we've learned enough, or God thinks we've evolved. I think it's a choice. There's a lot of free will involved with it.... I still think there's a choice.... Each little soul has their own choice of what they want to do. I believe that you're all given free will."

Even in a worldview that emphasized personal responsibility, nevertheless many thought they might get some help along the way. It was intriguing how this view could be held by very disparate people. Jack Acker, the rural Midwestern blue-collar factory worker from a conservative background, now a spiritual "explorer," told me with confidence that after death: "The soul goes back to the place that I call my celestial home. [There] I have mentors that say, 'You did this or that, or you didn't do this or that.'" And a very different sort of person, the biracial West coast spiritual retreat leader Tonya Bond, said something similar: "I believe we have attending spirits that are assisting us along the way. So, whether it's your past life, your attending spirits, that life, I think that it's all here to kind of assist us in our education."

The idea that a kind of re-evaluation process would take place for a period after death was a surprisingly common view. Jeff Wurtzel expressed it this way: "I think I'll pass on. My body will go away. My spirit will continue. I think there are multiple facets. I'll review my life with a group of more evolved beings and we'll figure out what I did and what I didn't do. We'll look at how I met the goals I set before I came here and there will be a period of rest and rehabilitation.... Then I'll be back. I'll get to do it again." In most cases, though, and even with the help of some "mentors," it was ultimately the person who evaluated him or herself, rather than any kind of external judge.

Bruce Carter, another rural Midwestern man, was an exception. He postulated that outsiders would judge people after death. In doing this, he conflated reincarnation, heaven, spirit mentors, and Jesus (who he called Jeshua). He said: "When you die you go to heaven and there [mentors] go over your life and everything you done and anything you need to do in many reincarnations.... Your soul will go there. You will be judged according to how you are. They'll go over many things with you.... You just kinda hang around there, like an open house. When Jeshua comes back here, he'll back it, so that there is no more pain and there will be only happiness for everybody who He chooses." Another exception was Gordon Hance, the young man who had been reared by a mother he labeled "New Age" but who had subsequently joined a church, to his mother's dismay. However, he still retained elements of his upbringing and, as many others, focused on choice: "I believe that eternal life is either heaven or hell. There is a choice now. There are people who make it easy to get into heaven. Some people make it impossible. In between, that is the reality, but I don't believe God sends people to hell. People might say, 'That's not for me.'"

Individual Continuity and Past Lives

Living in a country and an era where self-focus, self-esteem, self-knowledge, and self-love have risen to the level of dogma, it is not surprising that many interviewees expected to maintain some sort of individuality through successive lives. They explained this in various ways, often drawing upon the popular idea of remembering "past lives" and using this as a path to knowing one's "true self." Again, most asserted this would be ruled by personal choice. Tamara Birnbaum, the woman of Asian Buddhist and Christian parents, who was now an administrator in a spiritual retreat center, was very confident that no matter how many past lives, one would know oneself: "We do retain our identity....[but] I feel it's a choice...how deep I want to go." Sam Klein is the Silent Generation man raised by Jews and Baptists and now loosely connected to a liberal Protestant church. He was clear that one retained one's individuality, even in successive lifetimes.

> As far as losing our identity, I don't think so....The human experience is one of an infinite number of frequencies. I think reincarnation is a way of pointing to something eternal....The purpose of human life is to experience human life and become evolved....I like [the metaphor of] theatre because when you're born, the stage is already set. You're a walk-on....Our job is to become more aware of our freedom within the confines of your role. I feel very strongly about individuality. It's not like when you're born, this is your very first acting job. You couldn't even get on stage if it was. You come here with a history.

A few interviewees spoke of near-death experiences as proof of some kind of spirit continuity that could inhabit successive bodies. Wiccan Babs Chapman said that when she had this experience: "I didn't have any idea of being a body, but I had consciousness and I could see. I do believe that our spirit lives on, that we are spiritual beings and that we are electrical. You can't kill electricity. It lives on. I do believe in reincarnation. I believe we've lived more than one lifetime and we will live again. I don't see death as an end. I see death as a new beginning in a new form, doing something else.

One evening I conducted a focus group in a Midwestern city. It was held in the living room of a woman who was very interested in Sufi spirituality. She was able to gather a sizeable group of others. The conversation eventually turned to "past lives." Several focus group members insisted, as did a number of interviewees, that the experience of "déjà vu" proved that one had lived before. One said, to the eager nods of the others: "I believe—just in some of the things that have occurred in my life—that

I have to have been here before. From the age of 5, my Mom took me to a friend's house. I'd been in that house.... I knew the rooms. I knew where things were. I'd been there. That has happened to me several times in my life.... The 'déjà vu'.... So past lives versus reincarnation... for me they mean the same thing."

Westerner Tamara Birnbaum reiterated something similar, saying that anyone, upon meeting someone new, can "have the feeling like you know that person forever.... I've had that happen to me many times.... Instead of beating myself up and trying to figure out where this comes from, I just accepted the fact that it could possibly be a past life, that we've met before." Another woman used the popular reasoning that the reality of gifted children and great artists proves past lives: "How [do you] explain Leonardo Da Vinci [and those] who come with this incredible talent or Mozart, children who come... [as] prodigies? They come with a full deck." Dana Dove used past lives to explain why she was drawn to Native American and Eastern spirituality. "I do believe in reincarnation. I don't know how it goes but that makes sense to me. My experience goes back to the natives of Nepal and Tibet and Bhutan... and the other native peoples. It explains attraction... [because] my background has nothing to support my attractions to native things and art and religion and Buddhism."

Some interviewees not only speculated but also sought out "past life regression" seminars in order to facilitate their self-understanding. Often they were told that they had specific lessons to learn in each lifetime in order to progress. Mary Johansen, Silent Generation "dissenter," told me she went to a doctor for "chronic body problems and the way I was holding tension." This doctor sent her to "a weird Buddhist therapist. We would have 5–6 hour marathons.... Some of the stuff... was spontaneously coming out of me.... She told me that I was some high-up person in the church in England in the Middle Ages and I was nasty to people. I was kind of a harsh authoritarian person. She said part of what I was learning in this life was the law of hospitality and love."

"Channeler" Becky Stryker also conducted past life regression sessions. She was very firm in her beliefs but took the theory further than others had. She postulated that parallel universes contained parallel lives, and that, because of this, two people from the past could merge into one.

I do have this theory. It's not based on anything, because you can't prove any of this. I suspect that it's possible. Let's say that you and I were friends in a past life, or in a parallel life, and we decided to come into this life as one person. I believe it's possible for us to merge and do that. I don't know where that's coming from, because some people are so drawn to other people and it just doesn't make any sense why they would be.

But the most extensive conversation I had about the idea of past lives happened one day when Jack Acker, the rural Midwestern spiritual "explorer," walked into my seminary office, responding to my call for interviewees. His story deserves more elaboration now. Dressed in work pants and a partially buttoned tight plaid shirt, Jack seemed uncomfortable and out of place. Yet even though this was an unfamiliar environment for him, he was clearly eager to talk with me. He spoke at length about his hard times, including a wife who left him, being downsized from his factory job, struggling to find work and make ends meet. In the midst of his misfortune, he had become obsessed with discovering his past lives, thinking it would help him understand why his luck was so bad. He told me: "I asked a buddy because I think this life is very hard... 'How many times do you think I've been reincarnated?' He messed around with my fingers and said 'About 350,000 times.' I said: 'Oh God, no, don't say that.'"

In spite of this bad news, Jack continued to pursue the issue, signing up for regression workshops. I could see he was trying to find common threads that would help him understand himself better. He told me: "The first past life regression I went to, I thought I was in Germany. I was a news reporter during World War II....I kept going back to this beautiful brunette wife I had. I am literally enticed by brunette women." Another particularly meaningful session confirmed Jack's belief in past lives. "I had actually gone back 300,000 years to another time and another place. I could have not made that up in a million years....I saw buildings that no man could ever build and the message was just amazing. It still puts a smile on my face." This man kept using his scarce resources to sign up for additional sessions because he "desperately wanted to go back" to this positive experience. He clearly saw this continuity as a firmer footing than simply the idea of déjà vu. He said, "It's not déjà vu so much as we carry it through our DNA with us."

Before we parted, I asked Jack how long this process of reincarnation had to go on. He said: "I think you just keep coming back until you learn...until you forgive people. Then you go back to the Father and you don't have to go through this....Once I forgive myself for these negative emotions that I have when people do something to me—and get past that—then I won't have to forgive anybody, because there won't be any need to." Although his life had been hard, Jack focused on his response to it, his "negative emotions." One can also hear his efforts to combine ideas of reincarnation and past lives with his former conservative Christian background. This could be seen, for instance, in his idea that, once all issues are worked out, we "go back to the Father," as well as his insistence that forgiveness is the main issue.

I found the idea of both continuing and expanding "consciousness" to be a driving force in many people's ideas of reincarnation, karma, and ultimate goals. Even when they allowed a "judgment process," however, the goal was still personal development, rather than some assignation to a permanent status in the afterlife. Yet Western religious views kept getting mixed in. Even though Eastern religions are divided on whether one's individual identity is retained in successive lifetimes, many of my interviewees were convinced it was. Judy Eberstark, the "seeker" raised with only minimal religion, had gotten deeply into Buddhist teaching and, from this, had accepted reincarnation. Nevertheless, she blended in both traditional and progressive Christian views as well, such as preservation of some type of self-identity, forgiveness, judgment, and afterlife. In addition, she also included such New Age spiritual themes as evolution, growth of consciousness, self-judgment, and endless learning.

> I very much believe in continuing consciousness after death. That's a very basic thing in Buddhist teaching....It's not like going to heaven, hell or purgatory. You go through a judgment process. The only thing is that I know that my consciousness will go on and I will be able to see things and understand things that I don't see now. I will be able to see things that I will regret. My personal belief is that life, mind, or consciousness, are constantly evolving, whether it takes a form on this planet or in hell or heaven. Our life is a precious gift and as we learn more and more, than we can evolve and become more and more open. Our reality can become more and more stupendous, whether it happens in this lifetime or whether we get stuck in this lifetime. I believe in reincarnation, but I don't have this literalist idea of reincarnation where there is one soul. I do believe that many people can remember things from past lives but also that we are each unique. What I am trying to express is that I believe in existence after death and the forms that takes are

myriad and I'm an optimist in my faith. There is always an opportunity to forgive and to learn.

Not everyone, however, expected to remain the same person, have
conscious continuity, or even have any of their individuality preserved
in successive reincarnations. In fact, a few interviewees felt the goal was
to lose one's identity entirely. Dana Dove said: "To me the goal is to not
exist anymore. For me that would be liberation, nirvana, never forget-
ting the nature of reality." Amit Singh insisted: "There is a message of
hope that if you continue your actions towards your goal of God realization…then in one life you will realize the Lord and then there will be
no more lives."

But for most who did postulate some eventual "landing place," they
offered something like absorption into God, rather than the eradication of
the self entirely. Gail Asher, who kept her views on spirituality to herself
rather than sharing them at the congregation where she worked as secretary, likened self-realization with this absorption. She said: "Every person,
every soul on this planet is here because it is in process of finding that
source and becoming one with that source. Every lifetime has its goal of
how to get to the next level of realization." Spiritual "explorer" Michael
Blade said:

> I think the only goal for me, and ultimately for humanity, is to
> return to that from which we came.…Some people will do it in
> this lifetime. Some people will have to reincarnate.…I know that
> Buddhism teaches that there is no true self. I don't necessarily
> agree that that's the truth. I do think that there is some truth to
> this illusion of self. I do think we are all intertwined or interwoven.
> I think there is also something of the self that does exist in the now
> and that it could potentially carry on.

Alexandra Heim, Millennial and spiritual "casual," offered an interesting "eschatology" of re-absorption into "the blob." Earlier she used
it in relation to those who died in concentration camps (see chapter 6),
where she said: "In this blob is all the existence of everything that's living
and feeling. When someone is born, or when life is created.…there's a
little bit of this blob that is pinched off and pours into this vessel… but
when we are in the vessel we are not separate, we are all part of that
one blob."

Still, individuality was in some way preserved, she said, thus: "Whether I'm enjoying myself in this personal vessel....I'm still going to endure in myself somehow....I'm an eternal being and so I am going to exist....There's a sense of uniqueness and individuality that I have even if I still go back to that blob. I'm still me."

For most, the trajectory was also positive. Tonya Bond, spiritual retreat leader, felt confident that the path was "a progression toward uniting with the creator." The goal was inevitable, she said, using an analogy. "You will travel from New York to California. It doesn't matter how many detours you take to get there, or you could go straight there." Susan Cashman, who still attended church somewhat regularly along with her determined explorations into non-traditional spirituality, said something similar. "We see the cycles and the seasons, so I think we're cycles....I think we come back....I haven't gotten there, but I believe you can finish. Maybe that's what you do when in Christianity they talk about residing with God for eternity. After you've done whatever it is that you're supposed to do...you get finished. Kind of 'Beam me up, Scotty.'"

Naysayers

Like those who rejected ideas of heaven and hell, there were some interviewees who bucked the trend toward embracing the idea of reincarnation. However, their numbers were much smaller than those who rejected Western ideas of afterlife. Some who rejected reincarnation were firm in their refusal. A few disbelievers said they needed to be convinced, but allowed they might be wrong to reject the popular views. And some strongly criticized the eclectic quality of popular beliefs in reincarnation and past lives.

One woman in a focus group said, pragmatically, "I have had such a struggle getting through this life that I haven't had time to worry about others (lives)....Just...get me through this one and that will be enough." Spiritual "seeker" Pamela Ames felt similarly, but added more nuance to her statement. She had been raised with no religion, and had experimented with Eastern views, until choosing to join a church.

There was a period where I believed in reincarnation really seriously because that seemed to make the most sense. But I've since decided, especially as you get older, having to go through it over and over again might not be such a good idea...[It] might be a

terrible kind of empty and depressing thing. The belief in reincarnation...can be used to oppress people...in awfully terrible ways.

Gordon Hance had learned a lot from his "New Age" mother, fully
immersing himself into past life regression and reincarnation beliefs,
until he became "spooked" by them. He, too, had ended up joining a more
traditional church.

I believed in reincarnation for years but the gurus scared me. I got
spooked by some of it. I loved listening to Moody Blues and the
Indian thrust, but I knew people that would worship these gurus
and that freaked me out. I had so many hypnotic experiences, especially in my early to mid-teens. I'd see myself live out an entire life
of somebody from adulthood to death...I was working with different psychics....Instead of past life regressions, I took it a step
further.

Matt Adler, the conservative Christian turned Buddhist turned progressive Protestant, asserted he left his Christian background because of too
facile views of heaven and hell. But after several years of being deeply
involved in Buddhism, he decided he also had difficulty with the idea of
reincarnation. He gave the most extensive critique of any of my interviewees, raising questions no one else did.

In [my] childhood it was a choice of two afterlives. If I believe
the right thing, then when I perish I get to go to heaven. In
Buddhism, everyone gets reincarnated. What level you are on
depends on your karma of your past lives. Somebody I didn't
know. Something I have no control over. My problem with that
was if I have no memory of my past lives, then how can I know
that I'm reincarnated? If all we're taking on is the karmic baggage
of a previous life, then what's the point? Also there's the hierarchy to reincarnation. [And] how [do you] rationalize that humanity hasn't been getting that much better, but the population has
increased?...Or that Tibetan Buddhists are always reincarnated
in the East?...Who's to say that some sentient being wasn't born
in Houston?...That was where it started to break down. I can't
remember my past lives and yet I'm being punished for them by
this karma....Nobody could...[explain] whether it was a result

of a past life or some random act that was happening to you now in your current life. . . . I didn't like it from the beginning. I never believed in past lives.

Kimberly Takahashi, who had some minimal exposure to Buddhism from her grandmother, had abandoned all ideas of the afterlife and raised a similar critique. "It seems kind of weird, because a lot of bad things still happen to people that do good things. It seems . . . too perfect . . . a system. . . . It's too easy of a solution to say that the bad things that happen to you are something that you did in your past life." Several people, although they wanted to retain an open mind, said that they had difficulty believing in something without proof. One young woman said: "I don't know if I disbelieve in reincarnation and I don't know if I believe in it. But I have a hard time, I guess, visualizing a spirit from somewhere else. . . . I don't know what that would be like. I'm really visual and it's hard if no one has ever seen it or you don't have an idea of what it would be like. . . . It's something I just can't understand."

Other interviewees, often younger ones such as Kimberly Takahashi, challenged the idea of a constant and eternal soul. She explained: "When you die, that's pretty much it. Because if I don't believe in the whole concept of, like, heaven and hell . . . and I don't believe in reincarnation, then where does that really leave you? . . . I guess I would fall sort of semi along the lines of Buddhism, not in the sense that there is reincarnation, but that one doesn't really have a soul that goes on after death." Another young woman, like many, prevaricated: "I'm not one to believe in reincarnation per se. I don't totally believe the idea of a soul going to another place, but I can't dismiss it." Some, however, did dismiss it. Anne Heimlich, who said she wanted to grow and improve in this life, nevertheless rejected any sort of pay-off for this in an afterlife:

As I believe more and more in this universal life force energy, I think that we do have an energy inside us that leaves [when we die]. . . . I would like to just sort of be buried into the earth without anything around me and be recycled into the earth and be of service in that way. I don't have any notion that I need to be a certain way in this life to get to another place. This is it. I am awakening in my own life so I can be a better person. I am not doing any of this for some afterlife status.

Finally, several young people who had immersed themselves in New Age or Eastern religions eventually rejected the eclectic quality of many Americans' belief in reincarnation. Rebecca Henderson, the young woman from an Episcopalian background now seriously trying to adjust to Buddhism, really objected to the hybrid approach of many of her peers.

> People who start mixing Hindu and Buddhist or New Age stuff, that's where I start finding that those people are the most aggressive to my spiritual path. I would rather talk to somebody who is very exclusivist and says you are going to hell if you don't believe in God than somebody who says you're really a Hindu and it's all the same thing and if you just get in touch with your *chakras* everything will be okay.... That to me is more fundamentally aggressive.

And Alex Johnson, the young man who had devoted himself to the mission of a New Age retreat center, nevertheless had a similarly jaundiced view. He said of the center: "There's so much spiritual story going on here. It's mostly...not Hinduism...[but] California Hinduism. New Agey Hinduism...I don't think anybody is really practicing a strict Buddhism here, or Hinduism at all. It's mostly just playing with various California amalgams of, you know, a couple practices from this, a couple from that."

Is Everyone Hindu Now?

The widespread belief in reincarnation has prompted one article in a weekly news magazine to declare that "We are all Hindu now."[8] Is this supposed "turn to the East" correct? It is true that most of my interviewees reject what they deemed inadequate or unbelievable ideas of heaven and/or hell. Also, many have abandoned any idea of a divine judge who holds your fate in "his" hands, or even a loving God who "has a plan for your life." Many interviewees like the idea of an impersonal law of karma, where all your misdeeds inevitably bear consequences and all your good ones help you advance. They find this an improvement over any kind of external religious moral standards. Having overthrown more traditional Western views, it seems many of my conversation partners postulate reincarnation and karma as an alternative way to give meaning to life, even to bad things and misfortune.

But although the magazine article makes for a good story, for several reasons the contention that "we are all Hindu now" is simplistic, at least as it applies to my sample. First, in adopting some aspects of Eastern religions, my conversation partners rarely adhered to any one type of Hindu or Buddhist view on afterlife. For instance, few believed one could go backwards in a next life. Instead, most optimistically asserted they would endlessly improve their spiritual status. They insisted on this, even though the idea of endless progress, rather than regress, is not characteristic of most Eastern religious views. Also, when I asked if they retained self-consciousness and individuality, they often thought that they did. Yet Eastern religions often postulate the self or ego as more problem than prized possession, often expecting it to dissolve or merge with the "absolute." Finally, only a few interviewees speculated on some ultimate goal such as *nirvana* or *moksha* as Eastern religions often propose.

Second, an undercurrent of Western beliefs remained in many interviewees' comments. Many retained some variations on Abrahamic views, such as heaven and/or hell, a personal God with some level of control, and an eternal, identifiable soul or self. Third, mixed in with all this were many assumptions from American democratic principles, as well as the common "therapeutic" perspective. For instance, many held to a belief in endless second chances, where expanding consciousness and psychological growth would be inevitable. And although they liked karma as a substitute for a divine judge, most expected to have significant control over the whole process. Finally, although many often insisted that science is now or would soon be confirming their views, few interviewees paid much attention to the many common objections to reincarnation, such as over-population, or how one can have past-life memories when there is an entirely new brain and body in each lifetime.[9]

Instead, like the theodicy dilemma in Christianity which posits the quandary of a good and all-powerful God alongside the reality of evil, their positions end up with a set of difficulties which most chose not to address. Few questioned, for instance, whether some people suffered unfairly or whether misfortune was always commensurate with one's actions. There was not much talk of victimization or the idea that "bad things happen to good people." Few wondered whether there existed any divine sort of grace or mercy which might ameliorate the heavy price resulting from bad karma and multiple reincarnations.

In spite of potential quandaries, the majority of interviewees were satisfied to create their own mix, postulating an inexorable law of karma, endless opportunities, inevitable progress, expanding consciousness, and the very American idea of free will and personal choice. Rather than a complete eschatology—that is, belief in end-time trajectories, "last things," or a goal-oriented teleology—the belief in successive afterlives was, instead, a core aspect of interviewees' search for their "true selves" and a way to make meaning out of this life. In the end, the majority of interviewees simply liked the idea that each person had successive lifetimes to "work on" themselves. They liked the idea of endless time to grow and learn. They liked the idea that your life was in your own control. And they even seemed to like the idea that—no matter how bad your situation—you got what you deserved. It was especially striking to hear this latter view from socially liberal people, in a society where the reality of victimization is now taken for granted, where unfair suffering is the focus of many progressive organizations, and where many feel political systems are stacked against whole segments of the population.

9

Conclusions and Implications

A MOBILE HOME IN THE SPIRITUAL UNIVERSE

THERE IS NO simple explanation for why the people we have met here have felt compelled to minimize the importance of organized religion. As we have seen in earlier chapters, there are many aspects involved: cultural, historical, demographic, political, and others.[1] The belief—or theological—factor, however, has received scant consideration. We need more awareness of the belief issues playing into the decrease in religious affiliation. Therefore, my goal has been to ferret out the inchoate theology among a group of people in this growing population.

Some may think that in a postmodern era that is fragmented and shorn of meta-narratives, theology is not being done. But even in this context, people try to make sense of their lives, to find some compelling reason to get up each day, endure difficulties, find joy, and live with hope. In fact, a new "common parlance"—perhaps even a new theology—may be developing, as meaning-making shifts from religious and civic institutions to popularly mediated "gathering places," such as Internet, social media, self-help literature, television, and film. Against the common assumption that "spiritual but not religious" people do not have any particular theology, we have seen that these interviewees were often thinking theologically.

My goals in this research were several. I wanted to explore and better understand an aspect of the "none" world which has been neglected. That is, I wanted to hear how "spiritual but not religious" people construct and express their faith and beliefs. Rather than being alienated or puzzled by my invitation, many people found it both compelling and welcome. In the end, I had many more volunteers than I had time to interview. I also wanted to find the possible commonalities, overarching themes, or directions in their thoughts. I wanted to know if there were any theological concepts commonly rejected, adapted, or adopted. While my interviewees cannot be fully representative of everyone who is "spiritual but not religious," what they have said here can be heard in many other places. And, finally, I wanted to set their beliefs in relationship to theological ideas previously common in America. I did this so they and others—whether religious or not—could better understand this emerging ethos.

Theology is not just finding something to make you feel better or cope with life. These benefits may indeed result from careful theology. Instead, the common Western definition of theology is "faith seeking understanding." It is exploring the fact that you stand in relationship to something Ultimate, something larger than yourself. Both mysterious and revealed, this Ultimate undergirds and supports you while also having a claim on your life. Theology happens as we orient ourselves toward this Ultimate and have faith in its beneficence. We then become more confident as we tackle the existential—and ultimately theological—questions humans ponder such as: "Why are we here?" "For what can we hope?" "Why do we suffer?" "How can we thrive?" "Is death the end?"

Many interviewees were grappling with just these sorts of questions. Most, however, had not been given tools adequate for the task.[2] For them theology did not mean a systematic or consistent set of beliefs. It did not mean leaning on a catechism learned in childhood. It did not mean a permanent theological thought world which, once accepted, guides the rest of life. Thus, in many ways, these interviewees were not unlike the millions of "fuzzy faithful" that populate pews today, and perhaps always have. But theology was happening, nevertheless.

Theology may have looked different in eras when sheer survival needs predominated and people had to shelter under a common "sacred canopy" in order to work together. These interviewees seem less concerned than people in earlier eras to find a common theological narrative that can be held by a whole society. Nevertheless, they did search for a comprehensible and comprehensive meaning in which to situate themselves. Perhaps the need for a communal narrative still exists under the surface since a large percentage of my conversation partners held out a wistful hope of finding a group that believed as they did. The fact that the people we have met here search, read, and try different theories, practices, and teachers shows they are trying to pull things together. Spirituality, for them, may have become more a commodity than a lifeboat, but they were shopping for meaning nevertheless.

Many assume that people who reject religion must have had bad experiences there. Many assume that although these people have retreated from religion, they have kept many of the same beliefs. Others suggest that such people minimize belief and focus instead on eclectic practices. But studies show that people leave or reject organized religion for a variety of reasons. Some leave because of interpersonal conflict. Some find themselves unable to use the coping skills offered by religion.[3] Some are "structural nones," critical of religious organization in general and some are "marginal nones," people who choose to be socially detached. But many leave because they have theological difficulties with particular beliefs and values. These are "cultural nones" that is, those who disagree with some or all of the core principles of a particular religion or religion in general.[4] It is these people and their theological and cultural reasons which have engaged us here.

Although there was some mixing-and-matching and some holdover of earlier beliefs, by and large these interviewees were not "believing without belonging."[5] Nor did many interviewees report a history of interpersonal conflict or abuse experienced within religion. While some did demonstrate that religion had not helped them cope with life's problems, neither was this the only compelling reason. Instead, these interviewees show that a crucial aspect in their rejection of organized religion is the theological dimension. This fits with surveys that show two-thirds of former Catholics and half of former Protestants "say they left their childhood faith because they stopped believing in its teachings."[6] Thus, as we have seen, many of the problems my interviewees had with religion were as much intellectual as emotional, ideological as experiential. In other words, inadequate theology—or inadequately understood or interpreted theology—often played a large part in their lack of interest in religion.

And rather than simply representing eclectic beliefs and practices, the majority of my conversation partners held two important factors in common. This was the case in spite of their diversity in other ways and in spite of the different reasons why they prefer not to affiliate with any particular religion. First, the separation of spirituality from religion was more a "rhetoric" or an ideology than a deep disconnect. This is because, as we have seen, multiple core factors are held in common by both these designations. The people I met who resonated with the phrase "spiritual but not religious," did have beliefs, rituals, behaviors, and practices which

could legitimately be termed "religious." Some might say they are practicing "implicit religion."[7] They linked their own finite selves with something
larger. Their spirituality dealt with many of the same existential questions
which have occupied religions for ages. And they "performed" or lived
out their beliefs in various ways. In this process, the interviewees were
doing theology. That is, they were searching for and making meaning in
their own lives. They were looking for an ultimate reality. And they were
discerning theories or principles which could guide their behavior.

Second, it has become clear that a theological agenda and critique is a
crucial part of the rhetoric, and often more about repudiation than affirmation. Many interviewees homogenized and simplified core theological themes labeled as characteristic of Western religion—Christianity in
particular—and then rejected or radically altered them. For example, as
we have seen, people have rejected a God stereotyped as a judgmental
overseer and instead have substituted the idea of a sacred force which is
impersonal and benevolent. The positions disavowed by the majority of
interviewees include:

- an exclusivism that rejects all religions but one's own;
- a wrathful and/or interventionist God;
- a static and permanent afterlife of glorious heaven and tortuous hell;
- an oppressively authoritarian religious tradition;
- a non-experiential repressive religious community; and
- a view of humans as "born bad."

Through this process of setting up a malevolent archetype, the message
is able to reach and be clear to a great number of people, including people
with very little religious education. It works so well because many people
recognize these themes, whether they have learned them through hearsay
or inadequate teachings. That there may be some religious people or traditions which hold some or all of these positions is not the point. I found
no one interested in testing out the reality of these doctrinal assumptions.
Disproving them would hinder the rhetoric. Instead this strategy is a "language game" or "straw-man," which allows for a common enemy and thus
a crucial measure of agreement in a diverse group often thought to be
highly eclectic and transitory.

Interviewees' theology can be identified by its "detraditioning."[8] This is
not a total repudiation of the social order or even necessarily a call for radical social change. Instead, it is a revoking of religious authority in favor of

personal decision. Rowan Williams, the former Archbishop of Canterbury, explains this as a reaction to the ways this religious authority was sometimes practiced in the past.

> The traditional forms of religious affiliations…lose their integrity when they attempt to enforce their answers; and one of the most significant lessons to be learned from the great shift towards post-religious sensibility is how deeply the coercive and impersonal ethos of a good deal of traditional religion has alienated the culture at large.[9]

Although this detraditioning creates a vacuum, the vacuum does not remain empty. Instead, among many people like the interviewees we have met, a new ethos fills its place. This ethos includes an impersonalization of transcendence, a sacralization of the self, a focus on therapeutic rather than civic goals, and a self-needs orientation to community and commitment. To do this, concepts borrowed from non-Western religions (such as monism and reincarnation) or those borrowed from psychology, science, or alternative philosophies (such as positive thinking, "cellular" knowledge, energies, self-realization) are equally simplified, homogenized, or altered, and then brought in as alternatives. The end-product is distinctively American and it is widespread. For, as we have seen, a portion of this rhetoric, as well as some of its particulars, can be found inside as well as outside religion.

This is partly because many of the themes in the SBNR ethos are concepts adapted from earlier, common beliefs. It is as though many SBNRs are using the same tune but with new words. A few examples should make this clear. One very traditional-looking Midwestern church I visited had totally adapted itself to the SBNR ethos, thanks to the vision of its new preacher. The church took the cross down from the steeple, changed its name to something secular-sounding, and put a heavy shade over the stained glass picture of Jesus. Banners throughout the sanctuary proclaimed many tenets of the SBNR ethos. And yet this organization still met in a church building, had fixed pews, conducted services on Sunday morning, did service projects in the neighborhood, and had a type of adult education which one member described as "New York Times" discussion groups. It even called its leader "the minister" and had membership standards. The tune seemed familiar—but the meanings were entirely different.

On a trip to Mexico, I witnessed a wedding. It was conducted by a formerly Roman Catholic European woman whose business was "destination weddings," as well as teaching spiritual practices in this resort town. With an attractive website and a good following, this woman had a lively business. She set up the ceremony in ways that seemed familiar. Although held on the beach, even from a distance it was clear this was a wedding. Flowers lined the aisle that the bride marched down. The bride wore white. The celebrant wore an outfit that looked like a clerical alb. The couple stood under a floral arch, with guests sitting behind them in neat rows of folding chairs. Gentle music played in the background. Vows and rings were exchanged. Afterward there was a reception with dancing. Yet during the ceremony the celebrant's remarks were more about personal development, spiritual freedom, and individual needs coming together than about any kind of sacred presence who sanctified this union. The culmination of the ceremony was when the couple poured different colored sands from individual vessels into a common one. The picture looked familiar, but the message was quite different.

Although there is not a one-to-one comparison, it is possible to show how culturally Christian concepts, previously held by many Americans, are now transposed into alternative themes and held by the majority of these SBNR interviewees. By pairing them, one can see what is rejected and what is substituted. Again, some examples should help to make this clear. Starting with the idea of God, in the new ethos, God is transposed from transcendent actuality into the sacred or divine self. The "sovereignty" or freedom of God becomes instead readily accessible, even impersonal, divine energy to be used by the individual as he or she sees fit, with progress nearly guaranteed. The Spirit becomes less an agent of God than self-generating personal intuition. Instead of a savior figure or prophet, there may be multiple guides or gurus to provide help so the individual can heal him or herself.

As for the God–human relationship, other changes logically follow. Trusting God becomes trusting one's own inner voice which is said to hold all the answers one needs. Prayer, once seen as asking God to address needs, becomes instead self-generated positive thinking. One's own life-experience must likewise be reinterpreted. Rather than there being divine rewards or punishments, or unearned grace, now both beneficial and harmful outcomes are "attracted," thus becoming one's own doing or fault because the results are produced by one's own thought patterns.

Rather than a world ultimately shaped by God's mercy and justice, there is an impersonal law of karma which inexorably rules, with no grace possible. Guidance, no longer mediated through congregation, tradition, or God, becomes instead self-guidance ideally unaffected by external authority. Although nihilism would be a danger of this approach, it is somewhat prevented by the belief that the individual is also assumed capable of tapping into "ancient wisdom." There is a similarity here to other revitalization movements, such as the Reformation, in that it calls people back to earlier, fundamental beliefs. Although the "ancient wisdom" implied here may be a contemporary construction, the approach is similar.

What of the sin/salvation paradigm? In the new ethos, the idea of sin as offense against God is changed to violation of the authentic self. This latter type of offense is the result of negating or ignoring one's higher or inner truth. Justification, the idea that people must "get right" with God, becomes instead getting into alignment with one's own inner integrity. Sanctification, the idea that people become changed and purified through God's ongoing work, is changed into self-transformation and continuing self-improvement. Holiness is replaced by healing, and leans more towards the psychological than the physical.

There is less focus on community in the new ethos. Spiritual gifts, used by God for the good of church and world, become instead sacred power tools for the ongoing construction or revealing of the true self. Communal worship of an external deity becomes rituals to heal the self. Belief based on tradition or authoritative group consensus is transposed into personal experience as final authority, with desire or passion as the fuel. Life-changing commitment to a group's shared ultimate reality becomes instead ongoing experimentation with flexible, changing affiliations. Instead of a shared belief system, there are shared lifestyles or practices, which can be changed or supplanted on an as-needed basis. Finally, eschatology also gets a new face. Rather than an "ending" point and ultimate destination, based on God's grace, this self-improvement is a seemingly endless journey, often through multiple lives or multiple realities.

Although not every interviewee would hold each of these facets, the trajectory from external to internal is clear. Many of my conversation partners found this transposition liberating and even exhilarating. For those who found it difficult or confusing, they nevertheless agreed that it was the more "mature," contemporary, or ethical philosophy. In many ways, the effort to separate spirituality from religion is a derivation of the

"Romantic" movement. More an orientation than an actual theology, the marks of it are well described by Owen C. Thomas. These include:

> An emphasis on the interior life as distinct from the outer life of the body, the community, and history; a focus on individual and private life rather than public life; an emphasis on feeling rather than rationality; and…a sharp distinction between religion which is disparaged and spirituality which is honored. Along with these go a fascination with the ancient, the primitive, the exotic, the esoteric, the mystical, the mysterious, the apophatic, and the heretical.[10]

Because of all this, we need to find different ways to talk about the people we have met here. Common terms to describe "nones" really do not do justice to them. They are not simply "unchurched" or even "seekers," as though they are only waiting for the right fit, the right religious home, to come to their attention. They are not really "apostates" because that implies highlighting or putting a sectarian slant on one or more standard religious beliefs. They cannot really be called "atheists," since many affirm belief in "something" larger than themselves. They are not actually "doubters" because they may not so much doubt or struggle with religious claims as refuse their authority. Some may qualify as "deconverts,"[11] those who have had a conversion away from an earlier faith stance. But a large percentage do not fit here either, since many interviewees had little personal exposure to organized religion, while others we met were still occasionally attending religious services.

One study has suggested they might better be called "a-theists" in that they are not really trying to prove religion wrong nor demonstrate a "withering of religious instincts." Instead, it is said, they are displaying a "widespread decapitation of theistic construals."[12] That is, in setting up the schema I have been describing, they are moving authority, trust, belief, and divinity itself from "out there" to "in here." Some may call them "mystics" in their quest for an encounter with something ultimate and for a personally transformative spiritual experience. But, if so, it is a mysticism often cut off from larger religious thought worlds. Many of the "nones" we have met stand in an ambiguous relationship to religion, not completely in or out, lingering temporarily or permanently in a porous place where aspects can be taken in or thrown out, depending upon need and inclination. Because they live in the space between religion and secularity, people who claim to be "spiritual but not religious" could be called "liminal nones" standing "halfway in and halfway out of religious identity."[13]

What is not clear yet is the trajectory of this dramatic change. Although a qualitative study such as this one should avoid overgeneralizing its findings, most readers will be concerned about the larger meaning of this cultural change. They may ask questions like these: Is the SBNR movement a beacon of light or cause for despair? Is the SBNR ethos simply the interior decorating of the capitalist soul? Or is it a countervailing force to the materialism of consumer capitalism? In the end, will we be left with only two choices: the "hard" or conservative form of religion and the SBNRs? Or is this SBNR ethos really the triumph of religious liberalism, or even the revival of a more open, tolerant and active American religion? Although we are still in the midst of transition, here are some implications that seem to spring from our findings in this research.

Implications

For "Nones" Who are "Spiritual but not Religious"

There is much that is both good and necessary about this movement. From it we learn that rather than secularization or the "death of God," we may be seeing a shift in the location of the spiritual instinct. The echoes of religion and the residues of spiritual life are present in new creative ways. For many people this movement has produced personal benefits, such as inner peace, happiness, self-knowledge, and stress-reduction, which they were not able to achieve anywhere else.[14] The benefits may not just be personal, either, for all religious revolutions, revitalizations and reformations happened because people challenged the status quo, called people back to the core of faith, and returned their focus to the Ultimate. True spiritual seeking is a step in this direction and its preliminary phase, questioning and doubt, can function as a useful prompt for deepening or renewing one's faith.

There are many necessary correctives for American religion implicit in the "spiritual but not religious" ethos. For instance, many of the people we have met here are calling us back to the mystery and awe we should feel in the face of God or the Ultimate. They want us to transcend or find the sacred in the ordinary. They want both knowledge and liberation, not just temporary emotional experience. They are letting us know we all need experiences of liminality, so we can feel more than simply part of material reality in a technocratic world. They want a morality that more realistically responds to our changing and increasingly diverse culture. They are insisting we must love and care for our home, the earth, something clearly of pressing need. They are calling for us to practice tolerance in the face of increasing pluralism and globalization.

They are tired of religious conflict and want us to live in harmony. They have seen religion aligned too closely with civil society or politics and know that is corrupting. They feel disappointed in human structures, from government to family, and are wary of blind allegiance. They have seen religion used for negative purposes and they want no part in it. They affirm individual rights, personal responsibility, self-determination, and freedom, all core American values. They link this with a desire for compassion, peace, and mutual respect, values common to many faith traditions. Their openness to new scientific discoveries about consciousness may help us forge a new alliance between science and mysticism. Their openness to various spiritual perspectives may help us find common moral intuitions that span various cultures and religions. For women—often the majority in alternative spirituality circles—this ethos provides a way around social constraints, allowing a focus on self and personal satisfaction, things often hampered by traditional expectations about how women should act.

Although it may appear otherwise, many of the people we have met here have not consciously chosen this route. Instead, they find themselves on a spiritual journey made necessary by larger cultural changes. Many of their responses, including turning inward, wanting to affirm an authentic self, and carving out some space away from the distracting, fragmented external world are, in fact, self-preservative. They did not fold up the sacred canopy themselves, but inherited this waning of a common moral and religious narrative. Since they have been deprived of ascribed roles and inherited meaning, they have had no choice but to try to make meaning with the bits and pieces they find lying around. Of course, no one does this in a vacuum, so they are helping themselves to construction materials from any number of philosophical warehouses.

When seen this way, their affirmation of personal identity seems less like overwhelming self-focus and more like a defensive tactic in a bureaucratic, transient, mobile world where many people feel anonymous and unimportant. Their desire for personal purity, whether through thought control, diet, or a simpler lifestyle, indicates they, like most humans, recognize that all is not right with us. Their various ways of addressing human disorder show they believe change is possible. That they focus on self-work more than social change is, in many ways, an implicit recognition of how large, complex, and uncontrollable much of human society has become.

But are these approaches enough to bring about permanent personal and social transformation, even a "New Age?" This is not so clear, for many challenges are embedded in the "spiritual but not religious" ethos. We need to consider some of the difficulties inherent in this ethos. For instance, it is unwarranted to believe that simple or even complex techniques for self-calming, self-healing, and self-improvement will bring about thorough and deep-rooted personal transformation. The good feeling engendered by an inspiring lecture or group experience often fades away rather quickly without the ongoing hard work of community building. And even interviewees who worked on meditative techniques or gave themselves over to long periods of "sitting" often reported that the feeling of oneness they achieved did not last. Also, to couch spiritual search in largely therapeutic or functional modes runs the risk of trivializing it. Mysticism or piety can be expansive or self-limiting. It can be practiced in order to intensify one's connection to something larger than oneself, or it can simply be a quest for intensified feeling in an age that needs high stimulation to grab our attention.

As for finding truth within, it is unrealistic to assume you can strip away external influences, culture, and socialization and get inside to the sacred core. You may drink from many wells but you are not creating the water—and you still need water. Yet if one does try to distrust or eliminate all external sources of authority, how does one avoid the drift into nihilism? If all truth lies within, where do you turn when confused or in doubt? If one has no transcendent sense of good, how will one know what is evil? Some interviewees, often the older ones, avoided these dangers by assuming there were values and principles inherent in reality itself, and readily accessible to all. Sometimes these were mostly the "fumes" of religion or the bent poles of previously agreed-upon "sacred canopies."

But younger interviewees often succumbed to this popular "detraditioning" to such an extent that they questioned their own grasp on reality. Some retreated into comforting practices and connections. In this way they were not forced to confront how seriously the SBNR ethos—especially combined with the anti-foundationalism of our postmodern era—could destabilize their sense of meaning in life. On the other hand, rejecting "dogma" and religious authority, as well as distrusting human reason, could simply be a way to avoid intellectual commitment and the hard work it takes.

These responses are understandable, but are they enough? On the societal level, we are all suffering from a fragmented, information-overloading, bureaucratic world which constrains us in its grid. Turning inward can provide a measure of relief, but it does little to change the external conditions which are part of the real problem. Turning against institutions and organization is an overreaction that can be self-defeating. It keeps us wary of any kind of strong group identity which might actually be the basis of social action and more thorough personal transformation. However, in an ironic twist, if transcendence is simply taken to mean going beyond the ego—with no clear endpoint or goal—it is much easier to be manipulated or become part of a dysfunctional group.

Separating spirituality from religion is not the answer. At the least, it is an artificial dichotomy. If taken to extremes, it can also make people reluctant to form healthy long-term personal commitments in all sorts of arenas. Yet such commitments are a necessary component of change. To deal with the magnitude of the problems we face, we need an "engaged spirituality" rather than simply a privatized one. In fact, spirituality actually may be a smaller, not larger, category than religion. Religions have many interwoven ends, values, and goals, not just for self, but for community, the larger world, and after death. To try to homogenize all religions into a common spirituality, or to dismiss them all as only limited angles on reality, moves us further away from them, not closer, and it will not bring peace. It is not truly an inclusive perspective because it disrespects their distinctive characteristics, their history, their normative claims, and their unique visions.

Instead, by borrowing or "poaching" from organized religions, we may unknowingly be creating what Will Herberg called a "cut flower culture." A bouquet of flowers is beautiful for a time, but these blooms do not last very long because they are cut off from their roots. Perennials are plants whose flowers grow, wither, but come back again because the bulb in the ground provides life. If the bulb is removed from the soil, there will be no more blooms. Many of the values we still live by in this society are the fruits of the faith traditions and communal efforts of previous generations. Without keeping these plants in their proper soil, without tending them and leaving their roots intact, how long can they continue to flourish? Many SBNR people I met hope we will achieve a new cultural consensus, bringing oneness, peace, earth-care, human dignity, freedom, and equality. But how likely is that without the roots and soil that nurture commonly held values, and the structures to support and pass them on to subsequent generations? These are just some of the dangers in the SBNR ethos which will impede the hopes and dreams for change.

It is not likely, however, that the "spiritual but not religious" ethos or movement will die. In this market-driven environment where religion is privatized, commodified, and niche-marketed, it may well survive as a subset to which commercial enterprises cater. That is already evident by the increasing number of products which position themselves by, for example, yoga themes, meditation themes, organic themes, and so on. It is clear in all the health, psychological, educational, and business enterprises which now add "spirituality" to their list of offerings. In the face of all this, the search for authentic spiritual experience can seem daunting. But it is not impossible. For people who are genuinely seeking spiritually, I suggest they ask themselves some questions when they consider a spiritual group, practice, teacher, or affiliation:

- Does this theory or practice securely orient me to the Ultimate or does it promote an over-done or harmful focus on self?
- Does it give me more confidence to tackle the important existential questions of life? How does it deal with suffering and loss? Does it give me a sense of meaning and purpose? Or is this merely a technique to make me feel better temporarily?
- Is it a claim to exotic, esoteric, or ancient knowledge without much basis in historical and cultural realities? Does it promise to enhance my control over the uncontrollable?
- Does it lump all religions into one thing—whether claiming they are all similar or all harmful—rather than respecting each one's distinctive characteristics, traditions, and particular vision?
- How balanced is it? Does it balance reason with emotion? Is self-care balanced with concern for others? Is individualism balanced with group cohesion?
- What is expected from me and what character traits and outcomes do I observe in the other practitioners? Do I feel a spiritual connection with them?
- Are the practitioners working outward for the common good, as well as looking inward? Is there a concern for social justice, community, or political realities?
- Is the message largely one of repudiation, or one of affirmation? Are there common beliefs which give the practitioners unity and purpose, yet freedom is allowed for individual interpretation?

These and other such questions can help guide those who are genuine in their spiritual search.

For Society

Two main questions often come up when I speak to groups about the "spiritual but not religious" movement. First, people want to know if the United States is going the way of Europe (i.e., empty churches, few religious practitioners, a religious heritage lingering in general ways but no longer exerting the strong social and political authority it once had). In other words, they are referring to the debate around "secularism." Second, people are often concerned about the effects on American society as religion's public influence seems to be waning. While they sometimes repudiate the confluence of power politics and conservative Christianity which they witnessed in the 1990s and early 2000s, they also mourn the loss of moral and cultural custodianship which mainstream denominations held in the past, and by which they provided a set of common values which guided American public life.

The debate over secularism concerns both sociology and theology.[15] Secularism is not simply the separation of church and state. Instead, it is an ideology that privatizes religion, while according power and reason to the public domain. Once religion is considered merely a private affair, it is accorded little impact on the public realm. Or, alternatively, only some religions and their ideas are deemed compatible with social goals and allowed to provide influence. This type of secularism, which often holds a rather simplistic view of religion, is antithetical to the deep and holistic nature of faith.

Ironically, though, this view has its roots in a certain form of religion. Secularism is premised on a "chiefly Protestant notion of religion understood as private assent to propositional beliefs." Other religions and types of Christianity "do not frame faith in such rationalist terms....The very idea that it is possible to cordon off personal religious beliefs from a secular town square depends on Protestant assumptions about what counts as 'religion.' "[16] Thus, according to Mark C. Taylor, "religion and secularity are not opposites; to the contrary, Western secularity is a *religious* phenomenon." In practice, "religion is not a separate domain but pervades all culture and has an important impact on every aspect of society."[17]

Even with the inherent linkage between belief and behavior, however, simply knowing what people believe is not a complete predictor of how they will act. As one sociologist says, "The sociological problem is not what is or is not in the heads or practices of isolated individuals; it is in the ways in which ideas and practices become mobilized and institutionalized in concrete social structures."[18] Yet belief and behavior mutually reinforce each other. Lived religion cannot be kept at home; it affects belief and behavior in both private and public. This holds for the SBNR ethos as well. Given their large and rising numbers, SBNRs and their beliefs are sure to exert a growing influence. The change is, in fact, more profound than simply having less people sitting in pews. As Philip Hammond insists, we may be witnessing the third "disestablishment" of religion in American public life. In this case, organized religion is no longer an essential facet of American identity, but has become optional. Even for religious people, the meaning of their faith has become less collective and more individual.[19]

But does this mean we are becoming a completely secularized populace, or even a nation of atheists? Not according to the data we have examined here. The separation of the sacred from the secular spheres may be a feature of modernity, but it is not the end of religion. We may instead be moving into a "post-secular age." In this situation, religion is no longer given or stable, but optional and chosen. In fact, all worldviews are relativized. So, rather than society growing less religious, interviewees show us that the real change is in where authority resides. While the public influence of religion is waning, a private sort of religion seems to be growing. This, in fact, is one essential meaning of saying "I'm spiritual but not religious." As we have seen, SBNRs are "taking back" control over their own beliefs and spiritual practices, no longer bowing to creeds, structures, or religious authorities.

This may sound very liberating, very self-determined, and very American. In many ways, it is. But it also has a dark side on both the personal and the public levels. For when more people practice their faith alone, or away from wide communal structures, there is more isolation. With imagined, rather than actual, "others," an atmosphere of skepticism, confusion, and even fear can grow. We have seen some of this in interviewees who imagine repressive and rigid believers without actually knowing them. Even more troubling, the potential for manipulation can grow. For when isolated spiritual practice fails to deliver and people reach out for something more communal, they may have little experience in assessing social structures, theories, or teachers.

On the public level, too, there is potential for the SBNR ethos to cause profound changes to American society. Sociologists think about "pro-social" behavior and how it contributes to the common good. Research shows that people with strong religious beliefs are more likely to volunteer, take on civic obligations, vote, and generally work to improve society.[20] This comes partly from their beliefs but also from the social networks and experience they have gained in their congregations learning to collaborate with others based on mutual trust. One outcome of this is the extensive social services provided by religion, a deeply rooted feature of the American experience. Think of the many universities, schools, orphanages, hospitals, and agencies started by religious believers.

Of course, we cannot simply reduce religion to what it produces, although this trend toward "functionalist" definitions of religion is common.[21] Instrumental or utilitarian definitions cannot take into account the intangible aspects of faith or its truth claims. Yet research demonstrates that even for those who simply show up—whether or not they fully buy into the beliefs of the group—religion is good for people and for society. Whether looking at the health benefits of religious membership or the significant amount of volunteering that religious people do, religion makes a valuable contribution to the personal and the communal good of our civil society. We live in a world of loosening and more temporary connections. This can impede mutual ongoing social responsibility. In this light, we must ponder the importance of religious values and commitments that keep people engaged with the larger society.[22]

America has been an experiment with the tension between individual rights and equal opportunity. One way to prevent the dangers of inordinate self-interest—with its moral relativism and callous disregard for others—is to practice interdependence, civic duty, mutual trust, shared values, and collaboration of people from diverse perspectives. Democracy hinges on this. If we become more fragmented and isolated from one another, more withdrawn from public life, our social experiment will suffer. Many religions—not just Christianity—do, in fact, affirm an "engaged spirituality." But the SBNR freedom to borrow techniques and aspects from a variety of religions means that this perspective can be left off, in favor of individual needs and ends. In fact, many interviewees fit with the research that finds the religiously "unattached" less concerned about the moral conditions of the country, less optimistic about society's future (although optimistic about their own), more unsure or even hopeless about their ability to make an impact, unable to or wary of making moral judgments, and thus less civically "engaged" than the religiously committed.[23]

From listening to interviewees, it seems unlikely that a vast mobilization or the formation of concrete social structures will occur, at least partly because of the institutional wariness so inherent in the SBNR ethos. As we have seen from interviewees' views on community, many wish for a group that believes as they do, but are not often highly motivated to create or seek one, nor to stick with one that no longer meets their personal needs. In addition, a large majority of the people we have met are moral individualists. Some, usually older interviewees, think there are universal principles of right and wrong or some sort of "natural law," but many younger interviewees do not think there are any fixed social standards for everyone. They believe that moral positions are relative, historically constructed and/or chosen based on individual perceptions. If anything is immoral, they insist, it is imposing one's beliefs and standards on other people. Even were it beneficial to have some fixed standards, many feel it would be extremely difficult. They therefore base their own judgments on personal interest, minimizing harm, maximizing enjoyment, or intuition.[24] This does not bode well for finding the common ground that a democratic but diverse society needs to flourish.

Furthermore, all of this seems to work against any kind of permanent social structure or movement which could provide the "social capital" which religion has in the past provided. Whether or not some other type of social organization could replace what religion has provided—as has happened in socialist countries—this does not appear a logical outcome of the SBNR ethos itself. Of course, this may be changing. SBNRs could well organize around selected social positions, such as ecology. One scholar suggests as much. He says that although it took Baby Boomers thirty years waiting for "inner peace to flow from the individual hearts to the collective bloodstream...many now-middle-aged citizens realized that cosmic consciousness without skillful action will not solve real-world problems....The younger generation is not taking thirty years to get there."[25] Certain Christian scholars, too, are optimistic.[26] When I observe my younger theology students, with their passion for justice, service, and ability to adapt faith to the postmodern context, I am encouraged as well. However, other scholars disagree with this optimistic assessment.[27] And, frankly, I did not hear much about a structured and socially active spirituality from SBNRs of any age. Of course, both humans and history are full of surprises. Still, an engaged, organized, activist spirituality will require a profound adjustment to the SBNR ethos.

For Religion

One of the strengths, and yet the complexities, of American life is its freedom of religion, individual thought, and efforts to balance multiple points of view alongside social equality. The United States is increasingly a place of diverse religious perspectives, traditions, and cultures. In the face of the burgeoning population of "nones," all religions—not just white mainline Protestantism—are likely to be deeply impacted. From large and small denominations to ethnic enclaves to immigrant groups, many people hope to pass on their faith, their culture, and their values to their children. But this could be increasingly difficult if the SBNR ethos continues to grow. As we have seen, non-affiliation or disaffiliation from religion is especially common among younger people, and it is unlikely this is merely a youthful rebellion or a temporary phase.

Even so, all religions receive both benefit and challenge from the "spiritual but not religious" ethos. There is a message for religions inherent in the ethos. When people adopt a "generic" spirituality they are often trying to avoid religious conflict and be more inclusive, tolerant, and accepting of diversity. When people want to find the essential principles that inform all religions, when they search for "ancient wisdom" from which they claim all religions are derived, it is often for the sake of peace and cooperation. When people minimize beliefs and focus on practices, it is often an effort to avoid theological conflict. These are implicit criticisms that religions need to seriously consider. Sometimes, the perennialism which encourages persons to regard all religions equally can prompt a disaffiliated person to take another look at the religion they have left. They may find resources they did not know existed in it, perhaps prompting a reconciliation. And the "postmodern" climate which relativizes all truth claims can make it easier to talk about beliefs and faith with less rancor.

Still, no matter how benevolent the motives, the generic approach can be problematic, not just for Christianity, but for all religions. First, it minimizes the depth and range of religion. It is inauthentic to portray religion as dogmatic and rigid, to see it as simply "exoteric"—just external forms—divorced from "mysterious" substance. It is reductionist to portray religion as simply group assent to doctrines and procedures. And to primarily value religion or spirituality only for its therapeutic, behavior-modifying, or functional aspects is equally reductionist. All of these reductions trivialize religion. How can we really understand the profound content of any particular religion, if we leave out its metaphysical, conceptual, and intangible aspects? If you rip a religious practice out from the tradition's roots, you may well impede the prophetic and culture-challenging features of that religion. And what is the point of working to preserve and hand on a tradition if they are ultimately all the same? The SBNR ethos is very attractive in its promise of tolerance and freedom. Roger Kamanetz, exploring the phenomenon of Jews who align themselves with Buddhism, was reminded by a prominent rabbi that "modern cultures are more difficult to resist, because they are so kind and accepting." The rabbi said: "Because of persecution you get stubborn, but when you are kissed and hugged, you relax."[28]

At their best, religions provide an alternative vision that challenges power structures, politics, and solely materialistic views of reality. Consider that the most respected spiritual guides from all ages adhered to a religious tradition while also being prophetic, inclusive, and engaged with the wider world. There are also political consequences. On one hand, the generic approach has the potential to jeopardize each religion's constitutional freedom. For if all religions are ultimately the same, or equally inadequate, if religion is only a private affair and should stay at home, then perhaps religions do not need much legal or constitutional protection. But there is also a different, but equally dangerous, possibility. Some religious people, feeling misrepresented or ignored, might feel compelled to strongly highlight their distinctions, taking dogmatic or fundamentalist stances in reaction. A good example are those religious groups which take an extreme anti-gay or anti-abortion position because they think more liberal believers—or society in general—have "watered down" the faith in these (and other) areas.

Some of these problems should be of particular concern to minority and non-Western traditions, especially the ones to which many SBNRs are attracted. By minimizing their historical and cultural roots, by homogenizing them, by lifting parts from the whole, by using aspects without permission or oversight, we can easily misrepresent, misunderstand, and "colonize" minority traditions. Over-romanticizing the "other" is just as dismissive of actual practitioners as ignoring or trying to control them. In addition, it presumes that someone outside a particular religion has the right to say which parts are "universal" and thus "valid," and which parts are simply cultural products which can be put aside. Any religion borrowed for this generic task has every right to be wary rather than flattered by the attention. This is equally true for the Asian traditions often used to oppose Western religious views as it is for indigenous or "folk" religions.[29]

Whether we are witnessing further secularization or entering a post-secular era, all religions will have new difficulties. In a country where religious identity is chosen, rather than ascribed, and where choice also reigns regarding beliefs and practices, religions are in a more fragile and vulnerable state than in places where whole cultures are religious together. In our pluralist environment, new strategies are needed. It is unproductive to simply be defensive in the face of rising disaffiliation and the destabilizing of religious identities. Instead, as a first step, religious people need to remind themselves why religions are good for society. As Garret Keizer summarizes: "The virtues of organized religion include but are no means limited to the following: they give their adherents something solid against which to rebel; they allow one to see farther by standing on the shoulders of giants; they insist on the primacy of lived experience; they work against illusion and historical insularity; they point to the power of the collective and the merits of deep diversity; and they are capable of the kind of mobilization that can transform the world."[30]

In order to affirm this, we do not need to say that all religions propose the same ends or means.[31] They are not different paths up the same mountain. We must acknowledge that they each make different truth claims. Religious claims, by nature, require a person's loyalty and commitment. Yet all of them give us ways to recognize and bond with Ultimacy, even if the Ultimate is conceived differently in each tradition. Each provides a shared language and connection with others so that spiritual experience does not remain totally private. Each serves as a guide for others on a similar quest, providing ways to communicate with each other about our deepest needs and experiences. Religions understand that humans are meaning-seeking beings. They show us that we need an organizing center. They help us deal with suffering and evil by setting them within a theological framework. Each religion, in its own way, offers a coherent meaning narrative.

This is especially important in a postmodern world which fosters radical fragmentation and the individualization of values. In this sort of world, rather than religious belief causing distress, it is often the lack of deep beliefs that can harm individual psyches. The freedom for deep religious belief has also been good for America. For although the SBNR ethos seems to assume that strong religious belief is divisive for society, there is empirical data indicating that the freedom to be religious is "very good for social relations, for democracy, for equality, for women's advancement, for all the things we treasure in a liberal democracy."[32] Thus, while many contend that a secular society is necessary to promote tolerance, in actuality, religious ideals may be more salutary in protecting us from the reign of self-interest.

In fact, deep belief may be the best foundation for genuine pluralism in our increasingly diverse Western world. Rowan Williams, former

Archbishop of Canterbury, insists that religion which is corporate, sacramental, and doctrinal "becomes one of the most potent allies possible for genuine pluralism—that is, for a social and political culture that is consistently against coercion and institutionalized inequality and is committed to serious public debate about common good." It is not enough, he says, to simply acknowledge that human flourishing goes "beyond profit and material security." While this is helpful, it is "not well equipped to ask the most basic questions about the legitimacy of various aspects of the prevailing global system."[33]

When moving forward into inter-religious dialogue, we need not simply restrict ourselves to displaying our distinctive practices, food ways, or rituals—as important as that task is. We especially need to take on the greater challenge of explaining our respective beliefs, visions, and truth claims. In order for this to happen, though, we need to correct the problem of religious illiteracy in our country. Few people deeply understand their own, much less another's, religious beliefs. While we do not need a competition between conflicting theological claims, we do need to come to the table aware of the normative claims that shape us. This will be crucial not just for religious harmony but also for economics, politics, medicine, education, and business in our diverse nation and world. Only an honest approach will allow us to develop a theology of religious pluralism that does justice to the very real diversity that exists. This new theology, however, may well require us to rethink our positions and learn from each other.

Most important, we must appreciate our common humanity and find shared ground on which to cooperate in healing our society. Against popular assumptions, religion is not inherently violent. Instead nonviolence is a core of many religious claims. As one scholar graphically points out:

The most horrible genocidal atrocities of the past century and, indeed, in recorded history, Hitler's Holocaust in Central Europe, Stalin's purge of non-Communists in the former Soviet Union and Eastern Bloc... were all perpetuated in the name of atheistic ideologies that made no provisions for an afterlife and were sometimes directed at eliminating those who believed in an afterlife. What more compelling evidence could there be that it is misguided to point the finger of blame for this or the other humanly perpetrated atrocities at religion per se or at the belief in some form of life after death.[34]

In addition, religions have within themselves the ability to be self-critical. Therefore, it is important that we work against fundamentalist, intolerant, and conflictual tendencies within our own religions which hijack and distort the essence of the faith. If we are sincere in this whole complex task, we may help our society reconstruct a common narrative which accepts difference and yet formulates the shared values necessary for us to become less, rather than more, fragmented.

There are at least three different directions in which the SBNR ethos could push American religion. First, it might create more openness toward hybridity, "multiple religious belonging" (MRB) or "multiple religious participation." We may be moving into a religious world of very fluid boundaries. The idea of "multiple religious belonging" is not exactly the same as religious "parity," syncretism, or generic pluralism. Instead, individuals decide they profess allegiance to two or more religious traditions simultaneously. They do this even though the professed religions may well offer different visions, different truth claims, and different "salvations." Some of my conversation partners confidently insisted they are, for instance, both Jewish and Buddhist, a Shaman and a Christian, a Roman Catholic and a practitioner of *Santeria*, or a Black Baptist and a Rastafarian. This sounds promising in theory but, as we have seen, this blending is more difficult in actual practice.

It is true that many Asian countries lend themselves to a mixing of various practices and traditions. The Western world, however, with its monotheistic Abrahamic faiths each claiming authority, makes MRB an ostensibly countercultural option. Although actual religious practice may always have been somewhat "plural"[35] even in the West, today it seems that many who explore alternative spiritualities have already left their native religion, if they had one. And although meditation teachers and gurus tell people they can continue in their own religion—simply adding these new spiritual practices on top—those still associated with an organized religion often leave it once starting the new practices.[36] We might ask, then, whether this is really multiple belonging or simply one more aspect of "detraditioning" (i.e., a new way to free oneself from the duties and authority of any particular religion).

Second, we might be seeing the creation of a new religion altogether, one influenced by the SBNR ethos. This needs to be taken seriously.[37] Could the theological elements we have seen held in common by interviewees eventually coalesce into a new religion? Could anti-exclusivism become the foundational dogma, for example? Yet religion needs more than a generalized ethos. It needs both doctrine and structure to survive, and these are elements out of tune with the SBNR ethos. In spite of some important agreements, the interviewees' actions and inclinations do not yet seem to make this a viable outcome.

Third, we may simply be seeing the pervasive influence of the increasing contact between religions. This option may be the most likely. It builds upon the history of religious cross-fertilization which has been going on for a very long time. Religions that come in close contact with each other, such as through trading or immigration, often come away changed. As Diana Eck says: "Religions are not like stones passed from hand to hand through the ages. They are dynamic movements, more like rivers—flowing, raging, creative, splitting, converging. The history of religions is unfolding before our eyes. Perhaps nowhere in the world is it more interesting to study the process of dynamic religious change in this new century than in America."[38]

From the interviewees, we have seen especially the influence of what Lola Williamson calls HIMM (Hindu-inspired meditation movements)[39] which, along with the SBNR ethos in general, has clearly affected both religious and non-religious people. One author summarizes survey results and his own research, finding these common elements to be: spiritual independence, direct experience, tolerance, fluidity, nonliteralism, and a different kind of God.[40] More process oriented than conceptual, these elements already are working a transformation on popular American attitudes toward, within, and outside religion.

In the process of doing this research, I visited a new urban seminary that focused on "trans-spiritual traditions" or "inter-spirituality" for the training of interfaith ministers. The president graciously accommodated my request by assembling a large group of graduates for a dialogue. I learned that the curriculum required them to spend about one month per major religion, reading a summary chapter in a college-level religious studies text, hearing a speaker from that tradition, and participating in rituals and services. After they explained their educational process, I asked about the respective spiritual journeys that brought them here. Finally, I decided to explore how they practiced multiple religious participation or belonging. As interfaith chaplains, they had been trained to respect and offer services that accorded with the faith of the individual in front of them. They assured me their inter-spiritual orientation allowed them to live intentionally and with integrity across diverse religions.

Therefore, taking each religion they had studied in turn, I asked them the same sorts of questions. First, I asked them to raise their hands if they had been deeply impacted by Islam. All raised their hands. Then I asked them to keep their hands up if they prayed the requisite five times a day and obeyed other core aspects of Islam, such as fasting during Ramadan. All hands went down. Next I asked who had been profoundly impacted by Judaism, and again all hands went up. So I asked who kept kosher, attended Friday services, and observed the Day of Atonement. All hands went down. I did the same for all the other major religions they studied, including Christianity, and the results were the same.

I visited another seminary out West that trains interfaith ministers. I met one very intelligent young man who had a non-theistic Buddhist orientation and a Protestant background. He was already doing his internship as a hospital chaplain. I said to him: "Suppose I was in the hospital for surgery and requested a chaplain because I wanted someone to offer prayer before the procedure. You just told me you don't believe in a transcendent God who hears and answers prayers. So how would you minister to me given my Christian beliefs?" He responded, "Well, I would listen carefully as you explained your faith to me and then I would use the same words you used. If you spoke about God, then I would, too." Satisfied he had given a compassionate, sensitive answer, he confidently asked me: "So, wouldn't that be helpful?" I had to honestly confess that—although I appreciated his care and knew that God's existence did not depend upon his belief in it—it would feel inauthentic to ask him to pray for me.

Finally, I visited yet another seminary—this time a semi-urban school with a long heritage—which trains ministers but focuses on just three religious traditions. Students come from these respective faiths and learn about and from each other. I spent the day with a young Muslim woman who told me how exciting this program was for her, especially the chance to dialogue with believers from other religions. When I asked her about the many students who come to that school with a "spiritual but not religious" orientation, she became animated. "Oh, no, I don't enjoy them as much as the others. It becomes clear in class that they often don't know exactly what they believe. It's hard to talk with them. In fact, I would much rather talk with an evangelical Christian. At least they know what they believe and we have something substantial to discuss."

For the Church

I joke with my theology students that no matter what question I ask them, they always give "community" as the answer. It is true that we live in a fractured world which makes genuine community difficult. It is true that many churches are not providing as much community as they could. But, as we have seen, it is not the lack of community in the church, much less the presence of abuse, which has turned away many interviewees from religion. In fact, many missed the communal aspect of their previous religious experience. Nor is it simply the political positions of conservative Christians which have turned away these largely liberal thinkers, although they may get their stereotypes of Christian beliefs from the media focus on this group. If conservative politics were the only reason people left church, the more liberal congregations would be the logical places for them to go. There they would find a good fit in values and social positions. Yet few seemed attracted to the churches which potentially contain many like-minded people. In fact, these mainline churches are in the steepest decline of any.

The many SBNRs I met suggested they want a "re-sacralization" of the world. They want to see and experience the sacred in more areas of life. They want a spirituality which is vital and personal. If mainline churches are not attractive to them, perhaps such churches have adapted to our contemporary world all too well. In trying to respond, some churches have tried to further reduce belief content and concentrate more on spiritual practices. Some focus on health and wellness, perhaps offering more social services and less specifically religious ones. In their quest to minimize earlier orthodoxies and take up modern themes instead—trying hard to be practical, psychological, individualistic, focused on ethics rather than theology—many have buried the essence of the faith. Trying so hard to be relevant, non-demanding, and friendly, they have downplayed the awe, respect, and humility we should feel in the presence of God.

What about conservative churches? My interviewees were not drawn there, either. One might think Pentecostal or Charismatic churches, with their focus on experience and the living presence of the Spirit, would be a good fit. Yet most of the SBNRs I met were not interested, possibly because of conservative social and theological positions. And what about evangelical Christianity? It has continued to be clear about its beliefs and truth claims. It has also done a better job than the mainline in retaining its youth, although often at the cost of segregating them from the wider society. Still, many that leave conservative churches no longer fill the pews of more liberal ones, as used to happen, but now instead become SBNRs. Conservative social positions are not attractive to the liberal SBNR thinkers. In fact, conservative Christianity has contributed to SBNR distrust of religion. Many books document an evangelicalism seduced by political power which tried forcefully to take back the custodianship of American morals.[41] The rise of fundamentalism in all religions, in fact, has encouraged many SBNRs to feel that, when left to their own devices, religions naturally become extremist.

We might figure that Roman Catholicism, with its ethnic diversity, its rich and deep spirituality, and its well-developed theological tradition, might be attractive to some. It has worked hard to maintain its consistency and integrity. But studies show that many within that fold are increasingly as influenced by the "spiritual but not religious" ethos as Protestants.[42] This includes the Hispanic Catholics, too, even though their presence is helping prevent as sharp a decline as in other mainline churches. Even though many Catholics also display a loyalty to the institutional church and the sacraments,[43] when Catholics leave, many seem to stay away for good. Those still inside often become "cafeteria Catholics," taking only what they like and leaving the rest.

Formerly, Catholic mothers and nuns did more to insure the survival of the faith than anyone else, and many more women than men took religious vows. But now the Catholic Church is losing its women, especially young ones.[44] The former Roman Catholics I met—many of whom were women—were some of the most vocal, and often angry, of any of the unaffiliated. Many proclaimed that they were "recovering Catholics." I never heard anyone say that about their former Protestant ties. Often more doctrinally attuned because of their earlier formation, many had strong theological objections to the church's hierarchical structure, its exclusivism, morality, and gender roles. They resented the fact that their doubts and questions, as well as their leadership skills, were pushed aside.

As we have seen, the people in this book have distinctively theological reasons for being alienated from religion. Many have received inadequate or no teaching to help them with the existential questions of life. Many were not allowed to ask questions or air their doubts. And others have received skewed ideas of Christian beliefs which alienate them from the church. Minimizing Christian belief is not the answer to their critique. Focusing more on devotional practices is not the way to appeal to a group which can find stress-relieving and spiritual techniques in many places outside organized religion. Offering enjoyable events and social services will simply put the church in competition with the many secular places where sophisticated entertainment and help can be found.

Although belief is not its only lynchpin, Christianity is a religion that values reason and belief. Both creeds and congregations hold people together in this faith, helping give them structure, discipline, unity, and purpose. The synergy of affirming, assembling, moving inward and outward, focusing one's efforts for good, all work together. It is difficult to hold people together without some creed-like set of tenets or standards. To function as a moral body, people need a common set of principles and focus. These are axioms of Christianity with which many would agree.

Even so, churches have contributed to the theological problems interviewees raise. Only part of the difficulty stems from stereotype and hearsay. Few churches have provided the theological tools adults need to make faith decisions and understand diverse positions. Even among those interviewees with a religious background, only a few were able to frame their own positions with logic and consistency. There is also a lack of balance in the churches' own theological presentation. To refashion a Christianity that addresses SBNRs, much theological work will be needed.

For one thing, the tools of theological thinking need to be introduced, honed, and used. This is especially important in a nation as religiously diverse as our own. One cannot understand, much less appreciate, another's position if one cannot articulate or refine one's own. On the positive side, I did find an amazing openness to this task among my conversation partners. As we have seen, some did revel in holding inconsistent and incompatible positions. But many more were frankly astonished when I identified some of the mutually conflicting stances that they held. And not only were they surprised, they were grateful and pleased, saying I had given them something to "work on."

Also, we must beware of a "pick and choose" attitude toward beliefs. While individual judgment is a legitimate heritage of Protestantism, it has also led us to be rather cavalier and unsystematic regarding the "belief package." Like a puzzle, all the parts of a faith tradition are needed to make a complete picture. In fact, the very thing which SBNRs protest—the "take it or leave it" attitude—has actually been less prevalent in many churches than stereotype would suggest. Instead, it has become more common to over-focus on one or more aspects of the faith, divorced from the larger Christian theological structure and its safeguards. As a result, erosion has happened from inside. In fact, some of the themes rejected by the interviewees are doctrines that have gotten skewed in just this way. Both liberal and conservative Christians must avoid the unbalanced approach which not only fuels tension within Christianity but also helps fuel the SBNR ethos. There is ongoing danger to the "pick and choose" attitude.

Again, some examples are necessary, to demonstrate how a full-orbed theology can ameliorate excess, rigidity, or selective over-focus that can come from the "pick-and-choose" approach. For example, an over-focus on the Reformation idea of the "priesthood of believers"—that there need be no mediator between self and God—can devolve into unmediated claims of personal revelation. To avoid this, it must be held in tension with the theological consensus and experience of the larger church. An over-focus on the idea that God loves each person individually can degenerate into withdrawal from community. To avoid this, it must be understood as only one aspect of the body of Christ which must worship and serve God together. A mechanistic or literalistic focus on the Bible can force believers to stand on a narrow knife-edge of authority, vulnerable to having their faith threatened by anything that cannot be taken literally or at a loss when a particular issue is not directly addressed there. Biblical authority, although crucial for Christianity, must nevertheless be tempered by reason, tradition, and experience.

Out-sized attention to the inner testimony of the Holy Spirit or one's relationship with Jesus Christ can easily devolve into a focus on personal experience as the touchstone of sacred power. As a result, those without visceral ongoing spiritual experiences fear they are out of touch with the divine. To avoid this, the inner testimony must be buffered by tradition, scripture, and human reason as aids in interpreting that experience. And, amid the normal ebbs and flows of human emotion, we have to be reminded we are still held in the embrace of God. An over-focus on personal salvation can become distorted into a focus on the self. It needs to be mediated by a larger body of fellow believers who have mutual concern and common mission. And too much demand on demonstrations that one is "right with God," can become distorted into taking sole responsibility to justify and improve the self. This needs to be anchored in the assurance that God's trustworthy and benevolent grace is ultimately responsible for one's salvation.

Too much focus on outward mission—even though Christianity is an evangelistic and service-oriented religion—can deny the need for inward spiritual formation. But, then, an over-focus on Christian spiritual practices has its dangers, too, if we work so hard to feel God's presence that we dissolve the distinction between creature and creator. None of these caveats argues for a rigid orthodoxy or a return to a one-size-fits-all systematic theology. Instead, it is simply an observation that for a religion with such a strong conceptual heritage as Christianity, things can go out of balance easily. To avoid that, we must be holistic, and all aspects must be carefully tended and remain part of belief and practice.

There is much that is theologically pertinent about SBNR longings. That is where we must start the conversation when we engage this ethos. What can we affirm? How can SBNRs help us see our blind spots? For instance, does their humanizing of God challenge us to rethink the idea of God as unmoveable, wholly other, or utterly transcendent? Should it make us rethink both the Trinity and the incarnation of Jesus Christ not as some explanatory formula but as God's humble presence among us and invitation to collaborate in healing the world? Does their focus on human growth and inherent "divinity" urge us to remember we are all made in God's image and created for "theosis"[45] or union with God? Should it make us realize we often take sin too seriously and grace not seriously enough? Should their focus on human self-determination remind us that it is the humility and self-restriction of God which gives us freedom, dignity, and creativity? Does their rejection of original sin require us to restate that God created everything good? But should it also refocus our thoughts about humanity, taking seriously that we have both inherited and contributed to a dysfunctional system?

Does their focus on the sacred quality of the natural world encourage us to treat the earth with more reverence and care, especially as God's creation? Does their hope in endless self-improvement through multiple lifetimes make us reassert that eternal life is not some static place given over to buttressing God's ego? Could it help us realize, instead, that afterlife is an opportunity for the sanctification and deification of humans that is only possible in full communion with God? Does their rejection of religion as institutional and restrictive make us realize that God is as free to oppose the status quo as to affirm it? Does their longing for a spiritual community—where each can think freely, yet be accepted by others—qualify as a call to make the church a place where doubt, questions, and hopeful visions are welcomed? These and other theological challenges emerge from the SBNR ethos.

All is not lost for Christianity in the United States. Both Roman Catholicism and Orthodoxy continue to connect theology with spiritual practice. If women can be called into leadership, and the focus placed on core aspects of the faith, rather than politically charged social positions, it may well re-inspire devotion. Evangelical Christianity positioned itself well as a response to modernity, with its focus on the individual, making belief accessible, and success in appealing to segments of the American public. Still today it preserves a theological clarity and seriousness which can produce knowledgeable, faithful believers. Will it be able to respond as well to postmodernity? Could it also produce more ecumenically minded, socially active, and progressive alternative communities where faith is lived out intentionally and consistently? Some say that the "emerging" church is already doing these things, adapting itself to the current age and rejecting the linkage of Christianity with conservative politics.[46]

What about mainline Protestant Christianity? For all its losses and low self-esteem, this type may be better positioned to adapt Christianity to the postmodern context. With its tolerance for ambiguity, as well as its ecumenical interests, open-mindedness, social concern, and receptivity to other religions, this type of Christianity may be most able to speak with SBNRs compassionately and attentively. But the answer for such churches may be counterintuitive. What would happen if liberal or progressive Christians actually became more "religious"—in the sense of recognizing God's majesty and mystery—rather than less?

What would be the result if they renewed the core message of the faith and really lived it out corporately, while still retaining their liberal social and political values? What would happen if they focused more on, for example, immigrants, the disenfranchised, or the lonely? What would happen if they became more intentional about commitment and community, and less interested in appearing relevant and non-demanding? What would happen if they better understood and had more confidence in their beliefs? Could they do that and also allow room for doubt and individual interpretation? Could they promote a compelling Christian message which counteracts the conservative positions which have turned off SBNRs? Could they develop a leadership style which works well for a postmodern mentality? To do this, mainline churches will have to recover their prophetic edge, communal spirit, and devotion to the faith. Only a church that is intelligently faithful, ecumenical, and inter-religious stands a chance of convincing SBNRs that the church is truly forward-thinking, serious about spirituality, and an agent of change.

In the final analysis, all of us will need to sit down together. We are global citizens and cannot afford intolerance, ignorance, or dividing the world up into the "good guys" and the "bad guys." We all must cooperate together in healing our world. In fact, Jesus' Sermon on the Mount—the message all Christians revere—could very well promote the kind of tolerant, inclusive, and generous world which fits many SBNR longings. This new religious ethos may be more countercultural than status quo affirming. It is likely the best hope of responding to the SBNR ethos. As Rowan Williams says, Christianity may be developing "an articulate corporate voice which stubbornly resists being made instrumental to the well-being of an unchallenged Western and capitalist modernity."[47]

This may seem like hopeless idealism. Indeed, many of the churches and religious organizations I have visited do not feel excitement about the possibilities of reaching out to the growing unaffiliated population. Instead, many seem fearful and despairing, more worried about survival than revival. But God has a way of leading people through "dark nights of the soul" into a morning of new opportunities. Of course, we will have to approach the task with a mixture of realism and hope. Many SBNRs will remain uninterested in religion. Many will be so set against Christianity that it would take something cataclysmic to have them reconsider. But there are also many who are genuinely interested in a transformative spirituality which has roots and fruits. These "dynamic nones" are reachable. In fact, surveys show that the "none" designation is often a temporary one. When one study returned to former respondents a year later, some of them were involved or even affiliated with a religion.[48] The interviewees I recontacted, too, were often involved in something different than when I first met them.

Many SBNRs are open to outreach. But churches will have to approach them with a new attitude. They will have to help seekers gradually move from shoppers to participants. They may have to practice what Patricia Killen calls a "catch and release" approach,[49] and be aware that only a few may move on to become members. The concept of membership itself may have to be rethought, perhaps changed to something like what the Shakers practiced, with concentric circles of participation from the "gathering" order all the way to the fully committed.[50] House churches, cell groups, and other creative alternatives to traditional structures may open up the reality of religious community to more people.

In any case, churches need to remember that their primary job is not to make members, but to transform lives and produce mature, faithful Christians. Simply caving in to a consumerist approach, seeking only to serve surface needs and aim for "customer satisfaction," is inadequate. Nor should the American church, as in some other Western countries, be satisfied to provide "vicarious religion"[51] for those who want to be able to participate on an "as-needed" basis. Thus, although it is countercultural, churches do need to lovingly commend and demonstrate the benefits of commitment. Mentoring newcomers, identifying spiritual gifts, training for lay leadership, and more participant-involved experiential worship, all contribute to this.

Perhaps we should take a hint from the Buddhists. What would happen if we became more conversant in the "skillful means" necessary to make these claims compelling? How would it be if we encouraged people to "try out" aspects of the religion, without pressure or expectation of up-front commitment? What would happen if inquirers were able experience the benefits for themselves and then make a more informed decision? To make all this work, however, we will need careful teachers and wise guides. It would be a more "hands-on" approach, instead of simply expecting that assembling, watching, and listening would be enough to produce change.

It is important that Christians face forward into the theological and spiritual headwind of this burgeoning movement. If they do so, they may well repeat the feats of previous generations who overcame other seemingly impossible crises for the church. The church has been considered on its death-bed many times in the past, but it has arisen renewed. Today's Christians, like their ancestors, can reframe the gospel in ways that again speak to the deepest human longings and needs. They can create alternative faith communities which give persons a supportive context in which to live this out. And they can develop new ways to cooperate with God's healing work in the world.

Rita Rodriquez and the Resiliency of Religion

WHILE WRITING THIS book, my husband and I led a group of students to Cuba for a cross-cultural experience. After years of talking to "spiritual but not religious" people, hearing the laments of church members, and studying sociological research on the decline of religious affiliation in America, I was at an impasse. It was very evident that many churches and religious institutions felt they were experiencing irreversible decline. But I also heard genuine spiritual longings in my interviewees. I wanted to bring these two groups together. I wanted to help religious people hear these interviewees. And I wanted to bring the riches of theological thinking to my SBNR conversation partners. But I also needed some time away from this project. Although the Cuban cross-cultural course meant I would have to take a break from writing, I welcomed it. The Cuba context would be very unlike the American one because it would allow us to see what religion might look like in a society which was, until recently, officially atheistic.

During the height of the Revolution and for decades afterward, the Cuban government discouraged the practice of religion and actively repressed its institutional aspects. Many Cuban clergy left, foreign clergy were forced to do so, and some ministers were jailed. Religious schools and many churches were shut down or re-purposed. An active propaganda campaign was carried out that made religion look anti-intellectual, retrograde, and against the socialistic and Communistic values of the state. Santeria, an African spirituality which had always been underground or hidden behind church symbols, continued to exist, but remained concealed. Anyone who practiced religion or had religious beliefs would not be allowed in the Communist Party nor could they find good employment with the state. Since all jobs were essentially state-run, this would make finding a livelihood extremely difficult. In this climate, it was almost impossible to be religious. Thus, an entire generation was raised with virtually no religious education, exposure to, or memory of organized religion.

The socialist experiment gave people something to believe in, however. It created a meaning structure and a vision. It provided free education, medical care, and retirement. Racial and social disparities were officially discouraged. Everyone was supposed to be on the same level. During the height of the Revolution, even if there was some covert cynicism about the limitations of the experiment, a good sense of solidarity existed. While the US embargo hurt (and still hurts) Cuba, the socialism on this island, only 90 miles from the United States, seemed to be succeeding.

However, this was in large part because of the economic aid provided by the Soviet Union and other friends. In the 1990s, everything changed. With the collapse of the Soviet Union, Cuba was left largely on its own. This inaugurated what was called by Fidel Castro "The Special Period in Time of Peace." Food, medicine, and supplies were scarce. People earned little. Everyone lost a lot of weight. Few cats or dogs were seen in the streets. In the light of these and other factors, the system did not seem as successful an experiment as it once did. Younger people, even though they were raised without religion, began looking for something else to believe in. In the most unlikely of circumstances, they nevertheless rediscovered God and religion. Churches which had been shuttered or barely surviving came back to life. By the time we visited, churches were overflowing and the sense of vitality, joy, and community were more palpable than anything we had ever witnessed in the United States.

We visited a Presbyterian church in a beach-side town. During the Revolution, it had been reduced to one member, Rita Rodriquez. An itinerant minister came by every Sunday to hold services for her because Ms. Rodriquez insisted on attending, praying, and worshipping in spite of very unpromising circumstances. But by the time we got there, this church, too, was overflowing. It had grown exponentially since the time this one woman kept the church open. This congregation now runs a retreat center, hosts a baseball ministry, freely dispenses clean filtered water, and serves the community in many other ways. In fact, all the diverse churches we visited, no matter what their theological orientation, have created vital new ministries to help sustain society. In addition, they are engaged in active ecumenical cooperation with each other, even if they have different worship styles and theological emphases. Many, however, have also come up with a "theology of the revolution." This is a belief system which has found ways to affirm the gains of Cuban socialism while also ministering to its weak spots. Yet all the while the focus is kept on God.

After this trip, we were changed people. We are now more hopeful about God's faithfulness and human resourcefulness. We see that religion can thrive in all sorts of social systems. We realize that religion is amazingly resilient and significant. And we now know more deeply that this is not just because religions, at their best, try to heal the world, but especially because they offer more than this world can give.

APPENDIX

On Methodology

Process

AS A THEOLOGIAN, I am interested in how the changing American religious scene relates to beliefs formerly common among many Americans. One underlying question that informs this study is "what does a contemporary spiritual thought world look like as a dominant theology recedes?" When I first began thinking about this project, I was influenced by existing literature, media, and the ruminations of religious leaders worried about declining numbers. From this, it seemed the core issues were simply anti-institutionalism, rejecting the costs of commitment, or the "question authority" ethos inherited from the 1960s. But as I began listening more closely to the many SBNRs I was meeting, I began to hear actual theological complaints around certain core issues in Western religion. In the beginning of this study I did not have precise preformed categories or themes. But even after I developed them, I tried to walk a fine line between having some recognizable concepts to structure the research, and letting themes emerge organically from my conversation partners.

I also considered as "data" any other information I came across relating to the "spiritual but not religious" phenomenon, such as Internet sites, television programs, films, advertising, and so on. I read widely on the topic, including sociology, history, and psychology, as well as theology. I also studied the many surveys on changing trends in American religion. In all of this, I did not find much specifically on belief. I knew that surveys and quantitative work can only tell us so much. For instance, finding that a majority of Americans still believe in God or afterlife does not really tell us what kind of God or afterlife, or if these concepts would be recognizable to more traditional believers.

At first I thought I would simply survey SBNRs, focusing on participants in New Age retreat centers or classes as a likely petri dish of data. This proved logistically difficult, partly because people go to retreat centers and take classes for personal reasons, not to be objects of study. Retreat and class leaders were also wary of me, wondering if I was going to somehow take away business. Even so, through the gracious invitation of one director, I was able to create and administer a pilot survey at her retreat center where I had taught some spiritual memoir writing classes. I also administered the survey to several other individuals. Although I was not prepared to use a "mixed methods" approach for the whole project—formulating both quantitative and qualitative tools—this one survey experience allowed me to understand potential interviewees and their concerns much better.

Next I created an open-ended semi-structured interview format so I could explore SBNR beliefs in depth. I produced a consent form which assured respondents their real names would not be used in any presentations and their listed would be concealed. The form explained the purpose of the project, listed persons who could provide additional information, gave my professional status and contact information, and collected some basic demographic data. Our institution's "Human Subjects Review" committee supervised this aspect. Thus interviewee names are pseudonyms..

I used various methods to get volunteers for the interviews. I visited many types of retreat centers, yoga studios, book stores, coffee houses, and other logical venues. My project was announced at churches, inviting attendees to speak about the project to their non-affiliated friends and family. I announced the project on various websites and through email lists, created a website with blog, and physically posted notices in cafes, health food stores, meditation centers, bookshops. I sent out emails to interfaith organizations, spirituality, art, and music groups. I made an appeal for interviewees whenever I gave a public talk. I asked friends, fellow ministers, church members, and former students to contact persons they thought qualified. I had students in my "Theology and Culture" class (Spring 2010) find interviewees. I struck up conversations in coffee shops, yoga classes, alternative health clinics, and other places. Even when persons did not themselves identify with the phrase "spiritual but not religious," they almost always knew many others who did. Often they put me in touch with their children, spouses, friends, or former fellow church members. This is thus a "convenience" and "snowball" sample. People told each other about my project and then spontaneously contacted me to be interviewed. Word-of-mouth worked effectively to garner interest in this project. I did this research anywhere I had personal or professional reasons to go.

Other data came from the many "site" visits and participant-observer activities I pursued, going where SBNRs would go. I stayed at retreat centers, took yoga and meditation classes, participated in a sweat lodge, and did many other activities to which SBNRs were drawn. I have experienced and been initiated into reiki, have done "energy work," cranial-sacral therapy, acupuncture and other alternative health modalities, attended lectures and seminars by spiritual teachers, participated in a solstice service, and more. I have also offered many spiritual memoir writing workshops which allowed me to hear a wide variety of spiritual stories. In addition to having long talks with my interviewees, I have had hundreds of informal conversations with SBNRs. All of this informed my research and often brought me many prospective interviewees.

The main criterion for interviewees was to self-identify as a "spiritual but not religious" person. Even if interviewees did not personally use the term, they needed to resonate and agree with it. They also needed to be willing to talk in-depth about their spiritual journey and beliefs. I carefully pre-screened all volunteers, either in person, by telephone or email, talking with them about the project, their views, and how they felt about the phrase "I'm spiritual but not religious." In order to do justice to the label, which can be found within as well as outside religious congregations, I had to move beyond standard measures of religiosity and affiliation, such as attendance at services or a literal view of the Bible when accepting interviewees. Although age, education, economic status, or race and ethnicity were not primary criteria for selection, I did work hard to solicit a wide set of volunteers. Each interview represents only a snapshot of the person at a given time, but my decision to rely on each volunteer's self-identification as "SBNR" and eagerness to be interviewed worked well. Many people understood the phrase and responded very positively to it.

I conducted the bulk of the interviews myself, as well as leading several focus groups. Although most interviews were conducted in person, when this was not possible I did some interviews over the telephone, supplemented by email dialogue, or by Skype. This represented about 5% of the interviews. Another 5% were conducted in-person by students from my "Theology and Culture" class. They used the same consent form and interview format. All official interviews were recorded with full knowledge of the participant.

Interviews were usually conducted in public places such as churches, offices, libraries, or coffee shops, but I was careful to either be in a separate room or not within hearing distance of others. At the start of each interview, respondents filled out two copies of the form, one for them and one for me. I explained more about the purposes of the project, elaborating on the consent form's description and asked for any preliminary questions. Each interview started with a narrative of the respondent's "spiritual journey," including religious background if any, family history especially regarding religion, and current affiliations. Then we moved into the four conceptual areas. I used the same interview for each person, but allowed much freedom for respondents to tell their own stories and respond in their own ways. Interviews took between one and two hours. The focus groups lasted about two hours and followed the same format. I strove to maintain a warm, welcoming, and appreciative atmosphere. I mostly asked questions and did my best not to impose my own views on the subjects or their comments.

Although the SBNR phenomenon exists throughout North America and abroad, for this project I focused much of my attention on the American Midwest and the West. The West has the reputation of being spiritually open-minded, with less focus on tradition. The Midwest has the reputation of being more religious and traditional. I had an opportunity to spend several months in each of three consecutive years in a large Western metro area, including surrounding suburbs and a nearby mid-sized city. Not only did I find ample numbers of interviewees; I was able to re-visit many of them in following years. Since I teach in the Midwest, I was able to focus on a nearby large city and nearby smaller towns and suburbs. I have also visited other parts of the United States, including California, Michigan, and upstate New York, and have even gone outside the United States to Canada, Mexico, and Scotland. These last non-US interviews and site visits are interesting primarily because they often echo what I have heard from my US participants.

Interviewees

I formally interviewed ninety people and conducted two focus groups, totaling fifteen people. Interviewees and other conversation partners represent a fairly wide range of employment, ages, income, and educational levels. About one-third were male, about 10% racial or ethnic minorities, and an equal percentage of those with a non-heterosexual orientation. A few volunteers were atheists. I categorized my interviewees by age cohort and used the well-known groupings of: The Greatest Generation (born 1901–1924), The Silent Generation (born 1925–1945), Baby Boomers (born 1946–1964), Gen X (born 1965–1981), and Millennials (born after 1982). To see if there were potential geographic distinctions in SBNR beliefs, I compared the Midwestern and Western interviewees, since it is often assumed that people in the West are less tied to traditional religious patterns.[1] Although I found some geographic particularities in theological orientation, they did not overly affect belief, nor was finding them the main purpose of this project. The fact that more educated people and women volunteered likely means my call was attractive to people who are self-reflective, accustomed to talking to a professional about themselves, and/or had a dramatic story to tell.

"Silent Generation" interviewees comprised somewhat more than 10% of my pool. This cohort included nearly even numbers of men and women, most Caucasian, with one racial/ethnic minority. Although most were retired, they were among the more highly educated of any of my cohorts, nearly all holding college or advanced degrees. Most were now retired, many had served in professions, but only about one-third had incomes of $75,000 or above. Nearly equal numbers came from my two main interviewing areas, West and Midwest.

The Baby Boomers were the largest group of interviewees, more than 40% of the total. The majority were raised in mainline Protestantism, a few with conservative backgrounds, and about one-fifth from Roman Catholicism. Only one interviewee had a Jewish upbringing, although several others had one Jewish parent. Even with my efforts at diversity, in the end more than two-thirds of my Baby Boomer volunteers were women. These Baby Boomer interviewees, as a group, represented a wide economic scale, from returning students to retired professionals. Educationally, most had at least some college and only about 5% had stopped their education at high school. A small percentage had also earned a Master's degree. While the largest percentage of the total Baby Boomer pool was white and heterosexual, more than 10% openly claimed a GLBT identity, and about an equal percentage came from racial/ethnic minorities. Although I worked to recruit non-dominant-majority interviewees (gender orientation, racial, and class), the most avid volunteers among Baby Boomers were white college-educated middle-class women, lending some credence to the popular stereotype about who is likely to become SBNR. About equal numbers came from the West and Midwest.

Gen X interviewees represented about one-third of the total. More Midwesterners than Westerners were represented (about two to one) in this sample, and their income and educational levels were fairly evenly distributed. More than one-third were male; about one in four were either racial minority or self-identified GLBT participants. This group of interviewees was about two-thirds as large as the Baby Boomer cohort. Unlike the two earlier cohorts—and even though many were Midwesterners—significantly less than half of this group had a consistent, traditional religious upbringing. Many more respondents were raised with minimal exposure, eclectically, or with no religion at all. This could explain their low level of religious dissent, and high tolerance for "using" or enjoying spirituality without feeling an obligation to commit. Of those raised religiously, two-thirds of them were involved in mainline Protestantism, about one-sixth were raised conservative Christian, and a few grew up Roman Catholic. The small but significant number raised conservative Christian (about one in six of those with religious upbringing or about one in twelve of the total) mirrored the rise of evangelicalism during this period and also the decline in denominational identity. These people described a more "generic Christian" identity that nevertheless required much of them on a behavioral level.

There were about the same number of Millennial interviewees as there were of the Silent Generation. Nearly equal numbers of the Millennial interviewees were women and men, and nearly equal numbers were from the West and Midwest. True to the statistics on this group, more than half had divorced parents. This could affect any kind of continuity in religious upbringing they might have experienced otherwise. Two-thirds of them had been somewhat exposed to religion growing up, but that exposure varied greatly from a bare minimum, to "holiday" attendance, to a somewhat more regular routine. Several of these interviewees were taken to church irregularly until the middle of elementary school when parents ended all attendance. I hardly found anyone who sought out conventional religion on their own in spite of parental dis-involvement, even though in earlier cohorts this was a determination I always found in at least some of the interviewees.

Limitations

Most of my interviewees come from a Judeo-Christian heritage, whether religiously or culturally. I had only a few raised with Eastern religious or Native American heritages. The racial minorities who volunteered were often biracial. The only Latino volunteer did not show up for his interview and was not willing to reschedule. Thus, my pool was not as broad as I would have liked. Even though I networked with many racial and ethnic minority leaders to help find potential interviewees, many times my African American or Latino contacts would say "Oh, I don't know anybody like that." This was interesting because some surveys show that the rise in "nones" exists not just among Caucasians, but in racial and ethnic minorities as well.[2] However, the percentages are significantly higher among Caucasians.[3] Religious identity is often tied up with cultural identity, so in some communities being a spiritual seeker might not be something one wants to broadcast. The ethnic and minority interviewees I did find were often well-educated or professionals who had already moved some distance from a clear-cut identity with their roots. I would also have preferred to attract more Millennial interviewees but the topic, frankly, did not seem as compelling to them as it did to Baby Boomers and Gen X people. Still, the non-random nature of a convenience and snowball sample makes this limitation hard to avoid and may also say something about which audiences are most attracted to the SBNR label.

Analysis

Although my semi-structured interview did query interviewees' beliefs in certain very general areas, I was also able to allow themes to emerge organically. Thus, my method is most similar to a "thematic analysis," which discovers clusters of linked categories having similar meanings. I tried hard not to impose artificial structures on interviewee comments. Nor did I try to prove correlation between religious background and current beliefs, and the relationship did not appear determinative. This was not a purely phenomenological analysis, however, since I did start with some general topic areas. Neither did I set out to simply generate "thick descriptions" of or tell interviewee stories, although these are worthwhile goals. Instead, I wanted to discover if there are some recurrent belief patterns that would be recognized by others, both affiliated and non-affiliated. I did this purposely to allow readers to link interviewees' beliefs within existing theological frameworks. Readers can measure the validity of the themes by asking whether they are believable, recognizable, and can be corroborated in other settings and by other audiences.

Interviews were recorded, transcribed verbatim, and then loaded into NVivo software which is used for qualitative research. This program allows successive levels of coding, helps keep track of quotes, allows the researcher to run queries based on various types of data, and allows themes to emerge organically. I worked with several consultants to learn how to use the software most effectively. At the outset,

I immersed myself in the data and made initial notes about emerging themes or concepts. In subsequent passes through the material, I began to cluster these preliminary themes by their conceptual similarities, resulting in master and sub-themes. As meaningful units grew, I was able to construct the major themes that arose from the material. I coded data, according to many factors, including age, location, religious background, socioeconomic status, and so on. I spent considerable time first doing "open" coding on a broad collection of themes. Next I did "selective coding" (i.e., coding with respect to core concepts). Doing both types of coding helped me see clusters, similarities, and dissimilarities. To prevent imposing preconceived judgments, I looked for "outliers" and issues that did not fit the emerging themes.

This sort of research is time-consuming, labor-intensive, exploratory, and inductive. As a theologian in a small seminary, rather than a social scientist, I did not have access to a team of researchers or student assistants. However, I did work in frequent consultation with scholars in various fields. I wrote several grants for the project over a five-year period, thus subjecting the material to academic scrutiny. Because the project garnered me a Henry Luce III Fellowship in Theology, I was able to present my ongoing research to fellow Luce Scholars over a several year period. The project was also selected to be part of a two-year consultation on "Theologies of Religious Pluralism" sponsored jointly by the American Academy of Religion and the Luce Foundation. In this venue, I had many occasions to dialogue with scholars representing many different religious traditions. Throughout, I have also shared my findings with various SBNR conversation partners and religious affiliates.

Notes

A PERSONAL PRELUDE

1. Will Herberg, *Protestant, Catholic, Jew: An Essay in American Religious Sociology* (Garden City, NY: Doubleday, 1955).

2. Baltimore Catechism of 1891, "Question 391: Why did the Jewish religion, which up to the death of Christ had been the true religion, cease at that time to be the true religion? Answer: The Jewish religion, which, up to the death of Christ, had been the true religion, ceased at that time to be the true religion, because it was only a promise of the redemption and figure of the Christian religion, and when the redemption was accomplished and the Christian religion established by the death of Christ, the promise and the figure were no longer necessary."

3. My memoir, *Bloomfield Avenue: A Jewish-Catholic Jersey Girl's Spiritual Journey* (Lanham, MD: Rowman & Littlefield, 2006) contains the whole story.

4. See, e.g., Robert D. Putnam and David E. Campbell, *American Grace: How Religion Divides and Unites Us* (New York: Simon & Schuster, 2010), especially chapters 3–5. This is only one of the sources that comment on this fact. Much can be learned from the General Social Surveys (GSS) conducted since 1972 by the National Opinion Research Center (NORC), a social indicator that looks at, among other things, denominational affiliation, church attendance, religious upbringing, personal beliefs, and religious experiences. Earlier books show that concern was emerging in the mainline churches well before the rise in SBNRs was documented; see, e.g., J. Russell Hale, *The Unchurched: Who They Are and Why They Stay Away* (San Francisco: Harper & Row, 1977).

5. Barbara Ehrenreich, who had breast cancer herself, wrote about this phenomenon in her 2001 *Harper's Magazine* article "Welcome to Cancerland." Her focus is more on gender than spiritual issues. However, she does see the disease process being promoted as a passageway to a sort of spiritual "upward mobility" and even likens it to a cult or religion: "'Culture' is too weak a word to describe all this. What has grown up around breast cancer in just the last

fifteen years more nearly resembles a cult—or...perhaps we should say a full-fledged religion. The products—teddy bears, pink-ribbon brooches, and so forth—serve as amulets and talismans, comforting the sufferer and providing visible evidence of faith. The personal narratives serve as testimonials and follow the same general arc as the confessional autobiographies required of seventeenth-century Puritans: first there is a crisis, often involving a sudden apprehension of mortality (the diagnosis or, in the old Puritan case, a stem word from on high); then comes a prolonged ordeal (the treatment or, in the religious case, internal struggle with the Devil); and finally, the blessed certainty of salvation, or its breast-cancer equivalent, survivorhood. And like most recognized religions, breast cancer has its great epideictic events, its pilgrimages and mass gatherings where the faithful convene and draw strength from their numbers."

CHAPTER 1

1. For worldwide comparisons, see "The Global Religious Landscape," Pew Forum on Religion & Public Life, Dec. 18, 2012, and also its Oct. 2012 report "Nones on the Rise," http://www.pewforum.org. For a summary, see Kimberly Winston, Religious News Service, Dec. 19, 2012, "Unbelief is now the world's third largest 'religion,'" http://www.washingtonpost.com.

2. Barry Kosmin and Areala Keyser, *Religion in a Free Market: Religious and Non-Religious Americans, Who, What, Why, Where* (Ithaca, NY: Paramount Books, 2006), 24.

3. "In U.S., Rise in Religious Nones Slows in 2012," Jan. 10, 2013, http://www.gallup.com/poll/159785/rise-religious-nones-slows-2012.aspx.

4. Michael Hout, Claude S. Fisher, and Mark A. Chaves, "More Americans Have No Religious Preference: Key Findings from the 2012 General Social Survey," Institute for the Study of Societal Issues, University of California, Berkeley, March 2013.

5. Estimates vary, but research indicates that "nones" make up anywhere from 19% to 25% of Americans, and the amount is still growing. Surveys are a recent scientific tool, so it is difficult to speculate with any accuracy how many "nones" existed before polls began. Some say the 1950s and 1960s should not be taken as the historical norm. But for much of the twentieth and twenty-first centuries, this reality has been well documented by both scientific and popular surveys. See, for instance, the American Religious Identification Survey (ARIS 2008), Barry A. Kosmin and Ariela Keysar, Trinity College; the Pew Forum on Religion & Public Life, *Faith in Flux: Changes in Religious Affiliation in the U.S.*, 2009; also see their *Religion among the Millennials*, Feb. 2010; Knights of Columbus, Marist Poll, *American Millennials: Generations Apart*, Feb. 2010; *Newsweek*, "Spirituality

in America," Aug. 29–Sept. 5, 2005; *Parade*, "Has America Become More Spiritual?" Oct. 4, 2009. Estimates of the "nones" vary greatly. Putnam in chapter 1 of *American Grace* puts the percentage of "nones" at 17% and that of mainline Protestants at 14%; Robert Putnam, *American Grace: How Religion Divides and Unites Us* (New York: Simon & Schuster, 2012). The television show "Religion and Ethics Newsweekly" also did a three-part series on this group in the fall of 2012. In Jan. 2013, National Public Radio did a series of shows on "nones" on its popular "Morning Edition." For reference to decline in mainline Protestantism, see, e.g., William McKinney, "Crunching the Numbers," *The Christian Century*, Apr. 2, 2012.

6. In Jan. 2013, the Gallup Poll noted a slight reduction in growth, reporting "The percentage of American adults who have no explicit religious identification averaged 17.8% in 2012, up from 14.6% in 2008—but only slightly higher than the 17.5% in 2011. The 2011 to 2012 uptick in religious 'nones' is the smallest such year-to-year increase over the past five years of Gallup Daily tracking of religion in America." "In U.S., Rise in Religious Nones Slows in 2012," Jan. 10, 2013, http://www.gallup.com/poll/159785/rise-religious-nones-slows-2012. aspx.

   Even those surveys that focus on the faith of the remaining religious people are clear on the reduction in affiliation. See, e.g., Frank Newport, "Seven in 10 Americans are Very or Moderately Religious: But Protestant Population is Shrinking as 'Unbranded' Religion Grows," Gallup poll report, Dec. 4, 2012.

7. Pew Forum, *Religion among the Millennials*, 2010; LifeWay Research, Aug. 2009 survey of 1,200 Millennials.

8. Pew Forum, *Faith in Flux: Changes in Religious Affiliation in the U.S.*, 2009.

9. There are many books on these themes, from professing to analytical. Examples include: Nevill Drury, *The New Age: Searching for the Spiritual Self* (London: Thames and Hudson, 2004); Wouter J. Hanegraaff, *New Age Religion and Western Culture: Esotericism in the Mirror of Secular Thought* (Boston: Brill Academic Publishers, 1996); Courtney Bender, *The New Metaphysicals: Spirituality and the American Religious Imagination* (Chicago: University of Chicago, 2010); Paul Heelas, *Spiritualities of Life: New Age Romanticism and Consumptive Capitalism* (Oxford: Blackwell, 2008); Catherine L. Albanese, *A Republic of Mind & Spirit: A Cultural History of American Metaphysical Religion* (New Haven: Yale University Press, 2007). See also the best-seller by Greg M. Epstein, Humanist Chaplain at Harvard University, *Good Without God: What a Billion Nonreligious People Do Believe* (New York: William Morrow, 2009).

10. There are so many articles on this topic, from both Catholic and Protestants, that it is difficult to enumerate them. For accessible articles, see, for instance, Lovett H. Weems, Jr., "No Shows," *The Christian Century*, Oct. 10, 2010, 10–11; Amy

Frykholm, "Loose Connections," *The Christian Century*, May 31, 2011, 20–23. For a publisher's perspective, see, for instance, Marcia Z. Nelson, "Losing Their Religion," *Publishers Weekly* 260, no. 3 (Jan. 21, 2013): 16–17. For accessible and succinct expressions of the need to retain the intellectual heritage and contributions of religion, see, e.g., Garret Keizer, "Reasons to Join: In Defense of Organized Religion," *The Christian Century*, Apr. 22, 2008, 31.

11. Will Herberg, *Judaism and Modern Man: An Interpretation of Jewish Religion* (New York: Farrar, Straus and Young, 1951).

12. See, e.g., Kenneth Pargament, Bruce Smith, Harold Koenig, and Lisa Perez, "Patterns of Positive and Negative Religious Coping with Major Life Stressors," *Journal for the Scientific Study of Religion* 37, no. 4 (Dec. 1998): 710–24. See also Chris Baker and Jonathan Miles-Watson, "Faith and Traditional Capitals: Defining the Public Scope of Spiritual and Religious Capital—A Literature Review," *Implicit Religion* 13, no. 1 (2010): 17–69. The Gallup organization has a focus on this issue. For example, Frank Newport, Sangeeta Agrawal, and Dan Witters, "Very Religious Americans Report Less Depression, Worry," Princeton: Gallup, Dec. 1, 2010; Steve Crabtree and Brett Pelham, "Religion Provides Emotional Boost to World's Poor," Princeton: Gallup, Mar. 6, 2009; Frank Newport, Sangeeta Agrawal, and Dan Witters, "Very Religious Have Higher Wellbeing across All Faiths," Jan. 6, 2011; Frank Newport, Sangeeta Agrawal, and Dan Witters, "Very Religious Americans Lead Healthier Lives," Dec. 23, 2010; Frank Newport, Sangeeta Agrawal, and Dan Witters, "Religious Americans Enjoy Higher Wellbeing," Oct. 28, 2010.

13. Journalists John Micklethwait and Adrian Woodridge, in *God Is Back: How the Global Revival of Faith Is Changing the World* (New York: Penguin, 2009), give just some examples of this "mountain of evidence"; see, e.g., chapter 5.

14. Many prominent social theorists (e.g., Max Weber and Émile Durkheim) predicted that modernization and the rise of science would inevitably result in the decline of religion. Sociologists of religion have been debating aspects of this theory for decades. Although the outcome of the debate is still uncertain, the recent rise in religion calls into question the premise of inevitable decline and some theorists (e.g., Rodney Stark) actually predict a rise in religiosity. For the state of the argument and clarifications of various versions, see Phillip S. Gorski "Historicizing the Secularization Debate: Church, State, and Society in Late Medieval and Early Modern Europe, CA. 1300 to 1700," *American Sociological Review* 65 (Feb. 2000): 138–67. See also Charles Taylor, *A Secular Age* (Cambridge, MA: Belknap Press, Harvard University, 2007).

15. Micklethwait and Woodridge, in *God Is Back*, spend much time on this topic.

16. Robert Wuthnow, *After Heaven: Spirituality in America since the 1950s* (Berkeley and Los Angeles: University of California Press, 1998).

17. Jeffrey J. Kripal, *Esalen: America and the Religion of No Religion* (Chicago: University of Chicago, 2008).

18. The Network of Spiritual Progressives, "Spiritual But Not Religious," Feb. 25, 2009, http://www.spiritualprogressives.org/article.php/spiritual_butnot/.

19. http://www.sbnr.org/.

20. Mark C. Taylor, *After God* (Chicago: University of Chicago Press, 2007).

21. Chris Baker and Jonathan Miles-Watson, "Faith and Traditional Capitals: Defining the Public Scope of Spiritual and Religious Capital—A Literature Review," *Implicit Religion* 13, no. 1 (2010): 17–69.

22. Dr. Carolyn Schneider, a professor from Texas Lutheran University in Seguin, TX, asked her students to conduct interviews on people who were "spiritual but not religious." Dr. Schneider was surprised to learn that most of the students in her "Religion in the U.S." class had never heard the term. All under 21, they were nearly uniformly from conservative Christian backgrounds. They were confused by the phrase at first, thinking that spirituality must be a pejorative term if it was de-linked from religion. But after some explanation, they rapidly appropriated the popular connotation that "spiritual" meant one had a vital, living faith, and that to just be "religious" without it meant one was a hypocrite.

23. Heinz Streib and Ralph W. Hood, "'Spirituality as Privatized Experience-Oriented Religion: Empirical and Conceptual Perspectives," *Implicit Religion* 14, no. 4 (2011): 433–53.

24. See, e.g., Penny Long Marler and C. Kirk Hadaway, "'Being Religious' or 'Being Spiritual' in America: A Zero-Sum Proposition?" *Journal for the Scientific Study of Religion* 41 (2000): 289–300; and Simon Cassar and Pnina Shinebourne, "What Does Spirituality Mean to You?: An Interpretive Phenomenological Analysis of the Experience of Spirituality," *Existential Analysis* 23, no. 1 (Jan. 2012): 133–48; and Elaine Howard Ecklund and Elizabeth Long, "Scientists and Spirituality," *Sociology of Religion* 72, no. 3 (2011): 253–74.

25. This is a popular belief. For instance, George Lewis, host of "The Spiritual but not Religious Show," on The Spiritual Broadcasting Network (Internet) sees this as the only possible outcome of today's ferment. But also some writers claim a widespread transformation is happening within religion as well. See, e.g., Phyllis Tickle, *The Great Emergence: How Christianity Is Changing and Why* (Grand Rapids, MI: Baker, 2008).

26. One of the best known critics of the overly self-focused aspect, "religious privatism" or "Sheilaism"—called that after Sheila, a respondent who had constructed her own personal faith—is Robert N. Bellah, Richard Madsen, William M. Sullivan, Ann Swidler, and Steven M. Tipton, *Habits of the Heart: Individualism and Commitment in American Life, With a New Preface* (Berkeley and Los Angeles: University of California, 2007).

27. Rowan Williams, Archbishop of Canterbury, "The Spiritual and the Religious: Is the Territory Changing?" *Faith and Life Series*, Westminster Cathedral, Apr. 17, 2008.

28. See, e.g., Stephen Prothero, *Religious Literacy: What Every American Needs to Know—and Doesn't* (San Francisco: HarperOne, 2007).

29. See, e.g., Meredith B. McGuire, *Lived Religion: Faith and Practice in Everyday Life* (New York: Oxford University Press, 2008).

30. Harvey Cox, *The Future of Faith* (New York: HarperOne, 2009).

31. Owen C. Thomas, "Spiritual but Not Religious: The Influence of the Current Romantic Movement," *Anglican Theological Review* 88, no. 3 (Summer 2006): 404–5.

32. See, e.g., McGuire, *Lived Religion*.

33. R. Stark and C. Y. Glock, *American Piety: The Nature of Religious Commitment* (Berkeley and Los Angeles: University of California Press, 1968), 16; as cited in Neal Krause and Keith M. Wulff, "Religious Doubt and Health: Exploring the Potential Dark Side of Religion," *Sociology of Religion* 65, no. 1 (2004): 35–56, at 50.

34. Stephen Prothero has made this case in a very accessible way, *God is Not One: The Eight Rival Religions That Run the World—and Why Their Differences Matter* (San Francisco: HarperOne, 2010).

35. For a review of the literature, see Merlin B. Brinkerhoff and Marlene M. Mackie, "Casting Off the Bonds of Organized Religion: A Religious-Careers Approach to the Study of Apostasy," *Review of Religious Research* 34, no. 3 (Mar. 1993): 235–58.

36. Robyn L. Driskell and Larry Lyon, "Assessing the Role of Religious Beliefs on Secular and Spiritual Behaviors," *Review of Religious Research* 52, no. 4 (2011): 386–404.

37. See Adam B. Cohen, Azimn F. Shariff, and Peter C. Hill, "The Accessibility of Religious Belief," *Journal of Research in Personality* 42 (2008): 1408–17, for a summary of these studies.

38. Ibid., 1415, also citing the extensive work of Fazio and Powell. See especially R. H. Fazio and M. C. Powell, "On the Value of Knowing One's Likes and Dislikes: Attitude Accessibility, Stress, and Health in College," *Psychological Science* 8 (1997): 430–36.

39. Michele Dillon and Paul Wink, *In the Course of a Lifetime: Tracing Religious Belief, Practice, and Change* (Berkeley and Los Angeles: University of California, 2007), 192.

40. Christian Smith claims that "emerging adults" have very few resources to deal with the inevitable moral challenges that life presents. See *Lost in Transition: The Dark Side of Emerging Adulthood* (New York: Oxford University Press, 2011).

41. E.g. The Pew Forum, "Many Americans Mix Multiple Faiths," Dec. 2009.

42. In his 2009 presidential address to the Society for the Scientific Study of Religion, Mark Chaves challenged this problematic assumption. See "Rain Dances in the Dry Season: Overcoming the Religious Congruence Fallacy," *Journal for the Scientific Study of Religion* 49, no. 1 (2010): 1–14.

43. One study looks at this issue in Europe which has been longer on the trajectory toward the decline in religious affiliation. See David Voas, "The Rise and Fall of Fuzzy Fidelity in Europe," *European Sociological Review* 25, no. 2 (2009): 155–68.

44. Some have attended to the beliefs of Americans in general, rather than to the SBNR population in particular. See, e.g., Michele Dillon and Paul Wink, *In the Course of a Lifetime: Tracing Religious Belief, Practice, and Change* (Berkeley and Los Angeles: University of California, 2007); Stephen Prothero, *Religious Literacy: What Every American Needs to Know—and Doesn't* (New York: Harper Collins, 2007); and Rodney Stark, *What Americans Really Believe* (Waco, TX: Baylor, 2008).

45. Dick Houtman and Stef Aupers, "The Spiritual Turn and the Decline of Tradition: The Spread of Post-Christian Spirituality in 14 Western Countries, 1981–2000," *Journal for the Scientific Study of Religion* 46, no. 3 (2007): 305–20, at 308.

46. See, e.g., Simon Cassar and Pnina Shinebourne, "What Does Spirituality Mean to You?: An Interpretive Phenomenological Analysis of the Experience of Spirituality," *Existential Analysis* 23, no. 1 (Jan. 2012): 133–48, and Elaine Howard Ecklund and Elizabeth Long, "Scientists and Spirituality," *Sociology of Religion* 72, no. 3 (2011): 253–74.

47. Grace Davie wrote about this in the British context, *Religion in Britain since 1945: Believing Without Belonging* (Hoboken, NJ: Wiley-Blackwell, 1994), but the phrase is used more widely now, also describing results of U.S. research, which claims that Americans still believe what they always have, but without religious affiliation. See, e.g., Rodney Stark, *What Americans Really Believe*, (Waco, TX: Baylor University Press, 2008) and a paper given at the American Sociological Association, San Francisco, Aug. 8, 2009, by Michael Hout and Claude S. Fischer, "Unchurched Believers: Fewer Americans Have a Religion But Religious Beliefs Haven't Changed Much." But other studies, including the current book, claim New Age and other beliefs are growing; see, e.g., The Pew Forum, "Many Americans Mix Multiple Faiths," Dec. 2009.

48. Frank Newport, "Americans More Likely to Believe in God Than the Devil, Heaven More Than Hell, Belief in the Devil Has Increased since 2000," Gallup News Service, June 13, 2007.

49. Paul Froese and Christopher Bader, *America's Four Gods: What We Say about God—and What That Says about Us* (New York: Oxford University Press, 2010). But see also "The Quadrennium Project 2012: A Survey of US Religious

Preferences, Practices and Beliefs, A White Paper," Fall 2012, at http://www. MissionInsite.com.

50. Just a sampling of books on this topic include Robert Putnam, *American Grace: How Religion Divides and Unites Us* (New York: Simon & Schuster, 2012); Mark Chaves, *American Religion: Contemporary Trends* (Princeton, NJ: Princeton University Press, 2011); Claude S. Fisher and Michael Hout, *Century of Difference: How America Changed in the Last 100 Years* (New York: Russell Sage Foundation, 2006); Alan Wolfe, *The Transformation of American Religion: How We Actually Live Our Faith* (Chicago: University of Chicago Press, 2003); and more, some of which can be found in subsequent endnotes.

51. Linda Mercadante, *Victims & Sinners: The Spiritual Roots of Addiction and Recovery* (Philadelphia: Westminster John Knox, 1996).

52. See, e.g., K. I. Pargament, "The Psychology of Religion and Spirituality? Yes and No," *International Journal for the Psychology of Religion* 9 (1997): 3–16; D. O. Moberg, "Assessing and Measuring Spirituality: Confronting Dilemmas of Universal and Particular Evaluative Criteria," *Journal of Adult Development* 9 (2002): 47–60; J. Aten and B. Hernandez, "A 25-Year Review of Qualitative Research Published in Spiritually and Psychologically Oriented Journals," *Journal of Psychology and Christianity* 24 (2005): 266–77. R. W. Hood, Jr. and J. A. Belzen, "Research Methods in the Psychology of Religion," in R. F. Paloutzian and C. L. Park, eds., *Handbook of the Psychology of Religion and Spirituality* (New York: Guilford, 2005), 62–79. A study which has responded to the call of scholars in religion for more qualitative work is Matthew D. Graham, Marvin J. McDonald, and Derrick W. Klaasan, "A Phenomenological Analysis of Spiritual Seeking: Listening to Quester Voices," *International Journal for the Psychology of Religion* 18 (2008): 146–63.

53. Some studies, however, mix in smaller samples of interviews along with survey data. Rodney Stark reports on this in the area of belief, *What Americans Really Believe*, 2008.

54. Pew Forum, "Nones on the Rise," 2012, http://www.pewforum.org/2012/10/09/nones-on-the-rise/.

55. For more on how one can be atheist and spiritual, see, e.g., Elaine Howard Ecklund and Elizabeth Long, "Scientists and Spirituality," in *Sociology of Religion* 72, no. 3 (2011): 253–74.

56. I know that the term "religious" has acquired some pejorative undertones in the wider American culture. If a television evangelist like Joyce Meyers, who is clearly an evangelical Christian, can affirm that she is not "religious"—her tone having a veritable sneer in it—the word "religion" has become about as unpopular in America as the word "sin." When evangelicals use it, it generally means lifeless or rigid formal practice, rather than heartfelt faith in Christ.

57. Robert C. Fuller, *Spiritual but not Religious: Understanding Unchurched America* (New York: Oxford University Press, 2001).

58. Latin, usually translated "Through my fault," which is part of the Confiteor and can be said during Roman Catholic mass as a confession of sin. "I confess to Almighty God, to blessed Mary ever Virgin, to blessed Michael, the Archangel, to blessed John the Baptist, to the holy Apostles Peter and Paul, to all the Saints and to you, brothers (and to you Father), that I have sinned exceedingly, in thought, word and deed: through my fault, through my fault, through my most grievous fault. Therefore I beseech the blessed Mary, ever Virgin, blessed Michael the Archangel, blessed John the Baptist, the holy Apostles Peter and Paul, all the Saints, and you, Father, to pray to the Lord our God for me. Amen."

CHAPTER 2

1. Mainstream Protestantism, now sometimes also known as "old-line" Protestantism, is the name given to those churches with historic roots in the Reformation, such as Presbyterians and Lutherans, United Church of Christ, etc. Also included in this usage are Episcopalians and the United Methodist church, even though their roots and polity are more "Episcopal," meaning a hierarchy that includes bishops.

2. The term "fundamentalist," which unlike today once had luster, came from a series of twelve pamphlets, "The Fundamentals: Testimony to the Truth," sponsored by two lawyers from Los Angeles, setting forth core theological issues of the times, and sent to several million clergy and theologians from 1910 to 1915.

3. This 1960 movie about a con man and female evangelist duping small-town religious people, starring Burt Lancaster and Jean Simmons, was based on the 1927 novel by Sinclair Lewis.

4. The U.S. federal Johnson-Reed Act of 1924 put a quota on the number of immigrants who could be admitted from any country, based on 2% of their actual numbers living here in 1890. The intent was to preserve "homogeneity" by drastically limiting Southern and Eastern Europeans, including Jews, as well as Middle Easterners, East Asians, and Indians, after decades of dramatic immigrant influx.

5. An especially good reference is Catherine Albanese, *A Republic of Mind and Spirit: A Cultural History of American Metaphysical Religion* (New Haven, CT: Yale University Press, 2007).

6. Even Will Herberg notes this, but when he wrote in 1956 he suggested their numbers had considerably dwindled. Will Herberg, *Protestant-Catholic-Jew* (Garden City, NY: Doubleday, 1956), 59–60.

7. Gallup began tracking this in 1948. Frank Newport, "In U.S., Increasing Number Have No Religious Identity," Princeton, NJ, Gallup.com, May 21, 2010. Some

data on earlier years is included in John G. Condran and Joseph B. Tamney, "Religious 'Nones': 1957 to 1982," *Sociological Analysis* 46, no. 4 (1985): 415–23. Although there may have been somewhat more "nones" before the 1950s, their reasons for being "nones" were likely different. For an earlier look, see Glenn M. Vernon, "The Religious 'Nones': A Neglected Category," *Journal for the Scientific Study of Religion* 7, no. 2 (Fall 1968): 219–29. See also Michele Dillon and Paul Wink, *In the Course of a Lifetime: Tracing Religious Belief, Practice, and Change* (Berkeley and Los Angeles: University of California, 2007), 192. Robert Putnam, *American Grace: How Religion Divides and Unites Us* (New York: Simon & Schuster, 2012); and J. Russell Hale, *The Unchurched: Who They Are and Why They Stay Away* (San Francisco: Harper & Row, 1980).

8. Herberg, *Protestant-Catholic-Jew.*

9. The 1998 Warner Brothers fantasy film, "Pleasantville," by Gary Ross, depicted homogeneous small-town America and starred Tobey Maguire, Jeff Daniels, Joan Allen, William H. Macy, J. T. Walsh, and Reese Witherspoon.

10. Putnam, *American Grace.*

11. Newport, "In U.S., Increasing Number Have No Religious Identity."

12. A good example is the feminist "Evangelical Women's Caucus," which had its start in 1973.

13. Charles Taylor, *A Secular Age* (Cambridge, MA: Belknap Press, Harvard University, 2007).

14. Many millennialist books, like Hal Lindsey's blockbuster *The Late Great Planet Earth* (Grand Rapids, MI: Zondervan, 1970), were extremely popular with evangelicals during this period.

15. There are many sources documenting this alignment. For an entertaining personal narrative account of how apolitical fundamentalists turned into highly political conservatives, see Frank Schaeffer, *Crazy for God: How I Grew Up as One of the Elect, Helped Found the Religious Right, and Lived to Take All (or Almost All) of It Back* (New York: Carroll & Graf, 2007). Other sources include Randy Balmer, *Thy Kingdom Come: How the Religious Right Distorts the Faith and Threatens America: An Evangelical's Lament* (New York: Basic Books, 2006); and David Kuo, *Tempting Faith: An Inside Story of Political Seduction* (New York: Free Press, 2006).

16. Newport, "In U.S., Increasing Number Have No Religious Identity."

17. Michael Hout and Claude S. Fisher, "Why More Americans Have No Religious Preference: Politics and Generations," *American Sociological Review* 67 (Apr. 2002): 165–90.

18. David A. Roozen, "A Decade of Change in American Congregations 2000–2010," 14, http://www.faith communities Today.org.

19. Hout and Fisher, in "Why More Americans Have No Religious Preference," say their numbers doubled from 7% to 14%.

20. Newport, "In U.S., Increasing Number Have No Religious Identity."

21. See, e.g., C. Kirk Hadaway, Penny Long Marler, and Mark Chaves, "What the Polls Don't Show: A Closer Look at U.S. Church Attendance," *American Sociological Review* 58 (Dec. 1993): 741–52.

22. In 1968, Glenn M. Vernon noted the lack of interest in "nones." "The Religious 'Nones': A Neglected Category," *Journal for the Scientific Study of Religion* 7, no. 2 (Fall 1968): 219–29. But in the new millennium, after the surge, interest accelerated greatly. See, e.g., Hout and Fisher, "Why More Americans Have No Religious Preference"; Kevin D. Dougherty, Byron R. Johnson, Edward C. Polson, "Recovering the Lost: Remeasuring U.S. Religious Affiliation," *Journal for the Scientific Study of Religion* 46, no. 4 (2007): 483–99; Rodney Stark, *What Americans Really Believe: New Findings from the Baylor Surveys of Religion* (Waco, TX: Baylor University Press, 2008); Joseph O. Baker and Buster G. Smith, "The Nones: Social Characteristics of the Religiously Unaffiliated," *Social Forces* 87, no. 3 (2009): 1251–63.

23. Christian Smith with Kari Christoffersen, Hilary Davidson, and Patricia Snell Herzog, *Lost in Transition: The Dark Side of Emerging Adulthood* (New York: Oxford University Press, 2011), 21–22.

24. J. Russell Hale, *The Unchurched: Who They Are and Why They Stay Away* (San Francisco: Harper & Row, 1980), 175–76. He cites corroborating data from the 1978 Gallup Survey *The Unchurched American* (Princeton, NJ) and David A. Roozen, *The Churched and the Unchurched in America: A Comparative Profile* (Washington, DC: Glenmary Research Center, 1978).

25. Many express concern about the social consequences. See, e.g., Jean M. Twenge, *Generation Me: Why Today's Young Americans are More Confident, Assertive, Entitled—and More Miserable than Ever Before* (New York: Free Press, 2006). For a sensitive approach to contemporary challenges, see, e.g., Donald Capps, *The Depleted Self: Sin in a Narcissistic Age* (Minneapolis: Fortress Press, 1993). On helping to explain the emergence of small support groups, see Robert Wuthnow, *Sharing the Journey: Support Groups and America's New Quest for Community* (New York: Free Press, 1994). See also Robert Putnam's *Bowling Alone: The Collapse and Revival of American Community* (New York: Simon and Schuster, 2000). On reduced civic involvement, see, e.g., Philip Schwadel, "Individual, Congregational, and Denominational Effects on Church Members' Civic Participation," *Journal for the Scientific Study of Religion* 44, no. 2 (2005): 159–71.

26. See, e.g., Michele Dillon, Paul Wink, and Kristen Fay, "Is Spirituality Detrimental to Generativity?" *Journal for the Scientific Study of Religion* 42, no. 3 (2003): 427–42, and "Spiritual Seeking, Narcissism, and Psychotherapy: How Are They Related?" *Journal for the Scientific Study of Religion* 44, no. 2 (2005): 143–58.

27. Patricia O'Connell Killen, "The Religious Geography of the Pacific Northwest," *Word & World* 24, no. 3 (Summer 2004): 269–78, at 270. She explains that

in the Pacific Northwest, where religious adherents are the minority, 62.8% of the population is outside organized religion, with only 37.2% involved in some way. For a fuller treatment, see Patricia O'Connell Killen and Mark Silk, eds., *Religion and Public Life in the Pacific Northwest: In the None Zone* (Lanham, MD: AltaMira, 2004). The Pew Forum has documented this increase of "nones" in the former home of Protestantism, New England; see, e.g., "Nones on the Rise," http://www.pewforum.org.

28. Michael Hout and Claude S. Fisher, "Why More Americans Have No Religious Preference."

29. Many studies document these issues. See, e.g., Darren Sherkat, "Tracking the Restructuring of American Religion: Religious Affiliation and Patterns of Religious Mobility, 1973–1998," *Social Forces* 79, no. 4 (2001): 1459–93; Hout and Fisher, "Why More Americans Have No Religious Preference"; Wade Clark Roof's two works, *A Generation of Seekers: The Spiritual Journeys of the Baby Boom Generation* (New York: Harper Collins, 1993) and *Spiritual Marketplace: Baby Boomers and the Remaking of American Religion* (Princeton, NJ: Princeton University Press, 1999); Baker and Smith, "The Nones: Social Characteristics of the Religiously Unaffiliated"; and Philip Schwadel, "Period and Cohort Effects on Religious Nonaffiliation and Religious Disaffiliation: A Research Note," *Journal for the Scientific Study of Religion* 49, no. 2 (2010): 311–19.

30. Research is summarized in Baker and Smith, "The Nones: Social Characteristics of the Religiously Unaffiliated."

31. Paul Heelas and Benjamin Seel ask this question in "An Ageing New Age?" in Grace Davie, Paul Heelas, and Linda Woodhead, eds., *Predicting Religion: Christian, Secular and Alternative Futures* (Burlington, VT: Ashgate, 2003), 229–47, but they see New Age "spiritualities of life" continuing unabated. Others see a trend toward secularization in this. See, e.g., David Voas and Steve Bruce, "The Spiritual Revolution: Another False Dawn for the Sacred," in Grace Davie, Paul Heelas, and Linda Woodhead, eds., *Predicting Religion: Christian, Secular and Alternative Futures* (Burlington, VT: Ashgate, 2003), 43–61.

32. Robert Wuthnow, *After the Baby Boomers: How Twenty- and Thirty-Somethings Are Shaping the Future of American Religion* (Princeton: Princeton University Press, 2007).

33. Philip Schwadel contends this, based on the General Social Survey (GSS), reported in Daniel Lippman, "Young Americans More Loyal to Religion than Boomers," Reuters, Aug. 6, 2010.

34. "Religion among the Millennials: Less Religiously Active Than Older Americans, But Fairly Traditional in Other Ways," Pew Forum on Religion and Public Life, Feb. 17, 2010.

35. Peggy Long Marler and C. Kirk Hadaway, "'Being Religious' or 'Being Spiritual' in America: A Zero-sum Proposition?" *Journal for the Scientific Study of Religion*

41, no. 2 (2002): 289–300. While many Americans still see themselves as both religious and spiritual, the fact that these researchers identify a trend away from both among younger cohorts seems to support secularization theories. Other researchers claim younger people are more loyal to religion, but it is too soon to tell, especially with young adults maturing later than their predecessors. See, e.g., Philip Schwadel's study based on General Social Survey from 1973 to 2006 of more than 37,000 people. Schwadel, "Period and Cohort Effects on Religious Nonaffiliation and Religious Disaffiliation."

36. See the two works of Christian Smith, *Soul Searching: The Religious and Spiritual Lives of American Teenagers* (New York: Oxford University Press, 2005) and *Souls in Transition: The Religious & Spiritual Lives of Emerging Adults* (New York: Oxford University Press, 2009), as well as Stephen Prothero, *Religious Literacy: What Every American Needs to Know—and Doesn't* (San Francisco: Harper One, 2007), and a Pew study supporting Prothero's contentions, Pew Forum on Religion and Public Life, U.S. Religious Knowledge Survey, Sept. 28, 2010.

37. See, e.g., Mollie Ziegler Hemingway, "Faith Unbound: Why Spirituality is Sexy but Religion is Not," *Christianity Today*, Sept. 2010, 74; Stephen Cook, Patricia Borman, Martha Moore, and Mark Kunkel, "College Students' Perceptions of Spiritual People and Religious People," *Journal of Psychology and Theology* 2 (2000): 125–37; Kevin D. Dougherty, Bryon R. Johnson, and Edward C. Polson, "Recovering the Lost: Remeasuring U.S. Religious Affiliation," *Journal for the Scientific Study of Religion* 46, no. 4 (2007): 483–99. Lisa D. Pearce and Melinda Lundquist Denton, "What Being Religious Really Means to Young People," from the National Study on Youth and Religion, reported in *Huffington Post*, Jan. 14, 2011.

38. Many scholars have wrestled to untangle these terms, while others do not agree that it can be done. See, e.g., B. Zinnbauer, K. Pargament, B. Cole, M. Rye, E. Butter, T. Belavich, K. Hipp, A. Scott, and J. Kadar, "Religion and Spirituality: Unfuzzying the Fuzzy," *Journal for the Scientific Study of Religion* 36, no. 4 (1997): 549–64.

39. See, e.g., Michelle Dillon, "Old and New Spiritual Resources," *National Catholic Reporter*, Oct. 24, 2011, 1–5, http://ncronline.org. She found that large numbers of committed Catholics believe in many aspects of New Age spirituality, even more so among Hispanic Catholics, especially the ideas of "spiritual energy," reincarnation, and yoga as a spiritual practice.

40. Mark Chaves, *American Religion: Contemporary Trends* (Princeton: Princeton University Press, 2011).

41. Phillip E. Hammond, *The Dynamics of Religious Organizations: The Extravasation of the Sacred and Other Essays* (New York: Oxford University Press, 2000). See particularly the first essay: "The Extravasation of the Sacred and the Crisis in Liberal Protestantism" originally published in R. Michaelson and W. C. Roof, eds., *Liberal Protestantism* (Cleveland, OH: Pilgrim Press, 1986).

42. There is a very large debate on this theory, first credited to Roger Finke and Rodney Stark. See, e.g., their *The Churching of America, 1776–1990: Winners and Losers in our Religious Economy* (New Brunswick, NJ: Rutgers University Press, 1992). In fact, there is so much written on this that it prompted a literature review. See Mark Chaves and Phillip S. Gorski, "Religious Pluralism and Religious Participation," *Annual Review of Sociology* 27 (2001): 261–81. But cogent objections to this theory have been raised. See, e.g., David Voas, Daniel V. A. Olson, and Alasdair Crockett, "Religious Pluralism and Participation: Why Previous Research is Wrong," *American Sociological Review* 67 (Apr. 2002): 212–30.

43. Some claim it can revitalize the church; see, e.g., Phyllis Tickle, *The Great Emergence: How Christianity is Changing and Why* (Grand Rapids, MI: Baker Books, 2008); Harvey Cox, *The Future of Faith* (San Francisco: Harper One, 2009), says we are entering an "age of the spirit." Others disagree that this will help religion or insist this is simply more secularization. See, e.g., Heelas and Benjamin Seel, "An Ageing New Age?" 229–47. They see New Age "spiritualities of life" continuing unabated. While David Voas and Steve Bruce, "The Spiritual Revolution: Another False Dawn for the Sacred," in *Predicting Religion*, 43–61, see secularization. The "spiritual revolution" claim was tested in England in the "Kendal Project." See http://www.kendalprojec.org.uk and Paul Heelas and Linda Woodhead, *The Spiritual Revolution: Why Religion is Giving Way to Spirituality* (Oxford: Blackwell, 2005).

44. I call these "semi-spiritual" to distinguish them from organized religion, but others have also used the term "quasi-religious." See, e.g., Malcolm Hamilton, "Eating Ethically: 'Spiritual' and 'Quasi-Religious' Aspects of Vegetarianism," *Journey of Contemporary Religion* 15, no. 1 (2000): 65–83. For a critique of the money aspect of spiritual seeking, see, e.g., Joshunda Sanders and Diana Barnes-Brown, "How the Self-Help Industry Tied Spiritual Salvation to Spending Lots of Money," *Bitch*, July 2010, also on AlterNet.org, http://www.alternet.org/story/147454. On the "selling" of religion, see R. Laurence Moore, *Selling God: American Religion in the Marketplace of Culture* (New York: Oxford University Press, 1994).

45. Charles Taylor, *A Secular Age* (Cambridge, MA: Belknap Press, Harvard University, 2007).

46. See, e.g., Scott McKnight, "Five Streams of the Emerging Church: Key elements of the most controversial and misunderstood movement in the church today," *Christianity Today*, Jan. 19, 2007.

CHAPTER 3

1. Given their age, it may be that many have likely already come to terms with themselves, or have other issues, such as medical problems, on their

minds. Although later in life some people respond to the imminence of death by attending to their spiritual needs, it may seem too late to "changes horses."

2. Anabaptists emerged out of the "Radical Reformation," which wanted to take Martin Luther's reforms of Catholicism much further. They insist on believers', rather than infant, baptism, among other tenets.

3. See, e.g., Linda A. Mercadante, *Gender, Doctrine and God: The Shakers and Contemporary Narrative* (Nashville, TN: Abingdon, 1990) and *Victims & Sinners: Spiritual Roots of Addiction and Recovery* (Louisville, KY: Westminster John Knox Press, 1996) and my own spiritual narrative *Bloomfield Avenue: A Jewish-Catholic Jersey Girl's Spiritual Journey* (Lanham, MD: Rowman & Littlefield, 2006).

4. Merlin B. Brinkerhoff and Marlene M. Mackie, "Casting Off the Bonds of Organized Religion: A Religious-Careers Approach to the Study of Apostasy," *Review of Religious Research* 34, no. 3 (Mar. 1993): 235–58.

5. In the 1970s, when the rise in "nones" was starting to be of concern to American Christianity, J. Russell Hale interviewed and categorized them in his book *The Unchurched: Who They Are and Why They Stay Away* (San Francisco: Harper & Row, 1980). Then in an early book on the SBNRs, Robert C. Fuller categorized Americans into three "religious" types: the totally indifferent, those with an ambiguous relationship with organized religion, and the "spiritual but not religious"; *Spiritual but not Religious: Understanding Unchurched America* (New York: Oxford, 2001), 2–5.

6. George Barna, *FutureCast: What Today's Trends Mean for Tomorrow's World* (Carol Stream, IL: Tyndale House Publishers, 2011), 117–18.

7. J. Russell Hale, *The Unchurched: Who They Are and Why They Stay Away* (San Francisco: Harper & Row, 1980).

8. Nancy Ammerman, "Spiritual but not Religious? Beyond Binary Choices in the Study of Religion," *Journal for the Scientific Study of Religion* 52, no. 2 (2013): 258–78.

9. Paul Heelas calls this "wellbeing spirituality," but I found a more functional and less devoted approach to it among my interviewees. See his *The New Age Movement: The Celebration of the Self and the Sacralization of Modernity* (Oxford: Blackwell, 1996).

10. Michele Dillon and Paul Wink devote considerable attention to seekers in their *In the Course of a Lifetime: Tracing Religious Belief, Practice, and Change* (Berkeley and Los Angeles: University of California, 2007). They have found that "seeking and dwelling are different but overlapping approaches to religion; one does not preclude the other. An individual can be committed to church-centered religious practices and beliefs and at the same time be a highly active spiritual seeker engaged in intentional practices that negotiate among a range of religious and spiritual resources" (228).

11. The "spiritual revolution" claim was tested in England in the "Kendal Project." See http://www.kendalprojec.org.uk and Paul Heelas and Linda Woodhead, *The Spiritual Revolution: Why Religion is Giving Way to Spirituality* (Oxford: Blackwell, 2005).

12. See the many works by Robert Wuthnow, including *Sharing the Journey: Support Groups and America's New Quest for Community* (New York: Free Press, 1994) and also Wade Clark Roof, *A Generation of Seekers: The Spiritual Journeys of the Baby Boom Generation* (San Francisco: Harper, 1993).

CHAPTER 4

1. Robert Bellah, *Habits of the Heart* (Berkeley and Los Angeles: University of California Press, 1985), ch. 9, 221. Bellah and Madsen quote one of their interviewees, a young nurse they called "Sheila." She said: "I believe in God. I'm not a religious fanatic. I can't remember the last time I went to church. My faith has carried me a long way. It's Sheilaism. Just my own little voice.... It's just try to love yourself and be gentle with yourself. You know, I guess, take care of each other. I think He would want us to take care of each other." This suggests the possibility of "over 220 million American religions, one for each of us," and they see Sheilaism as "a perfectly natural expression of current American religious life."

2. Wouter J. Hanegraaff, *New Age Religion and Western Culture: Esotericism in the Mirror of Secular Thought* (Albany: State University of New York Press, 1998), 302. Another writer, in a more popular vein, does tackle some of the theological themes explicitly being rejected; see Dan Kimball, *They Like Jesus but Not the Church: Insights from Emerging Generations* (Grand Rapids, MI: Zondervan, 2007).

3. Catherine Albanese had done comprehensive work tracing these out. See Catherine Albanese, *A Republic of Mind & Spirit: A Cultural History of American Metaphysical Religion* (New Haven: Yale, 2007) and her edited collection, *American Spiritualities: A Reader* (Bloomington: Indiana University Press, 2001). Leigh Schmidt has also traced its roots in liberal Protestantism, see *Restless Souls: The Making of American Spirituality* (New York: Harper Collins, 2005). Robert Fuller, too, briefly summarized this historical trajectory in *Spiritual but not Religious: Understanding Unchurched America* (New York: Oxford, 2001).

4. Laurel Zwissler, "Pagan Pilgrimage: New Religious Movements Research on Sacred Travel with Pagan and New Age Communities," *Religion Compass* 5, no. 7 (2011): 326–42, at 326.

5. Peter Gregory, "Describing the Elephant," *Religion and American Culture* 11 (Summer 2001): 14, as cited in Fuller, *Spiritual but not Religious*, 87.

6. Fuller, *Spiritual but not Religious*, 85.

7. Joantine Berghuijs, Jos Pieper, and Cok Bakker, "Being 'Spiritual' and Being 'Religious' in Europe: Diverging Life Orientations," *Journal of Contemporary Religion* 28, no. 1 (2013): 15–32, at 16.

8. Paul Heelas, *The New Age Movement: The Celebration of the Self and the Sacralization of Modernity* (Oxford: Blackwell, 1996), 128.

9. S. Sutcliffe and M. Bowman, eds., *Beyond New Age: Exploring Alternative Spirituality* (Edinburgh: Edinburgh University Press, 2000), 11; as cited in Dick Houtman and Stef Aupers, "The Spiritual Turn and the Decline of Tradition: The Spread of Post-Christian Spirituality in 14 Western Countries, 1981–2000," *Journal for the Scientific Study of Religion* 46, no. 3 (2007): 305–20, at 306.

10. Robert Fuller's online response to Jeffrey Kripal, "From Altered States to Altered Categories (And Back Again): Academic Method and the Human Potential Movement," The University of Chicago Religion and Culture Web Forum, April 2007.

11. Laurel Zwissler explains the difference between New Age and Pagan, saying, "Contemporary Paganism is a rubric term for groups that practice recreations of pre-Christian religions or create altogether new rituals and belief systems that replicate the veneration of nature and spirit that they understand to have been part of human prehistory" ("Pagan Pilgrimage, 326–42, 326–27 for quote).

12. It is widespread in the Western world, too. See Houtman and Aupers, "The Spiritual Turn and the Decline of Tradition," 305. But it does not always imply the total repudiation of all tradition. See, e.g., Sergej Flere and Andrej Kirbis, "Comment on Houtman and Aupers, JSSR, September 2007," *Journal for the Scientific Study of Religion* 48, no. 1 (2009): 161–84.

13. He adds that "religion and secularity are not opposites; to the contrary, Western secularity is a *religious* phenomenon." Mark C. Taylor, *After God* (Chicago: University of Chicago, 2007), xiii–xiv.

14. Matthew D. Graham, Marvin J. McDonald, and Derrick W. Klaasen, "A Phenomenological Analysis of Spiritual Seeking: Listening to Quester Voices," *International Journal for the Psychology of Religion* 18 (2008): 146–63. See also Rodney Stark, Eva Hamberg, and Alan S. Miller, "Exploring Spirituality and Unchurched Religions in America, Sweden, and Japan," *Journal of Contemporary Religion* 20, no. 1 (2005): 3–23; Houtman and Aupers, "The Spiritual Turn and the Decline of Tradition," 305; Sergej Flere and Andrej Kirbis, "New Age, Religiosity, and Traditionalism: A Cross-Cultural Comparison," *Journal for the Scientific Study of Religion* 48, no. 1 (2009): 161–84; and Joantine Berghuijs, Jos Pieper, and Cok Bakker, "Being 'Spiritual' and Being 'Religious' in Europe: Diverging Life Orientations," *Journal of Contemporary Religion* 28, no. 1 (2013): 15–32.

15. Heelas, *The New Age Movement*, 18–28. See also Paul Heelas, *Spiritualities of Life: New Age Romanticism and Consumptive Capitalism* (London: Blackwell, 2008).

16. Miles Sherts, "Not a New Religion: Spirituality in Intentional Community," *Communities* 154 (Spring 2012): 61–62.

17. Nancy T. Ammerman, "Spiritual but not Religious? Beyond Binary Choices in the Study of Religion," *Journal for the Scientific Study of Religion* 52, no. 2 (2013): 258–78, at 268.

18. Heelas, *The New Age Movement*, 18–28. See also Paul Heelas, *Spiritualities of Life: New Age Romanticism and Consumptive Capitalism* (London: Blackwell, 2008). Another one of the few who takes New Age belief seriously is Hanegraaff, *New Age Religion and Western Culture*.

19. Transcript of "Spirit Wars: American Religion in Progressive Politics," The Pew Forum on Religion and Public Life, Key West, Dec. 2005, Leigh Schmidt, speaker.

20. For elaboration of this theme, see, e.g., Paul Heelas, Scott Lash, and Paul Morris, eds., *Detraditionalization: Critical Reflections on Authority and Identity* (Oxford: Blackwell, 1996).

21. According to the well-respected and comprehensive Pew Form on Religion and Public Life: "Most Americans agree with the statement that many religions—not just their own—can lead to eternal life. Among those who are affiliated with a religious tradition, seven-in-ten say many religions can lead to eternal life. This view is shared by a majority of adherents in nearly all religious traditions, including more than half of members of evangelical Protestant churches (57%). Only among members of the Church of Jesus Christ of Latter-day Saints and other Mormon groups (57%) and Jehovah's Witnesses (80%), which together comprise roughly 2.4% of the U.S. adult population, do majorities say that their own religion is the one true faith leading to eternal life." Pew Forum on Religion and Public Life, U.S. Religious Landscape Survey, 2010, http://religions.pewforum.org/pdf/report2religious-landscape-study-key-findings.pdf.

22. Gail Wells, "Nature-Based Spirituality in Cascadia: Prospects and Pitfalls," in Douglas Todd, ed., *Cascadia: The Elusive Utopia: Exploring the Spirit of the Pacific Northwest* (Vancouver, BC: Ronsdale Press, 2008), 246.

23. Patricia O'Connell Killen and Mark Silk, eds., *Religion and Public Life in the Pacific Northwest: The None Zone* (Walnut Creek, CA: AltaMira Press, 2004). See also Douglas Todd, ed., *Cascadia: The Elusive Utopia, Exploring the Spirit of the Pacific Northwest* (Vancouver, BC: Ronsdale Press, 2008).

24. Todd, *Cascadia*, 254–59.

25. Several have given comprehensive accounts of the various roots of this ethos. See, e.g., Hanegraaff, *New Age Religion and Western Culture*; Albanese, *A Republic of Mind & Spirit*; and Heelas, *The New Age Movement* and his *Spiritualities of Life*. For a historical treatment, see Schmidt, *Restless Souls*.

26. This is also the contention of Leigh Eric Schmidt who argues that the contemporary spirituality is simply the logical outworking of liberal Protestantism. See *Restless Souls.*

CHAPTER 5

1. See "More than 9 in 10 Americans Continue to Believe in God," http://www.gallup.com/poll/147887/americans-continue-believe-god.aspx. See also: http://www.religioustolerance.org/godpoll.htm.

2. Commenting on Gallup, another study says: "Since 1944, the Gallup Poll has been asking Americans whether they *'believe in God or a universal spirit.'* The answers have always been 94% or more affirmative. These numbers have been so widely reported in academic articles, and the media that they have been almost etched in stone. However, the ISSP results are under 63%. The wide gap is probably due to the different wording of the question asked. The ISSP requires a degree of certainty of belief in God that is not present in the Gallup Poll. This shows that many Americans who believe in God are not very certain about their conviction. An additional difference is caused by the term 'universal spirit' that Gallup has introduced into the question. Many Americans believe in some vaguely defined supernatural entity, but do not refer to him/her/it/them as 'God.'" B. A. Robinson, at http://www.religioustolerance.org, Ontario Consultants on Religious Tolerance.

3. One research group explicitly claims that for many years the Gallup poll wording obscured results. Two international surveys were conducted during 1991 and 1993 by the *International Social Survey Program* (ISSP). This is currently located at the *National Opinion Research Center* (NORC) at the University of Chicago.

   A comparison between the ISSP survey and common Gallup polls on religion is instructive. The ISSP seeks information on the level of strong beliefs in God and other religious topics. When the Gallup Poll conducts a poll on belief in God, it seems almost to design a question to obscure the results. It ask for belief in *God or a universal spirit.* Like the ISSP survey, Gallup does not differentiate between belief in monotheistic God as defined in Christian, Muslim, Jewish, Sikh, and other religions, and the creator God in Deism who has since disappeared, polytheistic pantheons of deities, the Goddess and God of Wicca, etc. Further, Gallup does not differentiate between any of these deities and some vague notion of a supernatural entity that is perhaps impersonal." B. A. Robinson, Ontario Consultants on Religious Tolerance. See also http://www.religioustolerance.org/godpoll.htm.

4. See "More than 9 in 10 Americans Continue to Believe in God," http://www.gallup.com/poll/147887/americans-continue-believe-god.aspx. See also http://www.religioustolerance.org/godpoll.htm.

5. See Michael Hout, Claude S. Fisher, and Mark A. Chaves, "Most Americans Have No Religious Preference: Key Findings from the 2012 General Social Survey," Institute for the Study of Societal Issues, University of California, Berkeley, Mar. 7, 2013. They report that the number of those who believe in God without any doubts has dropped significantly.

6. The question was: "*I know God exists and I have no doubts about it.*"

7. Here the religiously affiliated only register 79% of total adults (with Millennials dropping to 74%) who are sure there is a God. Here only 36% of the total adult population can say with confidence that they believe in God (Millennials at 34%). In 2008, even though the numbers are still strikingly low; 53% of Millennials said they had no doubt. Pew Forum on Religion and Public Life, U.S. Religious Landscape Survey, 2010, http://religions.pewforum.org/pdf/report2religious-landscape-study-key-findings.pdf.

8. Hout, Fisher, and Chaves, "Most Americans Have No Religious Preference." In 1972, people with "no religion" represented only 5% of the population. In 1975 it was 7%, in 1990 it was 8%, 2000 14%, 2010 18%, and 2012 20%.

9. See, e.g., Paul Froese, *America's Four Gods: What That Says about God and— What That Says about Us* (New York: Oxford University Press, 2010), and Rodney Stark, *What Americans Really Believe: New Findings from the Baylor Surveys of Religion* (Waco, TX: Baylor University Press, 2008).

10. A helpful article is Eckart Ruschmann, "Transcending Towards Transcendence," *Implicit Religion* 14, no. 4 (2011): 421–32. He makes a distinction between "horizontal transcendence," which is the more material or psychological form, and "transcending towards transcendence," which implies there is an ontological transcendent goal toward which one aims.

11. One Pew survey found 39% of the unaffiliated in the "moderate" political category, and 34% in the "liberal." If you include those who checked on the survey that they were Buddhists, Reform Jews, progressive Protestants, or even the choice of "New Age" the numbers rise considerably. For high percentages of these people claimed to be either "moderate" or "liberal" politically. http://religions.pewforum.org/pdf/table-political-ideology-by-religious-tradition.pdf. As we have seen, some of my SBNRs turned up within or on the fringes of some of these groups. However, an important factor was raised by my colleague Paul Numrich. He reminds us that "the Buddhists captured by Pew and other surveys are predominantly non-immigrants, which explains the liberal leaning. Immigrant Buddhists, who make up the majority, are more conservative" (personal correspondence, Sept. 7, 2012).

12. Brian Wren, *What Language Shall I Borrow? God-Talk in Worship—A Male Response to Feminist Theology* (London: SCM Press, 1989).

13. Christian Smith with Melinda Lundquist Denton, *Soul Searching: The Religious and Spiritual Lives of American Teenagers* (New York: Oxford, 2005).

14. This is a smaller instance of the broader program which Wouter J. Hanegraaff calls "the psychologization of religion and the sacralization of psychology." *New Age Religion and Western Culture: Esotericism in the Mirror of Secular Thought* (Albany: SUNY Press, 1998), 224.

15. Scholar Jeffrey Long added some points that clarify this understanding from a more traditional Hindu perspective, something with which my interviewees were not always familiar. He said: "I would say that Shiva destroys illusion. He is not just a randomly destructive force, but one who enables the process of creation by getting rid of what is no longer productive or necessary. This is done out of love.... The idea, not unlike in Christianity, is that God is still God— supremely blissful, infinite, etc.—even while being involved in our lives. The chaos being created has an ultimately creative purpose. One could call it 'tough love.' Does this resonate with your interviewees? It's how I at least understand the Hindu sensibility" (personal correspondence, Oct. 23, 2012).

16. However, consider the spreading popularity of the idea of "karma"—that is, logical, impersonal, unavoidable consequences for bad behavior—as a functional substitute for a moral law given by a personal God. With this latter view, divine sovereignty is the assurance that good will triumph in the end.

17. See, e.g., Froese, *America's Four Gods*; and Stark, *What Americans Really Believe*.

18. Scholar Jeffrey Long made a suggestive interpretation of this interviewee's journey: "Are you familiar with the work of Fr. John S. Dunne SJ, on 'crossing over'? I believe the relevant book is titled *The Way of All the Earth*. This young woman sounds like a case of someone who has done this: left her tradition of origin to delve deeply into another tradition, and then eventually returned to her home tradition with renewed insight" (personal correspondence, Oct. 23, 2012).

19. My colleague Paul Numrich reminds us how pervasive this term is, showing up on Oprah's shows as well as PBS pledge drives featuring Wayne Dyer. See, e.g., http://www.oprah.com/spirit/Learning-to-Live-Week-7-Getting-Help-from-the-Universe.

20. The Gospel of Thomas is not accepted by Christians as one of the canonical gospels and it does not appear in the New Testament. Instead, it is a non-canonical "secret sayings" document from early in the history of the Christian church, possibly originating from a "proto-Gnostic" group. It is not a narrative account of the life, death, deeds, or resurrection of Jesus, as the canonical gospels are, but instead a series of "logia" attributed to Jesus.

21. These had all encountered either Alcoholics Anonymous or another spin-off which uses the famous twelve-step method of addiction recovery. To explore the theological roots of this program, see Linda A. Mercadante, *Victims & Sinners: Spiritual Roots of Addiction and Recovery* (Louisville, KY: Westminster John Knox Press, 1996).

22. Paul Tillich and Spinoza might be considered Christian monists, as could "process theology" such as that of Alfred North Whitehead. A branch of Hasidic

thought might be considered Jewish monism. And some followers of Sufi thought might be considered Muslim monists.

23. Western Christians talk more about "sanctification" and partnership with God, while Eastern Orthodox traditions speak of "theosis," a closer identification. Neither goes to the extent of Mormonism, though, which posits the human possibility of becoming gods.

24. Pantheism, which we will soon examine, is not the same as "panentheism." Panentheism proposes that the universe, as God's creation, also resides "in" God. Process theology can be seen as a version of panentheism.

CHAPTER 6

1. Scholar of religion and practicing Hindu Jeffrey Long reminds us that "though theistic devotionalism is not absent from them in their original Asian contexts, [it is] an element often downplayed in Western representations of these traditions" (personal correspondence, Oct. 23, 2012).

2. Philip Rieff, *The Triumph of the Therapeutic: Uses of Faith after Freud* (Chicago: University of Chicago, 1987).

3. Jeffrey Long, scholar of Asian religions, reflected helpfully and at length on this: "Here, too, though this probably does reflect the views of your interviewees toward Eastern traditions, I would caution . . . that, in their original contexts, while these traditions do affirm that human sinfulness has deeper roots in ignorance, and while they do reject the idea of intrinsic evil or fallenness in favor of an idea of intrinsic goodness, they are as realistic and frank about the reality of human depravity on a day-to-day, pragmatic level as are the Abrahamic traditions. The idea that there is no concept of sin or evil in Hinduism or Buddhism is pure fantasy. It is simply that sin/evil is seen as the symptom of a deeper problem in these traditions—the problem of spiritual ignorance, as you note— rather than as THE problem, as seems to be the case in the Abrahamic religions (or at least mainstream versions thereof). And if anyone thinks that Hinduism and Buddhism are not judgmental, then they know nothing of the cultures of shame that these traditions sustain" (personal correspondence, Oct. 23, 2012).

4. Introduction to the *Big Book of Alcoholics Anonymous*. See also Linda A. Mercadante, *Victims & Sinners: Spiritual Roots of Addiction and Recovery* (Louisville, KY: Westminster John Knox Press, 1996).

CHAPTER 7

1. Paul Morris, "Community beyond Tradition," in Paul Heelas, Scott Lash, and Paul Morris, *Detraditionalization* (Malden, MA: Blackwell, 1999). Morris quotes Raymond Williams who says that community "unlike all the other terms of social organization (state, nation, society, etc.) . . . never seems to be used

unfavourably, and never to be given any positive opposing or distinguishing term." *Keywords* (London: Fontana, 1976), 66.

2. Paul Heclo, *On Thinking Institutionally* (Boulder, CO: Paradigm, 2008), 47. Heclo provides a chart of the many definitions of *institution* (48–50). He also notes that a key goal of institutions is to realize community values, at least according to the social systems school (53).

3. See the World Bank's definition at http://web.worldbank.org/WBSITE/ EXTERNAL/TOPICS/EXTSOCIALDEVELOPMENT/EXTTSOCIALCAPITAL/ 0,,contentMDK:20185164~menuPK:418217~pagePK:148956~piPK:216618~theS itePK:401015,00.html.

4. Heclo, *On Thinking Institutionally*, 11–12.

5. See, e.g., Robert Putnam, *Bowling Alone: The Collapse and Revival of American Community* (New York: Simon and Schuster, 2000); and also Robert Wuthnow, *Sharing the Journey: Support Groups and America's New Quest for Community* (New York: Free Press, 1994), who argues that small support groups are trying to fill that need.

6. "One can see religion as a set of developing attempts to apprehend spiritual reality, which will take on the forms of their particular historical and social contexts, but which are also felt to be responses, however incomplete and partial, to the presence or activity of such a reality." Keith Ward, *Religion & Community* (Oxford: Clarendon Press, 2000), 342.

7. Ibid., 1.

8. Ibid., 209.

9. Ibid.

10. Jeffrey Long, scholar of Asian religions, qualifies this connection. "There's a lot of contestation about the idea of Buddhism and Jainism emerging from Hinduism, much of it centering around the question of at what point in history it becomes valid to begin using the category of 'Hinduism.' I would argue, for example, that Hinduism as we now know it is a blend of ancient Brahmanism (which is different from contemporary Hinduism) and ascetic traditions such as Buddhism and Jainism" (personal correspondence, Oct. 23, 2012).

11. Ward, *Religion & Community*, 53.

12. Ibid., 79.

13. Perhaps, instead, the SBNR ethos is a particular "take" on religion, rather than something completely different. Perhaps, just to simplify matters, we might want—as two scholars have suggested—to refer to SBNR version as "privatized, experientially-oriented religion." Heinz Streib and Ralph W. Hood, "'Spirituality' as Privatized Experience-Oriented Religion: Empirical and Conceptual Perspectives," *Implicit Religion* 14, no. 4 (2011): 433–53.

14. There are several studies on this topic. Julie Juola Exline, "Stumbling Blocks on the Religious Road: Fractured Relationships, Nagging Vices, and the Inner Struggle to Believe," *Psychological Inquiry* 13, no. 3 (2002): 182–89. She has

categorized potential problem areas into four "stumbling blocks." First, people might experience "interpersonal strains," which can disrupt the powerful social support that religion provides. Second, individuals might develop negative attitudes toward God. This will make the comfort and coping devices of religion less effective. Third, individuals can suffer from "inner struggles to believe." Fourth, some people have problems with "virtuous striving" (i.e., trying to live up to ideal standards and coming to terms with one's imperfections). See also Neal Krause and Keith M. Wulff, "Religious Doubt and Health: Exploring the Potential Dark Side of Religion," *Sociology of Religion* 65, no. 1 (2004): 35–56; and Merlin B. Brinkerhoff and Marlene M. Mackie, "Casting Off the Bonds of Organized Religion: A Religious-Careers Approach to the Study of Apostasy," *Review of Religious Research* 34, no. 3 (Mar. 1993): 235–58.

15. See, for instance, Samuel R. Weber, Kenneth I. Pargament, Mark E. Kunik, James W. Lomas II, and Melinda A. Stanley, "Psychological Distress among Religious Nonbelievers: A Systematic Review," *Journal of Religion and Health* 51 (2012): 72–86.

16. For more information on twelve-step spirituality, see Linda A. Mercadante, *Victims & Sinners: Spiritual Roots of Addiction and Recovery* (Louisville, KY: Westminster John Knox, 1996).

17. This is suggested by Philip Goldberg in *American Veda: From Emerson and the Beatles to Yoga and Meditation—How Indian Spirituality Changed the West* (New York: Harmony Books, 2010). He states that New Thought leaders, especially the popular Emmet Fox, were "well acquainted with Alcoholics Anonymous founder Bill Wilson, and his sermons were quite the rage in early AA circles. Thus, it is conceivable that Indian philosophy...had some effect on the big bang phase of the twelve-step universe. Perhaps more to the point, Bill Wilson's formative years were in New England, where Emersonian ideals lingered like leaves in a warm November." Kindle edition.

18. For a detailed historical and theological analysis of AA and the twelve-step movement, see Mercadante, *Victims & Sinners*.

19. The Roman Catholic Church makes a distinction between mortal sin—which results in one's complete separation from God and eternal life—and "venial" sins which are less serious and more forgivable.

20. Paul Heelas, "Introduction: Detraditionalization and its Rivals," 1–20, in Heelas et al., eds., *Detraditionalization: Critical Reflections on Authority and Identity*, 2.

21. It is valid to ask whether this is an adequate interpretation of Eastern religions. Some scholars suggest it is not. See, e.g., Goldberg, *American Veda*. Scholar of Asian religions Jeffrey Long comments: "And these scholars are correct. What I think the interviewees are perceiving is that traditions like Hinduism and Buddhism are not primarily ABOUT belief, but see belief as a stage preliminary to direct experiential awareness: to knowledge" (personal correspondence, Oct. 23, 2012).

CHAPTER 8

1. Percentages vary but all hover around +/– 70%. The General Social Survey of 2010 puts that figure at 70.5%. In charting this belief from 1973 to 2010, the study showed it varied between 67% and 76%, fluctuating rather than steadily increasing or decreasing. In 2010, The Pew Forum found 74% so believing. This is not age-specific, it seems, for about 75% of Millennials believe in an after-life, according to the Religious Landscape Survey of The Pew Forum, "Religion among the Millennials: Less Religiously Active than Older Americans, but Fairly Traditional in Other Ways" Poll, February 17, 2010. In 2003, the Barna Group of Ventura, California, found 81% believing in an afterlife of some sort, 79% believing that each person has an eternal soul, and only about 10% believing this life is all there is. http://www.barna.org/barna-update/article/5-ba rna-update/128-americans-describe-their-views-about-life-after-death. In any case, surveys also find those affiliated with and practicing their religion are more likely to believe in life after death.

2. The popular term "JewBu" indicates this. See, e.g., Roger Kamenetz, *The Jew in the Lotus: A Poet's Rediscovery of Jewish Identity in Buddhist India* (San Francisco: HarperOne, 2007).

3. See Rodney Stark, *What American Really Believe* (Waco, TX: Baylor University Press, 2008), which makes use of the 2005 Baylor Survey; see especially chapter 8, "Heaven: We Are All Going."

4. The Pew Forum Religious Landscape report in 2011 summarizes: "Most Americans agree with the statement that many religions—not just their own—can lead to eternal life. Among those who are affiliated with a religious tradition, seven-in-ten say many religions can lead to eternal life. This view is shared by a majority of adherents in nearly all religious traditions, including more than half of members of evangelical Protestant churches (57%). Only among members of the Church of Jesus Christ of Latter-day Saints and other Mormon groups (57%) and Jehovah's Witnesses (80%), which together comprise roughly 2.4% of the U.S. adult population, do majorities say that their own religion is the one true faith leading to eternal life."

5. The Baylor study, among others, found that this confidence is widespread. See, e.g., Stark, *What Americans Really Believe*, chapter 8, "Heaven: We Are All Going." In 2003, the Barna Group of Ventura, California, found 76% believing in heaven, with 43% confident they will go there, and 71% believing in hell, although only one half of 1% actually expecting to go. http://www.barna.org/ barna-update/article/5-barna-update/128-americans-describe-their-views-abou t-life-after-death.

6. See, e.g., "Many Americans Not Dogmatic about Religion: Reincarnation, Astrology and the 'Evil Eye,'" Pew Forum on Religion & Public Life, Dec. 10, 2009. http://pewresearch.org/pubs/1434/multiple-religious-

practices-reincarnation-astrology-psychic. These views are popular enough to have made it to major media outlets. For example, "We Are All Hindus Now," *Newsweek*, Aug. 14, 2009; and the CBS television show "Sunday Morning" featured a story about this "Reincarnation: Believing in Second Chances," May 15, 2011.

7. According to Lisa Miller, the fascination with heaven has been going on for some time; *Heaven: Our Enduring Fascination with the AfterLife* (San Francisco: Harper & Row, 2010).

8. *Newsweek Magazine*, Aug. 14, 2009.

9. See, e.g., Paul Edwards, "The Case against Karma and Reincarnation," in *Not Necessarily the New Age: Critical Essays*, ed. Robert Basil (Buffalo, NY: Prometheus Books, 1988), 87–129.

CHAPTER 9

1. Many traceable sociological and historical factors are involved, including the thrust of general cultural change, demographics, political battles that seem to stack conservatives against liberals, the impact of globalization and pluralism, lack of religious background, influence of mass media, loosening mores, changes in family patterns, the "triumph of the therapeutic," religious illiteracy, and others.

2. The same finding is reported by Christian Smith with Kari Christoffersen, Hilary Davidson, and Patricia Snell Herzog, *Lost in Transition: The Dark Side of Emerging Adulthood* (New York: Oxford University Press, 2011), especially regarding young adults and moral reasoning. In explaining their assumptions and dismay, they say: "We think it is good for people to be able to think coherently about moral beliefs and problems, and to explain why they believe whatever they do believe....to be able to understand different moral positions, to consider how different assumptions shape moral beliefs, to think out some of the more obvious logical implications of taking certain positions. We think it is good for people to be able to carry on a basic, constructive discussion about moral differences with other people who disagree. We think these are especially important for people living in a culturally, religiously, and morally pluralistic society like the United States. And almost no emerging adult today is able to do much of that....We think that is a problem" (20).

3. See, e.g., Kenneth Pargament, "Patterns of Positive and Negative Religious Coping with Major Life Stressors," *Journal for the Scientific Study of Religion* 37, no. 4 (Dec. 1998): 710–24.

4. Joseph B. Tamney, Shawn Powell, and Stephen Johnson, "Innovation Theory and Religious Nones," *Journal for the Scientific Study of Religion* 28, no. 2 (1989): 216–29.

5. For more on "believing without belonging," see Grace Davie, *Religion in Britain since 1945: Believing Without Belonging* (Cambridge: Blackwell, 1994).

6. Pew Forum on Religion & Public Life, "Faith in Flux: Changes in Religious Affiliation in the U.S.," Executive Summary, p. 1, Apr. 27, 2009, http://www.pewforum.org.

7. Crystal L. Park, "Implicit Religion and the Meaning Making Model," *Implicit Religion* 14, no. 4 (2011): 405–19.

8. There is a debate among sociologists and others about what this means. See, e.g., Paul Heelas, Scott Lash, and Paul Morris, eds., *Detraditionalization: Critical Reflections on Authority and Identity* (London: Blackwell, 1996); Dick Houtman and Stef Aupers, "Christian Religiosity and New Age Spirituality: A Cross-Cultural Comparison," *Journal for the Scientific Study of Religion* 48, no. 1 (2009): 169–78; and Sergej Flere and Andrej Kirbis, "Comment on Houtman and Aupers, Sept. 2007," *Journal for the Scientific Study of Religion* 48, no. 1 (2009): 161–69.

9. Rowan Williams, "Archbishop's Lecture—Society Still Needs Religion," April 17, 2008, http://www.archbishopofcanterbury.org/1759.

10. Owen C. Thomas, "Spiritual but not Religious: The Influence of the Current Romantic Movement," *Anglican Theological Review* 88, no. 3 (Summer 2006): 397–415.

11. Heinz Streib and Ralph W. Hood describe three types of "deconverts" or ways of exiting religious groups: (1) the secular exit, those who terminate all concern with religious belief; (2) the "heretical exit," those who engage in "patchwork" religion; and (3) the "privatizing exit," those who continue to practice their religion in private. "Spirituality as Privatized Experience-Oriented Religion: Empirical and Conceptual Perspectives," *Implicit Religion* 14, no. 4 (2011): 433–53.

12. Simon Glendinning, "Beyond Atheism," *Think* 11, no. 32 (Sept. 2012): 37–52, 42.

13. Chaeyoon Lim, Carol Ann MacGregor, and Robert D. Putnam, "Secular and Liminal: Discovering Heterogeneity among Religious Nones," *Journal for the Scientific Study of Religion* 49, no. 4 (2010): 596–618. See also Rodney Stark, Eva Hamberg, and Alan S. Miller, "Exploring Spirituality and Unchurched Religions in America, Sweden, and Japan," *Journal of Contemporary Religion* 20, no. 1 (2005): 3–23.

14. Philip Goldberg makes this case persuasively in *American Veda: From Emerson and the Beatles to Yoga and Meditation—How Indian Spirituality Changed the West* (New York: Harmony Books, 2010), writing: "When I asked people what initially drew them to Vedanta-Yoga, most referred to the promise of tangible spiritual and psychological benefits; the rewards of...such [benefits]...as community and worldview, were usually considered secondary gains. The manner in which Eastern practices have improved the lives of adherents has been described in countless memoirs, research papers, and self-help manuals. The changes lean in the direction of improved well-being: greater peace, self-awareness,

happiness, and wholeness, and a connection to something bigger than them-selves." Kindle edition.

15. The debate over secularism is vast and deep. For some examples, see Charles Taylor, *A Secular Age* (Cambridge, MA: Belknap Press, 2007); William E. Connolly, *Why I Am Not a Secularist* (Minneapolis: University of Minnesota, 1999); Talal Assad *Formations of the Secular: Christianity, Islam and Modernity* (Palo Alto, CA: Stanford University Press, 2003); and Michael S. Hogue, "After the Secular: Toward a Pragmatic Public Theology," *Journal of the American Academy of Religion* 78, no. 2 (June 2010): 346–74. See also Nancy T. Ammerman, ed., *Everyday Religion: Observing Modern Religious Lives* (New York: Oxford University Press, 2007).

16. Molly Worthen reporting on the views of political scientist Elizabeth Shakman Hurd, "One Nation under God?" *New York Times*, Dec. 22, 2012, 4, http://www.nytimes.com/2012/12/23/opinion/sunday/american-christianity-and-secularism.

17. Mark C. Taylor, *After God* (Chicago: University of Chicago Press, 2007), Kindle edition.

18. Mark Chaves, "Secularization as Declining Religious Authority," *Social Forces* 72, no. 3 (Mar. 1994): 749–74, at 770. The secularization debate has resulted in too many articles and books to note here. But to gain a historical perspective on the secularization debate, see, e.g., Philip S. Gorski, "Historicizing the Secularization Debate: Church, State, and Society in Late Medieval and Early Modern Europe, ca. 1300–1700," *American Sociological Review* 65 (Feb. 2000): 138–67. See also Norval D. Glenn, "The Trend in 'No Religion' Respondents to U.S. National Surveys, Late 1950s to Early 1980s," *Public Opinion Quarterly* 51 (1987): 293–334.

19. Phillip E. Hammond, *Religion and Personal Autonomy: The Third Disestablishment in America* (Columbia: University of South Carolina Press, 1992). According to Hammond, the first disestablishment was allowance for pluralism when formerly state churches were legally separated from government. The second disestablishment was a result of the influx and increasing influence of Catholics and Jews, which fractured the pre–Second World War cultural hegemony of Protestantism.

20. There are many studies which affirm this. For a nuanced look, see Robyn L. Driskell and Larry Lyon, "Assessing the Role of Religious Beliefs on Secular and Spiritual Behaviors," *Review of Religious Research* 52, no. 4 (2011): 386–404. See also Penny Edgell Becker and Pawan H. Dhingra, "Religious Involvement and Volunteering: Implications for Civil Society," *Sociology of Religion* 62, no. 3 (2001): 315–35.

21. This is especially common in the psychology of religion. See, e.g., Ralph W. Hood, Jr., "American Psychology of Religion and the Journal for the

Scientific Study of Religion," *Journal for the Scientific Study of Religion* 39, no. 4 (Dec. 2000): 531–43. Charles Taylor in *A Secular Age* (Cambridge, MA: Belknap Press, Harvard University, 2007) also makes the point that religion needs no such justification.

22. See, e.g., Penny Edgell Becker and Pawan H. Dhingra, "Religious Involvement and Volunteering: Implications for Civil Society," *Sociology of Religion* 62, no. 3 (2001): 315–35.

23. See, e.g., George Barna, *FutureCast: What Today's Trends Mean for Tomorrow's World* (Carol Stream, IL: Tyndale House Publishers, 2011), 119; and Smith et al., *Lost in Transition*.

24. This accords with the findings of Smith et al., *Lost in Transition*. They find emerging adults to largely believe "that what people take to be moral truths are only socially constructed, historically and culturally relative items about morality" (30).

25. Goldberg, *American Veda*. In the full quote, he says: "Boomer spirituality was marked to a large extent by retreat from the sociopolitical battlegrounds of the era. Protest-driven activism was disparaged in many circles as lacking the vital ingredient of personal development. After a few decades of waiting for inner peace to flow from the individual hearts to the collective bloodstream like oxygen molecules, many now-middle-aged citizens realized that cosmic consciousness without skillful action will not solve real-world problems.... The younger generation is not taking thirty years to get there. Whereas the supercharged intensity of the 1960s and 1970s made Eastern spirituality seem antithetical to social activism, today, with the fate of the natural environment a burning issue, Vedanta-Yoga seems a natural fit, with its emphasis on connectivity and the sanctity of all living things.... Other devotees are offering the fruits of their inner work to service." Kindle edition.

26. See, e.g., Diana Butler Bass, *Christianity after Religion: The End of Church and the Birth of a New Spiritual Awakening* (San Francisco: HarperOne, 2012); and *A People's History of Christianity: The Other Side of the Story* (San Francisco: HarperCollins, 2009); Harvey Cox, *The Future of Faith* (San Francisco: HarperOne, 2009); and Phyllis Tickle, *The Great Emergence: How Christianity is Changing and Why* (Grand Rapids, MI: Baker Books, 2008).

27. After studying large numbers of "emerging adults" who are the future of the country, Christian Smith and his cohort said: "The idea that today's emerging adults are as a generation leading a new wave of renewed civic-mindedness and political involvement is sheer fiction.... Whatever any popular cultural or political observers have had to say about the political interests of emerging adults, we—without joy—can set the record straight here: almost all emerging adults today are either apathetic, uninformed, distrustful, disempowered, or, at most only marginally interested when it comes to politics and public life. Both that

fact itself and the reasons for it speak poorly of the condition of our larger culture and society" (*Lost in Transition*, 228–29).

28. As quoted in Roger Kamanetz, *The Jew in the Lotus: A Poet's Rediscovery of Jewish Identity in Buddhist India* (San Francisco: Harper Collins, 1994), Kindle edition.

29. This is especially true for Hinduism, which many SBNRs consider the forerunner in "universalizing" religion. Lola Williamson in *Transcendent in America: Hindu-Inspired Meditation Movements in America* (New York: New York University Press, 2010) shows that Hindu-inspired meditation movements are quite different from traditional Hinduism. Amanda J. Huffer comments on this misappropriation of Hinduism ("Hinduism Without Religion: Amma's Movement in America," *Crosscurrents* 61, no. 3 (Sept. 2011): 374–398). She says: "Universalizing discourses present general normative claims that aim to speak to and represent all of humanity.... In their claims to universality, proponents not only minimize the importance of the particularities of subjects' self-identities, but they claim to represent those particularities by supplanting them with general principles" (378–79). See also the comment by Jeffrey Long in chapter 6, note 3, above.

30. Garret Keizer, "Reasons to Join: In Defense of Organized Religion," *The Christian Century*, Apr. 22, 2008, 31.

31. See, e.g., S. Mark Heim, *Salvations: Truth and Difference in Religion* (Maryknoll, NY: Orbis, 1995).

32. Mary Ann Glendon, law professor at Harvard, as quoted in Gretchen Keiser, "Glendon Speaks on Threats to Religious Freedom," *The Georgia Bulletin*, Sept. 29, 2011, 1–4.

33. Rowan Williams, "Archbishop's Lecture—Society Still Needs Religion," Apr. 17, 2008, http://www.archbishopofcanterbury.org/1759.

34. Tom Pyszcznki, Shelden Solomon, and Jeff Greenberg, *In the Wake of 9/11: The Psychology of Terror* (Washington, DC: American Psychological Association, 2003), 148, as quoted by Ted Peters, "Christian God-Talk While Listening to Atheists, Pluralists, and Muslims," *Dialog: A Journal of Theology* 46, no. 2 (Summer 2007); 96, 84–103. See also David Martin, *Does Christianity Cause War?* (Vancouver, BC: Regent College Publishing, 2006) and his *The Future of Christianity: Reflections on Violence and Democracy, Religion and Secularization* (Burlington, VT: Ashgate, 2011).

35. This is the contention of Nancy Ammerman and other authors in *Everyday Religion*.

36. Williamson, *Transcendent in America*.

37. Scholars take different positions on this. Williamson, for example, thinks the HIMM (Hindu-inspired meditation movements) have already created something akin to a new religion or perhaps an American-style Hinduism. See her *Transcendent in America*. But Mark Chaves thinks this is not at all likely. He neither sees it reinvigorating existing religions nor providing the foundation

for a new religion. Instead, it simply shows that non-religious people are more interested in spirituality. See his *American Religion: Contemporary Trends* (Princeton: Princeton University Press, 2011).

38. Diana Eck, *The New Religious America: How a "Christian Country" Has Become the World's Most Religiously Diverse Nation* (San Francisco: Harper Collins, 2001), Kindle edition.

39. Williamson, *Transcendent in America*.

40. See Goldberg, *American Veda*. He also observes: "When asked about their religious and spiritual attitudes, a great many people sound vaguely Vedantic, and if you ask where they got those ideas, they don't always know." Kindle edition.

41. See, e.g., Frank Schaeffer, *Crazy for God: How I Grew Up as One of the Elect, Helped Found the Religious Right, and Lived to Take All (or Almost All) of It Back* (New York: Carroll & Graf, 2007). Other sources include Randy Balmer, *Thy Kingdom Come: How the Religious Right Distorts Faith and Threatens America: An Evangelical's Lament* (New York: Basic Books, 2006); and David Kuo, *Tempting Faith: An Inside Story of Political Seduction* (New York: Free Press, 2006).

42. For instance, see the Pew Forum, "Faith in Flux: Changes in Religious Affiliation in the U.S.," 2009.

43. Michelle Dillon, "Old and New Spiritual Resources," *National Catholic Reporter*, Oct. 24, 2011, http://ncronline.org/27167.

44. See, e.g., Patricia Wittberg, "A Lost Generation? Fewer Young Women Are Practicing Their Faith, How the Church Can Woo Them Back," *America*, Feb. 20, 2012.

45. A concept from Eastern Orthodox theology.

46. There are many works on this movement. For one overview, see Scot McKnight, "Five Streams of the Emerging Church: Key Elements of the Most Controversial and Misunderstood Movement in the Church Today," *Christianity Today* 51, no. 2 (Feb. 2007), http://www.christianitytoday.com/ct/2007/february/11.35.html.

47. Rowan Williams, "Archbishop's Lecture—Society Still Needs Religion," Apr. 17, 2008, http://www.archbishopofcanterbury.org/1759.

48. David Briggs, "Dynamic 'Nones' Hold Key to Future of American Religion," *Association of Religious Data Archives*, Feb. 16, 2012, https://blogs.thearda/trend/featured/dynamic. Based on the 2006–7 Faith Matters Study, it found that fewer than 70% of respondents were still "nones" when re-polled a year later.

49. Personal conversation, Aug. 25, 2008.

50. See, e.g., Linda A. Mercadante, *Gender, Doctrine and God: The Shakers and Contemporary Theology* (Nashville, TN: Abingdon Press, 1990).

51. For a discussion of this and other aspects of lived religion today, see Ammerman, *Everyday Religion*.

APPENDIX

1. This may be changing, however. While only recently, the Pacific Northwest was called the "none zone," now Vermont holds the title of least religious state.
2. The Pew Forum, "Faith in Flux: Changes in Religious Affiliation in the U.S.," 2009.
3. G. Jeffrey MacDonald reports the findings of the Pew Forum on Religion and Public Life, which finds Hispanics make up 11% and African-Americans just 8% of "unaffiliated" Americans. "Atheists' Diversity Woes Have No Black-and-White Answers," *The Christian Century*, Jan. 3, 2011.

Index